I0797882

Praise for *Wrestling with Paul*

Bold and original, compelling and honest. This book is not just about who Paul was, but about what he does and what we are willing to do with him. With verve, Sarah Emanuel provides a robust historical and metacritical engagement with Paul and his interpreters. She brilliantly wrestles them all to the ground and helps us face our worst fears about them—and discover, in some cases, that they're true. If we keep trying to rehabilitate Paul without truly facing him and what we've done with him, we are doomed to continue misusing him—to our own detriment. This is, quite simply, one of the most important books in Pauline studies in the past decade.

Isaac T. Soon, University of British Columbia

Masterful in her engagement of the topic, Emanuel takes her reader along while she wrestles with Paul and—more importantly—his interpreters. She asks the hard question of who benefits from interpreting Paul and shows how some contemporary understandings may be just as dangerous for Jews today as interpretations have been in the past. Elegantly written and astutely argued, this book should be read by scholars, students, and lay readers alike.

Shayna Sheinfeld, Augsburg University

Sarah Emanuel's *Wrestling with Paul* challenges our usual exceptionalist readings of the apostle, excavating the ethnocentric and exclusionary eschatology that slots him within, and not against, ancient Judaism's varied textual landscape. As clever as it is insightful, Emanuel's work does not shy away from hard questions—and even harder answers—about why New Testament Studies has worked so hard to erase Paul's rough edges. I dare you to put it down.

Stephen L. Young, Appalachian State University

Helpfully pushing against biblical scholarship's tendency to separate the personal from the professional, *Wrestling with Paul* offers an engaging reading of Paul alongside a compelling historiography. Addressing how Paul's modern interpreters have turned him into a Paul productive for dealing with their own anxieties about anti-Judaism, Emanuel models how to eschew convenience and comfort for earnest and brave analysis.

Jill Hicks-Keeton, University of Southern California

WRESTLING WITH PAUL

WRESTLING WITH PAUL

THE APOSTLE, HIS READERS, AND THE FATE OF THE JEWS

SARAH EMANUEL

FORTRESS PRESS
Minneapolis

WRESTLING WITH PAUL

The Apostle, His Readers, and the Fate of the Jews

30 29 28 27 26 25 1 2 3 4 5 6 7 8 9

Library of Congress Cataloging-in-Publication Data

Names: Emanuel, Sarah, author

Title: Wrestling with Paul : the apostle, his readers, and the fate of the Jews / Sarah Emanuel.

Description: Minneapolis : Fortress Press, [2025] | Includes bibliographical references and index. |

Identifiers: LCCN 2025001900 (print) | LCCN 2025001901 (ebook) | ISBN 9781506485898 hardcover | ISBN 9781506485904 ebook

Subjects: LCSH: Bible. Epistles of Paul—Criticism, interpretation, etc. | Paul, the Apostle, Saint | Jews in the New Testament | Christianity and other religions—Judaism

Classification: LCC BS2650.52 .E63 2025 (print) | LCC BS2650.52 (ebook) | DDC 227/.06—dc23/eng/20250514

LC record available at https://lccn.loc.gov/2025001900

LC ebook record available at https://lccn.loc.gov/2025001901

Cover image: Ancient Greek Olympic athletes wrestlers. Black and white silhouette, from Antonina Maslova/Getty Images

Cover design: Kris E. Miller

Print ISBN: 978-1-5064-8589-8

eBook ISBN: 978-1-5064-8590-4

For Zoë, my life.
And for Gus, a *good* boy indeed.

CONTENTS

ACKNOWLEDGMENTS

Writing a book is both a solitary and collaborative experience. My many interlocuters, even when we disagree, have made this book possible, as seen in both the body and the footnotes of this project. I must also acknowledge the many colleagues who shared their expertise and offered constructive feedback during the writing process. Some provided resources, some helped me think through ideas and organizational possibilities, some combed through paragraphs, some read full chapters, and some reviewed entire book drafts; all contributed to this book's development and no amount of assistance was too little. I am indeed indebted to (in alphabetical order): Christy Cobb, Stephanie Cobb, Cavan Concannon, Ashleigh Elser, Danna Nolan Fewell, Paula Fredriksen, David Freidenreich, Jill Hicks-Keeton, Jimmy Hoke, Melanie Johnson-DeBaufre, Layla Karst, Mark Letteney, Jessica Marglin, Stephen D. Moore, Jennifer Owens-Jofré, Ethan Schwartz, Shayna Sheinfeld, Sarah Abrevaya Stein, Matthew Thiessen, Tracy Sayuki Tiemeier, and Stephen L. Young. This book also benefits from the invaluable contributions of my research assistant, Emily Ward, and my former graduate student, Kayla Ray.

The final version of this manuscript would not exist without the significant grant support from the Louisville Institute (see especially chapter 5). Loyola Marymount University also provided me with considerable assistance, including a research and writing grant in summer 2021, a college fellowship in spring 2022, a sabbatical leave in fall 2023, and a research assistant from summer 2023 to spring 2025. I extend appreciation to my department chairs, Amir Hussain and Tracy Tiemeier, for their support during the different stages of research and writing and to Faith Sovilla and Fran Sanders for their assistance in handling grant funds. I am also grateful to my 2022 Wabash Center cohort and mentors for their comradery as I worked.

I had opportunities to workshop various parts of this project as it was in development. I am grateful to all the participants at the Biblical Studies and Political Theology roundtable conference at Villanova University in 2023 and to those in attendance at the University of Southern California's religion colloquium in 2021 and 2024. This includes the formal response from Rose Miller, a doctoral student at USC, who shared her constructive feedback at USC's religion colloquium in 2024. To all the students and faculty who shared comments and questions that day and in 2021: thank you. I received great feedback from colleagues at the Paul within Judaism section of the Society of Biblical Literature in 2021 and at the Metacriticism section of the Society of Biblical Literature in 2023. I presented part of this book's thesis for a two-part course I led at Brentwood Presbyterian in Los Angeles in 2021. I also presented some of its contents at the University of Oregon in 2024 and at a virtual mini-lecture series at Stanford University in 2025. I remain grateful for the feedback and candor at each setting.

Writing the fifth chapter of this book would not have been possible without the help of those at Avocet Playa Vista (Los Angeles, CA), Blue Ocean Faith Church (Ann Arbor, MI), St. Clare of Assisi Episcopal Church (Ann Arbor, MI), and Bnai Keshet (Montclair, NJ). I am thankful to Emily Swan, Anne Clarke, Caroline Kittle, Ariann Weitzman, and Eliott Tepperman for their considerable hospitality on these visits. I extend appreciation to the graduate students enrolled in my Loyola Marymount University course on Paul in summer 2024, whose feedback also helped me craft the fifth chapter. I am also grateful to those at Drew University, where I earned my PhD, and where I also gathered feedback for this book's fifth chapter. Many thanks to YoungHak Lee for organizing Drew's biblical studies colloquium and to all its participants; meeting new students, sharing space once again with Amy Chase and Dong Sung Kim (classmates from my own doctoral studies days), and being in conversation with my doctoral mentors, Melanie Johnson-DeBaufre, Danna Nolan Fewell, Althea Spencer Miller, Stephen Moore, and Robert Paul Seesengood, was an absolute joy. I am profoundly grateful to both the named and anonymized contributors in chapter 5. It is just as much your chapter as it is mine.

My editor at Fortress, Carey Newman, stood by me from start to finish, even as I insisted on breaking conventional styles of writing. He once asked me if I'd rather have this book function as a flashy solo cup or a boring-yet-standard cooking ingredient. When I countered with, "I'd like this book to be hot sauce," he went with it, and I am glad he did.

To Myles Clarke, my copyeditor for both my first book and now this one: thank you. To Fortress's copyeditors, typesetters, and full production team: thank you as well. Your keen eyes and attention to detail helped improve the final manuscript greatly. The typographical perfection of the Talmud section in chapter 5 is owed entirely to Kristin Miller. Its contents are also owed to Ethan Schwartz, Shayna Sheinfeld, and Ariann Weitzman. The index sections would not exist without Jimmy Hoke. The creation of the final product would not have been possible without this book's project manager, Chantelle Gibbs. And my family history, shared in short vignettes throughout the book, would not have been described without the archival assistance of my mother, Mara Lieberman, or our trip to Italy together in 2024. Her Italian language skills were particularly helpful in deciphering the nuances of family interviews. I am indebted to the interviewees as well, who, in addition to my mother, were my great-aunts: Annamaria Rotter, Mariella Maranzana, and Maria Luisa Rado. My uncle, James Lieberman, also assisted in family archival work, and I am grateful for his contributions.

There were parts of this project that were particularly difficult to research and write about. Shayna Sheinfeld was a beacon of light during the hardest of days—no one knows what writing this book was like as much as she does. Mary Foskett, too, provided considerable care and words of wisdom, as did Ashleigh Elser, Alexiana Fry, Meghan Henning, Heidi Kaufman, Julie Nemeth, Adele Reinhartz, Sarah Stein, and Carla Vidor. These women have my utmost praise. Cavan Concannon, Paula Fredriksen, and Matthew Thiessen also provided immense support as I was finishing drafts and applying for tenure simultaneously. To these friends and colleagues, my gratitude knows no bounds.

Finally, I owe a great deal of thanks to my spouse and our many nonhuman animals. Each of them bore the brunt of my preoccupation during the writing of this book; I have not taken their patience or encouragement for granted. Gus, you have now sat with me through the writing of three books, often without the exact amount of treats you insist you need. Thank you, sweet boy. Doug, Toby, Otis, Ru, and Ginger: You bring joy to my every day; thank you for your persistence in finding ways to peel me away from my computer screen. And Zoë, my wife, not only did you comb through pages of this book for tone and clarity, but you also provided emotional sustenance as I powered through. Thank you for consistently bringing love, joy, and comic relief to our family.

AUTHOR'S NOTE ON GENRE, AUDIENCE, TERMS, AND CONCEPTS[1]

> *What other discipline has been more anxious to separate the professional from the confessional, the public from the personal?*
>
> —Stephen D. Moore and Yvonne Sherwood[2]

The modern field of biblical studies, crafted under the impetus of the Enlightenment's "Dare to reason!" motto, customarily strives to maintain a separation between the confessional and the professional. Good academia is distanced academia, fueled by facts and philology as opposed to feeling, piety, and interpretive subjectivity. In its formative years especially, the goal of biblical studies was to situate biblical texts in their own historical contexts, often with an intellectual authority aspiring to the objective and universal. The sense was that, when read in the *right* way, the Bible would reveal the motivations of its authors and offer glimpses into the worlds in which it was made.[3]

There can, of course, be good reason to remove the personal. As biblical scholar Marc Brettler has shared, it would teeter into the realm of absurdity to suggest that the God-figure of Genesis 1 begins creation with ice cream and

---

1. This book is for scholars, students, and public audiences. The goal of this opening note is to help those readers who are new to biblical studies have a theoretical and historical foundation for the following chapters, although some explications of my overall argument and framework are also discussed here.

2. Stephen D. Moore and Yvonne Sherwood, *The Invention of the Biblical Scholar: A Critical Manifesto* (Fortress Press, 2011), xii.

3. I say "worlds" because biblical texts were written and edited by many people across different times and contexts. For more on the formation of the Bible, see, for example, David M. Carr, *The Formation of the Hebrew Bible: A New Reconstruction* (Oxford University Press, 2011); Lee Martin McDonald, *The Biblical Canon: Its Origin, Transmission, and Authority*, 3rd ed. (Baker Academic, 2007).

sorbet, as delightful as that may sound.[4] To my chagrin indeed, there are no frozen treats in the narrative. I've checked. While the text's lack of ice cream may come as no surprise—it is perhaps a more obvious misinterpretation of Genesis than an example of how personal or confessional upbringings can impact our readings—there are also more reputed elements missing from the Genesis narrative. On the topic of food, for example, there is no apple in the garden of Eden story. Instead, there is simply a *peri* or "fruit." There is also no mention of "Satan" or "sin," despite the common assumption that they are mentioned, and despite the oft-Christian assertion that both—especially sin—are central to the story.[5] That the Adam and Eve narrative is about sin and, moreover, "original" sin, is a later Christian interpretation, one fueled by an Augustinian reading of Genesis 3, Psalm 51:5, and Romans 5.[6] All of this is to say that, when conducting a critical analysis of the Bible, readers learn quickly that biblical stories tend to have a history of variegated interpretations that can be counter to, for lack of a better term, the authors' "original" intents. To put it bluntly, liking or sharing affinity with an interpretation does not make it historically or linguistically sound.[7]

Still, biblical texts, like all texts, cannot speak for themselves. Readers are required to interact with the Bible in order to generate meaning, and they do so in both conscious and unconscious ways that are dependent on a variety of factors, including but not limited to social, cultural, and educational conditioning. Who we are, put simply, impacts how we read. This is not to suggest we overlook Brettler's point and declare Genesis 1 the making of a sundae. Nor is it to endorse an "all interpretations of the Bible are equal" concept. Instead, it is to say that meaning-making is not tidy, universal, or wholly objective. The production of knowledge, including within the biblical field, is located beyond a singular approach, framework, or consciousness.

4. Marc Brettler, "Monopoly and Biblical Studies," *Ancient Jew Review*, August 9, 2023, https://www.ancientjewreview.com/read/2023/8/3/monopoly-and-biblical-studies.

5. Neither the Hebrew *chata* (transgression; sin) nor *satan* (adversary) appear at all.

6. Early Christianity scholar Paula Fredriksen provides an accessible overview, "Original Sin," *Bible Odyssey*, https://short-question.bibleodyssey.com/articles/original-sin/. See also Fredriksen, *Sin: The Early History of an Idea* (Princeton University Press, 2012).

7. On the topic of language, please note that all Bible translations in this book are in consultation with the NRSV and NRSVUE, with slight changes made throughout based on my own understanding of the terms and grammar.

In other words, while historical and linguistic grounding remains central to the biblical discipline, and while many thinkers continue to aspire to objectivism in their studies, many of them also maintain that unconditional objectivity is impossible. Some even highlight that focusing on a text's historical context generates meanings that are personal, since having an interest in (let alone the skills, tools, resources, and dialogue partners for) reading with critical, historical-contextual questions in mind tends to require a combination of education, relative economic privilege, available resources, and conversation partners with similar backgrounds who give such interests an outlet.[8] Thus engaging multiple modes of interpretation—including ones that are impacted by autobiography, church and secular history, or even a *desired* meaning of a text—has become a more prominent practice over the last few decades.[9]

---

8. Indeed, even "criticism is an act of autobiography," writes author and critic Christine Smallwood. "The work of making an argument, coming to a judgement, or simply choosing which books or objects to give time and attention to is inevitably, helplessly, an expression of values—and an expression of self . . . In the pursuit of explicating a text, observing its patterns and structure, how it works, what it means, I also explicate myself—revealing what catches my interest, where my attention lingers. I might do this more, or less, intentionally, but I always do it. Whatever is going on the life of the critic is going to show up in her reading; it can't not. Reading, writing, and thinking have experiential texture . . . I am a passionate adherent of close reading, the practice of being carefully attentive to words that are not our own. But close reading always involves the critic layering her own point of view over or next to the text's, even as she observes, explains, interprets, evaluates. What I should not do is pretend that my reading is definitive, neutral, objective, or somehow free of myself and my environment. I write criticism to encounter an object, and I read criticism to encounter another person encountering an object." See "A Reviewer's Life: The Material Constraints of Writing Criticism Today," *Yale Review*, June 10, 2024, https://yalereview.org/article/christine-smallwood-reviewers-life.

9. Autobiographical criticism, also known as "personal criticism," flowed into biblical studies from literary studies in the mid-1990s, initially through Jeffrey L. Staley, *Reading with a Passion: Rhetoric, Autobiography, and the American West in the Gospel of John* (Continuum, 1995) and Janice Capel Anderson and Jeffrey L. Staley, eds., *Taking It Personally: Autobiographical Biblical Criticism*, *Semeia* 72 (Scholars Press, 1995), attracting considerable attention. For more on the changing tides of biblical scholarship, see Fernando F. Segovia, "'And They Began to Speak in Other Tongues': Competing Modes of Discourse in Contemporary Biblical Criticism," in *Reading from This Place: Social Location and Biblical Interpretation in the United States*, ed. Fernando F. Segovia and Mary Ann Tolbert, vol. 1 (Fortress Press, 1995), 1–32. For a more recent case study, see Francis Borchardt, "CSTT and Gender #2: A Gender Theory Critique of the Historical-Critical Method," *Changes in Sacred Texts and Traditions*, July 6, 2017, https://blogs.helsinki.fi/sacredtexts/2017/07/06/

There is indeed a peculiar pathology to biblical studies, one that continues to exist even among the most traditional historical-critical modalities: Biblical scholars are trained to remain ostensibly distant from biblical texts—to hold impartiality when deciphering ancient meaning—while never forgetting the Bible's assumed cultural relevance, its supposed continuing ability to shape ideologies in its afterlife (ideologies that in turn shape one's reading of the Bible). The work of the biblical scholar, often, is to somehow keep the Bible in its past *yet also* recognize the ostensible power of the Bible in readers' presents *while never* obscuring the two. The purpose of this book is to interrogate this odd "then *not* now" but also "then *and* now" disciplinary norm *while also* being honest about the contexts, feelings, and interpretive subjectivities that shape such a multilayered approach.[10] Paul, in short, is not just a figure *in* history but also a figure *of* history, with a legacy that impacts how readers relate to him and his writings. Yes, this book is about ancient context.[11] But it is also about the changing "nows"—social, cultural, personal—that impact the intellectual imagination about Paul. To pretend that history and affect are mutually exclusive—to conduct scholarship in a way that obscures the humanity behind even the most "objective"

---

cstt-and-gender-a-gender-theory-critique-of-the-historical-critical-method/. See also Sara Parks, "'The Brooten Phenomenon': Moving Women from the Margins in Second-Temple and New Testament Scholarship," *The Bible & Critical Theory* 15 (2019): 46–64. For more on this in relation to Paul, Paul studies, and Christian anti-Judaism/philo-Judaism, see Matthew V. Novenson, "Anti-Judaism and Philo-Judaism in Pauline Studies, Then and Now," in *Protestant Bible Scholarship: Antisemitism, Philosemitism and Anti-Judaism*, ed. Arjen F. Bakker et al., vol. 200, Supplements to the *Journal for the Study of Judaism* (Brill, 2022), 106–124. As he writes, "In the history of Protestant interpretation, in particular, the collapsing of the distinction between Paul's view and the interpreter's view is, as we say nowadays, not a bug but a feature" (108).

10. On biblical studies and affect, see, for example, Maia Kotrosits, *How Things Feel: Affect Theory, Biblical Studies, and the (Im)Personal, How Things Feel*, vol. 1, Research Perspectives in Biblical Interpretation 1 (Brill, 2016).

11. To put it another way, I do not seek to "erase" the role and intents of biblical authors. I follow New Testament scholar Amy-Jill Levine's words in this regard. In her view, "While there is a theoretical concern that all meaning comes from the interpreter. . . . [this] strikes [her] as the erasure of the author and so a colonizing move on the part of the reader." See Amy-Jill Levine, "Supersessionism: Admit and Address Rather than Debate or Deny," *Religions* 13, no. 2 (2022): 156.

interpretation—would be to engage in a false positivism I do not wish to perpetuate.[12]

All of this is to say that scholars, as sophisticated as they may be in textual, historical, and philological criticisms, are not neutral. Even the construction of "enlightened" biblical studies had its hands clasped to the church, including its Paul-inspired belittlement of Jews and Judaism. In response, this book has its hands reaching for more earnest dialogue—a dialogue both within *and beyond* the biblical field (a beyond I am convinced has always existed)—about how our worlds shape our readings.[13] While this book maintains elements of Enlightenment episteme, which is to say it contextualizes Paul's writings in a first-century context so as to question what the historical Paul *might* have meant when he shared ideas of eschatological salvation, it also engages the ways in which interpretations of Paul continue to impress upon real communities, and in turn, their reading strategies.

The content of this book is for a wide audience, as is the writing style. It offers an accessible introduction to Paul's theology of salvation while recognizing that the boundaries between the academy and the laity, and the professional and the personal, are often more illusory than factual. At times, chapters will include sections of autobiography so as to render temporarily visible the ordinarily invisibilized zone where the personal impacts the professional or where the "now" impacts the "then" and vice versa. In order to upset these ostensible boundaries while still maintaining legibility, asterisks will be used to demarcate the more traditional scholarship from the questions, experiences, and confessions driving it.[14] In chapter 4, however, these asterisks will be removed to evoke a more earnest interaction among text, context, and interpretation. Again, this is not to discount the work of close readings, to render autobiography "better" than historical contextualization, or to underprivilege

12. "False positivism" is from Charles Strozier and used in Amy Johnson Frykholm, *Rapture Culture: Left Behind in Evangelical America*, 1st ed. (Oxford University Press, 2004), 4. See also Charles B. Strozier, *Apocalypse: On the Psychology of Fundamentalism in America* (Beacon Press, 1994), 11.

13. By "beyond," I mean that even when biblical scholars have striven to maintain a separation between the confessional and the professional, that separation has remained fluid.

14. I take my inspiration from a recent source, Cavan W. Concannon's *Profaning Paul* (University of Chicago Press, 2021), which also disrupts boundaries by way of autoethnography and the use of asterisks to separate his personal stories from more traditional ones of scholarship.

literary and archaeological evidence in the pursuit of historical reconstruction; it is simply to show how our environments—even the scholarly ones—impact our encounters with and expressions of the evidence. As readers will see, one of the theses of this book is that our environments, perhaps especially our environments' attitudes toward Jews, have consistently shaped our impressions of Paul. If I am to maintain this claim, I find it important to be honest about the environments shaping my own evaluations, too.

Finally, while I strive to explain terms and concepts as I write, below is an introduction to key topics, followed by a glossary and timeline on which to rely if needed. The remainder of this opening note, much like the information shared above, is more for those new to the conversation than for those already immersed in it. My goal in these opening pages is to help new readers have a theoretical and historical foundation for the following chapters.

Wrestling with Paul engages topics of apocalypticism, eschatology, and soteriology. While Paul did not write apocalypses, he did engage in apocalyptic eschatological thinking, which included soteriological contemplation. To better understand what I mean by this and how it relates to a broader ancient context, here is some background:

> Apocalyptic texts were first written by Jews in the late centuries BCE under Greek and Roman rule.[15] Leaning on the Greek term for "unveiling" (*apokalupsis*), an ancient "apocalypse" does not refer to the end of the world, but rather a genre of revelatory literature in which otherworldly beings unveil cosmic truths to human recipients. Such cosmic truths often included conceptions of the "end of days," or eschaton, which referred to a future time in which the world would change into something more God-centric. For many first-century Jewish writers, this new world order was thought to be experienced universally, ushered in by the God of Israel and that God's chosen messiah.[16]

---

15. 1 Enoch and the book of Daniel contain some of the earliest known apocalypses. The oldest parts of 1 Enoch are dated to ca. 300 to 200 BCE. Although the apocalyptic story in Daniel (chapters 7–12) takes place during the Babylonian exile, it was written in the Hellenistic period in the second century BCE.

16. Not all Hellenistic-Roman–era Jewish eschatological schemes had messiahs, however; for more on eschatology and messianism, see chapter 4.

Apocalypses carried with them a variety of theological ideas. In addition to eschatology (i.e., reflections on "the end"), they often included conceptions of cosmic goodness and badness. This dualistic worldview is known as "apocalypticism." And when these ideas of goodness and badness are wrapped up in apocalyptic worldly endings—in, for instance, the idea that the God of Israel will usher in a new world order in which the *good* will be rewarded—that is called "apocalyptic eschatology." Apocalyptic eschatology, in other words, refers to the belief that the world is composed of cosmic goodness and badness, and that at some point, with the help of God, the goodness will overcome the badness in the eschaton. Apocalyptic eschatology is also often soteriological in that it can include conditions for salvation (e.g., what kind of person will be ushered into the eschaton, when, and why).

Scholars consider Paul to be an apocalyptic eschatological thinker in that he envisions Jesus as God's chosen messiah, the one who will help usher in God's end of days. Paul's theology is also soteriologically driven in that he discusses the conditions for eschatological salvation, mostly for gentiles but also for Jews.

It is also important to keep in mind that none of Paul's writings—just as none of the New Testament texts—were written at a time when a systematic, doctrinal, or creedal Christianity existed. To put it another way, while there were followers of Jesus in the early centuries CE, there was not yet a developed tradition known as "Christianity." For this reason, I avoid the term "Christianity" when alluding to the historical context of New Testament texts. I also avoid the term "Christian," not only because Paul never used it—perhaps, in fact, because he did not *want* to use it—but also because it too easily carries the modern assumption that to be Christian means to not be Jewish.[17] In the New Testament period, a mix of Jews and gentiles followed Jesus as their Christ, and so for this reason I will refer to these followers as either "Jewish Christ-confessors" / "Jewish Christ-followers" or "gentile Christ-confessors" / "gentile Christ-followers" or members of the "Jesus movement."[18]

17. The word "Christian" appears in three instances in the New Testament, all in texts Paul did not write (Acts 11:26, 26:28; 1 Pet 4:16). That Paul may have deliberately not used the word "Christian" is New Testament scholar Matthew Thiessen's suggestion. See also Matthew Thiessen, *A Jewish Paul: The Messiah's Herald to the Gentiles* (Baker Academic, 2023), 12–13.

18. Cf. Josh Garroway, *Paul's Gentile-Jews: Neither Jew nor Gentile, but Both* (Palgrave Macmillan, 2012).

Similarly, I avoid the term "church" when discussing Jesus, Paul, and their early supporters. Yes, Paul did rely on the Greek word *ekklēsia* in his letters, which does often translate as "church," but this word often carries with it modern assumptions of Christian doctrine and worship spaces. *Ekklēsia* in Paul's time did not signal Christianity in the way it does today, as, again, Christianity as we know it did not yet exist. In Paul's time, *ekklēsia* was a generic word for "gathering," regardless of the identity of the gatherers. For this reason, I will rely on English terms such as "association," "gathering," or "assembly" to discuss groups and group meetings of early Christ-confessors.

This is not to say that first-century ideas about Jesus have no connection to later church practice. There were, for example, early theologies that *were* eventually declared orthodox by the church in the fourth century CE. These ideas are called "proto-Orthodox" theologies; they were precursors to Christian orthodoxy but not yet dominant at the time when writers such as Paul were writing. When alluding to these theologies, I will use the term "proto-Orthodox."

Glossary

apocalypse (1): A revelation or an unveiling of knowledge (in Greek, *apokalupsis*).

apocalypse (2): A genre of revelatory literature in which an otherworldly being discloses cosmic truths to an earthly recipient. Such revelations often include elements of eschatology and soteriology.

apocalyptic: That which takes on the qualities of apocalypse and/or apocalypticism (e.g., a text can exude an "apocalyptic" worldview).

apocalypticism: A social ideology maintaining that the world is mysterious and contains forces of good and evil. The present world, moreover, is thought to be corrupt and/or controlled by evil forces. God will thus intervene in the end-times to (1) destroy that evil and (2) inaugurate a new world order.

apocalyptic cure: The notion that apocalypses or apocalyptic thinking exudes a type of therapy for implied readers (e.g., reason[s] for why things are the way they are and hope that good will prevail).

apocalyptic eschatology: Ideas about the end-times that are apocalyptic.

Apocrypha: Greek for "hidden things"; refers to texts on the sidelines of a biblical canon. Because the Jewish, Catholic, and Protestant traditions have different biblical canons, the Apocrypha differ (e.g., 1 and 2 Maccabees are apocryphal in Jewish and Protestant traditions but canonical in Catholic tradition).

apostle: Greek for "herald" or "messenger." In later Christian tradition, the term often implies an important rank or closeness to Jesus.

Babylonian Exile: The period in which many ancient Israelites were sent from Judah into exile by the Neo-Babylonian Empire. While most of those exiled did not return to Judah after captivity, others did with the help of the Persian King Cyrus. Other Israelites had stayed in Judah during the time of exile, and others still went to the northern territories of Israel and nearby places.

Christ: From the Greek *Christos*, meaning "messiah." A title of veneration.

diaspora: Those who are scattered outside of their people's homeland (e.g., Israelites who did not return from exile or Jews who were scattered after the destruction of the Second Temple).

eschatology: The study of or knowledge about the end-times (*eskatos* = last; *logia* = study of).

eschaton: Final things or end of days.

Godfearers: Ancient gentile sympathizers of the Jewish God who involved themselves in varying degrees with the activities of Jewish synagogue communities.

Hebrew Bible: A catchall term to refer to both the Jewish Bible (a.k.a. the *Tanakh*) and the Christian Old Testament, regardless of the denomination. It is an incomplete term in that the *Tanakh* and Old Testament(s) differ slightly from one another, but it is still used as a way to be more inclusive of similar-yet-different canons.

Israel: An ancient land with changing borders residing alongside the Afro-Asiatic tectonic plates that meet in the Jordan River Valley. Prior to the Assyrian conquest of its northern highlands in 722 BCE, the northern area was called "Israel," while the southern highlands were called "Judah" (renamed "Judea" in the Greek and Roman periods). The northern and southern highlands collectively, however, were also called "Israel" for much of ancient Israelite history and into the early Jewish period.

Israelite: One of the people of Israel, who worshipped the God of Israel, prior to the use of the term "Jew" in the Persian and later periods. The God of Israel was imagined as being connected to the land of Israel but also pancosmic.

Jew: From the word "Judah." A person who ethnically identified with the Jewish people—a group that saw itself as connected to the God of Israel—in the Persian and later periods. Many Jews today may identify as ethnically or culturally Jewish without faith-based connections to the God of Israel or the modern State of Israel.

***kyrios*:** Greek for "Lord" or "master"; a term used in the New Testament to refer to the God of Israel.

messiah: Anointed one, such as a king or priest, often connected to King David (Hebrew = *Moshiach*; Greek = *Christos*).

messianic age: New world order ushered in by the messiah.

messianic expectation: Ancient Jewish hope that a messiah, often thought to be in the line of the ancient Israelite King David, would come and overthrow the powers that be to establish a new world order in which all humanity would worship the God of Israel.

New Testament: The second testament in Christian tradition. Written in Koine Greek, a common dialect in the Hellenistic period.

Old Testament: The Christian first testament, similar to the Jewish *Tanakh*, with slight differences depending on the tradition (e.g., the Catholic and Protestant Old Testaments have slight variations). Comprised of four sections: Pentateuch, historical books, poetical books, and prophets. Written mostly in Hebrew.

orthodoxy: Greek for "right opinion"; the version of Christianity, later called "catholicism" (i.e., "universal") by its proponents, that gained systematic support and became institutionalized as "Catholicism" in the fourth and later centuries (many of its defining beliefs are stated in the Nicene Creed, which was crafted in the fourth century). There was, however, a formal schism between the Roman Catholic Church and the Eastern Orthodox Church in the eleventh century CE.

Palestine: The land that some inhabitants called "Israel" was also, even in antiquity, called "Palestine." Already in the fifth century BCE, for example, the territory was called "Palestine" by some Greek writers, perhaps deriving from a wider consideration of the neighboring land of Philistia. After the second-century (CE) Roman expulsion of Jews from Judea, the empire renamed the territory "Syria Palaestina." From antiquity to today, the area has undergone border changes and sociopolitical renamings as a range of peoples have controlled and dwelled in the territory throughout the centuries.[19]

proto-orthodoxy: A collection of theologies that were retrospectively validated by one branch of the imperial Christian church in the fourth and later centuries.

Septuagint: A Greek translation of Hebrew scriptures dating from the third to second centuries BCE. Many New Testament writers utilized the Septuagint version of Jewish texts when making sense of Jesus as their Christ.

soteriology: Ideas of salvation.

supersessionism: The idea that Christianity supersedes and/or replaces Judaism. Can be thought of in conversation with other traditions claiming to be superior to or overriding competing groups.

***Tanakh*:** The Jewish Bible, similar to the Christian Old Testament. Comprised of three sections: Torah (Teachings), Nevi'im (Prophets), and Ketuvim (Writings). Written mostly in Hebrew.

---

19. For an accessible overview of this conversation, see Chance Bonar, "Myth: 'The Name Palestine Is a Roman Invention,'" *Everyday Orientalism*, September 23, 2024, https://everydayorientalism.wordpress.com/2024/09/23/myth-the-name-palestine-is-a-roman-invention-eopalestine-06/.

Timeline

Dates are based on the modern Gregorian calendar.

597 BCE	Beginning of exile of Israelites by the Neo-Babylonian Empire.
586 BCE	First Jerusalem Temple destroyed by the Neo-Babylonian Empire.
539 BCE	Beginning of the Persian Period.
538 BCE	King Cyrus issues a decree allowing Jews to return to Israel and rebuild the Jerusalem Temple.
515 BCE	Second Jerusalem Temple is completed and dedicated to the God of Israel.
332 BCE	Beginning of the Greek Period.
142 BCE	Beginning of the Hasmonean Dynasty in Israel.
63 BCE	Beginning of the Roman Period.
37 BCE	Rome appoints King Herod to serve as the client king of Jews in Judea and surrounding districts in Israel.
4 BCE	Jesus is born, and King Herod dies; Herod's sons take over Judea and surrounding territories.
30 CE	Jesus dies by Roman crucifixion.
50s–60s CE	Paul writes his letters; Paul dies around 65 CE.
70 CE	Romans destroy the Second Jerusalem Temple.
70–95 CE	Gospels eventually chosen for canonization are written.
135 CE	Romans expel Jews from Judea.
312 CE	Constantine embraces a Christ-following orientation.
313–325	Constantine gathers the council of Nicaea.
325 CE	The Nicene Creed is sponsored by the imperial church.
363 CE	The last non-Christ-following emperor, Julian, dies.
367 CE	Athanasius circulates a twenty-seven-book New Testament canon.
380 CE	Roman emperor Theodosius 1 declares the empire to be Nicene Christian.
393 CE	Athanasius's twenty-seven-book New Testament becomes canon (reaffirmed in 397 CE).

PREFACE

Wrestling

My first confession is that I used to be a wrestler. Before college, and long before my formal entrance into the academic world, I was one of the only girls in the state of Nevada to be on a high school wrestling team. Sometimes, I was the only girl, and at least during my tenure, was the only girl to earn a varsity letter in my state for the sport. This wasn't necessarily something to celebrate. Other girls wanted to wrestle but were not allowed on their schools' teams because of their sex. Many would approach me at matches and share how lucky I was to have such an open-minded coach. This knowledge often added an extra layer to the brawl. I was fighting for both a pin and a place. A place of belonging. A place of respect. A place in which girls—all of us—were allowed.[1]

I still have my wrestling shoes. I even still have my headgear, which might be one of the most unsanitary pieces of equipment I own. The headgear in particular reminds me of what it felt like to be on the mat. It was excruciating. I would twist my body as the side of my head would be slammed into the ground, doing just about anything I could to avoid being pinned. I would hear ringing in my ears and be on the verge of passing out before the buzzer would finally blast. Once, I threw up in the middle of a tournament. I had barely eaten to make the required weight, and by the time my third match started, I was too weak to fight.

There were good days, though. Great ones, even. My first tournament was exhilarating. I was fifteen years old, weighed in at ninety-five pounds, and won my first match 6-0. Almost everyone in the stands was cheering, I expect because many of them had never seen a girl competing in the sport.

1. I mean this in the most expansive sense.

The adrenaline—the badassery of it all, really—is what kept me going.[2] I liked fighting the system. I liked doing something that was hard and different. I liked fighting the norm, even if/when it felt like I was fighting with my own self.

And the system fought back. A parent once shared publicly how inappropriate it was for me to be on a "boys' team." He wouldn't even look at me when he spoke. He just wanted me to hear his anger and to see others nodding in agreement. I experienced animosity in subtler ways, too. There was no place for me to change, for example. While the boys on my team had a locker room, I had to find a bathroom in another part of the building. I often had to race doing this so I could be back in time for warm-ups. This happened at tournaments too. When weigh-ins would happen before matches, I wasn't allowed to join the locker room until the end—after everyone else had weighed in. Often, the opposing team—and sometimes a few wrestlers from my own—would make catcalls as I walked in. A handful of opponents would even forfeit their match with me so as to avoid grappling with a girl on the mat. I was never sure if this was their choice, their coach's, or their parents'. I was also never sure of the reason. Did they think a boy wrestling a girl would amount to a new kind of sexual spectacle?[3] Did they think I was "doing" femaleness wrong by joining a team of boys? Or did they simply not want to lose to a girl? All I know is that, for many, I had crossed lines. My existence on the mat was unnatural. I would be left alone to take a forfeited "win," which, despite earning points for my team, often felt like a personal loss.

Wrestling and biblical studies are not mutually exclusive either. In the book of Genesis, Jacob brawls with a disguised divine being, often interpreted

---

2. Much more can be said on this with regard to sex and gender. I suspect much of the cheering coincided with the fact that I was a cis girl wrestler. While I was breaking gendered boundaries, I wasn't breaking *too many* boundaries from the perspective of traditional onlookers in the early 2000s.

3. See Deborah Brake, "Wrestling with Gender: Constructing Masculinity by Refusing to Wrestle Women," *Nevada Law Journal* 13 (2013): 489. Here she writes, "Even the lingo of the sport is loaded with possible double entendres suggesting an undercurrent of sexuality (e.g., 'wrestling up the backside,' 'high crotch takedown,' the 'butt grab'). Wrestlers themselves, along with their coaches and educated fan base, know that the extraordinary, undivided focus required to compete in the sport leaves little room for distracting feelings of attraction or desire in the heat of a match. Still, more so than for other sports, the potential is there for sexualizing the sport in a way that is inconsistent with maintaining a strong hetero-masculine identity for the sport and its participants."

as Jacob's God (or an angel on behalf of that God), from night till dawn. For his skill and stamina, Jacob is renamed "Israel"—meaning "to wrestle with God" (Gen 32:4–36:43). In Rabbinic Judaism, this story is recited toward the beginning of the Jewish calendar year. The message behind it, however, carries through the entire solar-lunar cycle. In Judaism, it is okay to take philosophical risks. It is okay for us to enter theological brawls. I say "us" here because my second confession is this: I am Jewish. As members of *am-Israel*, it is part of our collective being to engage the struggle.[4]

The letters we call Paul's also invoke images of the wrestler. In 1 Corinthians, for example, the apostle attests that his work is that of a true athlete's; he aims for the ultimate prize: salvation (1 Cor 9:24–27). And in Ephesians, the author (almost certainly not Paul but rather a later imitator of Paul) attests to the power of wrestling for preserving intellectual and spiritual truth: "The wrestling [*palē*] for us is not against blood and flesh but against the rulers, against the authorities, against the cosmic forces of darkness, and against the spiritual powers of evil in the heavenly realms" (Eph 6:12).[5] Indeed, it takes a certain kind of athleticism to enter the world of ideas. For the ancient philosophers, wrestling was how meaning-making worked. Sometimes it was friendly, sometimes it was ruthless, but it was still viewed as a virtuous yet vulnerable give-and-take between two or more parties. "Try a fall with me," said Socrates, and "we shall both be the better."[6]

There are certainly aspects of Pauline studies that remind me of wrestling, and not just the theological contentions. One in particular is its effect on my nerves. I have the same nervous excitement—the *I cannot believe I am doing this* feeling—that I would get before every match. I suspect no small part of this has to do with the claustrophobic Christian-centeredness of Pauline

4. It is also a common metaphor that scholars engage in their work. See, for example, Phyllis Trible, "Biblical Views: Wrestling with Faith," *Biblical Archeology Review*, September/October 2014, https://library.biblicalarchaeology.org/department/biblical-views-wrestling-with-faith/; Phyllis Trible, *Texts of Terror: Literary-Feminist Readings of Biblical Narratives*, 40th anniversary ed. (Fortress Press, 2022), 4–5; Daniel Boyarin, *A Radical Jew: Paul and the Politics of Identity* (University of California Press, 1997), which has an introduction titled "Wrestling with Paul"; Pamela Eisenbaum, *Paul Was Not a Christian: The Original Message of a Misunderstood Apostle* (HarperOne, 2009), 3; Concannon, *Profaning Paul*, 6–7.

5. I return to issues of Pauline authorship in chapter 1.

6. From Plato's *Theaetetus*. See Richard Eva, "Wrestling with Philosophy," *Public Discourse*, August 8, 2021, https://www.thepublicdiscourse.com/2021/08/77088/.

studies, an area of inquiry that, as we will see, has, through most of its history, loved to talk about Jews and Judaism—but only so long as they are dead or presumed dead, spiritually at least, if not physically. Literary scholar Dara Horn sees this as a common phenomenon, one that highlights, for example, that "the entire appeal of Anne Frank to the wider world—as opposed to those who knew and loved her—lay in her lack of a future."[7] People don't like to hear from living Jews, Horn argues. Instead, they like the good-world-making stories of the dead ones—ones such as Anne Frank's, whose diary includes the now famous line "I still believe, in spite of everything, that people are truly good at heart."[8] Like my status as a wrestler, *Wrestling with Paul* is meant to be boldly countercultural. It will not end with a living Jew saying that a dead one, Paul, is truly good.

Another reason for the wrestling-like nerves may have to do with the shared misogynist contours of my wrestling experience and the male-centeredness of biblical studies, not least traditional Pauline studies.[9] In the pages to follow, readers will notice that men dominate the conversation on Paul and Judaism. Men and maleness also dominate Paul's own theological outlook, as readers will see most clearly in chapter 4. But the truth of the matter is that I never thought I'd write a book about Paul. Christian- and male-centeredness aside, I, for years, declared that Paul's ideologies made no sense to me. No matter how much I squirmed around the theological jargon, trying to twist and turn his and his interpreters' words to make them fit, I felt pinned on every read.[10]

7. Dara Horn, *People Love Dead Jews: Reports from a Haunted Present* (W. W. Norton, 2021), 8.

8. Horn urges readers to recognize that Frank wrote this sentence before she was murdered. She also urges readers to recognize how quickly the needs and insights of living Jews are dismissed.

9. Again, see Borchardt, "CSTT and Gender #2." See also Parks, "'The Brooten Phenomenon'"; and Stephen L. Young's final section in "Let's Take the Text Seriously: The Protectionist Doxa of Mainstream New Testament Studies," *Method & Theory in the Study of Religion* 32, no. 4/5 (2020): 328–363.

10. I am not alone in this contention. As New Testament scholar L. Ann Jervis summarizes, "Others argue that looking for coherence is a lost cause: Paul is not a coherent thinker. The reason it is hard to understand Paul is not the problem of interpreters, but the problem of the apostle—Paul's thought is full of inconsistencies." See L. Ann Jervis, "Paul the Theologian," in *The Oxford Handbook of Pauline Studies*, ed. Matthew V. Novenson and R. Barry Matlock (Oxford University Press, 2022), 73.

Writing instead on Gospels and Apocalypses, I thought I had dodged the apostle's views and the volumes of secondary literature about him. In a way, I was acting like the very athletes who refused to wrestle me.

My time of avoidance, however, has come to an end. I am finally ready to confront my nerves and meet my interlocuters on the mat. I imagine extending my hand out to Paul's, and also to his interpreters', knowing that I am about to suffer pain as I grapple with them. I imagine shaking their hands with uncertainty, worrying how they will respond to my interpretive throws, yet still emboldened by the drive of my claims.

Paul, I hope to show, was not a universalist. Instead, emanating from his Hellenistic Jewish worldview, he argued that Jews needed to maintain the law in Christ, including that which kept them ethnically distinct, and that gentiles needed to abstain from the law in Christ, especially that which kept Jews ethnically distinct. Both groups, in other words, needed to maintain ethnic difference in their particular Christ-following orientations lest they be "left behind" from Paul's imagined end of days (and many *were* left behind).[11] Furthermore, the way in which Paul understood these groups was through ethnonationalist, ethnocratic, and hierarchical means. By "ethnonationalist,"

11. I often put "left behind" in scare quotes because of the phrase's hold on modern conceptions of the end-times. Generally speaking, the concept of "left behind" refers to an eschatological idea popularized by an evangelical interpretation of 1 Thessalonians and Revelation. In 1 Thessalonians, for example, Paul explains that when Jesus manifests in the upper air in his resurrected state, the "good" will be rewarded by being invited into the eschaton—a new world order in which the God of Israel will be the God of all people. Paul adds that those who have already died will be ushered in first, followed by those who are still living. The latter group will be "caught up" (Latinized as *rapturo*) in the clouds to meet Jesus in the air. In popular evangelical imagination, this idea has been combined with readings of the book of Revelation. In Revelation, after the author's non-Christ-following enemies are destroyed by cosmic forces, Christ ushers in a new kingdom in which he and his God reign supreme. Modern evangelical rapture theology takes the destruction scenes of Revelation and inserts them into the *rapturo* of 1 Thessalonians. Those who are not "good" and thus not "caught up" with Jesus (1 Thess) are the ones who will face divinely sanctioned chaos (Revelation). Tim LaHaye and Jerry B. Jenkins's Christian book series, *Left Behind*, offers one of the most well-known contemporary discussions of this apocalyptic eschatology. Set in the modern era, it tells the story of righteous Christians being taken into the heavenly realm while the rest of humanity suffers in the earthly realm amid disorder and devastation. See also the section titled "Left Behind(s)" in Sarah Emanuel, "Down the Rabbit Hole . . . to the Humor of Apocalypse and the End of the World, LOL," in *Apocalypses in Context: Apocalyptic Currents Through History*, ed. Kelly J. Murphy and Justin Jeffcoat Schedtler, 2nd ed. (Fortress Press, 2025), 439–465.

I mean he viewed the end of days as a new, Israel-centric nation requiring particular polyethnic-cultural affiliation: Jews for Christ and gentiles for Christ.[12] By "hierarchical" and "ethnocratic," I mean that Paul valued Jews for Christ over gentiles for Christ (and also males over females and free persons over enslaved persons); after all, Paul's end of days was itself Israel-centered (i.e., Jewish-centered) with the God of Israel (i.e., the Jewish God) at the helm. Finally, none of these beliefs made Paul exceptional in his Judaism. On the contrary, they made him average in his Judaism.[13]

Such arguments are not popular in Pauline academia due in large part to their potential ethical ramifications. On the one hand, for many both inside and outside Pauline studies, Paul's writings constitute scripture. Therefore, if scholars assert that Paul was exclusive, ethnocentric, and hierarchical in his ideology, it follows that those who regard Paul's writings as scripture may adopt, or at least lean into, similar exclusive, ethnocentric, ethnocratic, and hierarchical perspectives. On the other hand, if Paul's ethnocentric, ethnonationalist exclusivity is seen as a negative quality, then it leads to a different moral issue; the Bible cannot be stained with such noxious ideologies. Furthermore, if these ideologies are seen as generated *from* Paul's Jewish worldview, then Judaism risks facing even more anti-Judaism. History has certainly demonstrated this dynamic, as readers will soon see.

I hope to wrestle with all of this—and not necessarily with the aim of tackling or pinning it into a confined hold. I intend instead to confront the ethical stakes: to name them, unpack them, acknowledge them, and most importantly not apologize for them. In brief, I am tired of bending Paul and his letters so as to make them ahistorically "good." That feels like a forfeit.

The following pages will orient readers to Paul's theology, especially his eschatological soteriology, with my own evaluations of Pauline inclusion and exclusion addressed throughout.

Let the match begin.

12. For more on nationalism in antiquity, see David M. Goodblatt, *Elements of Ancient Jewish Nationalism* (Cambridge University Press, 2006), chapter 1.

13. Note, however, that this paragraph is just one part of my three-part thesis. For a fuller explication, see the introduction, 11–13.

The author, age 17.

Introduction

Wrestling the "Good" of Paul and Pauline Studies

> *People who are destined for sainthood are human, and all humans have failings.*
>
> —E. P. Sanders[1]

Of the twenty-seven books within the New Testament canon, thirteen are attributed to the *apostolos* (i.e., herald or messenger) Paul. That's nearly half of the New Testament, making Paul, for many, the second most important person in the Christian tradition, just behind Jesus. Pauline theology, crafted through interpretations of Paul's letters, has had a profound impact on the development of Christian thought and practice, and it remains central to the Christian church.[2] One of Paul's most lasting impacts is his theology of eschatological salvation—his understanding of *who* will be saved in the end of days and *how* they will be saved.

Despite the popular assumption that the Christian church is absent from academic biblical studies—or that biblical scholars are on a quest to undermine Christian faith—Christian faith remains, like Paul to Christianity, central.[3] By way of background, biblical studies as an academic discipline emerged in the eighteenth century, primarily in Germany, as a field that focused on the humanity of biblical stories. The Bible became an object of cultural inquiry—a

---

1. E. P. Sanders, *Paul: The Apostle's Life, Letters, and Thought* (Fortress Press, 2015), 222.

2. By "Paul's letters," I mean more specifically "letters we call Paul's," as Paul relied on scribes to craft his work. Later writers/editors also added to Paul's corpus—how much, we do not know.

3. See, for example, Young, "Let's Take the Text Seriously." Here, Young argues that Christian (protectionist) instincts still dominate mainstream New Testament studies at the level of *doxa*, or disciplinary commonsense, such that it is overwhelmingly common (including among those who are not deliberately trying to produce Christian-friendly readings) for scholars to identify with biblical texts, repeat their own myths of origins in their scholarly analyses, and prefer readings that keep the Bible exceptional.

collection of stories created by humans with human subjectivities—as opposed to a divinely authored guidebook on faith. At first, many intellectuals resolved that the Bible merited uncensored critique. Its crime-ridden books—the near-sacrifice of Isaac, expulsion of Hagar, genocide of the Canaanites, sacrifice of Jephthah's daughter, and nearly the entire book of Revelation, to name a few—must be interrogated and named unfit for moral society. Not everyone agreed, however. Most declared that the Bible, even if historically distant from modernity and filled with painful plots of genocide, rape, and warfare, must encompass some sort of abiding moral core.[4] There must be a *reason* for the bloodshed. There must be a message that *exceeds* the pain. Some eighteenth-century biblical scholars thus became apologists, finding ways to dig around episodes of moral horror to excavate truer, more principled readings. The Bible, for them, needed to remain *good*.

By the nineteenth century, a quest for biblical morality was ostensibly forgotten. Rational readers do not engage irresolvable readings, and biblical morality was, according to rational minds, irresolvable. This does not mean that the theological zest of the early church fathers and later reformers was missing from the discipline.[5] Instead, it meant that theological convictions were shaping biblical interpretation in ways unexamined. Christianity, especially Protestant Christianity, became the unchecked mover of academic biblical scholarship, influencing the questions and conclusions biblical scholars were bringing to the text. Even for those whose specific theological convictions seemed to be out of sight from their writing projects, affirmations of a broader Christ-centered faith and the belief in a biblical "good" were palpably present in their projects. Indeed, much of academic biblical interpretation remains tied to some kind of Christian thinking. This includes the pursuit to render the Bible and especially the New Testament—or at least key figures within it such as God, Jesus, and Paul—righteous. Dara Horn, literary scholar and writer of the popular *People Love Dead Jews*, surmises that this is part and parcel of a

4. For examples on either side of the interpretive aisle, see Moore and Sherwood, *The Invention of the Biblical Scholar*, 47–75.

5. A sustained quest for morality was seen especially in the "first quest" for the historical Jesus, who regularly turned out to be a first-century preacher of nineteenth-century European morality. Moore and Sherwood, *The Invention of the Biblical Scholar*, 64–70.

Christian worldview. Happy endings are expected—needed.[6] Biblical scholar Jill Hicks-Keeton calls such good-making the "Bible benevolence project."[7] Christian interpreters often "make smooth" the Bible's "rough edges" by finding reasons for the harm.[8]

Like the Bible itself, however, the biblical field has ruptures. Within it are numerous intellectual fissures, challenges, and alternatives—which is to say, not everyone engages in good-book-making. For some, in fact, the ethical reading of the Bible renders it unethical (surely, at the very least, we can agree that the gang rape of Judges 19 and the god-ordained sexual assault of Revelation 2 are not okay).[9] Some scholars will also make clear that the

---

6. Horn, *People Love Dead Jews*, 78–79. For work on unhappy readings, see Rhiannon Graybill, *Texts After Terror: Rape, Sexual Violence, and the Hebrew Bible* (Oxford University Press, 2021). In relation to Graybill, see Trible, *Texts of Terror*.

7. Jill Hicks-Keeton, *Good Book: How White Evangelicals Save the Bible to Save Themselves* (Fortress Press, 2023), 8. See also Robert J. Myles, "The Fetish for a Subversive Jesus," *Journal for the Study of the Historical Jesus* 14, no. 1 (2016): 52–70; Stephen L. Young, "'Make Rome Great Again' Preceded 'Make America Great Again': The Ancient Romo-Nationalism of Biblical Writers," *Interpretation* 78, no. 4 (2024): 321–334.

8. Hicks-Keeton, *Good Book*, 7–8. We see this kind of "good-making" work at play in a wide variety of publications. In philosopher Simon Critchley's *The Faith of the Faithless*, for example, Critchley writes that Paul "is trouble" but in a positive, revolutionary sense. For Critchley, "the spirit of Paul is the movement of reformation. It is the attempt to clear away the corruption, secularism, and intellectual sophistry of the established church and to return to the religious core of Christianity." See Simon Critchley, *The Faith of the Faithless: Experiments in Political Theology* (Verso Books, 2012), 155. English philosopher Elaine Storkey offers a similar reading of Jesus in Mark 5. Jesus responds to the hemorrhaging woman with a breath of fresh air, she contends, simply for the fact that he did not publicly scold her for touching his cloak (as if readers should assume that she deserved to be treated badly). See Elaine Storkey, *Women in a Patriarchal World: Twenty-Five Empowering Stories from the Bible* (SPCK, 2020), 114. Even those who interrogate the Bible's androcentrism, patriarchy, and injustice find ways to excavate goodness for minoritized readers. See especially Eric C. Smith, *Paul the Progressive?: The Compassionate Christian's Guide to Reclaiming the Apostle as an Ally* (Chalice Press, 2019), in which he argues that Paul can be seen as a progressive ally for modern readers. Minoritized readers have themselves also often excavated goodness. See, for example, Lisa M. Bowens, *African American Readings of Paul: Reception, Resistance, and Transformation* (Eerdmans, 2020).

9. See Elizabeth Cady Stanton, *The Woman's Bible: A Classic Feminist Perspective* (Dover Publications, 2003); Yvonne Sherwood, *Biblical Blaspheming: Trials of the Sacred for a Secular Age*, 1st ed. (Cambridge University Press, 2012), chapter 1; Hicks-Keeton, *Good Book*, 4–7. For more on the Bible's sexualized violence, see, as just a few examples, Renita Weems, *Battered*

violence depicted in the Bible has been used to justify violence beyond the Bible, especially toward those who do not function at the center of societal systems. Readers interested in the livelihoods of women, BIPOC, LGBTQ+, disabled, and/or Jewish individuals, for example, will highlight how biblical interpretation has perpetuated harm against these persons and how the Bible might be used differently, if at all. Such interpretations of and for the marginalized, however, remain, in a word, marginal,[10] as do cross-examinations of the Bible's presumed goodness.[11] Academics, after all, are human. And as humans—many of them products of Christian cultural and social spaces, thus making the biblical field in many instances a Christian cultural one—they have found it easier to maintain that the Bible is not just a Good Book but a Great Book, carrying within its Good-God clutches a lasting cultural relevance that must be good—or at the very least *made* good—for humanity.

Such good-book-making is prevalent in Pauline studies and, in my view, most prominent in work on Paul's relations to Jews and Judaism.[12] For example, when Paul belittles Jews in his letters—saying that they are enemies of the gospel (Rom 11:28), under a curse (Gal 3:10), displeasers and opposers

---

Love: Marriage, Sex, and Violence in the Hebrew Prophets (Fortress, 1995); Amy Kalmanofsky, *Sexual Violence and Sacred Texts* (FSR Books, 2017); Tina Pippin, *Death and Desire: The Rhetoric of Gender in the Apocalypse of John* (Westminster John Knox, 1992); Sarah Emanuel, *Humor, Resistance, and Jewish Cultural Persistence in the Book of Revelation: Roasting Rome* (Cambridge University Press, 2020); Sarah Emanuel, *Trauma Theory, Trauma Story: A Narration of Biblical Studies and the World of Trauma*, Brill Research Perspectives in Biblical Interpretation (Brill, 2021); Lynn R. Huber and Gail R. O'Day, *Wisdom Commentary: Revelation* (Liturgical Press, 2023).

10. Moore and Sherwood, *The Invention of the Biblical Scholar*, 116–117.

11. Even the Deists, eighteenth- and nineteenth-century "freethinkers" extraordinaire, "seemed to recoil from the audacity of charging the biblical God with immorality and declaring Holy Writ antecedently unfit, impossible, or incredible on moral grounds." Moore and Sherwood, *The Invention of the Biblical Scholar*, 58.

12. Although not exclusively. As Sheila Briggs explains, the common "historicist approach" in New Testament studies is to read Paul's authentic letters with a supplemental "appeal to a normative emancipatory core," often with the intersectional Galatians 3:28 at the helm. See Sheila Briggs, "Slavery and Gender," in *On the Cutting Edge: The Study of Women in the Biblical World: Essays in Honor of Elisabeth Schüssler Fiorenza*, ed. Jane Schaberg, Alice Bach, and Esther Fuchs, 1st ed. (Continuum, 2003), 173. See also Marianne Bjelland Kartzow, "'Asking the Other Question': An Intersectional Approach to Galatians 3:28 and the Colossian Household Codes," *Biblical Interpretation* 18, no. 4–5 (January 1, 2010): 366. For more on Galatians 3:28, see chapter 4.

to everyone (1 Thess 2:15), and cut off from the economy of salvation (Rom 11:7)—modern scholars tend to sanitize his claims by asserting that Paul is speaking to gentiles who have mistaken their own position. Paul, according to these thinkers, is making Judaism only *appear* less attractive in an effort to persuade gentiles to *stay* gentile (i.e., to not convert to Judaism, an idea that will be discussed in more detail in chapters 3 and 4). Following this logic, Paul's rhetoric is not anti-Jewish but rather a showcasing of his swift politics. After all, Paul himself is a Jew—he says so repeatedly (2 Cor 11:22; Rom 9:3–5, 11:1; Phil 3:4–7)—and in Romans 11:26 declares firmly that "all Israel will be saved." Thus, Paul, both *as* a Jew and in his thinking *of* fellow Jews, is still *good*.

This interpretation—one that highlights Paul's positive investment in Jews and Judaism—has become so established in New Testament studies that it has its own name: the "Paul within Judaism" approach.[13] According to this newer perspective, Paul never intended to discredit all of Judaism.[14] Instead, and to repeat: He, a *Jewish* Christ-confessor, was trying to establish a distinct, gentile Christ-following movement, one that did not abide by most Jewish ethnic practices (such as circumcision and the maintenance of a particular diet), perhaps even as a way to fulfill the ancient Jewish hope that all people, both Jews *and* non-Jews, would honor the God of Israel in the end of days.[15] In other words, if gentiles stay gentile, one can better imagine an eschaton of Jews and non-Jews.

A newer perspective requires an older one.[16] Until the late twentieth century, scholars often adhered to the Christian interpretation that Paul *did* reject Judaism, and that the goodness of his message was its non-Jewish sentiment. The story supporting this interpretation goes something like this: In the mid-first century CE, there lived a Jewish man named Saul who antagonized followers of Christ. On his way to a synagogue in Damascus, however, he had a vision of Jesus as a resurrected messiah. Through this experience, Saul realized that Christ-followers were right: Jesus was indeed the messiah. He also realized

13. This approach is sometimes flattened into what is called the "New Perspective on Paul." Such flattening, however, overlooks the differences between the traditional New Perspective and pushbacks to that perspective. For this history, see chapter 3.

14. Again, for more on this perspective and other new(er) approaches, see chapter 3.

15. I say "most" because the exclusive worship of the God of Israel is a Jewish ethnic practice.

16. Not to be confused with the New Perspective, in capital letters, as outlined in chapter 3.

that Jewishness was marked by unattainable law codes. Humans needed grace through Jesus—not law—in order to attain salvation. Saul thus converted to Christianity and deemed Jewishness—most especially its halakhic (i.e., lawful/ethnic) traditions—"late," as in "dead."[17] He also changed his name from the Jewish "Saul" to the Roman "Paul" to signify his new convictions. In sum: Judaism, through Jesus, and later supported by Saul/Paul, became a sterile and overbearing tradition of works, while Christianity became the grace-filled tradition of love. Jews who did not rid themselves of their ethnic ties to Judaism and convert to a non-ethnocentric Christianity would be left out of this love, and in turn be left out of the end of days. This, in a nutshell, is called the "Old Perspective on Paul."[18]

Dismantling the Old Perspective to Make the Bible Good

The Old Perspective has contributed to the hatred, repudiation, and even killing of Jews. Stories, put simply, shape ideologies, and the Old Perspective's narrativizing of Jews as targets of divine wrath has made the Othering of Jews in the name of Christianity seem appropriate. The Holocaust is obviously the most extreme example of this, in that much of Hitler's anti-Jewish successes can be attributed to the prevalence of anti-Jewish Christian theology.[19] This is not to say that Nazi ideology was represented as a Christian ideology—it was not—but rather that Nazi propagandists could rely on Christian rhetoric to bolster their anti-Jewish claims and even persuade Christians to support their politics.[20] Some Nazi sympathizers even relied on Nazi race theory to "prove" that Jesus was not Jewish but in fact an anti-Jewish, antisemitic Aryan.[21]

17. See Konrad Schmid, "The Interpretation of Second Temple Judaism as 'Spätjudentum' in Christian Biblical Scholarship," in *Confronting Antisemitism from the Perspectives of Christianity, Islam, and Judaism*, ed. Armin Lange et al., vol. 2, *An End to Antisemitism!* (De Gruyter, 2020).

18. This is also sometimes called the "Lutheran Perspective"; see chapters 1 to 3 for explication.

19. Susannah Heschel, *The Aryan Jesus: Christian Theologians and the Bible in Nazi Germany* (Princeton University Press, 2008), 6–7.

20. See, for example, Robert Ericksen, *Complicity in the Holocaust: Churches and Universities in Nazi Germany* (Cambridge University Press, 2012).

21. For more on the relationship between anti-Judaism and antisemitism, see chapter 2.

This was indeed persuasive for some Christians, so much so that Lutheran pastor Siegfried Leffler wrote that Jesus was "the most positive anti-Semite of all time."[22]

But the Holocaust is not the only site of Christian-fueled anti-Jewish hatred. Already in the New Testament, there are examples of Jesus being rhetorically removed from his Jewish heritage and Jewish theology (e.g., John 8:44).[23] In the fifth century CE, Augustine declared that Jews read their own texts with blind eyes (*City of God* 18.46). And by the twelfth century, stereotypes of Jews as satanic murderers who baked Christian children into their Passover matzah became widespread.[24] It is perhaps no wonder, then, that in the sixteenth century, Michelangelo produced a sculpture of Moses with horns, or that Martin Luther reformed Christianity with an accompanying declaration that Jews were Christianity's enemy.[25]

Thankfully, the "goodness" of the Old Perspective, anti-Jewish Paul has not won the day. While there were thinkers who interrogated Christian anti-Judaism prior to World War II,[26] for New Testament scholarship, the Holocaust was the breaking point. With two-thirds of the worldly Jewish population dead, New Testament interpreters finally felt called to reevaluate the canon's place in anti-Jewish history.[27] So did the Catholic Church—and

22. Mary M. Solberg, trans., *A Church Undone: Documents from the German Christian Faith Movement, 1932–1940* (Fortress Press, 2015), 351.

23. When Jesus calls Jews "children of the Devil," John is rhetorically distancing Jesus from his own Judaism, setting the stage for gentile Christ-following anti-Judaism. See Adele Reinhartz, *Cast Out of the Covenant: Jews and Anti-Judaism in the Gospel of John*, illustrated ed. (Lexington Books / Fortress Academic, 2018).

24. Pamela Eisenbaum, *Paul Was Not a Christian: The Original Message of a Misunderstood Apostle* (HarperOne, 2009), 49.

25. There is also linguistic reason for this. *Karan*, from the Hebrew root *keren*, often means "horn," but it can also be interpreted as "glorified" or "emitting light." When Jerome translated this Hebrew word into his Latin Vulgate, he used the Latin *cornuta* (i.e., "horned"). Based on his commentaries, it is likely Jerome understood this word as signifying "glorified," but readers misinterpreted it as literal horns.

26. See "A Few Good Men" in chapter 2.

27. It is a sad truth indeed that it took something like the Holocaust for scholars to interrogate their Pauline assumptions. It is also ironic, given that there were a fair number of Nazis who adhered to what we might call a proto-New Perspective ideology. According to the Nazi academic Paul de Lagarde, for example, Paul the apostle was "a Pharisee from head to toe" and

at a faster rate than much of biblical scholarship. With the publication of *Nostra aetate* in 1965 by the Second Vatican Council, the Catholic Church renounced the wholesale vilification of Jews. Meaning "In Our Time," *Nostra aetate* was very much a response to Christianity's role in the making of modern antisemitism.

A remarkable archaeological discovery aided the academic shift to read Paul differently. Between 1946 and 1956, numerous texts—some known and many previously unknown—were found in caves on the northern shore of the Dead Sea in the modern West Bank. Among other things, the texts showcased the extent to which Jews in the late centuries BCE and into the first century CE not only thought apocalyptically, eschatologically, and soteriologically, but also argued with each other about how best to make sense of these theologies. While the theologies of the New Testament may *appear* different from some of the ideas we see in the Hebrew Bible, they suddenly looked very Jewish in relation to these newly discovered Jewish sources.[28]

In doing re-evaluative work on the heels of the Shoah and the discovery at Qumran, many biblical scholars started to argue that rather than dismantling Jewish ideologies, the New Testament reflected a Jewishness of its time. Scholars asserted that the New Testament in fact is at its core a remarkably Jewish text, filled with Jewish characters imagined by Jewish authors, preserving much information on a type of Second Temple Judaism. Jesus (a.k.a. Joshua, if we transliterate the Aramaic to English) was *not* Aryan but in fact a Jewish teacher from the Jewish region of Galilee who was motivated to share his interpretations of Jewish theology with fellow Jews. To believe that Jesus was the Christ meant to believe that he was the Jewish messiah—the one who would usher in the Jewish eschatological hope of a better future, a future in which humans regained their immortality, and in which all nations would see that the God of Israel is the one, True God. Even if Jesus did maintain

---

responsible for Judaizing a historically Aryan Jesus. Unlike Lagarde, however, who sees Paul's Jewishness as a problem, some Newer Perspectives see this as a positive for Jewish-Christian relations. See Heschel, *The Aryan Jesus*, 37–42. See also chapter 3 of this book.

28. I emphasize the word "appear" because there *was* evidence prior to the discovery of the Dead Sea Scrolls that the ideas within the New Testament relate to those in early Jewish texts and even some of the messianic and eschatological ideas within the Hebrew Bible. I think what the Dead Sea Scrolls did was affirm and compel readers to take more seriously Jewish texts *outside* of the New Testament that discussed issues related *to* the New Testament. For more on this, see chapter 4.

gentile followers (this occurred more frequently after his death),[29] they were still entering a fundamentally Jewish conversation.

Paul, a self-described Jew (2 Cor 11:22; Rom 9:3–5, 11:1; Phil 3:4–7), was also entering Jewish conversations. Although he was writing letters to a predominantly gentile audience, he still, in doing so, quoted the Torah and the Prophets, engaged matters of Jewish faith and practice, observed the Jewish commandments, believed in the God of Israel, and prayed for the coming of a Jewish messiah. Paul's belief in Jesus as the *Christos*—the *Moshiach*—did not diminish Paul's Jewishness, but rather added to it. Sure, not every Jew agreed with Paul, but Paul also did not agree with every fellow Jew. Like Jacob, Jews in Paul's time wrestled with their theologies. Paul's theological conviction of Jesus as Christ was just another nuance (albeit an important one!) to his personal understanding of appropriate Jewishness. While various "partings" between what we now call Judaism and Christianity have certainly occurred (i.e., most modern Jews and Christ-followers would *not* call the belief in Jesus as Christ a Jewish nuance), Christ-centered theologies in the earliest centuries, and certainly during the years of Paul's writings (ca. 50–60 CE), were not antithetical to Jewish thought or, for many, Jewish practices.[30]

The discovery of the Dead Sea Scrolls helped prove that the New Testament writers in fact never hated Jews, and that readers of the New Testament, for centuries, had it all wrong. An increasing number of scholars have ushered this into their readings of Paul's eschatological soteriology. This wasn't just good history; it was also good ethics. In a post-Holocaust world specifically, "goodness" meant to no longer justify the hatred of Jews by way of Christian text. Paul, like Jesus, was Jewish. And as a Jew, he could not have argued that Jews were left out of his conception of the end of days. As another newer perspective maintains: Jews don't even need to believe in Jesus as the

29. It is possible that Godfearers (gentile sympathizers of Jewish theology) were part of the earliest movement, although I suspect, if so, they were in small number.

30. For an accessible summary of the "parting of the ways" narrative(s) and counternarrative(s), see Adam H. Becker and Annette Yoshiko Reed, "Introduction," in *The Ways That Never Parted: Jews and Christians in Late Antiquity and the Early Middle Ages*, ed. Adam H. Becker and Annette Yoshiko Reed (Fortress Press, 2007), 1–33.

Christ. They, through their faith in Abraham, are automatically included. The story of Christ is simply for the gentiles.[31]

So What Is the Problem?

The problem is that much of the field's newer perspectives fall prey to the Bible benevolence project. Just as Paul "leaves behind" non-Christ-following Jews in his theology, interpreters have come to "leave behind" difficult analyses in favor of more comforting narratives. Yes, New Testament writings are shaped by contemporaneous Jewish theology. And yes, Paul was Jewish. He did not convert from Judaism to Christianity, and his letters must be read with this Jewishness in mind. Such contextualized work, however, must also leave room for Paul's Jewish ethnocentrism and Jewish particularism. The purpose of this book is to showcase how, akin to the polemics of the Dead Sea Scrolls, Paul thinks that some Jews had it "right" and other Jews did not. Some gentiles also had it "right," at least in terms of eschatological salvation, and others did not.[32] This extends to his understanding of the eschaton. When Paul says that "all Israel will be saved," he means a particular all: a *True* Israel of superior ethnic Jews and inferior ethnic gentiles who believe in Jesus as the Christ. For Paul, only Christ-confessing Jews, just as only Christ-confessing gentiles, can be ushered into the end-times. Moreover, Jews and gentiles must *maintain* these ethnic distinctions in order to receive salvation.[33] The Christ-following Jew will be first. The Christ-following gentile will be second.

---

31. This is otherwise known as the *Sonderweg* model. For an overview of this argument, see John G. Gager, *Reinventing Paul* (Oxford University Press, 2002), 59–75. See also chapter 3.

32. As I articulate in chapter 4, Jews for Paul are the preferred group, making gentiles automatically less "right."

33. By "ethnic Jews," for example, I mean persons who maintained Jewish ethnic practices in their orientations toward Jesus as the Jewish messiah. This focus on Jews maintaining their ethnic particularity through bodily materiality, as readers will see, is what differentiates my reading of Paul's particular universalism and ideas of "true Israel" from that of Daniel Boyarin, who sees Paul as condoning a *ridding* of ethnic particularity for Jewish Christ-confessors (an argument he uses, moreover, to confirm his own ideas about the modern state of Israel). In Boyarin's words, "The Law was rather given to the Jews, as a temporary measure for specific historical reasons, meant to be superseded by its spiritual referent, faith, when the time would come, which, of course, it has . . . Paul dreamed of a day in which all human distinctions that led to hierarchy would be erased." Boyarin, *A Radical Jew*, 156, 216. And in mine, "Paul's messianism adheres to the common Jewish hope that ethnically and hierarchically distinct

My overall thesis is thus threefold: First, I argue that Paul, as a Jew, was not a universalist. Instead, he was ethnocentric in his ideology, including his theology, which spanned into his assertions of eschatological supremacy for Christ-following Jews and gentiles. Jews needed to maintain an ethnic-specific law in Christ, and gentiles needed to abstain from such ethnic-specific law in Christ. Both groups, in other words, needed to maintain particular ethnic differences in allegiance to Christ, lest they be "left behind" from Paul's end of days. Paul, moreover, understood these groups through ethnocentric, ethnonationalist, and ethnocratic means. Although both were important for his

---

Jews and gentiles would follow the God of Israel in the end of days. For Paul, eschatological deliverance was bestowed to the ethnically righteous Jewish Christ-confessor first—the remnant—followed by the ethnically gentile Christ-confessor. Jewish males would [also] continue to be treated as first in the end of days" (chapter 4, page 201; see also footnotes 78 and 108 in that chapter). My argument on Paul's theology in fact aligns most closely with Paula Fredriksen's. In her words, "Not only must eschatological gentiles remain gentiles: so too Israel must remain Israel, that family group, God's 'sons' and Paul's blood brothers, united by the covenants, the Law, the temple cult, the promises, the patriarchs, and—again the family, 'flesh' connection—by the Christ, the son of David (Rom 9.4–5; cf. 1.3, 15.9)." Matthew Thiessen has also made a similar argument, although, at least on my reading, with less emphasis on Paul desperately needing Jews to maintain their ethnic particularity for eschatological deliverance. See Paula Fredriksen, *Paul: The Pagans' Apostle* (Yale University Press, 2017), 165; Matthew Thiessen, *A Jewish Paul: The Messiah's Herald to the Gentiles* (Baker Academic, 2023), 33. See also Paula Fredriksen, "How Jewish Is God?: Divine Ethnicity in Paul's Theology," *Journal of Biblical Literature* 137, no. 1 (2018): 193–212. Major differences between my work and Fredriksen's and Thiessen's are my definition of "Israel" for Paul, at least in Romans 11; my overall reading of Romans 11; the forcefulness with which I read Paul as a Jewish ethnocentric, ethnonationalist, and hierarchically oriented thinker; and the overarching metacritical framing I am bringing to this study. All this will be fleshed out in more detail in chapters 3 and 4, but readers should know that much of my work on the ethnic particularity of Paul, Jesus, and the Israelite God is in conversation with and building upon theirs. For their view on "Israel," which counters my own, see Matthew Thiessen and Paula Fredriksen, "Paul and Israel," in *The Oxford Handbook of Pauline Studies*, ed. Matthew V. Novenson and R. Barry Matlock (Oxford University Press, 2022), 371–388. Of course, Caroline Johnson Hodge's work is also of great importance to this discussion, as is the work of a number of other great thinkers. I will do my due diligence in citing them whenever I can. For now, see, for example, Caroline Johnson Hodge, "The Question of Identity: Gentiles as Gentiles—but also Not—in Pauline Communities," in *Paul Within Judaism: Restoring the First-Century Context to the Apostle*, ed. Mark D. Nanos and Magnus Zetterholm (Fortress Press, 2015), 153–173; Caroline Johnson Hodge, *If Sons, Then Heirs: A Study of Kinship and Ethnicity in the Letters of Paul* (Oxford University Press, 2007); Caroline Johnson Hodge, "Paul and Ethnicity," in *The Oxford Handbook of Pauline Studies*, ed. Matthew V. Novenson and R. Barry Matlock (Oxford University Press, 2022), 547–561.

messianic age (i.e., his imagined new nation), Paul saw Jewish Christ-followers as the superior assemblage in Christ and gentile Christ-followers as the inferior assemblage in Christ.[34]

Second, I show how scholarly readings in a post-Holocaust world have often "left behind" Paul's ethnonational exclusivism in order to make him "good" for modern Jews, guilt-ridden interpreters, and broader Jewish-Christian relations. To play on Hicks-Keeton's most recent metacritical project, *Good Book: How White Evangelicals Save the Bible to Save Themselves*, this one might well be called—in lieu of *Wrestling with Paul*—*Good Paul: How Post-Holocaust Scholars Save Paul to Save Jews to Save Themselves*.[35] This book, in short, attempts to highlight that there are indeed Pauline materials that create Us-versus-Them dialectics—ones that, ironically (given Paul's own privileging of Jewish Christ-following views), have become fodder for gentile Christian exceptionalism, supersessionism, and the fetishization of proselytizing to modern Jews.[36] It argues that Paul "leaves behind" most Jews (not to mention most gentiles) in his theology *and* that the biblical field has "left behind" difficult analyses in favor of tidier, more comforting narratives.

Third, I demonstrate that the Bible's lasting cultural relevance—the many ways it has been used to justify anti-Judaism and antisemitism—has not only made the aforementioned scholarly "objectivity" unattainable, but has also led interpreters to *consistently* manipulate its verses so as to make it subjectively and ahistorically "good." To put it another way, the way we think about Jews has—for millennia—impacted the way we think about Paul.[37] The changing

34. Paul's ethnonationalist and hierarchical understanding of the end of days will be explained more fully in chapter 4.

35. See Hicks-Keeton, *Good Book*. Adele Reinhartz has also made similar moves in Johannine studies. See Reinhartz, *Cast Out of the Covenant*.

36. A jarring irony indeed of *Wrestling with Paul*, especially if we think of supersessionist ideations more expansively (e.g., as referring to the idea that one tradition is better than or supersedes another), is that it argues that Paul promoted a type of *Jewish* Christ-following supersessionism—he was a *Jewish* Christ-follower who presumed that *Jewish* Christ-followers reigned supreme. While gentile Christ-followers were included in Paul's visions of the eschaton, they were included as the inferior group, all in line with contemporaneous *Jewish* expectations of the eschaton. Those without Christ, including non-Christ-following Jews, were not entitled to his eschaton.

37. I extend gratitude to Judaism scholar David Freidenreich for helping me think through this framing. For more on how changing "presents" consistently change conceptions of

"goodness" of Paul's perspective on Jews wrests from our *own* changing social consciousnesses, *not* from Paul's.

* * *

I recognize the dangers of my non-universalist argument. I am well aware, in fact, that teaching this in my classrooms may result in perpetuating further antisemitism or losing my students' trust. The reasons for this are multiple. On the one hand, my reading can be used to justify the exclusion of Jews in modern Christian imagination (i.e., if Paul excludes non-Christ-confessing Jews, then so should modern Christians). On the other hand, it can be interpreted as blaming Paul's Judaism for his ethnocentrism and particularism, two attacks Christianity and the biblical field have made repeatedly on Jews, as readers will see. Furthermore, if Paul's exclusivity is seen as a negative quality—even without his Jewishness—then it raises another moral concern; the Bible's moral integrity (as if it has such a thing without the work of its readers) cannot be compromised by such a "bad."

These assumptions, however, are part of the problem. For example, the first assumption infers that interpreters must carry an allegiance toward Paul's theology—that his thinking is sound, divinely sanctioned, and should be emulated in one's treatment toward modern Jews and Judaism. The second implies that all Jews and Judaism, from antiquity to today, support Jewish ethnocentrism at the expense of others. And the third suggests that the Bible's sense of morality must always, no matter what, align with ours. I carry no such views. But to make this abundantly clear, perhaps it is time I reiterate my second confession: I am Jewish. Unlike Paul, I do not consider myself blameless before the law (as a teenager, I once ditched Yom Kippur services to get a cheeseburger; if you're Jewish or study Judaism, you know how transgressive that is), and I do not confess Jesus as my Christ. According to my own argument, in other words, I am firmly left out of Paul's end of days. I have also been the target of Christian supersessionism, including attacks of ethnocentric egoism simply for being Jewish (Jews are self-obsessed, Jews are loyal to

---

pasts, see Melanie Johnson-DeBaufre, "Historical Approaches: Which Past? Whose Past?," in *Studying Paul's Letters: Contemporary Perspectives and Methods*, ed. Joseph A. Marchal (Fortress Press, 2012), 13–32. For another accessible overview of Paul and interpretive history, albeit without this metacritical framing (or perhaps, more rightly, fram*ings*), see, for example, Robert Paul Seesengood, *Paul: A Brief History* (Wiley-Blackwell, 2010). See also Eisenbaum, *Paul Was Not a Christian*, 32–66.

law over love, Jews are exclusive ethnonationalists—I've heard it all). To put it otherwise, I know the dangers of an ethnocentric, exclusivist Jewish Paul. But as both a biblical scholar and a Jew, I'd rather name Paul's ethnocentric exclusivism than pretend it does not exist. To ignore Paul's ethics not only requires bending history and bending text but also making Paul's conception of "good" fit our conceptions of "good" as if our conceptions are somehow all the same. I suspect they aren't.

* * *

Rather than wrestle with these ethical stakes alone, I have asked others if they might consider alongside me the ethical stakes of my argument. No writing, as we have seen, exists in a monolith; we are all shaped by our interpretive neighbors, even those who pen their stories as solo authors (just look at the footnotes or endnotes of any academic book). A major difference here is that I am inviting my neighbors to add their own text to these pages. In the last chapter, interlocutors will emerge from the background. They will join me upfront, on the mat. In doing so, they will contribute to this book being what I call a "metacritical double crossover."[38] While I am attempting to share with a wide audience how biblical scholars have constructed and related to Paul—a construction, I contend, that continues to develop based at least in part on fears, assumptions of, and even close relations to the wider public—I am also trying to bring a taste of what the public has to say back to academia.[39] In other words, this book is metacritical in that it investigates how scholars have related to their objects of study: in this case, the Bible, Paul, and Jews. It is a double crossover in that it first brings scholarship on Paul to a more public audience (crossover one) and then brings responses back to academia (crossover two).

Overview of Chapters

In addition to introductory and concluding notes, this book consists of five chapters. Chapter 1, "A Good Anti-Jew," begins with an introduction to Paul and Paul's letters. It then moves to early interpretations of these letters,

38. If a "double crossover" is not already a niche wrestling move, perhaps it should be!

39. I understand metacriticism to be the study of how scholars analyze and relate to their objects of inquiry.

focusing on the history of proto-Orthodox renderings and how they, in conversation with certain "heretical" perspectives, created a foundation for reading Paul as rejecting Jews in his imagining of the end-times. Ancient thinkers such as Marcion and Augustine will be discussed, followed by their relations to Luther's Protestantism: the theological backbone of modern biblical studies.

Chapter 2, "A Good Anti-Semite," reveals the origins of modern biblical scholarship and, in doing so, unpacks the field's reliance on Luther and his Christ-following predecessors to make the more "academically reasoned" argument that Paul rightfully rejected Jews. It also showcases the developing field's dependence on nineteenth-century conceptions of race. As readers will see, biblical scholars were conditioned to read Paul through an amalgamation of theological *and* scientific antisemitism. This concoction fermented into its most toxic state under twentieth-century Nazi Germany, a state that, along with its Christian anti-Jewish antecedents, has come to haunt the post-Holocaust biblical scholar, so much so that many thinkers now bend Paul's writings so as to make them "good" for Jews and their own changing ethics. In many ways, this chapter outlines the stakes of biblical interpretation, including some of the dangers of my own argument, which is that Paul *was* ethnocentric in his Judaism—even ethnocratic—and that he *did* reject non-Christ-following Jews in his eschatological soteriology.[40]

Chapter 3, "A Good Jew," begins by tracing the geographical move of biblical studies from Germany to North America and the United Kingdom after the Holocaust. It then puts into conversation these new environments with considerations of post-Holocaust New and Newer Perspectives on Paul, including especially the more apologetic good-Paul-making models. Particular attention will be given to the *Sonderweg* (i.e., "two paths" or "special path") solution, which is the idea that Jews and gentiles have two distinct paths to salvation: Jews through the grace of Torah and gentiles through the grace of Christ. The chapter will conclude with an introduction to the "Paul within Judaism" approach, which is the approach I implement in the fourth chapter, albeit stripped of its often good-Paul-making tendencies.

Chapter 4, "An Average Jew," will turn to my own reading of Paul. Tracing ancient Jewish understandings of apocalyptic eschatology alongside that of Paul's, it will show that while Paul was not anti-Jewish—he was a Jew who

40. Not to mention non-Christ-following gentiles, a group that seems to be repeatedly "left behind" from ethical considerations of Paul within the changing tides of biblical studies.

believed the best way to be Jewish was to follow Jesus as the Christ—he still, like many of his contemporaries, was ethnocentric, ethnonationalist, hierarchical, and exclusive in his thinking. Non-Christ-following Jews, alongside non-Christ-following gentiles, were left out of his Jewish understanding of the messianic age. Paul, moreover, valued Jewish Christ-confessors above any and all gentiles. He also expected Jews to remain Jewish in their Christ-following orientations, just as gentiles needed to maintain their own ethnic particularity in theirs. Such distinctions, I will show, were required for eschatological deliverance; not even Galatians 3:28, a verse frequently praised as advocating for a universal, nonethnic or hierarchical Christ-following orientation, can erase Paul's ethnocentric hierarchical soteriology. In fact, as readers will see, Galatians 3:28 promotes it.

While the fourth chapter may be described as the most traditionally "academic" of this book, the fifth chapter, "In Our Time," steps out of this mold. Here, readers will have the opportunity to consider for themselves the ethical stakes of this book's tripart thesis, particularly for Jewish-Christian relations. Throughout the chapter, I will include transcripts of conversations on the topic—conversations with those from the academy, yes, but also from the church, the synagogue, and wider secular spaces. Readers will be invited to take part in these conversations both internally and with others in their own lives, thereby offering avenues to evaluate the dimensions of these stakes and issues for themselves. This chapter also discusses issues around the systematics of historical Paul scholarship; as readers will see, the Paul we study is not necessarily the historical Paul but rather the Paul given to us by the New Testament. To put it another way, the historical Paul of this book is more accurately the *scholarly* historical Paul, a figure constructed from a collection of limited and fragmented source material.

In addition to offering a review of the project, the conclusion—titled "What's Left?"—gestures broadly toward where we might go next.

CHAPTER ONE

A Good Anti-Jew

Jesus may be the core of the Christian message, but Paul became the key to unlocking the message.

—Pamela Eisenbaum[1]

Paul and His Letters

The New Testament canon is a small collection of literature, containing only twenty-seven writings. Of those twenty-seven, thirteen are attributed to Paul, a smaller collection still. Quite remarkable it is, then, that Paul's theology impacted so greatly the trajectory of Christian history. Paul may not have written much, but what he did write changed the world.[2]

In canonical order, the thirteen texts attributed to Paul are Romans, 1 and 2 Corinthians, Galatians, Ephesians, Philippians, Colossians, 1 and 2 Thessalonians, 1 and 2 Timothy, Titus, and Philemon. An additional four, however, carry some kind of Pauline affiliation: Acts of the Apostles charts Paul's journey of establishing Christ-following assemblies across the ancient Mediterranean; the Epistle to the Hebrews has a history of being attributed

1. Pamela Eisenbaum, *Paul Was Not a Christian: The Original Message of a Misunderstood Apostle* (HarperOne, 2009), 35.

2. Or, really, what he dictated changed the world. Ancient writing often took the form of "writers" dictating to literary laborers. As Candida Moss has shown, many of these laborers were enslaved. For more, see Candida Moss, *God's Ghostwriters: Enslaved Christians and the Making of the Bible* (Little, Brown, 2024). See also Sarah Rollens, "Why We Have Failed to Theorize Scribes in Antiquity," in *Scribal Practices and Social Structures Among Jesus Adherents: Essays in Honour of John S. Kloppenborg*, ed. William E. Arnal et al. (Peeters, 2016), 117–133.

to Paul in Christian tradition;[3] 2 Peter, although not about Paul, mentions Paul's letters; and James addresses issues arising directly from Paul's teachings. This means that over half of the New Testament is in some way connected to Paul.[4] Even the Gospel writers may have crafted their stories about Jesus in light of what Paul wrote.[5]

Despite Paul's hold on the New Testament—and the New Testament's hold on Paul—it is difficult to know who Paul was, at least from a historical perspective. Much to scholarly chagrin, Paul never wrote a systematic autobiography, that is, a clear description of his life, ministry, and theology in one place. Instead, for over a decade, he wrote letters to different communities across the ancient Mediterranean, letters that changed in tone, motive, and perspective depending on when and to whom he was writing. Most of Paul's letters seem to be responses to ones he received—ones we do not have—which means it is impossible to know the fullness of his letters' intents. To what, specifically, was Paul responding? Were they questions pertinent to Paul's overarching theology, or were they insignificant from his perspective? Did Paul intend for his responses to be read and revered so widely? How established

3. Even though it is anonymously written.

4. There is even a theory that the letters of James, Peter, John, and Jude (i.e., the "Catholic Epistles") may have been written to counter Paul's influence. See David R. Nienhuis, *Not by Paul Alone: The Formation of the Catholic Epistle Collection and the Christian Canon*, reprint ed. (Baylor University Press, 2007).

5. The Gospels were written anonymously after Paul wrote his letters, which means the authors may have been familiar with, persuaded by, or even in conflict with Paul's teachings. See, for example, Heidi Wendt, "Secrecy as Pauline Influence on the Gospel of Mark," *Journal of Biblical Literature* 140 (2021): 579–600; David Sim, "Matthew's Use of Mark: Did Matthew Intend to Supplement or to Replace His Primary Source?" *New Testament Studies* 57 (2011): 176–179. Scholars have similarly argued for Pauline influence on non-Gospel New Testament texts. See, as just a few examples, David Frankfurter, "The Fiction of the Seven Letters in the Apocalypse: Representing Heavenly Authority in the Shadow of Paul," *Harvard Theological Review* 117 (2024): 79–98; David Frankfurter, "Jews or Not?: Reconstructing the 'Other' in Rev 2:9 and 3:9," *Harvard Theological Review* 94 (2001): 403–425; David Frankfurter, "The Letter of James as a Document of Paulinism?" in *Reading James with New Eyes: Methodological Reassessments of the Letter of James*, ed. R. L. Webb and J. S. Kloppenborg (T&T Clark, 2007), 75–98.

were these communities anyway?[6] The answers to these questions are ones we will likely never know.

We also lack access to Paul's original manuscripts. Every surviving Pauline letter, even when dated to antiquity, is a copy of a copy of a copy (etc.), with textual variants existing between it and other copies. The earliest known Pauline fragment dates to the second or third century of the common era, a half century to a century and a half after Paul's letters were written.[7] This means we cannot know for sure which verses were written by the historical Paul and which ones were added later. It also means that if there were additions to Paul's letters—and there were—then there were also likely deletions.

Translation adds another barrier. Paul shared his ideas in Koine Greek, which humans no longer speak as a native language. And even if they did, they would not be speaking it from Paul's first-century context. This means it is easy to miss the nuances and idioms of Paul's prose. The earliest copies of Paul's letters are also script continua, which means the words run together without breaks or punctuation. Even the New Testament scholars who are the most knowledgeable in ancient Greek disagree on how to translate and/or parse certain words and phrases from the Pauline corpus.

It is also unclear how many of the thirteen letters Paul actually wrote.[8] Based on historical and textual study, most scholars agree that seven of the thirteen—Romans, 1 and 2 Corinthians, Galatians, Philippians, 1 Thessalonians, and

6. Some New Testament experts argue that it is unclear Paul was really writing to "communities" so much as trying to reshape collections of people into the kind of "community" (with his preferred hierarchies and norms) he wanted. For more on these hierarchies and norms, see chapter 4. For more on this evaluation of community, and with gratitude to Stephen L. Young for his insights and assistance in research on this, see Stanley Stowers, "The Concept of 'Community' and the History of Early Christianity," *Method & Theory in the Study of Religion* 23 (2011): 238–256; Hugo Mendez, "Did the Johannine Community Exist?" *Journal for the Study of the New Testament* 42 (2020): 350–374; Rollens, "Why We Have Failed to Theorize Scribes in Antiquity"; Stephen L. Young, *Paul Among the Mythmakers: Sins, Gods, and Scriptures* (Studies in Religion in Antiquity; Edinburgh University Press, forthcoming).

7. This fragment is known as Papyrus 46 and contains verses from a number of Pauline texts.

8. Or at least cowrote. Paul often names a coauthor in his greetings. Of the undisputed letters, see 1 Corinthians 1:1, 2 Corinthians 1:1, 1 Thessalonians 1:1, and Philemon 1:1. Of the disputed, see 2 Thessalonians 1:1 and Colossians 1:1. See also the work below on "Tertius" in Paul's letter to the Romans.

Philemon—were written by the historical Paul.[9] Scholars call these seven the "undisputed" Pauline letters.[10] The Pauline authorship of Ephesians, Colossians, and 2 Thessalonians is debated, whereas most biblical scholars agree 1 and 2 Timothy and Titus were not written by the historical Paul but instead are the earliest residua of his literary afterlives. None of this is to say that these latter letters lack import. In antiquity, it was common for people to write pseudepigraphically. Those who wrote in Paul's name likely wanted to be understood *in earnest* as Paul—and luckily for them, they have been. What it does mean, however, is that the historical Paul may have disagreed with some or all of what the pseudepigraphers wrote. Relatedly, it also means that Paul may have disagreed with some of the changes made to his own seven letters.

Even when examining Paul's undisputed letters, readers notice discrepancies. Again, Paul was not always consistent; he changed tone, motive, rhetoric, and perspective depending on when and to whom he was writing. This was intentional. Since most of Paul's letters were responses to ones he received, he contoured his messages depending on the needs and attitudes of those who wrote to him (and, moreover, the needs and attitudes he had of/toward them).[11] Paul may have also changed his mind between one letter and the next. It is easy to imagine Paul, writing for over a decade, tweaking his theology as he encountered new peoples and ideas. A bigger issue, however, is that even a *singular* text can be difficult to decipher. Some of Paul's letters contain so many internal tangents, ambiguities, and intertextual diatribes that searching for meaning can feel daunting. Paul was not just speaking *to* differing communities but also *with* different texts he found sacred. When Paul interjects his interpretations of them, he does so without much clarity.

Such confusions, whether across letters or within a singular text, could also speak to the effects of amanuenses, literary scribes and copyists—often enslaved—who transcribed someone's oral dictations and/or created written

---

9. Cf. Nina E. Livesey, *The Letters of Paul in Their Roman Literary Context: Reassessing Apostolic Authorship* (Cambridge University Press, 2024).

10. Scholarly consensus also holds that the historical Paul did not write or dictate Hebrews.

11. See, for example, Stanley K. Stowers, "Kinds of Myth, Meals, and Power: Paul and the Corinthians," in *Redescribing Paul and the Corinthians*, ed. Ron Cameron and Merrill P. Miller (Society of Biblical Literature, 2011), 105–150; Robyn Faith Walsh, *The Origins of Early Christian Literature: Contextualizing the New Testament Within Greco-Roman Literary Culture* (Cambridge University Press, 2021). See also footnote 6 above on community.

copies of previously written works.[12] Romans 16:22, for example, names a scribe called Tertius (literally "Third"), which suggests either that Paul relied on an enslaved literary worker to craft his original letter or that a copyist inserted this name into a later edition.[13] Either way, it is clear that Paul was not the only person crafting his letters. Just as a scribe could have changed what Paul dictated, a copyist could have altered his original words, purposefully or by accident. This brings us back to the issue of not knowing for sure what the historical Paul actually wrote or said, an issue I bear far less frustration toward when taking into account the possibility that enslaved scribes changed Paul's writings as a form of rebellion or subversion to the deplorable institution that was the Roman slave market.

Suffice it to say the author of 2 Peter was correct when he wrote that "there are some things [in Paul's letters] that are hard to understand . . . you are forewarned" (3:16–17).[14] Some scholars even confess that we cannot do historical Paul studies; the information about him is too complicated and too scarce. Indeed, conducting research on Paul is in many respects akin to playing a game of detective. Readers are forced to consider all evidence when deciphering his ideas: When is Paul writing? To whom is Paul writing? To what might Paul be responding? Did Paul write the letters himself, or did a scribe write—or later edit—for him? How many *sentences* do we even know reflect Paul's own thinking? Scholars often do not know the answers to these questions, at least not fully.

None of this is to suggest that attempts to construct the historical Paul—who he was, where he came from, what he believed—never occur. They do. Despite the difficulties, many scholars still try to piece together information from Paul's undisputed letters so as to arrive at some sort of picture, even if faint, of the apostle's life and mindset. What all this does suggest, however, is that any analysis of Paul must be taken with a bucket of salt, including the analysis offered in this book.

---

12. Again, see Moss, *God's Ghostwriters.*

13. This also complicates the idea that Romans was not written with a coauthor. Whereas most of Paul's letters mention a coauthor in the salutations, Romans does not. The mention of Tertius in chapter 16, however, challenges the assumption of Paul having authorial autonomy in Romans.

14. See also Matthew Thiessen, *A Jewish Paul: The Messiah's Herald to the Gentiles* (Baker Academic, 2023), 1.

What to Do About Acts

Readers may want to privilege Luke's second volume, Acts of the Apostles, as it includes a well-structured narrative about Paul's Christ-following mission.[15] It was also intended to be read as an introduction to Paul by those who decided on the order of the New Testament canon. Acts is positioned in the canon as the first foray into Paul's life and mission. All subsequent letters were envisioned as being read in light of Acts's introduction.

Structure and intention, however, do not guarantee accurate information. This is unfortunate, as Acts positions Paul as a Christ-follower who takes part in Jewish practice publicly, thus showing his continued adherence to Judaism as part of his Christ-following orientation (Acts 18:18, 21:24). In short, this book could be great for trying to assert Paul's lasting Jewishness![16] And in fact, according to Paul scholar Matthew Thiessen, Acts *is* great, at least for Christian readers. On his reading, faithful Christians should make sense of Paul in light of the authorized canon, which is to say they should read Paul as Jewish because Acts sets him up and consistently narrates him as Jewish.[17]

While I agree with Thiessen that Paul remained Jewish throughout his ministry, I disagree with his view that Christians should privilege Acts in their navigation of Paul as a Jewish thinker. Instead, I urge readers of all backgrounds to consider the fact that the canon could have been crafted differently—that other devout followers of Jesus wanted a different set of texts; they just lacked the power to make it happen—and that the information within the canon is not always historically accurate.[18] In antiquity, theologically invested biographers were less interested in charting facts than in persuading readers to their points of view. Not everything Luke wrote, in other words, is historically verifiable.

---

15. Luke's Gospel, like all the canonical Gospels, was written anonymously. The name "Luke" was attributed to the author by later Christ-confessors. For brevity, I will refer to this author as "Luke."

16. Acts 18 and 21 also indicate that Luke understood Paul as advocating for ethnic maintenance and distinction between Jewish and gentile members of the movement, which is an integral aspect of my argument. For more on this, see chapter 4.

17. Thiessen, *A Jewish Paul*, 28.

18. Thiessen, of course, agrees that not all information within the canon is historically accurate, and that general audiences should keep this in mind.

In fact, in many respects, Acts mirrors the genre of ancient fiction more than history or even biography. The book is action-packed with chases, escapes, and even a shipwreck, all plot points well-known to the genre of ancient fiction.[19] All that's missing is a romance! But even if Acts was written as history and/or biography, modern readers must keep in mind the differences between contemporary genres and those of antiquity. To write about the history or life of a person was much more about capturing the spirit of that person than transcribing facts. And even if a writer did want to transcribe historical specifics, tracing them could be rather difficult. There were no recording or typing devices in antiquity, and only a small percentage of people were literate. Interpreters who rely on Acts thus need to be careful about how they do so and for what reasons.

I tend to avoid Acts in piecing together the life of the historical Paul.[20] Not only is the genre questionable, but too many of the biographical aspects in Acts contradict what Paul writes elsewhere. For example, while Paul writes that he was appointed by God to preach the news of Jesus as the Christ to gentile communities, he in Acts speaks to them as a last resort. The details around Paul's "conversion" experience are also different from what Paul writes in his undisputed letter to the Galatians. In Galatians, Paul attempts to prove his dependability by insisting that his revelation of Jesus as the resurrected Christ comes directly from the divine realm (Gal 1:15–18). He also tries to counter the assumption that it comes from leaders of the Jesus movement in Jerusalem by adding that he did not speak with anyone in Jerusalem after his time in Damascus. Luke, however, writes in Acts that Paul *did* go to Jerusalem after Damascus, which highlights a major textual discrepancy (Acts 9:10–30).

---

19. For more on ancient fiction and its relations to canonical and non-canonical Acts, see Shelly Matthews, "Teaching Fiction, Teaching Acts: Introducing the Linguistic Turn in the Biblical Studies Classroom," in *Reading and Teaching Ancient Fiction: Jewish, Christian, and Greco-Roman Narratives*, ed. Sara R. Johnson, Rubén R. Dupertuis, and Christine Shea (Society of Biblical Literature, 2017), 213–231. See also Marília P. Futre Pinheiro, Judith Perkins, and Richard Pervo, eds., *The Ancient Novel and Early Christian and Jewish Narrative: Fictional Intersections* (Barkhuis, 2012). Please note that I am citing Pervo with dismay, as he was a convicted sexual predator.

20. I often align in fact with those who avoid too robust a historical-Paul project at all in that Paul's understanding of himself is both scarce and varied. In most cases, I refer to Paul and his letters as a collective "archive" as opposed to a clearly known historical figure writing clearly legible historical documents. This is why my qualification of what constituted "typical" or "average" ancient Jewry in chapter 4 is so important.

While it's certainly possible that Paul changed his story to add credibility to his mission—or that both versions are in some ways incorrect (e.g., maybe Paul spoke with leaders of the Jesus movement outside of Jerusalem)—most scholars deduce that Luke's version is incorrect since (1) Luke did not know Paul and (2) Acts contradicts Paul.

Whether a work of fiction or biography or a mix of both, Acts paints a clearer picture of how Luke understood Paul than how Paul understood himself. While it is possible that Paul was an unreliable narrator and that Luke's version is more accurate, we currently have no evidence to be persuaded by this. Despite Paul's own discrepancies, as well as the later move to situate Acts within the canon alongside Paul's letters, scholars still privilege Paul's undisputed letters over the disputed ones and also over Acts.[21] But there is good news for those who interpret Paul as a Jewish Christ-confessor: There is evidence for Paul's Jewishness in his own letters.[22] Acts is not needed to prove Paul's Jewishness.

The Importance of Romans

Of Paul's undisputed letters, Romans stands out. Unlike the others, Romans was neither written to a community Paul helped organize nor composed as a response to the specific needs and questions of others as far as we know. Instead, it seems to have been crafted as an introduction to a prominent Christ-following assembly in Rome—one Paul had never met.[23] Paul's hope was that this community would find his ideas persuasive enough to help fund his anticipated mission to Spain. While the letter is filled with its own

21. For more on the development of the biblical canon, see Edmon L. Gallagher and John D. Meade, *The Biblical Canon Lists from Early Christianity: Texts and Analysis*, 1st ed. (Oxford University Press, 2018).

22. Thiessen asserts this as well. In his words, "Lest anyone conclude that we must allow Luke's account of Paul to override the evidence of what Paul himself wrote, I suggest that Paul's own letters point in this direction *when properly read*." Thiessen, *A Jewish Paul*, 29; emphasis in the original.

23. Related, see Yii-Jan Lin, who stresses how Paul's naming of (women) leaders in Rome is trying to authorize himself to them, in "Junia: An Apostle Before Paul," *Journal of Biblical Literature* 139, no. 1 (2020): 191–209.

theological complexities and obscurities, its premise as an overview of Paul's thought makes it unique.[24]

It is also in Romans that Paul discusses the mystery of salvation for Jews and gentiles. In chapters 9–11, he argues that, aside from a remnant of Israel (i.e., a small group of Jews), God has temporarily disabled the people of Israel from recognizing Jesus as the Christ: "God gave them a sluggish spirit, eyes that would not see, and ears that would not hear" (Rom 11:8).[25] As a result, many Jews have been excluded from God's salvific plan. There is reason for this, however. In Paul's view, it is for the sake of gentiles: "Through [Israel's] stumbling, salvation has come to the gentiles" (Rom 11:11). Paul adds, however, that those of Israel who come to believe that Jesus is the Christ may be grafted back into God's saving grace (this is presumably when God is no longer disabling them, although the subject of Jewish free will here is unclear). Using an olive tree as a metaphor for the new world order, including who is saved and how, Paul says that Jewish and gentile believers in Christ represent the tree's (i.e., the eschatological nation's) lasting branches: A remnant of believing Jewish branches have stayed, while unbelieving Jewish branches have fallen/been cut off;[26] believing gentile branches have been grafted in, and Jewish branches can be grafted *back* in through a stopping of unbelief. He then concludes with a summary and added note: "I want you to understand this mystery: a hardening has come upon part of Israel until the full number of the gentiles has come in [this is the summary]. And so all Israel will be saved [this is the addition]."

Chapters 9–11 are often described as the climax of the letter, at least by those attempting to make sense of Paul's overarching eschatological soteriology. Because Paul spends so much time in his other letters discussing gentile Christ-confessing thought and practice, the fact that he in Romans 9–11 is also discussing Jews makes these chapters at the very least stand out. What Paul means in these chapters, however, remains, to borrow from Romans, a

24. It is also in Romans where Paul states that Christ-followers are "justified by faith." This, alongside passages in Galatians that discuss the importance of faith over works for gentiles, has been a staple for Christian interpreters, especially Protestant ones, for whom the idea of justification by faith is paramount. This is likely another reason why Romans (with Galatians) is given such import within the (Protestant) biblical field.

25. See Stephen L. Young, "Ethnic Ethics: Paul's Eschatological Myth of Jewish Sin," *New Testament Studies* 70 (2024): 235–248.

26. Paul uses both images but culminates in the latter. See Romans 11:20–22.

mystery. On the one hand, it is clear that gentiles must believe in Jesus as the Christ in order to obtain eschatological salvation; surrounding verses paired with Paul's other undisputed letters reveal that gentiles must "come in" to the Christ-following faith for such deliverance. The placement of Jews, on the other hand, remains hotly debated. If, for example, "all Israel will be saved," as Paul writes in Romans 11, does that mean "all Jews" will be saved? If so, how? Why? When? *Who or what* is Israel at this point in the explication?

Until recently, most answers have fallen prey to Christian supersessionism—the idea that the gentile church is the new, True Israel, and that only gentiles in Christ will be saved. Jews, in other words, can only be saved in the eschaton as "Israel" if they rid themselves of their Jewishness and honor Christ, like gentiles do. In a post-Holocaust world, however, many Christian interpreters no longer want to uphold a tradition that, at its core, displaces others. Some modern New Testament scholars, most of whom are Christian, have even suggested a *Sonderweg*, or "special path," approach—one that claims Jews have their own route toward salvation. "All Israel," according to this theory, refers not to a gentile church or even a predominantly gentile church but rather to "all Jews" regardless of whether they followed Jesus. The fact that this is a theory driven by post-Holocaust ethics cannot be overstated. As one Paul scholar and retired Anglican bishop expressed, the threat of Christian supersessionism has become "waved around as a magic wand to cast a spell of guilty silence over any suggestion that Paul might have meant what he said . . . namely that the answer to Jewish salvation is the new covenant established through Jesus Christ."[27] But as readers will see, there is no spell that can make Paul's eschatological soteriology inclusive of non-Christ-following Jews. Jews without Christ, for Paul, are left behind. Romans 11 and the "special path" will be engaged more thoroughly in chapters 3 and 4, but for now, suffice it to say it's time to put the *Sonderweg* wand down.[28]

27. See N. T. Wright, "Romans 9–11 and the 'New Perspective,'" in *Between Gospel and Election: Explorations in the Interpretation of Romans 9–11*, ed. Florian Wilk and J. Ross Wagner (Mohr Siebeck, 2010), 50. See also Jeremy Cohen, *The Salvation of Israel: Jews in Christian Eschatology from Paul to the Puritans* (Cornell University Press, 2022), 22–23.

28. Fellow readings against the *Sonderweg* model include, but are not limited to, Daniel Boyarin, *A Radical Jew: Paul and the Politics of Identity* (University of California Press, 1997); Terence L. Donaldson, "Jewish Christianity, Israel's Stumbling and the *Sonderweg* Reading of Paul," *Journal for the Study of the New Testament* 29, no. 1 (2006): 27–54; Thiessen, *A Jewish Paul*; and Paula Fredriksen, *Paul: The Pagans' Apostle* (Yale University Press, 2017). For more on their views and how my reading of Paul engages theirs, see chapters 3 and 4.

The Historical Paul

Taking the textual and historical limitations into perspective, what can be said about the historical Paul is this: Paul (maybe also Saul) was a literate, Greek-speaking Jew of the first century CE.[29] He lived under the auspices of the Roman Empire, a Hellenized imperial system that honored the divinity of any number of gods and goddesses,[30] including emperors, mostly posthumously, and also in the quotidian. Paul's god, however, was the God of Israel, who was sometimes referred to as Yahweh by ancient Israelites or, in modern Jewish parlance, *Adonai* or *HaShem*. In Paul's time, this god was often simply called God (*Theos* in Greek), or Lord or Master (*Kurios* in Greek). Paul was also a follower of Jesus as his Christ, believing Jesus to be the Jewish messiah who would overthrow the powers that be, including Rome, and usher in a new world order in which his god—the God of Israel—would reign supreme. For the duration of Paul's life, the Roman Empire did not adhere to such ideologies, and often marginalized those who did. Despite such power imbalances, however, Paul still promoted his beliefs, including to non-Jews, whom Paul referred to as "gentiles." But Paul also, like most Jews of the first century, Christ-confessing or not, interacted with the broader Greco-Roman culture. Paul read in Greek, spoke in Greek, and crafted his soteriology alongside Jewish *and* Greco-Roman philosophies.[31]

* * *

29. It is unclear if "Paul" was ever "Saul" or even if "Paul" was actually always "Saul." The story of Saul changing his name to "Paul" is found in Acts, which was not written by the historical Paul. The apostle's name being "Saul" makes sense given his Jewish heritage. I question, in fact, if his name remained "Saul," and if later writers simply changed his name to "Paul" when editing his letters. It is also possible the apostle's name was always "Paul," thus never "Saul," given his Hellenistic context.

30. Please note that I am not lowercasing "gods" and "goddesses" here to make any sort of hierarchical point between the God of Israel and others. I am lowercasing them here, as I continue to do elsewhere, because the sentence is not referring to a specific deity (whereas the God of Israel is specific).

31. Some readers might assume that Paul's Roman citizenship adds to this robust relationship with the broader culture, but such citizenship is named only in Acts (16:37–38, 22:25–29, and 23:27). While it is possible that Acts is correct on this point, I find it odd that Paul did not mention this in the letters we have, especially given his related explications of state violence and imprisonment. Hence, I will still not be assuming Paul was a citizen of Rome.

If transparency is a key aspect of this book, then another confession is long overdue. Sometimes I think the above is all I can say with historical confidence. As scholarship continues, it is becoming evident that we cannot know for sure which parts of Paul's letters are from the historical Paul and which are from later editors. Even Romans 9–11, again to borrow from Romans, *is a mystery*. Did the historical Paul write these verses, in part or in full? I honestly have no idea.

What follows, then, and what follows for the rest of this book, is an attempt to craft a portrait of the historical Paul by way of the field's own tools and mindsets. In other words, scholars do generally, as of now, take the bulk of Paul's seven letters to be reflective of the historical Paul in some way, including Romans 9–11.[32] The point of this book is to take the current scholarly model—to use its foundations and its tools—to show how one can indeed arrive at an ethnocentric, even ethnocratic Paul.

Studies of the historical Paul are really studies of the New Testament's Paul. Not even the seven "undisputed letters" can give us a Paul unaltered by later writers.[33] Does this declare everything said about Paul in this book void? No. The New Testament's Paul is still the Paul who has shaped the biblical field. This Paul is the one whom scholars probe to construct their version of the historical figure. And this Paul is the one who has shaped later Jewish-Christian relations. In other words, the New Testament's Paul is still the Paul with whom I want to wrestle.

All this said, *could* some of this book be a real reflection of the historical Paul? Absolutely. All I'm saying is to keep in mind that the "historical Paul" of biblical scholarship is based off of the Paul of the New Testament—a collection of limited and fragmented source material.

* * *

The historical Paul, which is to say the Paul I am constructing based on the literary and cultural evidence related to the New Testament, was originally against the Jesus movement. Although Paul had never met the historical Jesus, he was adamant that he could not be the Christ, and thus persecuted those

32. This may become more nuanced in the coming years due in no small part to new Marcion scholarship attesting that Marcion's version of Paul's letters may have been closer to what the historical Paul actually wrote. See this chapter's section on Marcion below.

33. In this way, Paul's letters aren't really even Paul's letters. They are the letters *we call* Paul's.

who believed he was (Gal 1:13–16; 1 Cor 15:9–10; Phil 3:4–6).[34] After having a vision of Jesus as the resurrected messiah, however, Paul changed his mind. He writes that Jesus revealed to him not only his messianic status, but that it was Paul's God-given mission to spread the news of Jesus to non-Jewish audiences (i.e., gentiles). Thus while Jews were already privy to the conversation—one must remember that Jesus was Jewish and spoke predominantly to fellow Jews—Paul helped expand the movement by preaching beyond the original Jewish fold.

Throughout his preaching, Paul told gentiles that if they wanted eternal life, they had to stop worshipping their own gods and switch to his. He also said they needed to trust in Jesus's messianic status and, relatedly, Jesus's resurrection. According to contemporaneous Jewish theology, resurrection would occur at the onset of the eschaton. Thus, if Jesus was resurrected, then he not only overcame death—an even greater force than the earthly powers that be—but he also signaled to others the oncoming of the messianic age, the age in which Jesus would be ruler (i.e., *kyrios*, or "master/lord," a colloquial understanding of "messiah" or "king") alongside the Israelite God.[35] Perhaps most interesting of all, however, is that despite God and Jesus being so connected to Israelite and Jewish tradition, Paul insisted that gentiles need not convert to Judaism in order to be ushered into their new world order. Righteous gentiles-for-Christ would not be left behind in the end of days. In fact, such gentiles *needed* to stay gentile in order to be saved.

While this information may seem wanting—and I'm not saying it isn't—it is more than we can say about most people in the first century. Some might argue it is even more than we can say about Jesus. This is because the sources that say the most about him are the canonical Gospels, texts that were written decades after Jesus's lifetime and in a language Jesus likely did not speak. Jesus, put simply, did not write for himself. Paul did. But even when examining Paul's letters, it is important to remember that there existed no printing presses or recording devices in antiquity, making any source we have about someone's

---

34. Jeremy Williams argues that *diōkō* should be translated as "prosecute" instead of "persecute," especially since "persecute" connotes martyrdom myths that, in his view, don't fit first-/second-century models. See Jeremy L. Williams, *Criminalization in Acts of the Apostles: Race, Rhetoric, and the Prosecution of an Early Christian Movement* (Cambridge University Press, 2023).

35. Fredriksen, *Paul: The Pagans' Apostle*, 138–139 and accompanying footnote 16 on page 139.

life—even if written or stated autobiographically—questionable. Changes to lives were made through both the oral storytelling process and the written copying one. Furthermore, the majority of the population was illiterate. Most lives were never documented. The fact of the matter remains that we have little to no access to most people from the first century. Taking all this into account, it becomes easy to see how the few paragraphs above are nothing short of remarkable.[36]

Still, there are aspects of Paul's life that are contested, including how he felt about salvation and what he thought it was. While I've already asserted that Paul did not believe in eschatological deliverance for non-Christ-following Jews, such is still debated within biblical studies. It is even debated whether Paul thought about salvation in a systematic way at all. In other words, because Paul did *not* write a comprehensive autobiography—he instead wrote letters to different audiences for over a decade—it is difficult to know whether he inserted into each source a unified theological premise (i.e., a systematic theology), or whether he simply wrote to different people about different things depending on the context.[37] We don't even know if Paul imagined his letters being read together at all. I suspect he didn't.

The Old Perspective assumes a systematic Paul. It argues that Paul's undisputed letters, when read in the "right" way, show that Paul believed Christ was needed in order to achieve salvation, and that Jewishness as a whole needed to be left behind. Despite the movement's Jewish roots, following Christ without Jewish law and practice was the only way to receive God's grace. "All Israel" is not "all Jews" or even a mix of Jews and gentiles but instead the gentile church. Below is the story of how and when this theory got its legs.

From Relatability to Reliability

Not everyone agreed with Paul during his lifetime. His letters alone showcase the extent to which there was a wide variety of thought and practice within the Christ-following assemblies. Paul, for example, crafted an entire

36. It would be even more remarkable if Paul were a woman, slave, or child—that is, someone of lower status according to Roman standards. Again, see Moss, *God's Ghostwriters*.

37. I extend gratitude to Cavan Concannon and the metacriticism section of the Society of Biblical Literature 2023 (at which Concannon presided) for raising this aspect of the conversation.

letter in disagreement with the devotional practices urged by competing Christ-teachers in Galatia.[38] Apparently, gentiles in Galatia received circumcision as a way to show their reverence for Jesus, a man who was also circumcised. In Paul's view, this is a rite reserved for Jews. He takes great offense that gentiles are co-opting the tradition. His letter makes clear that gentiles in Christ were arriving at different conclusions on how best to follow Jesus as their messiah.

Still, Paul made an unusual impact. One possible reason for this was his way of making the Jesus movement accessible to gentiles, in that he did not want gentiles to take on the bulk of Jewish ethnic practices (e.g., circumcision, a practice many gentiles, Galatians notwithstanding, likely did not want to undergo). Another possible reason, however, was his relatability. Like most Christ-confessors of the first century, Paul never knew the historical Jesus; he joined the movement after Jesus's death. Paul's "coming to Christ" moment thus required nothing short of faith—a faith that went against the grain of the Roman polytheistic norm. While the Roman Empire tolerated more traditional Jewish thought and practice—that is, Jewishness without Christ—it was suspicious of Christ-followers. From the Roman perspective, Jesus followers lacked a foundation, something it admired in Judaism's long history, and were suspicious of treason when followers called Jesus "king." To follow Jesus was to risk cultural discrimination and, at times, death. While the details of Paul's passing are unknown, he is venerated in Christ-confessing memory for enduring imperial-imposed hardship. As the author of First Clement writes ca. 100 CE, "[Paul] was set free from this world and transported up to the holy place, having become the greatest example of endurance."[39] Paul's faith mirrored most others' in the prejudices placed on him. The idea was that if Paul's faith could persevere without Jesus physically present and without support from the powers that be, perhaps theirs could too.

In many Christ-believing circles, this relatability morphed quickly into reliability.[40] Thinkers from a variety of Christ-following perspectives came to

38. See Galatians. For more on the differences and debates within the early Jesus movement, see chapter 4.

39. See 1 Clement 5.7. The text is anonymous but could have been written by Clement of Rome. Translation from Bart D. Ehrman, trans., *The Apostolic Fathers* (Harvard University Press, 2003), 45.

40. Eisenbaum, *Paul Was Not a Christian*, 35.

trust that Paul's letters revealed how best to follow Jesus and, in turn, how to be accepted into the end of days. As the epigraph above states, "Jesus may be the core of the Christian message, but Paul became the key to unlocking the message." To have faith like Paul meant to have faith in Paul, not as the Christ, but as the one who understood the Christ.

Marcion's Paul

The Christ-confessing gentile Marcion (85–160 CE) certainly seemed to believe this. While not much can be said about the historical Marcion, as there are no known copies of his own work, his proto-Orthodox opponents attest that he was deeply attached to Paul.[41] From one perspective, we could say that such attachment was not the problem for proto-Orthodox thinkers. Marcion's adversaries agreed that Paul was central to the Christ-following mission, showcasing the speed at which followers from a variety of sects considered Paul an important messenger. The problem in this sense was that, at least from a proto-Orthodox perspective, Marcion agreed with Paul in the wrong way.[42] But from another perspective, we could say that Marcion's opponents *did* have a problem with Marcion's attachment to Paul, in that they were competing with him over who truly got to claim the apostle. In this sense, proto-Orthodox thinkers needed to discredit or delegitimize Marcion's association with—and therefore attachment to—Paul.

According to his contemporary Justin Martyr (100–165 CE), Marcion believed that Jesus's God was indeed the ultimate God, but that this God was

---

41. Interpreters are forced to rely on the information written by Marcion's opponents, who differ in content and are bound up in anti-Marcion biases. These opponents include second-century Christ-followers Justin Martyr, Irenaeus, and Tertullian, each of whom is in hindsight categorized as "proto-Orthodox" thinkers and each of whom rhetorically mythologized Marcion, at least in part. See Judith M. Lieu, *Marcion and the Making of a Heretic: God and Scripture in the Second Century* (Cambridge University Press, 2015), 9.

42. By the second century CE, there were a wide variety of Christ-centered theologies and practices, and theologians relied on rhetorical sparring to disprove their opponents. The theological forerunners to the Nicene Creed—those that supported the ideas that were deemed "orthodox" in the fourth century CE—are considered "proto-orthodox" thinkers, while their opponents are called, at least by orthodoxy's standards, heretics. Because orthodoxy agreed with proto-orthodoxy, it is mostly the proto-orthodox texts that have survived into modernity. Had other theologies "won," they would likely be the ones to which we'd have better access.

different from the God of Israel. In Justin's words, Marcion "teaches to deny God the maker of everything in heaven and earth."[43] Aligning with contemporaneous ideas of a false god imprisoning the world in material chaos, Marcion contended that the Israelite God was a vengeful and jealous deity, power hungry for unjust supremacy.[44] This position extended into how Marcion read Jewish texts. According to Irenaeus (130–202 CE), Marcion cut apart the Gospel of Luke and aspects of Paul's letters in an effort to render only parts of them (e.g., the non-Israelite-God parts) authoritative.[45] Scholars more recently, however, are contending that even if Marcion's letters of Paul were shorter than the versions found in the New Testament, that does not necessarily mean he cut them up. Instead, it is possible that Marcion had texts closer to what Paul actually said, and that other Christ-followers in the second century added to Paul's materials.[46] It is also possible that those adding to Paul created justification for their additions by saying Marcion's version was corrupted.

Marcionite scholarship is changing rapidly, so much so that what I write here may need serious revision in the next year. But as of now, what can be said is this: If we follow thinkers like Justin and Irenaeus, then Marcion, regardless of whether he cut up Paul's letters or had copies that were closer to what the historical Paul wrote, had an issue with traditional Jewish sources because they celebrated, in Marcion's view, a lower deity.[47] While what eventually

43. Apol 58.1. Marcion's "other" God refers to a greater, more compassionate deity, one for whom the Israelite God is an enemy. Unlike the "Demiurge," meaning "producer" or "creator," this greater God was non-bodied, detached from material want. Because of this, Marcion's Jesus also needed to be non-bodied. Marcion ostensibly believed that Jesus only appeared to have a body for the sake of his mission on earth, a mission informed by the knowledge of the Demiurge.

44. I.e., that the Israelite God was the Demiurge.

45. *Against Heresies* 1.27.2. Tertullian writes similarly in *Against Marcion* Books IV and V.

46. See, for example, Markus Vinzent, *Resetting the Origins of Christianity: A New Theory of Sources and Beginnings* (Cambridge University Press, 2023); Jason D. BeDuhn, *The First New Testament: Marcion's Scriptural Canon* (Polebridge Press, 2013); Markus Vinzent, *Christ's Torah*, English ed. (Routledge, 2024); Markus Vinzent, *Paul's Literary Metamorphosis: Translations of Marcion's Apostolos and Canonical Counterparts*, version 1.01, ed. Jack Bull, trans. Mark G. Bilby (LODLIB, 2023), https://doi.org/10.5281/zenodo.8271824.

47. As Tertullian, who thought the traditional Jewish sources foretold the story of Christ, bemoans, "To Abraham were the promises made. . . . Fie on Marcion's sponge!" (*Against Marcion* V).

became known as the "Old Testament" was significant to Marcion in that it proved to him that its God was the lesser-than demiurge (i.e., "creator" of earthly substance), Jewish sources were not considered sacred in the same way his Luke and Paul were. Those who have trusted that Marcion did indeed cut up Paul's texts have postulated that Marcion's redactions were devoid of any Pauline quotes that seemed to favor Jewish tradition.[48] Instead, his version highlighted that Judaism was a movement marked by law and bodily practices that take one away from true spiritual knowledge. The assumption in this is that Marcion's Paul would never say something positive about Judaism; all such statements must have been inserted into Paul's letters by his adversaries. That Paul considers himself as an apostle to the gentiles, and that Luke depicts Jesus as a light for the non-Jewish nations, are likely reasons why Marcion privileged them over others.[49]

For Marcion, and for Marcion's Paul, promoting a distinctly gentile Jesus movement was integral. The God of Israel, after all, was the God of the Jews, and if we follow thinkers like Justin and Irenaeus, Marcion thought that this God was a malevolent, jealous deity of a higher order. While we cannot know what Marcion said specifically about Romans 9–11—as, again, we have nothing written by the historical Marcion—it is likely he believed that Jewish worshippers of the Israelite God (or any worshippers of the Israelite God) would *not* be granted eternal salvation. A major note of clarification, however, is needed here. In reconstructions of Marcion's Pauline corpus, Romans 9–11 is not there. In other words, it is possible that Marcion either cut these verses out of Paul's letter, or that they were created and added in by others. Following the latter possibility, it is still possible that Marcion knew about these verses, even if they were added in by his contemporaries. Regardless of whether one thinks Marcion's corpus was closer to the historical Paul's or not, the point is that, for Marcion—or so scholars currently think—Paul was great, and Jews were not.

Marcion's Paul did not win the day. Neither did his ostensible demiurge-driven views. Other Christ-confessors declared that the God of

48. Specifically Jewish law (e.g., Rom 3:31 and Gal 3:21); interestingly, Rom 7:12 is in reconstructions of Marcion's materials. See also Paula Fredriksen, "The Birth of Christianity and the Origins of Christian Anti-Judaism," in *Jesus, Judaism, and Christian Anti-Judaism: Reading the New Testament after the Holocaust*, ed. Paula Fredriksen and Adele Reinhartz (Westminster John Knox, 2002), 24–25.

49. See, for example, Galatians 2:7–8, Romans 15:16, and Luke 2:32.

Israel was indeed the Good God of Jesus, and that sources about this God were Holy Scripture.[50] This doesn't mean that Judaism was supported by Nicene Christianity, however. Already in the early centuries CE, ecclesial leaders from a variety of backgrounds denigrated Jews as a way to bolster their self-acclaimed un-Jewish principals. Such opposition, in fact, was integral to the survival of any kind of a gentile Christ-following norm, including an Orthodox one. As historian Robert Michael attests, gentile Christ-confessors "needed Jews and Judaism as a kind of antitype to define nearly everything [they were] and stood for."[51] After all, Jesus was Jewish. A clear way to prove that conversion to Judaism was unnecessary was to discount the tradition altogether. Thus, the way Jews followed God had to be wrong. The way Jews read their scriptures had to be outdated. The way Jews performed their ideology on and through the body (e.g., circumcision and diet) had to be demonic. While Jesus may have been *born* a Jew, early leaders in favor of a gentile assembly for Christ needed to assert that Jesus's God-given mission was to establish something *different*—something *better.*

Proto-Orthodox and later Orthodox thinkers also relied on disagreements with Marcion—their claims that Marcion's way of "establishing something better" was heretical—to bolster their own views. From the Greek word *hairesis*, or "choice," heresy referred to "wrong choice" in ideology. To name-call Marcion a heretic—to even accuse him of manipulating Paul's texts and worshipping a false god, regardless of whether he did or not—served as a tool of emotional persuasion. "To my dear supporters!" a proto-Orthodox might say. "Don't listen to Marcion's theology on the God of Israel; he claims that

50. Not all texts about this God were canonized, however, and they are thus rendered "apocryphal." Something to keep in mind, too, is that while Orthodoxy may on the surface appear friendlier to Jews than, say, the ideologies of Marcion, it is not. Orthodoxy, as readers will see, asserted that Jews misunderstood their God and sacred texts, unlike proper Christ-followers. Paula Fredriksen has even postulated that if Marcionite theology remained over and against Orthodoxy, there might be less Christian antisemitism, in that Jews and Christians would not be arguing over the same origin story and collection of texts. In short, Judaism and Christianity might be less of a threat to each other, and might in turn come in contact with each other less. Fredriksen, "The Birth of Christianity and the Origins of Christian Anti-Judaism," 29.

51. Robert Michael, *A History of Catholic Antisemitism: The Dark Side of the Church* (Palgrave Macmillan, 2011), 27. See also Luke T. Johnson, "The New Testament's Anti-Jewish Slander and the Conventions of Ancient Polemic," *Journal of Biblical Literature* 108, no. 3 (1989): 425–426.

our God is not the real God! Don't believe what he says about Paul; he *changed* Paul's writings! Truly I say to you, Marcion is a *heretic*!" The idea was that, if enough listeners came to associate Marcion with something *wrong*, then they were that much closer to being seen as *right*.[52]

Of course, in the fourth century CE, the proto-Orthodox *were* seen as right. Romans 9–11 *was* seen as inherently Pauline. The God of Israel *was* declared the God of Christians. Traditional Jewish texts *were* rendered sacred. To go against these tenets—to leave *all* of Jewishness behind—became a violation of the newly developed Nicene Creed. What this meant, in turn, was that Nicene Christians needed to address how to reflect upon Jews and Judaism, even if doing so was at an anti-Jewish distance.[53] To put it otherwise, by inheriting the proto-Orthodox view that Marcion's theories about the Israelite God and Jewish texts were "heresy," Nicene Christians had to consistently *engage Jewishness*, even as they declared themselves *necessarily not* Jewish.

Augustine's Paul

Augustine was one of the most influential Nicene supporters to simultaneously engage with and distance himself from Jewishness. Born in 354 CE in North Africa, he theologized at an exciting time. He lived to see the establishment of the Christian canon, as well as Theodosius I's edict that Nicene Christianity

---

52. Readers can see this tactic at play in Justin Martyr's *Dialogue with Trypho*. As George Foot Moore so aptly put it, "The literary form of dialogue was chosen because it enabled the writers to combat Jewish objections as well as to develop their own argument in the way best adapted to their purpose. . . . [Trypho] raises his difficulties and makes objections only to give the Christian opportunity to show how easily they are resolved or refuted, while in the end the Jew is made to admit himself vanquished. This of itself shows that the authors did not write to covert Jews but to edify Christianity, possibly also the convince Gentiles wavering between the rival propaganda of the synagogue and the church." In the same vein, the proto-Orthodox called people like Marcion "heretical" in order to edify *themselves* and, in turn, persuade more to follow them. See Justin Martyr, *Dialogue with Trypho*. George Foot Moore, "Christian Writers on Judaism," *Harvard Theological Review* 14, no. 3 (1921): 198.

53. Such need to reflect on Jews and Jewishness, even if at an anti-Jewish distance, continued through the Protestant Reformation. For example, as Matthew Novenson writes on Protestantism, "Protestants needed the idea of Jews and Judaism in order to know what [they], Protestants and Protestantism, were." See Novenson, "Anti-Judaism and Philo-Judaism in Pauline Studies, Then and Now," 109. For more on Protestantism and Judaism, see the work on Luther below and chapter 2 of this book.

was the official religion of the Roman Empire.[54] With Marcionism institutionally supplanted by this edict, Augustine did not need to convince those in power that the best way to follow Christ was to believe in the Jewish God and rely on Jewish texts. He did, however, feel the need to articulate *how* Nicene Christians should relate to such Jewishness—as well as to Jews more generally—and often did so through his readings of Paul.

Augustine saw himself in Paul. In his *Confessions*, a work often heralded as the first autobiography, Augustine parallels his relations to Christ to those of the apostle. He does this by connecting his desire to rid himself of bodily yearnings to what Paul writes in Romans 13: "[Let us live] not in riots and drunken parties, not in eroticism and indecencies, not in strife and rivalry, but put on the Lord Jesus Christ and make no provision for the flesh in its lusts" (Rom 13:13–14).[55] This understanding of Christ—as one who helps humanity turn away from licentiousness—came from Paul, who, in Augustine's view, similarly suffered from material want. It was after reading Romans 13, however, and considering Paul's own turning to Christ, that Augustine wrote: "I neither wished nor needed to read further. At once, with the last words of this sentence, it was as if a light of relief from all anxiety flooded into my heart. All the shadows of doubt were dispelled."[56] For Augustine, Paul was the ultimate convert, one whom he aspired to be.[57]

Augustine's theologies are acutely related to his ideas of Jews. Again, contra Marcion, Augustine believed that the God of the Jews is the same as the God of Christ. But he also believed that humans are bound to fail if they do not understand the real purpose of that God's demands.[58] According to

54. Theodosius I was the last Roman emperor to rule until the Roman Empire's split into east and west.

55. This is Augustine's quote of the passage; see *Confessions* 8.12.29. See also Augustine, *Confessions*, trans. Henry Chadwick (Oxford University Press, 2008), 153. Mastering or elimination of passions was a standard way that intellectuals in Greco-Roman antiquity envisioned progress in virtue.

56. *Confessions* 8.12.29; see also Augustine, *Confessions*, trans. Henry Chadwick, 153.

57. Augustine was baptized as an infant, but he did not fully turn to or embrace the Christian tradition until adulthood. He even subscribed to Manichaeism for about a decade before turning (back) to Christianity.

58. Augustine relies on Romans 7 to make this point: "For I do not do the good I want, but the evil I do not want is what I do" (Rom 7:19).

Augustine, God's laws are not meant for lifelong abidement but are instead designed to remind humans that they are destined to sin (which he says can be blamed on the behaviors of Adam and Eve in Gen 2).[59] Like Marcion's relations to traditional Jewish scriptures, which are valuable to Marcion insofar as they demonstrate the inadequacies of the Israelite God, God's laws for Augustine are valuable in that they demonstrate the inadequacies of humanity.[60] In short, no one is able to follow God's laws sufficiently, and that is their point. Laws cannot save. Only God's grace, which is accompanied by Jesus's forgiveness of sins, can rescue humans from tragedy.[61] After all, writes Paul, those without Christ are "captive to the law of sin" (Rom 7:23).

It is often argued that the logic of Christ saving humans from sin stems from ancient cultic practice. The typical assumption is that, prior to the destruction of the Second Temple in 70 CE, Jews, like pagans, offered their God animal sacrifices as a way to connect with and atone for their wrongdoings. Thus, Paul, shaped by this understanding and his belief in Jesus as the Christ, came to believe that Jesus, in the form of a human being, was the world's *ultimate* sacrifice. As he writes in Romans, "God has done what the law, weakened by the flesh, could not do: by sending his own son in the likeness of sinful flesh and as a sin offering" (Rom 8:3). Christ-followers are thus "justified by [God's] grace as a gift, through the redemption that is in Christ Jesus, whom God put forward as a sacrifice of atonement by his blood" (Rom 3:24–25). Jesus's death, in this interpretation, justified humans (i.e., made them right before God) as long as they believed that Jesus's death was "for" or on behalf of their sins, and that God's resurrection of Jesus brought about their ultimate salvation (e.g., Rom 4:23–24, 10:9–10). It is unclear, however, if Paul actually connected his ideas of Jesus's death to the Jewish sacrificial system in this way, as his understanding of that system would not have been structured

59. For more on Augustine and his conceptions of original sin, see, for example, *On Merit and the Forgiveness of Sins and the Baptism of Infants*.

60. See also Romans 3:20.

61. See Augustine's *Ad Simplicianum* I. ii; Paula Fredriksen, "Paul and Augustine: Conversion Narratives, Orthodox Traditions, and the Retrospective Self," *Journal of Theological Studies* 37, no. 1 (1986): 22–23. Augustine does seem to find value in following the law, however, prior to Christ's arrival on earth. See John Y. B. Hood, "Did Augustine Abandon His Doctrine of Jewish Witness in Aduersus Iudaeos?," *Augustinian Studies* 50, no. 2 (2019): 178. Here, Hood is in conversation with Fredriksen's work (e.g., Paula Fredriksen, *Augustine and the Jews: A Christian Defense of Jews and Judaism* [Yale University Press, 2010]).

around the later concept of a "fall" or "essential brokenness" or "original sin" that Augustine posits onto Genesis 2.[62] Still, for *Augustine's* Paul, and thus for Augustine, this is how Jesus's death and resurrection worked.[63]

Augustine also wrote that Jews were beneficial. On his reading, Jesus needed to be crucified by his enemies, which Augustine believed were Jews: "It was the Jews who held him; the Jews who insulted him; the Jews who bound him; the Jews who crowned him with thorns; who soiled him with their spit; who whipped him; who ridiculed him; who hung him on the cross; who stabbed his body with their spears."[64] But as he also writes, "Now, the price of our redemption is the blood of Christ, who could manifestly not be killed except by his enemies. Here is the use of wicked men [Jews] for the benefit of the good."[65] To put it otherwise, Augustine seemed to believe, at least when writing this letter, that Jews did indeed have a purpose: to kill Jesus. He also seemed to believe, through his understanding of Paul in Romans, that Jews provided space for a plenitude of gentiles to be welcomed into God's covenant

---

62. See Stanley K. Stowers, *A Rereading of Romans: Justice, Jews, and Gentiles* (Yale University Press, 1994), 207.

63. See, for example, Augustine, *Propositions from the Epistle to the Romans*, 32–34, 48, 51, in Paula Landes Fredriksen, trans., *Augustine on Romans: Propositions from the Epistle to the Romans and Unfinished Commentary on the Epistles to the Romans* (Society of Biblical Literature, 1982).

64. Augustine, "Sermo ad Catechumenos: De Symbolo," Tractatus IV, 40:634. Cited in Robert Michael, *A History of Catholic Antisemitism*, 17–18. See also Jules Isaac, *Genèse de l'Antisémitisme* (Calmann Lévy, 2014), 167. The ahistorical belief that Jews were responsible for Jesus's death was likely in circulation by the end of the first century CE, as the Gospels were already rhetorically constructing animosity between Jewish leaders and Jesus in Jesus's final days. Pontius Pilate, in fact, insinuates in the Gospel of Matthew that Jews for all time are to blame for Jesus's death (Matt 27:25), despite the fact that Pilate, in non-Christ-centered sources, is depicted as a ruthless leader who would be doubtful to care about Jesus's life or death. Paul—or perhaps someone in Paul's name who later added to Paul's work—also says that Jews killed Jesus and their prophets (1 Thess 2:15–16). Still, the belief that Jews killed Jesus—and that Pilate was trapped under Jews' clutches—grew over the centuries as the Christ movement became an increasingly gentile one. For more on the Christ-killer myth and its various expressions, see Jeremy Cohen, *Christ Killers: The Jews and the Passion from the Bible to the Big Screen* (Oxford University Press, 2007). See also J. Christopher Edwards, *Crucified: The Christian Invention of the Jewish Executioners of Jesus* (Fortress Press, 2023).

65. Letter to Paulinus, 149.20; see Augustine, *Letters, Volume 3 (131–164)*, trans. Wilfrid Parsons (Catholic University of America Press, 1953); see also Cohen, *The Salvation of Israel*, 51.

and, in turn, the end of days—perhaps another way of benefiting "the good." As Paul explains, "Through their stumbling, salvation has come to the gentiles" (Rom 11:11). And as Augustine affirms, in conversation with Paul in Romans, "As concerning the Gospel, indeed they [Jews] are enemies for your sake."[66] Thus, for Augustine, the wickedness of Jewish disbelief is all part of God's beneficial—albeit mysterious—plan for human salvation.

Augustine adds, however, that at least *some* Jewish believers in Christ will be joining believing gentiles in the end of days. Referencing again Romans 11, he writes that "not all of them were blind; there were some among them who recognized Christ."[67] This "some" is important, especially when it comes to deciphering Paul's line that "all Israel will be saved" in Romans 11:26. For Augustine, "all Israel shall be saved because *of the* Jews [i.e., the some] and *of the* gentiles [i.e., the plentitude] who have been called according to the plan, and there arises a truer Israel."[68] All Israel, in other words, constitutes a New Israel: a small collection of Jews and a great collection of gentiles who understand that Jesus fulfills the law of atonement and, in doing so, saves the world's believers. Augustine then adds, as if in anticipation of unwanted confusion, that the removal of sin, and thus initiation into this New Israel, is "not, indeed, [for] *all* the Jews, but [for] the *elect*."[69]

Finally, in what is called Augustine's "Doctrine of Witness," which is expressed to varying degrees across a number of his works, Augustine argues that Jews continue to serve two additional purposes.[70] First, because

---

66. Letter to Paulinus 149.20; see Augustine, *Letters, Volume 3 (131–164)*, trans. Wilfrid Parsons.

67. Letter to Paulinus 149.20; see Augustine, *Letters, Volume 3 (131–164)*, trans. Wilfrid Parsons.

68. Letter to Paulinus 149.20; see Augustine, *Letters, Volume 3 (131–164)*, trans. Wilfrid Parsons; emphases mine.

69. Letter to Paulinus 149.20; see Augustine, *Letters, Volume 3 (131–164)*, trans. Wilfrid Parsons; emphases mine. See also Romans 11:27.

70. See *Contra Faustum Manichaeum*, his exposition of Psalm 59, and *The City of God* 18.46. See also his *Aduersus Iudaeos*, which John Y. B. Hood argues carries a different tone from his earlier works. For more on this doctrine and the nuances therein, see Jeremy Cohen, *Living Letters of the Law: Ideas of the Jew in Medieval Christianity* (University of California Press, 1999) 35–66; Fredriksen, *Augustine and the Jews*, xii, 371; Eisenbaum, *Paul Was Not a Christian*, 47; and Hood's "Did Augustine Abandon His Doctrine of Jewish Witness in Aduersus Iudaeos?", in which Hood also argues that by the time Augustine's life was ending,

Augustine believed that Jewish scripture foretold the story of Christ, Jews added credibility for Nicene Christians. Outsiders, in short, could not argue that Christians "made up" the Old Testament or its prophecies to benefit themselves.[71] Second, Jewish ways of being (e.g., disbelief in Christ and the literal observance of God's laws) offer examples to Christians of what *not* to do. The fact that Jews were continually subjugated and displaced was seen as proof that they were being punished for their crimes—crimes that also included the perceived persecution and execution of Jesus—which, again, served as a guiding light for Christians. Thus, Augustine attests, in conversation with Psalm 59:12, "Slay them not." Jewish texts show the validity of Christian theology, and Jewish oppression demonstrates that Christians are God's new chosen people.

This is certainly interesting, given the development of Christian Roman law. At the end of the fourth century CE, the Roman emperor Theodosius I forbade the practice of non-Nicene Christianity—all Christians "shall embrace the name of Catholic Christians," he decreed—but there is no record of him forbidding Judaism.[72] This does not mean that Jews were treated as equals to Nicene Christians, however. Evidence, in fact, shows the opposite. In the fifth century, Theodosius II put into effect a codification of Roman law—a compilation of Roman codes that had been in development since the emperor Constantine called the *Codex Theodosianus*—in which it was avowed that Jews were "polluted with the Jewish disease."[73] Nicene Christians were thus prohibited to "cease being a [Nicene] Christian and adopt the abominable and disgusting name of the Jews [that is,] to adopt the Jewish perversity, which is alien to the Roman Empire which has now become Christianized. . . . For it is an issue of life and death when someone rejects the Christian faith and

---

he no longer believed that Christians should let Jews live as Jews—their Jewishness is a witness to the rightness of Christianity and they therefore serve a purpose *as* Jews—but that they should focus on converting them to Christ (180).

71. Eisenbaum, *Paul Was Not a Christian*, 47.

72. *Codex Theodosianus*, 16:1:2. The main "heretical" threat to Nicene Christianity at this time was Arianism, which claimed that God and Jesus were of distinct essences, with God alone being immutable. According to the *Codex*, these heretics were deemed "demented and insane." See Clyde Pharr, trans., *The Theodosian Code and Novels, and the Sirmondian Constitutions* (The Lawbook Exchange, 2001), 440.

73. *Codex Theodosianus* 15:5:5; cited as such in Michael, *A History of Catholic Antisemitism*, 36.

replaces it with the disgusting Jewish form of perverse belief."[74] Or as classics scholars Clyde Pharr translates it: "Indeed it is more grievous than death and more cruel than murder if any person of the Christian faith should be polluted by Jewish disbelief."[75] In other words, Judaism itself may have been legal, but turning to it was like turning toward death.

Theodosius II also made sure Jews did not receive the same legal rights as Nicene Christians. The code states that Jews were barred from working as attorneys, bringing criminal cases against Christians, and serving in the army unless they were baptized. By legalizing invective against Jewish behavior, blood, and body, the Christian Roman Empire, in both its Eastern and Western posts, not only essentialized Jews—perhaps even racialized them, as readers will see in the next chapter—but also made such degradation "good" in the eyes of its more centralized citizens.[76]

A few key ideas regarding Paul and Jews were solidified in Christendom through its reception of Augustine. One is that Paul rejected Judaism, and in so doing, converted to a proper Christianity.[77] Another is that Judaism remained inferior to Christianity, due in no small part to Jewish attachment to law instead of grace—an attachment preached as sin according to Augustine's reading of Paul.[78] Another still is that studying Jewish (reframed

---

74. *Codex Theodosianus* 16:8:19; cited as such in Michael, *A History of Catholic Antisemitism*, 37.

75. Pharr, trans., *The Theodosian Code*, 469.

76. J. Kameron Carter suggests that early Christians biologized and in turn racialized Jews through such essentializing attitudes. He even suggests that origins of contemporary constructions of race and racism reside in the essentialism behind Christian anti-Judaism. See *Race: A Theological Account* (Oxford University Press, 2008). For more on how Jews were treated in the ancient Mediterranean once the empire became Nicene Christian, see Ross Shepard Kraemer, *The Mediterranean Diaspora in Late Antiquity: What Christianity Cost the Jews* (Oxford University Press, 2020).

77. Paula Fredriksen helpfully nuances this, stating that, for Augustine, "the source of [Paul's] former religion . . . had been demons, but the source of Jewish law was the true God." Again, the law for Augustine was good in that it educated people about the inevitability of human sin. See Paula Fredriksen, *Ancient Christianities: The First Five Hundred Years* (Princeton University Press, 2024), 27.

78. In the words of Krister Stendahl, who will be discussed in more detail in chapter 3, "It was not until Augustine that the Pauline thought about the law and Justification was applied in a consistent and grand style to a more general and timeless human problem." See Krister Stendahl, *Paul Among Jews and Gentiles and Other Essays* (Fortress Press, 1976), 85.

as Christian) texts and believing in the Jewish (reframed as Christian) God were integral to maintaining a proper Christian norm. In other words, not only were Jews to live, but their traditions—reread through a Christian lens—were to live too.

These ideas shaped Christianity's attitude toward Jews for centuries. From the fourth century onward, the papacy declared Jews a collective public opponent, diseased killers of Christ who deserved divine damnation. Such hostility continued to extend into how Jews were treated by Christian governments.[79] Throughout the Middle Ages, the Catholic Church passed laws limiting Jewish employment, travel, marriage, dress, housing, and interpersonal relations with Catholics.[80] In the thirteenth century, Jews were even required to wear distinguishable clothing such as a yellow badge or pointed hat, and they were also by then accustomed to being relegated to the ghettos.[81] In fact, even when laws were set to protect Jews (perhaps in light of Augustine's Doctrine of Witness), they were rendered dangerous, and the laws were not always followed.[82] By the time Martin Luther was born in the late fifteenth century, Jews were long called the collective enemy of Christendom, blamed even for killing Christian children and baking them into their Passover matzah—the proto-Titus Andronicus and Sweeney Todd, yet without the fanfare.[83] Perhaps it is time we Jews get some royalties.

Luther's Paul

Martin Luther inherited Christianity's supersessionist and anti-Jewish ideologies. He was also trained in the Augustinian order and inherited Augustine's

---

79. According to Robert Michael, Pope Damasus I provided the first evidence of a papal position toward Jews. See Michael, *A History of Catholic Antisemitism*, 76.

80. Richard S. Harvey, *Luther and the Jews* (Wipf and Stock, 2017), 62. For more on the history of Catholic antisemitism, see Michael, *A History of Catholic Antisemitism*.

81. Badges were not always yellow, however. See Michael, *A History of Catholic Antisemitism*, 81–82.

82. For example, Pope St. Gregory's Jewish policy in the sixth century. Michael, *A History of Catholic Antisemitism*, 76, 81–85.

83. That Jews killed Christian children in their rituals was otherwise known as "blood libel." See also chapter 2 of this book.

theology of sin and salvation.[84] Agreeing with Augustine that humans are destined to fail, he maintained that the Jewish law was useful insofar as it showcased the wretchedness of humanity. Rather than privilege Romans 7, however, as Augustine had done centuries prior, Luther privileged Romans 1: "For the righteousness of God is revealed in it from faith for faith, as it is written, 'The righteous one shall live out of faith.'"[85] From this verse, Luther argued that human effort is fruitless in the quest to please God. Anyone who suggested otherwise was missing the point and, moreover, showcasing their own ineptitude and self-righteousness. The problem, however, was that rather than stray from a works-righteous model, the Catholic Church had leaned into it by promoting the idea that Christians could buy forgiveness through deeds, confessions, and indulgences. In the face of this contemporaneous Catholic standard, Luther declared a different set of Christian truths: *sola scriptura*, *sola fide*, *sola gratia* (scripture alone, faith alone, grace alone). What he meant by these truths is that scripture shows that forgiveness of sins occurs solely through God's grace, which is available only to those who have faith in Christ. Salvation, in other words, never comes from works but instead only through grace. This theology, which is in many respects a repackaging of Augustine's, is often referred to as a "justification by faith" model, meaning that a person is "made right with God" (i.e., "justified") by believing in the grace of God through Christ, as opposed to following Catholic deeds or, worse, Jewish law.

The traditional Catholic Church, in short, was too Jewish for Luther. It focused too much on a material and transactional relationship with the divine, which he believed led to self-satisfaction and, in turn, damnation. It was thus from Luther's *non*-Jewish doctrine of justification by faith—a doctrine proclaimed through his readings of Paul and Augustine's dichotomy of grace and works—that the Protestant Reformation was formed.

Throughout his career, Luther had much to say about Jews, although four projects stand out: *That Jesus Christ Was Born a Jew* (1523), *Against the Sabbatarians* (1538), *On the Jews and Their Lies* (1543), and *The Last Words*

84. Luther also had a turning moment, akin to Paul and Augustine. After being nearly struck by lightning and praying for survival, he quit his path toward becoming a lawyer and joined the monastery.

85. Specifically, Romans 1:17.

of David (1543).[86] Luther's ideas sometimes change from text to text. For example, despite viewing Jews as descendants of Christ-killers and living an unjust life, Luther at first believed that Jews needed to be approached with care and kindness; only then could they trust Christians and be turned to Christ. But by the time Luther wrote *On the Jews and Their Lies*, his views were filled with vitriol. He, like Augustine, observed that the sustained oppression of Jews—they have been a "wandering" people for over 1,400 years, he repeats ad nauseam—was proof of God's rightful rejection of them.[87] But unlike Augustine, he turned away from an attitude of witness and at times even the goal of converting Jews to instead one of God-ordained violence. In *On the Jews and Their Lies*, he advised Christians to burn down synagogues and destroy Jewish homes, writing that Moses himself would do so if he could. After all, as true inheritors of God's promises, Christians are the real offspring of the Israelite patriarchs and prophets; Jews, with their refusal to honor God's gift in Christ, are "not Abraham's but the Devil's children."[88] To be a good

86. Brooks Schramm and Kirsi I. Stjerna, eds., *Martin Luther, the Bible, and the Jewish People: A Reader*, illustrated ed. (Fortress Press, 2012), 147; Harvey, *Luther and the Jews*, 69.

87. As one example, he writes, "They [the Jews] have failed to learn any lesson from the terrible distress that has been theirs for over fourteen hundred years in exile . . . If you have to or want to talk with them, do not say any more than this: 'Listen, Jew, are you aware that Jerusalem and your sovereignty, together with your temple and priesthood, have been destroyed for over 1,460 years?' For this year, which we Christians write as the year 1542 since the birth of Christ, is exactly 1,468 years, going on fifteen hundred years, since Vespasian and Titus destroyed Jerusalem and expelled the Jews from the city. Let the Jews bite on this nut and dispute this question as long as they wish." See Martin Luther, "On the Jews and Their Lies, 1543," in trans. Martin H. Bertram, *Luther's Works*, Vol. 47, *The Christian in Society IV*, ed. Franklin Sherman (Fortress Press, 1971), 138. For more on how this text was used to legitimize later antisemitism, see, for example, Christopher J. Probst, "Luther Scholars, Jews, and Judaism During the Third Reich: From the Hallowed Halls of Academia to the Sacred Spaces of German Protestantism," in *The Betrayal of the Humanities: The University During the Third Reich*, ed. Bernard M. Levinson and Robert P. Ericksen (Indiana University Press, 2022), 114–153.

88. Luther, *On the Jews and Their Lies*, referencing John 8. Luther adds that this "coincides with the judgement of Christ, which declares that they are venomous, bitter, vindictive, tricky serpents, assassins, and children of the devil [John 8] who sting and work harm stealthily wherever they cannot do it openly. For this reason I should like to see them where there are no Christians. The Turks and other heathen do not tolerate what we Christians endure from these venomous serpents and young devils. Nor do the Jews treat any others as they do us Christians. That is what I had in mind when I said earlier that, next to the devil, a Christian has no more bitter and galling foe than a Jew. There is no other to whom we accord as many

Christian was thus to be a watchful Christian, one who fought for the Paul-inspired *sola scriptura*, *sola fide*, and *sola gratia* at the much-desired expense of Jews and Judaism.

So, according to Luther, will Jews ever be saved? Of Paul's soteriology in Romans 9–11, Luther wrote that it is obscure. In Luther's words, "The text is the basis of the common opinion that at the end of the world, the Jews will return to the faith. However, it is so obscure that, unless one is willing to accept the judgement of the fathers who expound the apostle in this way, no one can, so it would seem, obtain a clear conviction from this text."[89] Luther's views are also obscure, so much so that he seems to have entirely different views at one point in his life versus another. In his lectures on Romans, dated to 1515–1516 CE, he argued that all Jews would eventually realize that Jesus is the Christ and thus be saved: "In that future day not a part but all Israel shall be saved. Now only in part are they saved, but then all shall be."[90] In fact, just as much as Jewish disbelief would help gentiles join the Jesus movement and thus be saved, Luther argued that gentile *belief* would help Jews realize that they needed to follow Jesus and thus be ushered *back into* the movement they left behind: The Jews' "fall is the salvation of the gentiles; yet this was not its final purpose, but the fact that they fell was to induce them to emulate the good of those who rose up."[91] Later, however, Luther changed his mind entirely. Jews were so evil in essence, he surmised, that there is no way the lot of them could find Christ. In 1543, he wrote: "Although there are many who derive the crazy notion from the 11th chapter of the Epistle to the Romans that all Jews much be converted, this is not so. St. Paul meant something

---

benefactions and from whom we suffer as much as we do from these base children of the devil, this brood of vipers [Matthew 3:7, 12:34–36]." See Luther, "On the Jews and Their Lies, 1543," trans. Martin H. Bertram, 141; and Martin Luther, "On the Jews and Their Lies (1543)," in *Luther the Expositor: Introduction to the Reformer's Exegetical Writings* 47: The Christian Society, trans. Martin H. Bertram (Fortress, 1971), part 11, respectively.

89. *Epistola ad Romanos* 56:436–37 in the Weimarer Ausgabe; Martin Luther, *Lectures on Romans*, trans. Wilhelm Pauck (Westminster John Knox, 1961), 315; see also Cohen, *The Salvation of Israel*, 26.

90. *Epistola ad Romanos* 56:438 in the Weimarer Ausgabe; Luther, *Lectures on Romans*, trans. Wilhelm Pauck, 315; see also Eric W. Gritsch, *Martin Luther's Anti-Semitism: Against His Better Judgment* (Eerdmans, 2012), 39–40.

91. *Epistola ad Romanos* 56:434 in the Weimarer Ausgabe; Luther, *Lectures on Romans*, trans. Wilhelm Pauck, 311; see also Cohen, *The Salvation of Israel*, 68.

quite different."[92] Luther, unfortunately, did not expand upon what such difference was.

Luther's doctrine of faith remains the central focus of Protestant Christianity today and was even adopted by the Catholic Church in 1999 through the shared Catholic-Lutheran construction of the *Joint Declaration on the Doctrine of Justification*.[93] In it, Luther's theology is evoked at the outset, with Pauline texts cited as proof of God sending Christ as a gift of salvation: "'for freedom Christ has set us free' (Gal 5:1–13; cf. Rom 6:7) . . . 'the righteousness of God is revealed through faith for faith' (Rom 1:16f) and that grants 'justification.'"[94] The World Methodist Council espoused this declaration in 2017, and the World Communion of Reformed Churches followed suit in 2017.[95] While interpretations of Romans 9–11 remain in dispute (including if the historical Paul even wrote it), most Christians are taught that believing in Christ is necessary in order to receive salvation. Jews, like gentiles, must be justified by faith. The law, misguided at best and sinful at worst, will not help one obtain salvation. These views, moreover, are frequently discussed in relation to ideas of Jewish "particularism" and Christian "universalism." Jews, from a Lutheran perspective, which is also to say an Augustinian one, are attached to a particular, ethnocentric ideology—one that favors self-righteous works, matters of the flesh, and an elitist-nationalistic relationship with God over a fully spiritual, fully universal Christianity. Christians, by this dichotomy, are not only not Jewish, they are also not ethnic.[96]

Luther's work was so influential that many scholars refer to his understandings of Paul as reflective of a modern Christian majority, including from within the biblical field. Biblical studies, as readers will see, was not founded upon a professional-versus-confessional dichotomy, but instead a predominately Protestant ideology hailed as Scientific Reason. Until the end of the

92. Martin Luther, *Vom Schem Hamphoras* 53:579–80 in the Weimarer Ausgabe; Gerhard Falk, *The Jew in Christian Theology: Martin Luther's Anti-Jewish Vom Schem Hamphoras* (McFarland and Company, 1992), 167; see also Cohen, *The Salvation of Israel*, 68.

93. It was also adopted by later Reformers, including John Calvin and John Wesley. See Eisenbaum, *Paul Was Not a Christian*, 53–54.

94. Section 1, paragraphs 8–9.

95. Some, however, suggest that it had little impact practically.

96. Hodge, "Paul and Ethnicity," 547.

twentieth century, even the most reputable scholars rendered anti-Judaism the rightful way of Paul and thus the rightful way of the world. New Testament texts and "good" interpreters of them showcased the truth that is Jewish inferiority: Jews were a tormented particularistic people, unable to see the truth that lies in their own texts or their own God. Jesus and his greatest apostle are for the gentiles, the ones who have "ears that hear" and "eyes that see" (2 Cor 2:9).

* * *

Perhaps it is no wonder I get asked so frequently why I study the New Testament. I am often even asked if I was raised in a Christian family; only with such an upbringing does it seem plausible to have a pronounced interest in Jesus and Christian origins. Such curiosity is not entirely off-base. To be Jewish in New Testament studies is so uncommon that I am often the only Jewish person in a room of fellow New Testament scholars. I can count on one hand the number of Jews I know who have graduated with a doctorate in the field in the last ten years, to put it mildly.

I was immersed in Jewish life and learning from infancy, initiated into the Jewish peoplehood on one of my first Shabbats by way of a Jewish baby-naming ceremony. I began attending Hebrew School as a toddler and felt like our second home was the synagogue, if only because we were there so frequently. I was not raised in a theistic household; I cannot remember conceptions of God ever being discussed, at least not in a serious way. Even when the *Tanakh* was rendered sacred, its sacrality was attached to its centrality for Jewish history and identity as opposed to a unified reflection of a divine realm or being. I was, however, taught to value Judaism as my family's culture and tradition. To provide just one example, here are the words my parents shared with me and our Jewish community upon wrapping me in my first tallit—a ritual fringed garment—at my bat mitzvah:

> When people get married, their lives center around themselves. But when they have children, the children take over. Suddenly, it's not our house, but Sarah's house. Phone calls aren't for us, they're for Sarah. And social lives revolve around children's concerts, school activities, and birthday parties. And we have never regretted it. We, your brother David, and your little sister Anna, all love you.
>
> You have accomplished so much in your young life, from school to the Temple, from sports to music. You are a beautiful young

> woman, outside, and more importantly, on the inside. You are a credit to the Jewish community and to the community at large.
>
> You will soon read from the Torah, which has guided us for thousands of years and given meaning to our lives. You will then have the responsibility to carry out the teachings and traditions of our Jewish heritage, symbolized by this tallit. Wear it well.

Nothing about God. Nothing about faith. Nothing about the Torah representing the divine. Even at one of the most traditional Jewish ceremonies, the focus was on being part of a peoplehood.

Many would say that my family's lack of a theistic orientation added to our Jewishness, and I agree. Unlike Christianity, Judaism has no creed. There is no profession of faith or systematic theology by which to abide, at least not in any kind of robust or agreed-upon way. In fact, on the day of my bat mitzvah, my Torah portion was *Parashat Emor* (Lev 21:1–24:23), which includes the Israelite God's infamous "eye for an eye" law. After chanting the Hebrew text directly from the Torah—a part of the service often considered the most sacred—I gave an entire *d'var*, or talk, on how much I disagreed with a lot of the passage. My focus, too, was on people—how humans create and relate to laws—not an almighty godhead. My congregation welcomed this approach, reflecting Judaism's tradition of encouraging difference, asking questions, and being open toward opposing or even lack-of-faith perspectives. "Two Jews, three opinions" is the long-standing joke within Judaism—perhaps the closest thing we have to an overarching theological system.[97]

In fact, it was not in spite of but rather *because* of my Jewishness that I became so interested in the study of Jesus and early Christianity. This happened early. One of my youngest memories is of being babysat by a family friend during the Christmas season. I was at her house, saw the Christmas tree, and saw what looked like figurines with which to play underneath it. I was particularly excited about the small baby whom I thought was resting in a basket.

"Look!" I exclaimed to the sitter. "It's baby *Moses*!"

"No, Sarah." The sitter replied. "This is *Jesus*."

---

97. Or perhaps I should say *things*—that is, difference/debate *and* jokes. For more on Jews and humor, see Jeremy Dauber, *Jewish Comedy: A Serious History* (W. W. Norton, 2017); Jennifer Caplan, *Funny, You Don't Look Funny: Judaism and Humor from the Silent Generation to Millennials* (Wayne State University Press, 2023).

"No! You're wrong. This is *Moses*. Trust me. *I* go to Hebrew School!"

"*No*, Sarah. This is *Jesus*!"

Obviously, I cannot know if this is how the conversation actually went. I was maybe three years old, and the specifics of the interaction remain fuzzy at best. What I do recall, however, is the extent to which the conversation felt heated, at least to my young mind. I thought we were in a legitimate argument over these men, in utter failure of what has since been called the Bechdel test.[98]

More important than knowing the details is the fact that the feelings behind this conversation stuck with me. Throughout my childhood and adolescence, Jesus continued to pique my interest. By the time I got to high school, I started attending church services, Bible groups, Sunday school classes, early morning seminary, and even church dances so as to gain a better understanding of Christianity. This was never because I was personally or spiritually drawn to Christian doctrine(s), but because I remained curious about Christian thought and practice. My curiosity deepened once I realized that so many Christians were being taught that Jesus was indeed Jewish, but that Jews also needed to become Christian. I did not understand how the central figure of the Christian faith—a Jew—could be used to justify the cultural Othering of Jews or, worse, the systematic slaughtering of them. Christian anti-Judaism and Christian supersessionism seemed utterly counterintuitive to me.

To put it otherwise, my upbringing as a Jew informed my subsequent research, including the history of Christian anti-Judaism discussed in this book. I learned from an early age that modern antisemitism, including the belief that Jews cannot be saved (or, for some, that Jews are not even worth trying to save), was not created in a secular vacuum. The centuries of Christian hostilities toward Jews both preceded and preconditioned it. These chapters thus hold the information I wish I had known when I was searching for *reasons* why Christianity seemed to revolve around such a confusing and painful hypocrisy.

* * *

The hypocrisy that is Christian supersessionism grew as the academic study of the Bible developed, and it grew by way of Pauline studies. In the face

98. From author Alison Bechdel, the Bechdel test is a measure used to evaluate the representation of women, which includes the criterion that a conversation focus on something other than a man or men.

of seventeenth- and eighteenth-century European Enlightenment, "biblical studies" as an area of scholarly pursuit separate from the church began to emerge. Until then—that is, from the early church fathers through the Reformers—the guiding principal of biblical interpretation was one of faith and theological conviction.[99] With modern skepticism turning its head, however, thinkers began to rely on new evaluative techniques to negotiate the Bible's meaning and ultimate relevance.[100] The Bible, in becoming the "Enlightenment" Bible, also became the "Heritage" Bible, a collection of texts reflecting ancient human contexts, as opposed to a perfect and methodical reflection of the divine.[101]

While Luther and his fellow supersessionist predecessors may seem absent from this new orientation, rest assured: They are there. Their seeming hiddenness from this new orientation in fact adds much to the drama that is the creation and preservation of biblical studies. It is precisely their role in the creation of biblical studies to which we now turn, a creation that became fodder for the academic understanding of what is now called the Old Perspective on Paul.

99. As Stephen Moore and Yvonne Sherwood put it, "The essential and enabling rule for biblical scholarship from the second-century apologists down to the sixteenth-century Reformers was the rule of faith; it was that rule—actually a complex congeries of minute regulations and encompassing assumptions—that determined the enterprise of biblical scholarship down to its details, however much those details might shift, slide, disintegrate, and reform in the ceaseless ebb and flow of the historical tide." See Stephen D. Moore and Yvonne Sherwood, *The Invention of the Biblical Scholar: A Critical Manifesto* (Fortress Press, 2011), 47.

100. As seen, for example, in the philological work of Richard Bentley and John Mill. Jonathan Sheehan, *The Enlightenment Bible: Translation, Scholarship, Culture* (Princeton University Press, 2013), 46–47; Moore and Sherwood, *The Invention of the Biblical Scholar*, 77.

101. Sheehan, *The Enlightenment Bible*, x.

CHAPTER TWO

A Good Anti-Semite

Christian interest in Jewish literature has always been apologetic or polemic rather than historical.

—George Foot Moore[1]

Nazism was not born in the desert. We all know this, but it has to be constantly recalled. And even if, far from any desert, it had grown like a mushroom in the silence of a European forest, it would have done so in the shadow of big trees, in the shelter of their silence or their indifference but in the same soil.

—Jacques Derrida[2]

By challenging the monopoly of Catholic teaching, the Protestant Reformation opened the doors to widespread reflection, skepticism, and diversification of thought. Conjoined with the Renaissance's revitalization of classical text study, the Scientific Revolution's advancements in observational analyses, and the Enlightenment's emphasis on reason, individualism, and progress, the Reformers' appeals to new modes of meaning-making helped pave the way for the creation of biblical studies in the eighteenth century and, with it, the field's Old Perspective on Paul. Particularly influential was Luther's promotion of individualized biblical interpretation—a desire for Christians to read the Bible for themselves—followed by modern attachments

1. Moore, "Christian Writers on Judaism," 197.

2. Jacques Derrida, *Of Spirit: Heidegger and the Question*, trans. Geoffrey Bennington and Rachel Bowlby (University of Chicago Press, 1989), 109. Also cited as an epigraph by Shawn Kelley, *Racializing Jesus: Race, Ideology and the Formation of Modern Biblical Scholarship* (Routledge, 2013), 89.

to philology and taxonomy in the Enlightenment and post-Enlightenment periods.[3] In many respects, the nascent biblical scholar became an amalgamation of Lutheran and taxonomized reason—a theologized, rationalized, and (as readers will see) racially invested concoction that was rendered both morally and reasonably sound.

The purpose of this chapter is to introduce readers to some of the techniques and frameworks early biblical scholars used to solidify an Old Perspective mindset. There is an additional focus to this, however, that readers should not overlook. What is shared below demonstrates the real fear many biblical scholars now have, which is that if thinkers see Paul as rejecting Jews in the world to come, then many of the world's inhabitants will reject Jews in the here and now. History has shown this to be an understandable dread; interpreters *have* read Paul as rejecting Jews and *have* followed suit. The contents of this chapter, in other words, could just as well be called "the stakes." While biblical scholarship typically refers to the Holocaust as the breakpoint between anti-Jewish approaches to Paul and those of a reparative spirit, it is also the Holocaust's anti-Jewish antecedents—the biblical interpreter's role in the development of an anti-Jewish racism that culminated in the atrocities of the death camps—that shake the biblical field so strongly. What follows is thus an attempt to unpack this history—to unveil readers' eyes, as Paul would say[4]—and show how a combination of Christian supersessionism, modern antisemitism, and "enlightened" biblical scholarship not only created the Old Perspective on Paul but also, if only in hindsight, led to a change of ethics in biblical studies.

The Enlightened Scholar

A cultural movement of seventeenth- and eighteenth-century Europe, the Enlightenment heralded reason, individualism, and suspicion of conventional

3. As Jonathan Sheehan writes on the individual study of the Bible, "Even more than *gratia* [grace] and *fides* [faith], the Bible powered the very project of the Reformation. Whatever the theological controversies that arose . . . the Bible lurked, as a force of chaos for many Catholics, a force of righteousness for Protestants . . . To say 'scripture alone' was to invest reform and reformers with the very authority of God, before which no human institution—church or state—might stand." Sheehan, *The Enlightenment Bible: Translation, Scholarship, Culture* (Princeton University Press, 2013), 1.

4. See 2 Corinthians 3:13–16; see also page 91 on the prayer for the "perfidious Jew."

authority. Inheriting a number of religious and philosophical principles from the Renaissance, Reformation, and Scientific Revolution, it promoted scientific exploration and the pursuit of rationally based knowledge at full speed. This impacted contemporaneous treatment of the Bible, especially in Protestant circles. While the Catholic Church did not yet support the idea of intellectuals implementing modern methods for interpreting what was deemed as scripture—methods that prioritized historical and linguistic contextualization over the theological authority of the Church[5]—Protestant thinkers were granted broad cultural and local theological permission to utilize modern principles to interrogate biblical writings (within limits, of course).[6] German Protestants in particular relished the opportunity to bring new questions—and in turn, new answers—to their studies.

Such interrogations prompted a widespread awareness that fallible humans were part of the transmission and translation of biblical writings. Not only were the ancient manuscripts seen as variegated—recall, there was no ability to mass produce a single file—but so were translations and interpretations of them. The Reformation alone made this clear. Catholics and Protestants followed different canons.[7] A major query for eighteenth-century Protestants thus became: If, according to Luther, a cornerstone of good faith

5. Beginning in 1943 with the papal encyclical *Divino Afflante Spiritu* and reiterated by the Second Vatican Council in 1962–1965, Roman Catholic scholars were encouraged to use modern methods for biblical analysis (this can be compared with the dogma of infallibility expressed in Vatican I, Pope Leo XIII's late nineteenth-century *Providentissimus Deus*, and Pope Pius X's early twentieth-century *Pascendi Dominici gregis* and Oath Against Modernism). Earlier Church doctrine, however, does not mean all Catholics agreed. Some Catholic scholars (e.g., George Tyrell in the late nineteenth century and Alfred Loisy in the early twentieth century) *did* attempt to use modern lenses to study the Bible, albeit in a way that still centered Christian views and garnered much pushback (this latter point can be compared with Strauss's experience articulated in footnote 6 just below). Still, and to the point of biblical studies maintaining a Protestant orientation, these Catholic thinkers are typically left out of intellectual histories on the origins of the biblical field.

6. For example, David Friedrich Strauss, whose *Das Leben Jesu kritishch bearbeitet* ([*The Life of Jesus, Critically Examined*], vol. 1, 1835; vol. 2, 1836), although now seen as a landmark in the quest for the historical Jesus, cost him his chair in theology at the University of Zürich and caused him to be burned in effigy in the streets of the city.

7. Michael Legaspi highlights the import of the canon's expanded opacity post-Reformation for the creation of the biblical scholar. See Michael Legaspi, *The Death of Scripture and the Rise of Biblical Studies* (Oxford University Press, 2010), 4.

is *sola scriptura*, which translations, interpretations, and canons were best? Is it the Septuagint's ancient Greek version? Jerome's fourth-century Latin? Luther's sixteenth-century German? Tyndale's sixteenth-century English? The many English voices of the sixteenth-century Geneva Bible or the seventeenth-century King James Version?[8]

By the mid-eighteenth century, scholars began to conclude that even the New Testament texts—the ones constructed in Greek in the years closest to Jesus's lifetime—exhibited biases. Just as scribes altered passages as they made their copies, scholars of the Enlightenment period contended that the authors of the New Testament crafted their works based on their own views, needs, and referents. This wasn't to render the Bible insufficient, but was rather an earnest, *human* reach for the divine. As ever-the-rationalist Protestant theologian Johann Salomo Semler wrote, "Holy Scripture and the Word of God must be differentiated because we know the difference. . . . not all of [the Bible's] *books* called *holy* belong."[9] In other words, while the Bible contains biases and discrepancies, "the word of God," for Semler, was "outside of, and above, all critique."[10] But the Bible, in this way, became protected too. Rather than containing a singular truth about the divine, it became a collection of *relatable*, even if fallible, evaluations that differed depending on the author. No longer was the Bible the singular word of God—or even the representative word of God in all of its books—but instead a collection of texts that reflected

8. These questions were being asked primarily by English and German Protestants, but with the latter group becoming more vocal. While English thinkers found it best to keep their findings from the public, Pietistic Lutherans in Germany—Christ-followers who valued one's individual relationship with biblical texts—celebrated the idea. The general argument from English schools was that by keeping the philological debates insular (i.e., beyond the pulpit but still within contained intellectual circles), Protestantism had a better chance of being preserved. Additional translations were seen as offering Christians new possibilities of connection, which was an integral part of the Pietist project. Individuals could choose which translations would help them best connect to Christ's love, thereby constructing the idea that to be a good Christian meant to be a good reader. Never, however, did these readers agree upon a "right" Bible translation. Instead, more and more options were produced, thereby creating further questioning. For more on this, including seventeenth-century mobility and stability of Bibles, see Sheehan, *The Enlightenment Bible*, chapter 1.

9. Semler is often regarded as a principal figure of German rationalism. See Johann Semler, *Abhandlung von freier Untersuchung des Canon* (Halle, 1771), 1:73.

10. Cited in Sheehan, *The Enlightenment Bible*, 90.

ancient human contexts, ones that later humans interpreted, inherited, and integrated into their own worldviews.[11]

Through these moves was born what historian Jonathan Sheehan calls the Enlightenment Bible: a canon bound by the cultural and temporal subjectivities of its authors, editors, canonizers, and translators.[12] With this also came the invention of the biblical scholar: a thinker tasked with analyzing the Bible's human origins with the assistance of rationalism, empiricism, and historical contextualization. But just as these moves opened space for new types of questions—ones that privileged messiness over theological unification—they also brought a dismissal of others. While, for example, questions of biblical morality were, at least for a time, blended with questions of historical reliability (e.g., *Were* the Canaanites annihilated? And *would* that be morally sound?), the search for moral meaning within the biblical canon was eventually cast to the margins. Magic was treated the same. Because Jesus's miracles could not be assessed on the grounds of empiricism, scholars focused instead on what Jesus's followers might have *believed* about Jesus's actions.[13] All this is ironic, of course, as many biblical scholars still assumed the Bible contained a moral core.[14] Many even performed their own kind of interpretive magic so as to render Paul systematically "good"—that is, in keeping with their own moral compass.[15] But I am getting ahead of myself.

As much as the Enlightenment Bible was rendered a post-theological text—a text scholars could study from a variety of historical, linguistic, and literary angles, all while keeping in mind the humanity behind its sources—interpretations of it often remained tied to Protestantism. The goal for many, in fact, was not to diminish the Bible, but rather to let it live—to help it survive

---

11. See Sheehan, *The Enlightenment Bible*, x.

12. Sheehan, *The Enlightenment Bible*, xii.

13. For more on miracles and magic in the early centuries CE, see, for example, Laura Salah Nasrallah, *Ancient Christians and the Power of Curses: Magic, Aesthetics, and Justice* (Cambridge University Press, 2024). Shaily Patel, "Magical Practices and Discourses of Magic in Early Christian Traditions: Jesus, Peter, and Paul" (PhD diss., University of North Carolina, 2017).

14. See Moore and Sherwood, *The Invention of the Biblical Scholar*, 61.

15. More will be discussed in chapter 3. See also Hicks-Keeton, *Good Book*, 151–155.

modernism and the more radical minds of a developing secular Europe.[16] Thus, even as biblical scholars no longer rendered the Bible in its entirety a perfect, divinely made, or even coherent theological system, they often still affirmed some sort of faith conviction in their analyses. Most interpreters remained Protestant and contended that appropriate interpretation reflected and supported appropriate Christianity. The conviction that good scholarship and good faith were inextricably bound was presumed at even the highest levels of scholarship and continued into the post-Enlightenment era. Typical of that conviction was the insistence by F. C. Baur, German patriarch of biblical historical criticism, in his 1845 classic, *Paul the Apostle of Jesus Christ*, that the Protestant faith should be allowed "its inalienable right to be restricted by no false concerns, at least not by fear of the truth; that is, its right to freely investigate the scriptures and beyond the scriptures. Whoever does not acknowledge this right—and . . . in acknowledging it also abandons the foolish prejudice that striving for truth and searching for truth could be to the detriment of the church, is no friend of the Protestant Church."[17] To be sure, the Enlightenment Bible was quintessentially a Protestant Bible. But it was also hotly debated.[18] Not only were there many translations, variants, and canonical possibilities to be studied, but this was all discussed across disciplines, sects, and in more public discursive settings such as newspapers, salons, and coffeehouses.[19] The Enlightenment Bible thus made space for religion to be fully part of, and keep pace with, a rapidly transforming culture. Rather than die with secularism, the Bible was granted a second chance at life, a life that could withstand skeptical tides of the modern age. With minimal self-reflection, moreover, the

16. Sheehan, *The Enlightenment Bible*, 27.

17. Ferdinand Christian Baur, *Paul, the Apostle of Jesus Christ*, "Preface to the First Edition," trans. Robert F. Brown and Peter C. Hodgson (Wipf and Stock, 2021), xxvi.

18. Indeed, there is no "one" version of Protestantism, just as there is no "one" version of Catholicism, just as there is no "one" way to read the Bible. While those considered to be the "founding fathers" of biblical studies were indeed self-identifying Protestants, these thinkers also developed their ideas through their own local and contextual lenses. Those who set the agenda for much of biblical studies in the nineteenth and twentieth centuries, as readers will see, were affiliated with the Tübingen School.

19. Sheehan, *The Enlightenment Bible*, 91; Moore and Sherwood, *The Invention of the Biblical Scholar*, 95. On the discursive role of the coffeehouse, see also Brian Cowan, *The Social Life of Coffee: The Emergence of the British Coffeehouse* (Yale University Press, 2011).

ever-expanding field of biblical scholarship—including the demographics of scholars *within* that field—became, as intimated above, a Protestant one.

The Racialized Scholar

As the nineteenth century saw the institutionalization of a Protestant-based biblical studies, another development infected public consciousness and in turn the biblical field: a reformulated hierarchy of race. Biblical scholar Shawn Kelley writes that this new hierarchy had much to do with Christianity. On the one hand, as European attachments to Christianity were declining, thinkers yearned for a more secular foundation through which to view the world.[20] On the other hand, this new foundation—race and racism—proved hardly secular at all, at least when examined in tandem with Christian history. Europe's newly "scientific" turn to race was supported by the already racialized view that Jews, in rejecting Jesus, were an innately and irrevocably inferior class of human.

These two areas—a growing secular Europe and an already anti-Jewish Christian prejudice—proved especially productive for Christian biblical scholars, in that they could now combine Christianity's long history of anti-Judaism with the scientific racism of modernity in order to prove that Paul saw it all along: Jews *are* a problem, even *the* problem. This view, moreover, was rendered ethically and intellectually good. As Kelley expounds further, racism for most modern white Europeans was "*a morally and empirically justifiable way of thinking* . . . repulsion in the face of overt racism is a relatively recent phenomenon."[21] Even the most respected biblical scholars found the category of race to be a helpful tool to better address the truths of the Bible and what it says about the Jewish problem. For Paul scholars specifically, Jews became the rightfully and radically inferior Semites, whereas Paul became the enlightened harbinger of a non-Semitic and even proto-Western elite civilization. For these scholars, Paul may have been *born* a Jew in the Near East, but his intellect reached for the Christian, the West, and the white.

Below is an overview of how scholars came to these conclusions, beginning with an introduction to the scientific foundation that helped get them there: nineteenth-century race science. I should note, however, that the information

20. See Kelley, *Racializing Jesus*, 3.

21. Kelley, *Racializing Jesus*, 3; emphasis in the original.

below is not a ground-up history but rather a summary of what secondary scholarship tells us about this topic.[22] My overall argument, as readers will see, is less about the changing tides of race science definitions and more about how certain ideologies of race science—such as the ideologies shared below—were interpolated into the biblical field.[23]

What Is Race Science?

Race science of the nineteenth century is best described as pseudoscience, parallel to the ideas of social Darwinism.[24] As European exploration and colonization penetrated new territories throughout the sixteenth through eighteenth centuries, European thinkers developed new methods for studying the natural world and to connect human difference to that natural order.[25] With this came a paradox: Human nature was thought to be uniform—humans knew when they encountered other humans—but, like plants and animals, also inherited differences due to climate and environmental variants.[26] Hypotheses about

22. And there is much secondary scholarship, far more than what can be cited here. I suggest combing through the footnotes, knowing that this is still just a glimpse into the conversation.

23. Also note that I am providing a more specifically New Testament trajectory. For a more Hebrew Bible–focused trajectory, see, for example, Joel S. Baden, *Source Criticism* (Wipf and Stock, 2024); Bernard M. Levinson, "The Impact of Johann Wolfgang von Goethe's Discovery of the 'Original' Version of the Ten Commandments upon Biblical Scholarship: The Myth of Jewish Particularism and German Universalism," in *Confronting Antisemitism in Christianity, Islam, and Judaism*, vol. 2 of *An End to Antisemitism!*, ed. Armin Lange et al. (Walter de Gruyter, 2020), 121–138; Bernard M. Levinson, "Gerhard von Rad's Struggle Against the Nazification of the Old Testament," in *The Betrayal of the Humanities: The University During the Third Reich*, ed. Bernard M. Levinson and Robert P. Ericksen (Indiana University Press, 2022), 154–204.

24. The English term "race" emerged in 1508. It was used in relation to humans starting in 1580, and was then applied to nineteenth-century race science. See David Theo Goldberg, *Racist Culture: Philosophy and the Politics of Meaning* (Blackwell, 1993), 63. For an overview of the definitions of "race" and "racism," including their relations to prejudice in antiquity, see Benjamin Isaac, *The Invention of Racism in Classical Antiquity* (Princeton University Press, 2004), introduction.

25. The first modern attempt to taxonomize humans comes from François Bernier in his seventeenth-century "A New Division of the Earth." See also Nicholas Hudson, "Introduction," in *A Cultural History of Race in the Reformation and Enlightenment*, ed. Nicholas Hudson (Bloomsbury Academic, 2023).

26. Hudson, "Introduction," 6–8.

these variants, which connected to ideas of beauty and culture, permeated the Enlightenment period and extended into the modern era.

By nineteenth-century modernity, European philosophies of human difference began to coalesce.[27] With a more developed desire to theorize and taxonomize human variety based on subjective ideas of beauty and progress, thinkers across disciplines relied on phylogeny and the Linnean taxonomy model to classify human variation. To put it otherwise, philosophers and medical leaders superimposed their biased cultural theories onto human bodies and called it science.[28] With cross-field agreement, Western European intellectuals rendered themselves the ones possessed of highest worldly consciousness: They were not only the most aesthetically pleasing, but also pioneers in global human advancement through their understandings of arts and sciences. Humans of different physiognomies, politics, and beliefs from those in Western Europe were in turn classed as degenerate, lesser-than people (sometimes even classified as lesser than—as in *not actually*—people). This was all preconditioned and further supported by European colonization, the process whereby European countries annexed other territories and named their peoples alien, ugly, and culturally inferior.[29]

Antisemitic Race Science

Antisemitism is bound up in this history. Coined by Austrian Jewish scholar Moritz Steinschneider in the mid-nineteenth century and then popularized

---

27. On the coalescing of theories, see Hudson, "Introduction."

28. Dennis Austin Britton, "Definitions and Representations of Race," in *A Cultural History of Race in the Reformation and Enlightenment*, ed. Nicholas Hudson (Bloomsbury Academic, 2023), 21.

29. Historian Michelle Gordon writes, "Studies that place the Holocaust within this wider framework of European [colonial] violence are not undertaken to be 'fashionable.'" But as she also writes that "this approach [is] an attempt to 'universalise' the Holocaust and remove its specificities—notably the key role of antisemitism: 'The idea that anti-Semitism was the essence of the Holocaust is perfectly compatible with the idea that such anti-Semitism can also be understood as related to colonial ideologies.'" Michelle Gordon, "Selective Histories: Britain, the Empire and the Holocaust," in *The Palgrave Handbook of Britain and the Holocaust*, ed. Tom Lawson and Andy Pearce (Palgrave Macmillan, 2020), 224. Here she is citing Tom Lawson, "Coming to Terms with the Past: Reading and Writing Colonial Genocide in the Shadow of the Holocaust," *Holocaust Studies: A Journal of Culture and History* 20, no. 1–2 (2014): 135, 147.

by German agitator Wilhelm Marr in the late nineteenth century, it maintains the idea that Jews are a class of human that did not evolve at the highest speed.[30] With it, however, came the century's new texture of race science cross-disciplinarity: Jews were a philosophically, theologically, philologically, psychologically, and medically inferior class of human. The extent to which ostensible secular science supported this classification cannot be overstated. Physicians argued that the ugly Jewish psyche and ugly Judaic-Yiddish language were reflections of the ugly Jewish body and therefore the ugly Jewish gene.[31] For many nineteenth-century European scientists, anti-Blackness, anti-Eastness, and anti-Jewishness went hand in hand: Jews were a "mongrel" race with ancestral ties to the Middle East and North Africa (i.e., the "Orient") who carried similar physiognomies to fellow inferior Blacks and Orientals.[32] In the words of nineteenth-century anatomist Robert Knox, "The [Jewish] contour is convex; the eyes long and fine, the outer angles running towards the temples; the brow and nose apt to form a single convex line; the nose comparatively narrow at the base, the eyes consequently approaching each other; lips very full, mouth projecting, chin small, and the whole physiognomy, when swarthy, as it often is, has an African look."[33] Jews were also thought to have an ugly psyche, or at least a diseased one. An "ugly" outside meant an "ugly" inside; aesthetics and pathology were inescapably linked.[34]

The widespread understanding of Jews as a degenerate race extended into the twentieth century and went beyond the "color line." By this time,

---

30. Steinschneider used the phrase *antisemitische vorurteile* ("antisemitic prejudices") when engaging the racist theories of Ernest Renan, a French philosopher discussed later in this chapter. Marr wrote of *semitismus*, or Jewry, in his 1879 pamphlet, "The Victory of Germanism over Judaism." He then wrote of *antisemitismus* in his 1880 pamphlet, "Way to Victory of the Germanic Spirit over the Jewish Spirit," and again in his 1881 *Zwanglose Antisemitische Hefte*, which was printed widely. Because of Marr's specific verbiage, he is sometimes credited as creating the term instead of Steinschneider.

31. The word "gene" was not coined until the early twentieth century, but conceptions of biological heredity predate its usage.

32. The idea was that dark Jewish skin was due to disease (e.g., "plica polonica," possibly from impoverished living) and interbreeding with those from Africa. See Sander L. Gilman, *The Jew's Body* (Routledge, 1991), 172–173.

33. Robert Knox, *The Races of Men: A Fragment* (Forgotten Books, 2018), 133.

34. Gilman, *The Jew's Body*, 173.

the apparent blackness of the Western European Jew was replaced with the contention that second- and third-generation Jewish immigrants had lost their darkness due to long-term occupancy in the Global West.[35] Jews were more regularly seen as presenting as white in color, sometimes even Aryan, with accompanying blond hair and blue eyes. This did not mean Jews were "truly white," however. Despite their white-like phenotype, Westernized Jews remained Jewish—that is, their own distinct race. That these Jews were "wandering" in the West, in fact, made their inferiority all the clearer. Jews had no homeland. Jews had no self-governance. All they had was repeated expulsion—and for good reason, if one recalls Luther. Thus, interestingly and ironically, Jews were at once not "True Israel" for most Christians *because of* their nationalistic particularity and also not "True Whites" for most nineteenth- and twentieth-century thinkers (including Christian thinkers) because they *lacked* national self-governance. Indeed, perhaps one of the most glaring lessons of racism is that its logics are illogical.

Black American activist W. E. B. Du Bois reflects upon the changing logics of racism in the early twentieth century. Whereas he once understood race as solely a color issue, he wrote that witnessing the Nazi treatment of fair-skinned Jews made him see race and racism in more expansive terms. In his words, "It had never occurred to me until then that any exhibition of race prejudice could be anything but color prejudice . . . the ghetto of Warsaw helped me to emerge from a certain social provincialism into a broader conception."[36] Race *is* a broader conception, yes. But it is also a conception that requires constant manipulation in order to sustain itself.

Physiognomy was scarcely forgotten, however. Racial considerations of the Jewish nose, chin, hair, and general mannerisms permeated twentieth-century discourse as a way to preserve Jews as racially Other. Conceptions of the Jewish nose in particular replaced ideas of the Jewish

---

35. Gilman, *The Jew's Body*, 176–177.

36. Quoted in this way by Glynis Cousin and Robert Fine, "Brothers in Misery: Reconnecting Sociologies of Racism and Anti-Semitism," in *Race, Color, Identity: Rethinking Discourses About "Jews" in the Twenty-First Century*, ed. Efraim Sicher (Berghahn Books, 2013), 309. See W. E. B. Du Bois, "The Negro and the Warsaw Ghetto [1952]," in *The Social Theory of W. E. B. Du Bois*, ed. Phil Zuckerman (Pine Forge Press, 2004), 45–46. After coming to this conclusion, Du Bois edited out his own antisemitic remarks in a later edition of his *The Souls of Black Folk*. See, for example, the fiftieth anniversary jubilee edition (Blue Heron Press, 1953).

skin, which included the idea that Jewish noses were a physical reflection of Satan.[37] Thought to resemble the number six—a number affiliated with Satan (see, e.g., Rev 13:18)—the Jewish nose became a reflection of an inner darkness that speaks to an even deeper truth about the darkness of the Jew.[38] For some twentieth-century thinkers, in fact, a Jew's lighter skin made them all the more dangerous—the Jew could more easily hide among the true whites—which also meant that spotting the Jewish nose or other Jewish features was all the more urgent. In 1938, Nazi loyalist Julius Streicher even published a children's book, *Der Giftpilz* (*The Poisonous Mushroom*), as a way to help Europeans of all ages distinguish the Jew from those of legitimate Aryan ancestry (see figure 2.1). The Jewish body is discussed as follows: "The Jewish nose is wide at the end and looks like the number six . . . Every Jew does not have these characteristics. Some do not have a proper Jewish nose, but real Jewish ears. Some do not have flat feet, but real Jewish eyes. Some Jews cannot be recognized at first glance. There are even some Jews with blond hair. If we want to be sure to recognize Jews, we must look carefully. But when one looks carefully, one can always tell it is a Jew."[39]

Could one always tell if someone was Jewish? Probably not. Historian Benjamin Isaac urges us to remember that racism exists even "where physical

---

37. Unless, for example, one underwent cosmetic rhinoplasty, in which a "Gentile contou[r]" was created, but even that route of creating Jewish invisibility was replaced with the enforcement of the Jewish star badge. Gilman, *The Jew's Body*, 187.

38. The number seven in Jewish antiquity was thought to reflect divine perfection, thereby making the number six deviant (a "wannabe" seven, so to speak). Three sixes are even worse (see Rev 13:18)! The gentile Christ-following movement and in turn Christianity appropriated this understanding for themselves and then applied it onto Jewish bodies. The Jewish nose was also thought to reflect Jewish sexual difference. For more on this, see Gilman, *The Jew's Body*, 188–189.

39. A full English translation of *Der Giftpilz* with accompanying illustrations is available through Calvin College's German Propaganda Archive: https://research.calvin.edu/german-propaganda-archive/thumb.htm.

The book was authored by Ernst Hiemer and illustrated by Philipp Rupprecht. See Ernst Hiemer, *Der Giftpilz* [*The Poisonous Mushroom*] (Stürmerverlag, 1938). For more on Nazi children's literature, see Daniel Feldman, "Reading Poison: Science and Story in Nazi Children's Propaganda," *Children's Literature in Education* 53, no. 2 (2022): 199–220; Kathleen Gallagher Elkins, "The Jews as 'Children of the Devil' (John 8:44) in Nazi Children's Literature," *Biblical Interpretation* 31, no. 3 (2022): 374–390.

Figure 2.1. "The Jewish nose . . ." illustration by Philipp Rupprecht from "Der Giftpilz" by Julius Streicher. United States Holocaust Memorial Museum, courtesy of *Der Giftpilz: Erzahlungen* [*The Poisonous Mushroom*] - Hiemer, Ernst - Der Sturmer.

differences are insignificant."[40] Again, the idea that any Jew could be spotted based on specific physical traits is a social perception, not a biological one, despite the extent to which thinkers of this time period asserted otherwise.[41] In fact, in order to be sure Jews *were* revealed, the Nazis enforced the wearing of a yellow star badge. If Jews could really be spotted using the right techniques, the Nazis would not have needed this tool.

40. Isaac, *The Invention of Racism in Classical Antiquity*, 19.

41. Matthew Frye Jacobson, *Whiteness of a Different Color: European Immigrants and the Alchemy of Race* (Harvard University Press, 1998), 174.

None of this is to say that all understandings of antisemitism were or are consistent.[42] Historian Albert S. Lindemann is quite right when he says that antisemitism can be difficult to pin down because Jewishness can be difficult to pin down. Jewishness escapes categories, so much so that many cannot seem to agree on exactly what it is.[43] Is it a religion? A culture? An ethnicity? A race? Is it all of the above or only some of the above, or does the answer change depending on the context and the person answering? How do we know when hostility toward Jews is a religious hostility and when is it a racial one?

Of course, the terms surrounding antisemitism are also difficult to define. What, for example, counts as hostility? What, moreover, *is* race? Is the answer to *that* consistent? No, it is not consistent. As alluded to above, where it was once defined as a biologically determined state, race is now rendered a social construct.[44] This is because genetic variation is in fact not

---

42. It is also not to suggest that Jews necessarily disagreed with race science. Historian John M. Efron, for example, has shown that there were Jews involved in race science between the years 1882 and 1933. A general difference he found, however, was that, compared to their gentile colleagues, who often relied on race science to promote a hierarchy of superior and inferior races, Jewish scientists engaged its methods to better make sense of and even define Jewish peoplehood. These scientists, he adds, were also able to build "a trend within racial science: Jewish resistance." They could rely on the "appropriate and professional discourse of modern science to challenge the biological and medical evidence brought to bear against them." See John M. Efron, *Defenders of the Race: Jewish Doctors and Race Science in Fin-de-Siècle Europe* (Yale University Press, 1994), 8–9. Historian Albert S. Lindemann also discusses the Jewish attraction toward Jews as a race, especially in relation to matrilineage, identity by descent (including patrilineal for many modern Jews), and many Jews' understandings of themselves *as Jewish* but without any kind of theistic or even "religious" orientation. Albert S. Lindemann, *Anti-Semitism Before the Holocaust*, 2nd ed. (Routledge, 2014), 8–9.

43. Lindemann, *Anti-Semitism Before the Holocaust*, 8.

44. For an accessible overview of race as a social construct and not a biological one, see Alan Goodman, "Race Is Real, But It's Not Genetic," SAPIENS, March 13, 2020, https://www.sapiens.org/biology/is-race-real/. For more on the relationship between Jews and race, see Cousin and Fine, "Brothers in Misery"; Evelyn Torton Beck, "The Politics of Jewish Invisibility," *NWSA Journal* 1, no. 1 (1988): 93–102; Karen Brodkin, *How Jews Became White Folks and What That Says About Race in America* (Rutgers University Press, 2002); Cheryl Greenberg, "'I'm Not White—I'm Jewish': The Racial Politics of American Jews," in *Race, Color, Identity: Rethinking Discourses About "Jews" in the Twenty-First Century*, ed. Efraim Sicher (Berghahn Books, 2013); Noa Sophie Kohler and Dan Mishmar, "Genes as Jewish History? Human Population Genetics in the Service of Historians," in *Race, Color, Identity: Rethinking Discourses About "Jews" in the Twenty-First Century*, ed. Efraim Sicher (Berghahn

stable across "races"; two people designated to the same race group can have greater genetic differences than those designated to different ones. Biological anthropologist Alan Goodman thus understands genetic variation as having much more to do with geography. "Ultimately," he explains, "the farther apart groups of people are from one other geographically, and, secondly, the longer they have been apart, can together explain groups' genetic distinctions from one another."[45] Race, in other words, is very much real in terms of social identity, social connectivity, and even social stigma. It's just not genetic. And it's certainly not taxonomized "naturally"—that is, without the insertion of profound human prejudice.

Still, and questions of variation aside, the idea that Jews were a racially inferior class of human served as the backbone of twentieth-century Nazism.[46] The same, unfortunately, can be said for much of nineteenth- and twentieth-century biblical scholarship. It is to this history we now turn.

Books, 2013), 234–246; Howard Winant, "Behind Blue Eues: Whiteness and Contemporary U.S. Racial Politics," in *Off White: Readings on Power, Privilege, and Resistance,* 2nd ed., ed. Michelle Fine et al. (Routledge, 2004); Jonathan Branfman, "Teaching for Coalition: Dismantling 'Jewish-Progressive Conflict' Through Feminist and Queer Pedagogy," *Frontiers (Boulder)* 40, no. 2 (2019): 126–166; Jacobson, *Whiteness of a Different Color*; Efraim Sicher, ed., *Race, Color, Identity: Rethinking Discourses About "Jews" in the Twenty-First Century* (Berghahn Books, 2013); David Baddiel, *Jews Don't Count* (HarperCollins, 2021); Jeanne Favret-Saada, "A Fuzzy Distinction: Anti-Judaism and Anti-Semitism (An Excerpt from *Le Judaisme et Ses Juifs*)," *HAU: Journal of Ethnographic Theory* 4, no. 3 (December 2014): 335–340; Shaul Magid, "The Price of (Non) Whiteness," Contending Modernities, September 18, 2020, https://contendingmodernities.nd.edu/theorizing-modernities/the-price-of-non-whiteness/; Michelle Fine et al., eds., *Off White: Readings on Power, Privilege, and Resistance*, 2nd ed. (Routledge, 2004).

45. He explains that genetics change over time and place, regardless of a "racial" background. Genetic variation affects all humans and has much more to do with geography. Depending on where one lives, there can be a greater difference between two persons of the same "race" than two persons of different "races." See Goodman, "Race Is Real, But It's Not Genetic."

46. That the Holocaust had anything to do with race, however, seems to be repeatedly forgotten. For example, one might recall, closer to our own time, Whoopi Goldberg's assessment in 2022: "This is white people doing it to white people." The Holocaust was not "about race." But this happened earlier too. Even the renowned philosopher Frantz Fanon once said that the Holocaust was a product of "little family quarrels," suggesting the European Jews were and always will be white. There were moments in which Fanon made clear he was horrified by Nazi antisemitism, but often viewing race in black-and-white terms, he concluded that European Jews are distinguished in their ability to hide behind their white skin and therefore their overall whiteness. Fanon, of course, was not the only person to think in these

Antisemitism and the Biblical Field

As biblical studies developed into an academic discipline, the ideologies of earlier Christian theologians were combined with the racialization of the post-Enlightenment era. In the nineteenth and much of the twentieth centuries especially, it was common for biblical scholars to use modern methods of investigation—those of history, yes, but also ones of biased racial taxonomy—to prove the superiority of Christianity to Judaism.

There was, however, a particular nuance to Christian antisemitism that made it distinct from non-Christian models: Christians believed that they still shared a God and first testament with Jews.[47] This meant that Christian biblical scholars, which is to say most biblical scholars, needed to justify the existence of Jews—to find a goodness *somewhere* in Jewish history—but only to a point. Many thinkers understood Paul as that point. While Jesus provided a departure from Judaism through his teaching, it was really Paul who, in spreading the good news of Jesus to gentiles, institutionalized that departure.[48] Below is a summary of how three of the most influential biblical scholars utilized a racialized Christian mindset to craft this reasoning. While what follows is by no means exhaustive, it is designed to give readers a taste of what nascent biblical studies looked like, and how its racialized

---

terms. As Andy Pearce writes, "The dominance of colour-centric 'racialised politics' left little space to accommodate the particularity of the Jewish experience under Nazism." Although Pearce is writing from a post-Holocaust British context, he contends that this transcended British borders. See Ashley Shannon Wu, "Whoopi Goldberg Returns to *The View* After Her Suspension," *Vulture*, February 14, 2022, https://www.vulture.com/2022/02/whoopi-goldberg-holocaust-comments-late-night-show.html; Jamelle Bouie, "On Whoopi Goldberg's Comments and the Origins of Racism," *New York Times*, February 5, 2022, https://www.nytimes.com/2022/02/05/opinion/whoopi-goldberg-race-history.html; Frantz Fanon, *Black Skin, White Masks*, trans. Richard Philcox (Grove Press, 2008), 115; Andy Pearce, *Holocaust Consciousness in Contemporary Britain* (Routledge, 2014), 15. See also Cousin and Fine, "Brothers in Misery," 309–310.

47. A testament with differences. The Jewish *Tanakh* and the Catholic, Protestant, and Eastern Orthodox Old Testaments are all different from each other.

48. The scholarly idea that Jesus rejected Judaism was usually explicated along parallel lines with how they saw Paul doing so. Jesus stressed love; Jews stressed law. Jesus was inclusive; Jews were exclusive. Jesus preached grace; Jews preached deeds and earning salvation. Still, Paul is the one who has, to quote biblical scholar Lloyd Gaston, "provided the theoretical structure for Christian anti-Judaism, from Marcion through Luther and F. C. Baur down to Bultmann." Lloyd Gaston, *Paul and the Torah* (University of British Columbia Press, 1987), 15.

attitudes toward Jews coalesced into what is now called the Old Perspective on Paul.

Ferdinand Christian Baur

Ferdinand Christian Baur (1792–1860) was one of the principal philosophical minds of nineteenth-century biblical scholarship. A German Protestant and leader at the Tübingen School—a school that set the agenda for much of biblical studies in the nineteenth and twentieth centuries—Baur sought to prove the ethical truths of the Bible using the historical-critical techniques of the modern age. Particularly influential for him were Luther and the German philosopher George Wilhelm Friedrich Hegel (1770–1831). Baur relied on Luther and Hegel to show that Paul rejected Judaism in favor of a more universal, spiritual Christianity.[49]

Hegel posited that every new evolutionary stage in world history brought with it a higher human evolvement. In his view, newer (i.e., better) culture was still negated at least in part by older (i.e., lesser) culture, but the combination of the two—newer and older—still moved humans toward constant higher evolvement.[50] Hegel, put simply, created a racialized understanding of world history, one in which each people—each *Volk*—could be simplified into an essence that was then surpassed by newer and better *Volk*. A global turning point for Hegel was the emergence of Hellenistic culture. For him, the Greeks were the epitome of spiritual beings, the originators of Western

---

49. Meanwhile, the Afroasiatic world from which these traditions emerged was completely ignored. In the words of Shawn Kelley, "Hegelian biblical scholarship, and all of those influenced by Hegelian biblical scholarship [e.g., the Tübingen school], will implicitly deny the possibility of an African spirit and will effectively erase Africans from the biblical world." Kelley, *Racializing Jesus*, 66. For more on the effects of this erasure within the biblical field, see, for example, Angela N. Parker, *If God Still Breathes, Why Can't I?: Black Lives Matter and Biblical Authority* (Eerdmans, 2021), especially chapter 1. For more on scholarship by faculty at Tübingen, see Anders Gerdmar, "Jewish Studies in the Service of Nazi Ideology: Tübingen's Faculty of Theology as a Center for Antisemitic Research," in *The Betrayal of the Humanities: The University During the Third Reich*, ed. Bernard M. Levinson and Robert P. Ericksen (Indiana University Press, 2022), 205–262.

50. Although not countering Hegel specifically, Sheila Briggs offers what might be called a rebuttal: "History does not run like a train schedule with fixed points spread out in linear development. Like the physical universe of which it is a part, human history is marked by nonlinear events and conditions that are not predetermined by and predictable through a precisely definable set of preconditions." Briggs, "Slavery and Gender," 175.

sophistication. Once the Jewish God was given to Hellenistic people by way of Paul, a Greek-like consciousness—which for Hegel was also a gentile-like consciousness—became unstoppable. For Hegel, then, Jews were "good" in the sense that they operated as movers between East (Jewish) and West (Greeks). But once the West acquired such goodness, Jews and Jewishness could be left behind.

Baur combined Hegel's understanding of world history with a Lutheran view of Jewish particularism and Christian universalism. He argued that Paul, in the name of Jesus, was rightfully and radically opposed to the non-spiritual, lesser-than Judaism of his time. In Baur's words, "The conversion of the Apostle Paul to Christianity is so important an event in the history of the recently established Church."[51] For example,

> everything that was national and Jewish in the Messianic idea . . . was at once removed from the consciousness of our apostle [Paul] by the one fact of the death of Jesus. With this death, everything that the Messiah might have been as a Jewish Messiah disappeared; through his death, Jesus, as the Messiah, had died to Judaism, had been removed beyond his national connexion [*sic*] with it, and placed in a freer, more universal, and purely spiritual sphere, where the absolute importance which Judaism had claimed till then was at once obliterated . . . The apostle [Paul] therefore saw in the death of Christ the purification of the Messianic idea from all the sensuous elements which cleaved to it in Judaism, and its elevation to the truly spiritual consciousness.[52]

Thus, even though, in Baur's view, Jesus is the one who died to Judaism, it was Paul who was "first to lay down expressly and distinctly the principle of [Jesus's] Christian universalism as a thing essentially opposed to Jewish particularism. From the first he set this Christianity principle before him as the sole standard and rule of his apostolic activity."[53]

51. Ferdinand Christian Baur, *Paul the Apostle of Jesus Christ*, vol. I, "Preface to the First Edition," trans. Robert F. Brown and Peter C. Hodgson (Wipf and Stock, 2021), 115.

52. Baur, *Paul the Apostle of Jesus Christ*, vol. 2, 125–126. See also Kelley, *Racializing Jesus*, 77.

53. Ferdinand Christian Baur, *The Church History of the First Three Centuries*, vol. 1, trans. Allan Menzies (Williams and Norgate, 1878), 47. See also Kelley, *Racializing Jesus*, 75.

In short, Baur applied a Lutheran-Hegelian theory to biblical studies and concluded that the earliest followers of Jesus—Jews—were too immature to properly know God and Jesus. When Paul joined the Jesus movement in the mid-first century, he not only rejected Judaism as wrongfully particular (this is Luther) but also, in doing so, promoted a scientifically superior form of human: the gentile Christ-follower (this is Hegel).[54] Thus through Jesus's death—which is to say through Paul's preaching of Jesus's death—gentile Christ-followers were not only freer than Jews, but finally free from Jews. In Baur's words, "It is only in Christianity [in explicit contrast to Judaism] that man can feel himself lifted up into the region of the spirit and of the spiritual life: it is only here that his relation to God is that of spirit to spirit."[55] Once again, we see a self-conception of Christianity as not only not Jewish, but also not ethnic.

Ferdinand Wilhelm Weber

German Pietist Ferdinand Wilhelm Weber (1836–1879) arrived at similar supersessionist conclusions, ones that were bound to Luther and the antisemitism of his time. Weber's is hardly the household name in biblical studies that Baur's is, but his influence should not be underestimated. E. P. Sanders assigned special significance to Weber in *Paul and Palestinian Judaism*, the formative book for the New Perspective on Paul, as readers will see in the next chapter. Sanders noted how "Weber's general view of Judaism lives on in New Testament scholarship," and devoted several pages to summarizing it.[56] Indeed, Weber epitomized the (mis)conception of Judaism that fueled the Old Perspective on Paul. Weber's overall thesis was that Judaism instituted a detrimental theology of legalism and works-righteousness. While Paul corrected this for gentile Christ-followers, Jews continued to miss the memo. Rabbinic sources, he argued, sustained a legalistic system that lacked earnest commitment to or connection with God.

54. On the role of Baur and Christian antisemitism, see also M Adryael Tong, "Banishing Baur: The Antisemitic Origins of White Supremacy in Biblical Studies," *Political Theology Network*, December 3, 2020, https://politicaltheology.com/banishing-baur-the-antisemitic-origins-of-white-supremacy-in-biblical-studies/.

55. Baur, *Paul the Apostle of Jesus Christ*, vol. 2, 212. See also Kelley, *Racializing Jesus*, 77.

56. E. P. Sanders, *Paul and Palestinian Judaism: A Comparison of Patterns of Religion* (Fortress Press, 1977), 36–39.

Despite focusing studies on rabbinic texts, Weber connected the plight of Jewish legalism to earlier experiences in ancient Israelite history. He argued that in ancient Jewish history, God gifted the Israelites the commandments at Mount Sinai as a way to extinguish the consequences of Adam's and Eve's fall (cf. Augustine). But because the Israelites disobeyed God by worshipping a golden calf at the mount,[57] the Israelites underwent another, distinct fall: a loss of their elect status, which Weber coined *Israel's Südenfall* (i.e., "Israel's downfall").[58] Then, in the wake of this lost status, God became a distant deity, and the Israelites became a legalistic people that strove to save itself by way of a works-righteous model. Thenceforth, Jews believed that every good deed and every bad deed were put onto a scale, and that the final weight of one's life determined one's place in the next world. Jews, moreover, worked for salvation without any care for a true and meaningful relationship with God.

For contemporary readers immersed in pop culture, the idea of counting merit may sound familiar. Similar to NBC's 2016–2020 hit comedy series *The Good Place*, Weber saw Judaism as, in effect, assigning numerical scores to human behavior. But just as the characters within *The Good Place* insist that keeping score does not adequately attend to the nuances of life and living, Weber insisted that Jewish law did not adequately attend to the nuances of morality. Life is complicated, ethics are complicated, and Jewish law could not possibly navigate such complexity. Instead of being open to Jews' own views toward nuance, however, Weber concluded that Judaism writ large was self-righteous, empty, and futile. Jews *think* they are on a path toward salvation, but they are not. Jewish law cannot save. Only law-free grace through Christ can.[59]

---

57. See Exodus 24–32.

58. Ferdinand Wilhelm Weber, *Jüdische Theologie auf Grund des Talmud und verwandter Schriften* (Dörffling & Franke, 1897), 274. See also E. P. Sanders, *Paul and Palestinian Judaism*, 36–39; E. P. Sanders, "Covenantal Nomism Revisited," *Jewish Studies Quarterly* 16, no. 1 (2009): 26.

59. This anti-Jewish rhetoric was also repurposed to vilify Catholicism as mired in works-righteousness. My instinct, along with others', is that the anti-Catholic competition/polemic among Protestant theologians was also very much a driving force of how they constructed ancient Judaism and how they interpreted passages in Paul's letters they took as "opposition to Judaism" (e.g., they read ancient Jews as ciphers for the polemical image of Catholics they were rejecting). This instinct was fleshed out in conversation with Stephen L. Young. My additional instinct is that this anti-Catholic vilification contributed to the sidelining of

As strange as Weber's two-fall analysis sounds—it is not one upheld in the scholarly literature—his conclusion that Jews were a self-righteous and legalistic people became standard by the end of the nineteenth century. For some, in fact, Weber's theories were more than just standard; they were a service. In the words of Reverend Nathaniel West, "No one can rise from the reading of Dr. Weber's book without feelings of the profoundest gratitude to God, through Christ, for redemption, not only from Sin and Death, but from '*Legality*.' It shines with the sunlight clearness, that the *whole* difference between the Christian and Jewish Soteriology is that between Grace and Law."[60]

Grace, in short, ushered in by Jesus and affirmed by Paul, is what brought relationality between God and God's *true* people (gentile Christ-followers). Law is what kept—and keeps—God and salvation away. Luther, of course, displayed a similar conviction in his own time, but through Weber, modern readers learned (or thought they did) that it wasn't just Christian texts proving the inadequacy of Jews and Judaism. It was Jewish ones too.

Rudolf Bultmann

The combination of Baur's and Weber's theories infiltrated Pauline scholarship like a virus. In the twentieth century, Rudolf Bultmann (1884–1976), commonly said to be the most influential New Testament scholar of the century, grabbed the vein that was post-Enlightenment New Testament studies in the Lutheran mode, and, like so many of his contemporaries but with special vehemence, inserted an IV drip of Baur and Weber.[61] Trained at the "history

---

Catholic modernists in the biblical field. It is worth repeating, for example, that in expositions on the invention of the modern biblical scholar, Catholic modernists tend to be missing. In other words, the field's Protestant orientations remain all the more Protestant based on scholars' own reconstructions of the field's productions of knowledge. Interestingly, Ernest Renan, who was educated in Catholic seminaries (although he left Catholicism in 1845), is frequently cited, but to highlight his harmful exegesis: Renan was profoundly antisemitic; he used modern lenses to argue that Jesus was Aryan. Protestant biblical studies was, of course, also grounded in antisemitism, but it is still noteworthy that the nuances of Catholic thinking in the modern period tend to be missing from the conversation (whereas nuances of Protestant thinking—e.g., James Parkes and George Foot Moore—are present).

60. Nathaniel West, "The Old Hebrew Theology," *The Old Testament Student* 3, no. 1 (September 1883): 18.

61. Bultmann is often praised for his stance against the National Socialist regime. His stance, however, which focused on a resistance to the so-called "Aryan Paragraph" on the church,

of religions school" at the University of Göttingen, a place heavily influenced by the scholarship of Tübingen, Bultmann, too, was convinced that Judaism was a self-righteous religion of works, while Christianity fostered a true love and respect for God through its understanding of God's grace.

Paul is the one who, for Bultmann, decisively established this works-grace dichotomy.[62] While Jesus remained an important figure for Bultmann—Jesus is the one who "overcame the flaws of late Judaism"—it was Paul's Hellenistic preaching of Jesus that saved humanity.[63] After all, Bultmann contended, "[Paul's] letters barely show traces of the influence of Palestinian tradition concerning the history and preaching of Jesus."[64] But "when Paul does refer to *Christ* as an example, he is thinking not of the historical [Jew] but of the pre-existent [non-Jew]."[65] In other words, by reading Paul through a twentieth-century racialized lens, Bultmann contended that Paul understood Jesus not through Judaism, but through the more sophisticated, spirit-oriented way of life—which is to say, a Greek or Hellenized way of life. Freedom itself, he wrote, is counter to the Jewish way of life, which he contends is "ministry of death."[66] As such, it cannot originate in Jesus or Judaism, but rather "in the Greek world. It is here that it is comprehended and developed along definite lines. It then acquired a peculiar stamp in Christianity," thanks to the apostle Paul.[67]

Sin and salvation had their place here. Akin to Luther, Bultmann read Paul's letters as showing that the law grants humans the *knowledge* of their never-ending sin, but not their survival of it. Jews, stuck to the law, were never

---

does not negate his anti-Jewish theologies. For more on this conversation, including a detailed discussion of Bultmann's views on Jews and Judaism, see Anders Gerdmar, *Roots of Theological Anti-Semitism: German Biblical Interpretation and the Jews, from Herder and Semler to Kittel and Bultmann* (Brill, 2009), 373–411.

62. Kelley, in fact, asserts, "The most unusual aspect of Bultmann's work comes in the relatively limited role he assigns to Jesus." *Racializing Jesus*, 145.

63. Kelley, *Racializing Jesus*, 145.

64. Rudolf Bultmann, *Theology of the New Testament*, trans. Kendrick Grobel (Charles Scribner's Sons, 1951), 188.

65. Bultmann, *Theology of the New Testament*, 188; emphasis mine.

66. Bultmann, *Theology of the New Testament*, 247.

67. Rudolf Bultmann, *Essays Philosophical and Theological*, trans. J. C. N. Greig (SCM Press, 1955), 306; see also Kelley, *Racializing Jesus*, 146.

really free. Only those detached from Jewish legalism—detached from the law's promotion of fear, anxiety, and self-aggrandizement—had access to God's grace and eternal salvation.[68] While Bultmann did not limit this freedom to solely those of the German *Volk*—something scholars note, given Bultmann's mid-twentieth-century German context—he does make clear that it comes neither from nor for Jews. To a certain extent, it doesn't even come from Jesus. Whereas Jesus protested legalism, Paul showed how to overcome it: through the gift of faith.

Indeed, for Bultmann, Christianity emerged less from the rural Galilean Jesus and more from the cosmopolitan Greek Paul, the one who theologized Jesus's message for the masses through the lens of a free, universal Spirit. And for Bultmann, Paul made it rightfully clear: gentile over Jew, Greek over Jew, grace over law. In his view, Jews cannot save, and Jews cannot be saved. Paul, in fact, knew this so well that he, writes Bultmann, underwent his own "conversion" from the bad Judaism to the good, "Torah-free Gentile Christianity."[69] He then preached this Torah-free gentile Christianity to help save the world.

The Old Perspective on Paul

While the tides were shifting throughout twentieth-century biblical scholarship, historical-critical New Testament studies still relied on Protestant-invested thinkers such as Baur, Weber, and Bultmann to imagine Christian origins. These, of course, were not the only thinkers shaping the field—neither was Luther—but their ideas helped instill within the field of biblical studies an anti-Jewish Pauline consensus, one that is now called the Old Perspective on Paul.

This perspective is as follows: A Pharisee named Saul, in realizing Jesus was God's chosen grace-giving Christ, rejected legalistic Judaism.[70] He converted to Christianity, changed his name to the Greek-sounding Paul, and spread the good news of a gentile, faith-based Christian tradition. It's almost impossible to overstate how central and defining a "believing versus doing"

68. Bultmann, *Theology of the New Testament*, 243–247.

69. Bultmann, *Theology of the New Testament*, 243–247; see also 187–189 and 108.

70. Relying on Acts's narrative of Paul changing his name from "Saul" to "Paul" adds to the drama that is, from an Old Perspective view, Paul converting from Judaism to Christianity.

(i.e., grace/faith versus works/earning) principle is for this construction. Paul represented a new soteriology, one in which humans were granted salvation through faith in Christ, not self-righteous works. As such, Judaism became *Spätjudentum*: late, dead, and sterile.[71] For enlightened modernists invested in faith, this "good" history showed that to be a "good" Christian meant to believe that Jewishness cannot save, and perhaps more insidious, that Jews cannot *be* saved. This, for them, was the essence of Paul's theology, and thus the essence of the gospel.

A Few Good Men

With any ideological structure, there will be ideological dissenters—which is to say, not every academic agreed with these views. For example, a thinker who has been "rediscovered" and celebrated in post-Holocaust biblical studies is a Christian clergyman named James Parkes, who in the early twentieth century dedicated his life to combating antisemitism by way of scholarship. In his 1934 monograph, *The Conflict of the Church and the Synagogue*, Parkes went to great lengths to show that neither Jesus nor Paul would support the schisms of Old Perspective orientations. Jesus was not trying to create a separation between Jews and Christians, he argued, and neither was Paul.[72] Parkes was not alone in his discontentment. The German scholar and rabbi Abraham Geiger discounted Baur directly, contending that he reconstructed history through the lens of anti-Jewish stereotype.[73] Additionally, from 1943 to 1963, in the years between his wife's and daughter's deaths at the hands of Nazis and that of his own death, the Jewish French historian Jules Isaac dedicated his career to discussing Christian antisemitism and the ahistorical claim that the earliest followers of Christ were not embedded in Judaism.[74] And even before Parkes, Geiger, and Isaac, Claude Joseph Goldsmid Montefiore, a Jewish intellectual and the founding president of the World Union for Progressive Judaism,

---

71. For more on this, see Schmid, "The Interpretation of Second Temple Judaism as 'Spätjudentum,'" 141–154.

72. James W. Parkes, *Conflict of the Church and the Synagogue: A Study in the Origins of Anti-Semitism* (Soncino, 1934).

73. Susannah Heschel, *Abraham Geiger and the Jewish Jesus* (University of Chicago Press, 1998), 112–119; Kelley, *Racializing Jesus*, 81.

74. More on this in chapter 3.

criticized Christian scholars for asserting their anti-Jewish views without reading Jewish sources closely.[75] God, he argued, was *not* a distant deity for ancient Jews, but was in fact regularly referred to as a compassionate and accessible one. For Montefiore, if Paul understood Judaism as purely legalistic and devoid of human-God interaction, then Paul understood Judaism wrongly. Presbyterian historian of religion George Foot Moore arrived at similar conclusions regarding the weight of Christian-centered reading strategies. In 1921, he critiqued Christian interpretation of Jewish sources fiercely, writing that "Christian interest in Jewish literature has always been apologetic or polemic rather than historical."[76] In his view, Christian scholars had repeatedly and ahistorically pit Jesus against Jews as a way to attest the supremacy of Jesus's later followers: gentiles.[77] Of Weber's systematic Judaism in particular, Moore wrote, "The fundamental criticism to be made of Weber's 'System' is precisely that it *is* a system of theology, and not an ancient Jewish system but a modern German system."[78]

The problem, however, was that these pushbacks were overwhelmed by an even louder ideal: Christian antisemitism. This ideal set the stage for an Old Perspective academic consensus, one that declared Judaism "late" by Jesus and later confirmed by Paul. Naming the field's antisemitic orientation is not to suggest that all nineteenth- and twentieth-century biblical scholars were at their core antisemitic, but rather that they were indeed "trapped," to quote Shawn Kelley, by the "[racialized] resources that permeated the discipline."[79]

Ghosts and Guilt

But they were also trapped—and were later haunted by—an even deeper set of social discriminations, ones that go beyond the writings of Marcion,

---

75. Claude Goldsmid Montefiore, *Judaism and St. Paul: Two Essays* (Max Goschen, 1914).

76. Moore, "Christian Writers on Judaism," 197.

77. This, at least, is how I interpret his remark that in the modern field of biblical studies, "the 'essence' of Christianity, and therefore its specific difference from Judaism, was for the first time sought in the religion of Jesus . . . the piety assumed to be distinctive of Jesus and his teaching, demanded an antithesis in Judaism."

78. Moore, "Christian Writers on Judaism," 229.

79. Kelley, *Racializing Jesus*, 5.

Augustine, or even Luther. With the discovery of six million Jews systematically murdered in the name of antisemitic ideals—ideals justified through scholarly readings of the Bible—biblical scholars were forced to confront Christianity's role in the development of anti-Jewish racism and its impact upon 1930s and 1940s thinking. This meant recognizing that legal, social, and essentializing discriminations—what modern critical race theorists describe as the core ingredients of race and racism—had been lauded against Jews by gentile Christ-followers for centuries. Indeed, for many biblical scholars, the post-Holocaust question was "not simply whether individual Christians had added fuel to modern European antisemitism," as New Testament scholar John Gager put it, "but whether Christianity *itself* was, in its essence and from its beginnings, the primary source of antisemitism in Western culture."[80]

Even if not *the* source of modern antisemitism, Christianity, scholars found, was certainly *a* source, traceable back to some of the earliest Christ-following groups. In other words, while race science, the origins of academic biblical studies, and the events of the Holocaust remain specific to modernity, biblical scholars asserted that their shared relations to earlier anti-Jewish prototypes could not be ignored. To be sure, this double-take on Christian antiquity derived in many respects from a guilty, if not trembling, collective conscience. Christianity's anti-Jewish past became a ghost, so to speak, haunting the scholarly living, demanding a reckoning. The following section is thus reflective of what theories of hauntology call a disruption of linear storytelling; it conjures back where we've already been.[81] Let me be clear when I say this work is not superfluous. If, in other words, the anti-Jewish racism of the Holocaust became the crux of Paul Perspective shifts, then looking back at Christianity's relations to that racism becomes necessary. Historian Sarah Abrevaya Stein calls this kind of work an "extended flashback," a retelling "that allows for a more complex understanding"—a "thick[er] reportage" of, in this

80. John G. Gager, *The Origins of Anti-Semitism: Attitudes Toward Judaism in Pagan and Christian Antiquity* (Oxford University Press, 1985), 13; emphasis mine.

81. In the words of Mark D. West, "Hauntology posits a state of being between presence and absence, disrupting linear temporality and exploring the haunting traces left by unresolved pasts upon the present." See Mark D. West, "Necro-Waste and Hauntology: Ghosts, Specters, and the Infinitive Responsibility of the Past," *Social Epistemology Review and Reply Collective* 12, no. 10 (October 31, 2023): 65.

case, the various Christian beginnings outlined in this book's first chapter.[82] As readers will see, Christian anti-Judaism was never solely about theological differences. It was about racial ones, too.

I want to also be clear, though, about not just why I am telling this story, but also how I am telling it. Rather than inserting the following history on premodern anti-Jewish racism into, say, chapter 1 on Marcion, Augustine, and Luther—in other words, I could have narrated the following cultural trappings alongside *their* interpretations of Paul—I have chosen to insert it here in a way that disrupts this book's temporal flow. I feel bound to tell this story like this precisely because it has entered into the biblical field *as a haunting* or *as an extended flashback*, epitomized in the Gager quotation above. Yes, what is outlined below *did* shape readings of Paul as those readings were occurring (e.g., Marcion was shaped by these broader cultural understandings of Jews, as was Augustine, as was Luther). But it *also* shaped the invention of the biblical scholar in the eighteenth and nineteenth centuries, the authority of the Old Perspective in the first half of the twentieth century, and the eventual guilt-ridden split toward Newer Perspectives in the late twentieth century. Put simply, there is no perfect way to tell this story. But because the biblical field has so frequently produced a double-take on this anti-Jewish past—a double-take that probes whether racialized antisemitism is embedded within earlier Christ-centered anti-Judaism, often starting with and then leading readers back to the Holocaust—I have chosen to do so here as well. Again, the history below is not superfluous. It is the history that shaped—and then reshaped—the biblical field.

An Extended Flashback: Christian Anti-Judaism as Proto-Antisemitism

A product of European race science as it may be, antisemitism has roots in earlier forms of Christian anti-Judaism.[83] That Jews were distinctly Other was not

82. Indeed, if studies of the changing perspectives on Paul so frequently begin and end with Christianity's relations to the Holocaust, then reflecting again on how and why Christianity relates to the Holocaust is not superfluous but imperative. Sarah Abrevaya Stein, *Saharan Jews and the Fate of French Algeria* (University of Chicago Press, 2014), 10.

83. And perhaps deeper ones still, such as in the imperial persecutions of Israelites and later Jews under Egyptian, Assyrian, Babylonian, Persian, Greek, and pre-Christian Roman rule.

a random perception within the Christ-following movement, but rather part of a deliberate framework used to rationalize the emergence and dominance of a gentile Christ-following populace. This framework was established early. Already in the first century, the author of Matthew insinuated a charge of deicide against Jews by having Pontius Pilate fault Jews collectively for Jesus's death.[84] The writer of John then intensified this perception by having Jesus refer to "the Jews" as murderers and children of the Devil.[85] These accusations aimed to solidify the identity of a Jesus movement with a non-Jewish core and fuel the belief that Jews of all time and all places were demonic beings who carried within them the hereditary blame for Jesus's death. John, in other words, supported a lens through which Jews could become theologically *and* racially antithetical to a proper gentile Christ-following. This is not to cast blame on John for the history of antisemitism or to suggest that he was the first to essentialize Jews (he was not), but rather to bring to light, as John himself would say, the dehumanization of Jews that occurred within the early Jesus movement.[86]

Of course, it is important to keep in mind that ideas of peoplehood change depending on the zeitgeist. Race as a construct is both localized and filled with contradiction, gaining significance through ever-shifting means.[87] For this reason, scholars are often wary of using the terms "race" and "antisemitism" when referring to prejudice prior to modernity so as not to superimpose the particularity of nineteenth-century taxonomized race science onto the past.

For a metacritical investigation of how Jews discuss anti-Jewish history—the feeling of eternalness beyond historical specificities—see Shaul Magid, "Judeopessimism: Antisemitism, History, and Critical Race Theory," *Harvard Theological Review* 117, no. 2 (2024): 368–390.

84. Matthew 27:24–25. See also 1 Thessalonians 2:14–16, although many authors consider these verses to be pseudo-Pauline. See, for example, Gager, *The Origins of Anti-Semitism*, 255–256. Of course, even if pseudo-Pauline, someone wanted them there, and in the name of Paul.

85. See John 8:37–47. Unlike the other Gospels, John uses the definite article when speaking of Jews: They are *oi ioudaioi—the* Jews.

86. John uses "light" as a symbol for good and "dark" as a symbol for evil. This has had lasting consequences for Jews and people of color. For an accessible introduction to this issue, see Wilda C. Gafney, "White Supremacy in Biblical Interpretation," 2020, https://www.youtube.com/watch?v=7hemIaya_Ic.

87. See, for example, Geraldine Heng, *The Invention of Race in the European Middle Ages* (Cambridge University Press, 2018), chapter 1.

"As in real estate, the bottom line is always location, location, location," writes historian Sander Gilman.[88] Race is defined differently depending on place, time, and the changing particularities of one's sociocultural assumptions.

And yet, in the many published studies on race and racism, premodern attitudes toward Jews and Judaism permeate the pages.[89] Just because ancient concepts of "peoples" do not correlate *exactly* with modern theories does not mean ancient stereotypes were devoid of racist attitudes. After all, no racisms correlate perfectly. Not even in modernity. In many instances, the attitudes of antiquity may in fact seem more similar to modern antisemitism than distinct: Jews *were* essentialized and dehumanized based on the idea that their physiognomy, psychology, and heredity were linked.

The above conception regarding Jews "of all time and all places" is thus important here. Anti-Judaism was so pervasive—so embedded in Christian cultural consciousness prior to the coinage of terms such as "race," "racism," and "antisemitism"—that one could well rewrite Dr. Seuss's *Oh, the Places You'll Go* tale into an *Oh, the Places Anti-Judaism Will Go* drama. The examples below may appear disjointed, but that is in part the point: Anti-Judaism had the potential to occur anywhere/everywhere, and at any time. In order to further demonstrate some kind of coherency, however, I will focus on four interrelated foci: heresy, morality, blood, and body.[90]

---

88. Sander L. Gilman, "Foreword," in *Race, Color, Identity: Rethinking Discourses About "Jews" in the Twenty-First Century*, ed. Efraim Sicher (Berghahn Books, 2013), xi.

89. Robert Stacey has claimed that medieval England's treatment of Jews can be viewed as archetypal of Western Europe's, albeit in "high relief." Geraldine Heng responds to this notion with a nuanced affirmation, stating that England's anti-Judaism is both "situation-specific *and* resonate." David Nirenberg similarly urges readers to not forget the particularities of violence depending on context. I take Heng's and Nirenberg's points throughout this chapter. Each instance of Christian anti-Judaism is both specific *and* resonate of other instances in Christian-centered Europe. Robert C. Stacey, "Jews and Christians in Twelfth-Century England: Some Dynamics of a Changing Relationship," in *Jews and Christians in Twelfth-Century Europe*, ed. Michael Alan Signer and John H. Van Engen (University of Notre Dame Press, 2001), 340. See also Heng, *The Invention of Race in the European Middle Ages*, 58. See Nirenberg's introduction to *Communities of Violence: Persecution of Minorities in the Middle Ages* (Princeton University Press, 2015) for an overview of his intervention against *longue durée* argument regarding the history of anti-Jewish hate. But see also Magid, who engages the insights of Afropessimism to question if "ahistorical erasure of such distinctions is not haphazard but rather intentional and calculated." Magid, "Judeopessimism," 379.

90. I extend gratitude to theologian Layla Karst for helping me parse out these foci.

Dirty Heresy as Dirty Morality as Dirty Blood and Body

In the early centuries CE, gentile leaders from a variety of Christ-following perspectives disparaged Jewish ideology as heresy in order to strengthen their self-acclaimed un-Jewish orthodoxy. This ideological sparring quickly attached onto perceptions of Jewish behavior, blood, and body. For many, Jews thought badly. Thus, Jews behaved badly. Thus, their bodies and blood were spoiled.

We see evidence of this kind of thinking across early Christ-centered texts and contexts. Here are just a few examples: In the second to third centuries, the gentile North African church father Tertullian wrote that Jews "are always stained, forever red with the blood of the Prophets and of our Lord Himself" and are "conscious . . . of this hereditary stain of their fathers."[91] In the fourth century, the gentile church father Jerome asserted that anyone who followed Jewish rituals was "doomed to the abyss of the Devil," while his contemporary, Ambrose, bishop of Milan, wrote that Jews are "possessed by the unclean spirit of demons."[92] When solidifying the Nicene Creed in the same century, the emperor Constantine affirmed that Jews are "a people who, having imbrued their hands in a most heinous outrage [killing Jesus], have thus polluted their souls and are deservedly blind . . . therefore [Nicene Christians] have nothing in common with that most hostile of people the Jews."[93] Shortly after the establishment of Nicene Christianity as the imperial religion, archbishop of Constantinople John Chrysostom preached that Jews are not human but rather beasts and demons.[94] Of their bestial condition,

91. Tertullian, *On Prayer*, 14. See Tertullian, *Disciplinary, Moral, and Ascetical Works*, trans. Rudolph Arbesmann, Emily Joseph Daly, and Edwin A. Quain (Fathers of the Church, 1959), 170. See also David Patrick Efroymson, *Tertullian's Anti-Judaism and Its Role in His Theology* (PhD diss., Temple University, 1975). In the words of John Gager, in conversation with Efroymson, Jews for Tertullian were "the very anti-type of true virtue: they resisted the prophets and Jesus; they insult and persecute Christians; they rebel against God. Their crimes are manifold. They embody the principle of *vetustas*, or obsolescence. In short, what emerges in Tertullian is a rekindling of traditional Christian anti-Judaism in which the full burden of Marcion's assault of the God of the Jews is deflected onto the Jews themselves. And in his case, the intensity of language clearly crosses the boundary between anti-Judaism and anti-Semitism." Gager, *The Origins of Anti-Semitism*, 164.

92. Cited in Michael, *A History of Catholic Antisemitism*, 29, 40.

93. Cited in Michael, *A History of Catholic Antisemitism*, 34.

94. Cited in Michael, *A History of Catholic Antisemitism*, 30.

he wrote, "their condition is no better than that of pigs or goats." Of their demonic state, he said that Jews "themselves are demons" who "danced with the Devil." Chrysostom asserted that evil is so imprinted upon the Jewish body that Jews are carriers of absolute disgust, and in turn, are "fit for slaughter."[95] Indeed, it is precisely when one comes across emphatic animalizing and demonizing language directed at Jews that the line between theological anti-Judaism and racial antisemitism becomes blurriest. The implicit postulating of an ontological difference between Jews and Christians pushes it from one kind of anti-Jewish hatred to another.[96]

These anti-Jewish expressions impacted Christian Roman law. As discussed in the previous chapter, Theodosius II put into effect a codification of Roman law issued under Christian empires (*Codex Theodosianus*) in which it was avowed that Jews were the "worst of men" in both spirit and body. By legalizing invective against Jews, the Christian empire not only essentialized them but also made their degradation "good" in the eyes of its more centralized citizens.[97] The pain of this history cannot be ignored. Scholars of trauma have long articulated the extent to which social and institutional debasement ruptures the psyche. For the gentile church to succeed—for it to take the Jewish Jesus and the Israelite tradition as its own—it had to deny the humanity of Jews, a denial that psychologist Eduardo Duran calls a "collective raping process of the psyche/soul."[98] As much as the gentile Christ-following movement was

---

95. Susanna Drake, *Slandering the Jew: Sexuality and Difference in Early Christian Texts*, Divinations: Rereading Late Ancient Religion (University of Pennsylvania Press, 2013), 93–94.

96. I extend gratitude to Stephen Moore for this observation.

97. As noted previously, J. Kameron Carter suggests that early Christians biologized and in turn racialized Jews through such essentializing attitudes. He even suggests that origins of race and racism rest in the essentialism behind Christian anti-Judaism. See chapter 1, footnote 76, and Carter, *Race: A Theological Account*. But again, even before the Christianization of the empire, Jews were treated as social and legal outcasts. From the Assyrian onslaught in 722 BCE, to the Babylonian captivity in 587 BCE, to the Roman conquest of Judea in 63 BCE, ancient Israelites and later Jews had to fight repeatedly for cultural persistence. But when the Romans destroyed the Jewish Temple in 70 CE and then expelled them from Judea in the second century, Jews were forced to consider how they might maintain cultural existence in the face of what could be (and ultimately was) long-term displacement.

98. Eduardo Duran, *Healing the Soul Wound: Trauma-Informed Counseling for Indigenous Communities* (Teachers College Press, 2019), 23.

excluding Jews from its perception of the end-times, it was already excluding them from experiencing full personhood in its here and now.[99]

None of this is to say that the essentializing Self/Other dichotomies utilized by the proto-Orthodox and Orthodox church fathers were necessarily new. Ancient historian Benjamin Isaac writes that this kind of prejudice—the kind that goes beyond theology or ideology and into conceptions of ethnic essentialism and genetic determinism—is common across cultures.[100] It is part of the human preoccupation with social group making and the drive to assert ideological dominance over opposing views. What made Nicene Christianity distinct, however, was the extent to which its views entered the global arena. Its Self/Other imaginings were acquired by Rome, a locus of power across Eastern and Western provinces. Written polemics against Jews, restrictions of Jewish civil liberties, and anti-Jewish social discriminations were widespread and lauded from imperial positions of power. To be sure, pre-Christian Romans were already constructed to think poorly of Jews. The pre-Christian empire destroyed the Jewish temple in 70 CE, overwhelmed the Jewish revolts, levied additional taxes against them, expelled Jews from Judea, sold them into slavery, and in 135 CE renamed their ancestral land Syria Palaestina. But the combination of the already Self/Other imaginings between Jews and gentiles was heightened all the more when the empire became Nicene Christian in the late fourth century. Despite letting Jews live (i.e., naming Judaism a legal tradition), Christian Roman law shows that Christians fretted over the rights and existence of Jews. This is not to say that Jews never had privileges—they did (e.g., Jewish holy days were legally authorized in the fifth century and affirmed in the sixth century)—but that, broadly speaking, Christian Roman law, alongside developing doctrinal principles, constrained Jews to the margins of Christian society.[101]

Things took a drastic turn in the eleventh century. Throughout the medieval period, stereotypes incited violence, and violence incited stereotypes. Much of this occurred on the grounds of circular theological reasoning.

99. Again, see also Kraemer, *The Mediterranean Diaspora in Late Antiquity.*

100. Isaac, *The Invention of Racism in Classical Antiquity*, 3.

101. For more on Christian Roman law, see Andrew S. Jacobs, "Christianizing the Roman Empire: Jews and the Law from Constantine to Justinian, 300–600 CE," in *The Cambridge Companion to Antisemitism*, ed. Steven Katz, Cambridge Companions to Religion (Cambridge University Press, 2022), 100–117.

Anti-Jewish interpretations of the Gospels made the Gospels themselves anti-Jewish, which then made the medieval riots against Jews justifiable.[102] The Crusade wars from the eleventh century onward, for example, were waged primarily against Muslims but also against Jews, all in the name of an ostensibly anti-Jewish Christ.[103] In fact, for most crusaders, the pogroms against the Jewish people were holy ones supported by the already established conspiracies of Jews as cheats and murderers. As one person described the mass murder of Jews in 1096, "We desire to attack the enemies of God in the East, although the Jews, of all races the worst foes of God, are before our eyes."[104] Jews throughout Christian Europe were thus tortured and slain as crusading knights sped toward Jerusalem. This is a problematic history, writes scholar Emily Rose: "It is difficult to reconcile images of Jewish children torn from their mothers, young people tossed into rivers and purposefully drowned, and Jewish bodies burned in makeshift cemeteries with descriptions of crusading as 'an act of love.' But that is how the crusades were promoted to their participants who were told that they were defending Christ's honor."[105] Unbelievers needed to suffer, and killers of Christ needed to be avenged.

One of the most powerful and widespread medieval myths purported against Jews was that of blood libel. Jews were imagined as killing Christian children in mockery of Jesus, and then using the deceased's blood for baking Passover matzah or healing a circumcision cut.[106] Connecting the blood libel

102. The arguments, in other words, were circular. As Daniel Feldman writes of racialization and storytelling in the modern period, "Racist science and ideological narrative tautologically reinforce each other." Feldman, "Reading Poison," 199–200. Stories of stereotype shape broader climates and vice versa.

103. While efforts were made to overthrow Muslims to the East, killing the more proximate Others—Jews—was an appropriate extension of the Crusade cause.

104. This quotation is from the memoirs of contemporary French abbot Guibert of Nogent. See Cohen, *Christ Killers*, 121.

105. Emily M. Rose, "Crusades, Blood Libels, and Popular Violence," in *The Cambridge Companion to Antisemitism*, ed. Steven Katz, Cambridge Companions to Religion (Cambridge University Press, 2022), 197. See also Jonathan Riley-Smith, "Crusading as an Act of Love," *History* 65, no. 214 (1980): 177–192.

106. Christians were not the first to accuse Jews of this. Although popularized in medieval Europe, the charge of ritual murder directed against Jews dates to at least the first century CE and likely earlier. In the first century CE, the historian Flavius Josephus wrote that an Alexandrian man named Apion blamed Jews for sacrificing and eating Greek strangers

to Abraham's near sacrifice of Isaac and the belief that Jews executed Jesus, Christians saw Jews as being so off course that they continued to murder innocents in the name of their God.[107] The irony here, of course, is that Christians honor the same God, read Genesis 22 as scripture, believe the crucifixion was not just an execution but also God's sacrifice of God's son, and then eat that son through the Eucharist rite. By this logic, Jews, Christians, the Israelite God, and the Christian Devil do not look so different. That Christians mirrored their own understanding of Jews is heightened when taking into account the fact that Christians actually did murder people in the name of their God.

Jews were also accused of desecrating the Eucharist host. Medieval sources claim that during Holy Week in 1290, a Jew in Paris attacked the Eucharist wafer by stabbing it, hammering it, or submerging it in boiling water.[108] The belief was that other Jews followed suit, and did so, purportedly, as a way to continue their assault on Christ. Libels like this spread across Christian Europe and contributed to the death of thousands of Jews in 1298 under the Rintfleisch movement, and again later during the Black Death pandemic, a time in which Jews were also accused of poisoning wells and causing people to fall ill.[109] These allegations also contributed to the widespread racialization of Jews in art and text. Depictions of Jews having dark skin, horns, tails, and even noses similar to that of the Devil were so common across medieval Europe that Jews began to stand on their own as a collective representation

---

annually. Interestingly, this charge was eventually extended onto Christ-followers. Tertullian, for example, lamented that followers of Jesus were being accused of partaking in sacrificial baby killing. "We are thought to be the most criminal of men," he writes, "on the score of our sacramental baby-killing." For Christ-followers to later take this myth and thrust it again on Jews demonstrates both a survival tactic and another method of Self/Other denouncement. Jews are the real criminals. They are the ones who take our blood and mix it with their own. Again, by defining Jews as the problem, gentile Christ-followers were able to define themselves as the righteous. By defining Jewish blood as demonic, gentile Christ-following blood became pure. See Tertullian, *Apology. De Spectaculis. Minucius Felix: Octavius*, trans. T. R. Glover and Gerald H. Rendall (Harvard University Press, 1931), 145–220. See also Tertullian, *Apology*, VII.1.

107. Cohen, *Christ Killers*, 38–44. See also E. M. Rose, *The Murder of William of Norwich: The Origins of the Blood Libel in Medieval Europe*, 1st ed. (Oxford University Press, 2015).

108. This, interestingly, is the same year that Jews were expelled from England. See Cohen, *Christ Killers*, 103–109.

109. Cohen, *Christ Killers*, 103–109.

of the Devil and vice versa.[110] *Christ Carrying the Cross*, from the school of Hieronymous Bosch, epitomizes in the visual arts this perception of Jews quite well (see figure 2.2).[111]

Figure 2.2. "Christ Carrying the Cross" by Hieronymus Bosch or follower (circa 1450–1516). Public domain.

I would not be surprised at all, in fact, if representations of "Saul" to "Paul," if only in an individual's mind, included a man with a nose job.

Medieval writers also often depicted Jews as emitting a disturbing odor known as the *foeter judaicus*, or "Jewish stink."[112] This, too, was theologized.

110. For more on this history, see Robert Jütte, *The Jewish Body: A History* (University of Pennsylvania Press, 2020), 18–26.

111. This piece is from the early sixteenth century, but it helps bring to light these earlier understandings. I extend gratitude to Stephen Moore for guiding me to it.

112. For work on odor and its cultural effects (or, rather, affects), see Drew Daniel, "Early Modern Affect Theory, Racialized Aversion, and the Strange Case of Foetor Judaicus," in *Race and Affect in Early Modern English Literature*, ed. Carol Meija LaPerle (ACMRS Press, 2022), 57–75. Citing Janet Adelman, Daniel adds, akin to the discussions of physiognomy in the "Antisemitic Race Science" section above, that this was an imagined reality. In Adelman's words, "Jews . . . are generally depicted as physically unmistakable, with red or black curly

Just as Jews were imagined as "wanderers" for their crimes against God and Jesus, they were also perceived as emitting a foul odor wherever they went. This odor, moreover, was associated with evil spirits and even the Devil's farts.[113] The *foetor judaicus* thus worked to further connect Jews with the demonic realm, including the idea that Jews and Satan shared a "personality type," if not a shared gastrointestinal ailment.[114]

Even when Jews were perceived as competent, it was a problem. This is seen perhaps most clearly in stereotypes about Jews and moneylending. Despite the fact that many countries channeled Jews into finance,[115] Jews were at risk of being expelled if they performed too well.[116] This happened in the wave of Jewish expulsions across Western Europe in the thirteenth century, beginning with Edward I of England's edicts in the 1280s and 1290s. Despite England's small Jewish population and there being only a handful of successful Jewish financiers, Edward I branded its entire Jewish population as "coin clippers and hence criminals" who needed to be ejected.[117] Jews, for many, weren't just "too good" at finance, but were seen as usurers who used money to dishonor

---

hair, large noses, dark skin, and the infamous *foetor judaicus*, the bad smell that identified them as Jews. But apparently Jews could not be counted on to be reliably different: although allegedly physically unmistakable, Jews throughout Europe were nonetheless required to wear particular styles of clothing or badges that graphically enforced their physical unmistakability—as though they were not quite different *enough*." Cited in Drew Daniel, "Early Modern Affect Theory, Racialized Aversion, and the Strange Case of Foetor Judaicus," in *Race and Affect in Early Modern English Literature*, ed. Carol Meija LaPerle (ACMRS Press, 2022), 70–71; emphasis in the original. See also Janet Adelman, *Blood Relations: Christian and Jew in the Merchant of Venice* (University of Chicago Press, 2010), 79.

113. Rose, "Crusades, Blood Libels, and Popular Violence," 205.

114. Jonathan Reinarz, *Past Scents: Historical Perspectives on Smell* (University of Illinois Press, 2014), 95. See also Joshua Trachtenberg, *The Devil and the Jews: The Medieval Conception of the Jew and Its Relation to Modern Anti-Semitism* (The Jewish Publication Society, 1983), 47–48.

115. This occurred for a number of reasons. Christians, for example, were forbidden to take interest, and money was portable for Jews if/when they were expelled.

116. Historian Julie Mell thus urges readers to put into conversation antisemitism and philosemitism: Appreciation for Jewish success has a history of turning into a distrust of them. Julie Mell, "Jews and Money: The Medieval Origins of a Modern Stereotype," in *The Cambridge Companion to Antisemitism*, ed. Steven Katz, Cambridge Companions to Religion (Cambridge University Press, 2022), 213.

117. Jews made up 4,000–5,000 of 5 million people in thirteenth-century England. See Robert C. Stacey, "Anti-Semitism and the Medieval English State," in *The Medieval State:*

Christ and Christians.[118] Eventually, this stereotype entered the discourse so deeply that Jews were deemed usurers regardless of whether they worked in finance or not.[119]

The negative association of Jews with money remains one of the most persistent. By the modern period, Jews were not only rendered diabolical killers of Christ but also money-obsessed mongrels who repeatedly cheated their way through faulty economics. Especially during World War I, German antisemites promoted the idea that Jews were succeeding while Germans were suffering, all due to Jewish control of international communism and capitalism.[120] Eventually, Adolf Hitler became concerned with "reverse colonization," the idea that the wandering Jew would overtake the indigenous German *Volk*.[121]

But even this has an earlier prototype. According to the Gospels, one of Jesus's last acts was overturning Jewish money-changing tables while accusing the Jewish merchants of turning the Jewish Temple into a "den of robbers."[122] Judas Iscariot, Jesus's disciple-turned-traitor, also has a long "afterlife" as the exemplar of the money-grubbing Jew (*Judas*, in fact, is the Greek rendering of the Hebrew *Judah*, from which the word "Jew" derives).[123] In Matthew, for

---

Essays Presented to James Campbell, ed. John Maddicott and David Palliser (The Hambledon Press, 2000), 165; Heng, *The Invention of Race in the European Middle Ages*, 64.

118. Mell, "Jews and Money," 229.

119. Mell, "Jews and Money," 229.

120. A. Dirk Moses, "Colonialism," in *The Oxford Handbook of Holocaust Studies*, ed. Peter Hayes and John K. Roth (Oxford University Press, 2010), 72.

121. Moses, "Colonialism," 74.

122. Matthew 21:13; Mark 11:17; Luke 19:46; John 2:16; cf. Jeremiah 7:11. Money-changing at the temple occurred so that Jews could exchange their Greek and Roman coinage into Jewish and Tyrian shekels to purchase animals for sacrifice or for paying Temple taxes.

123. This afterlife extends into modernity. In 2005, for example, a Protestant minister from the Netherlands shared the following in his sermon (later nicknamed "The Anti-Semitic Sermon of Rev. Mos"): "Behind Judas in the New Testament we find the Jews. This is already clear from the name: Judas, Judah, Jews. But it is even clearer from the way in which his story is being told. Everything he says and does is Jewish through and through. The biblical story does not hide that in any way. On the contrary, it seems that this is precisely the reason that the story of Judas is told so elaborately, to show: this is the way Jews are . . . Thus Judas reveals what sin is, what the Bible calls Jew . . . The Bible says: 'The Jew in us is our worst adversary.'"

example, Judas is depicted as handing Jesus over to the authorities for thirty pieces of silver (Matt 26:15–16, 27:3). In Luke, he is a money-loving traitor (Luke 6:16, 22:3–6). And in John, he is called a "thief" and "the Devil" (John 12:6, 6:70–71).[124] Each of these Gospels makes monetary greed and deicide conveniently combined in the same person. The fifth-century church father John Chrysostom relied on a similar combination in his series of homilies *Against the Jews*, in which he wrote that the Jewish synagogue is "not only a brothel and a theater; it also is a den of robbers . . . When God forsakes a place [such as this], that place becomes the dwelling of demons."[125]

Of course, it is often assumed that Christianity left room for Jews to rid themselves of their demonic ties by way of baptism. Writing on race and smell, for example, historian Jonathan Reinarz notes that the medieval "barrier between the two religious communities was regarded as one between barbarism and civilization but was not considered insurmountable. If a Jew were converted to Christianity, it was said, the Jewish stench transformed immediately into a fragrance sweeter than ambrosia."[126] While the early church did

---

Cited and translated by Arie W. Zwiep, "Judas and the Jews: Anti-Semitic Interpretation of Judas Iscariot Past and Present," in *Jesus and Paul: Global Perspectives in Honor of James D. G. Dunn. A Festschrift for His 70th Birthday*, ed. B. J. Oropeza, C. K. Robertson, and D. C. Mohrmann, Library of New Testament Studies (T&T Clark International, 2009), 72. See also in Arie W. Zwiep, *Judas en de Joden: Een onderzoek naar antisemitische interpretaties van Judas Iskariot* (Onderzoeksverslag in opdracht van het Openbaar Ministerie n.a.v. de preek van ds. N.C. Mos, gehouden op zondag 13 maart 2005 in de Messiaskerk te Wassenaar; februari 2007).

124. Cf. the Gospel of Mark, whose author does not demonize Judas as do Matthew, Luke, and John. For more on the characterization of Judas in the Gospels, see Zwiep, "Judas and the Jews," 73–75.

125. *Adversus Iudaeos* 1.3.1. Much can be said about Chrysostom's connection between money and sex. In his homilies, Chrysostom slams Jews for being oversexed and overly effeminate as they count their money like prostitutes, thus relying on what Jill Hicks-Keeton has since coined "pornodoxy": "the regulation of right belief and practice while imaging sex, sexiness, or sexual desire" in his disparagement of Jews. That Jews were money-stealing effeminates—regardless of legal status, anatomy, or gender expression—was and remains a well-established anti-Jewish trope. (Please note that I am not making a moral claim about sex work; Chrysostom is.) For more on pornodoxy, see Jill Hicks-Keeton, *Good Book*, 80. For more on the effeminization of Jews, see Drake, *Slandering the Jew*. For the embracement of such an alternative form of maleness, see Daniel Boyarin, *Unheroic Conduct: The Rise of Heterosexuality and the Invention of the Jewish Man* (University of California Press, 1997).

126. Reinarz, *Past Scents*, 95.

not pray for the baptism of the stinky Jew, it certainly did for the perfidious one. By the seventh century CE, a prayer for their conversion was included in the church's Good Friday liturgy, although versions of it circulated earlier.[127] The traditional prayer goes as follows:

> Let us pray also for the faithless Jews [*perfidis Judaeis*]: that Almighty God may remove the veil from their hearts; so that they too may acknowledge Jesus Christ our Lord. [No instruction to kneel or to rise is given, but immediately is said:] Almighty and eternal God, who dost not exclude from Thy mercy even Jewish faithlessness [*Judaicam perfidiam*]: hear our prayers, which we offer for the blindness of that people; that acknowledging the light of thy Truth, which is Christ, they may be delivered from their darkness. Through the same our Lord Jesus Christ, who liveth and reigneth with thee in the unity of the Holy Spirit, God, for ever and ever. Amen.

In its earliest iterations, the prayer's "perfidious" may have been understood in relation to Paul's words in 2 Corinthians: "A veil lies over [Jewish] minds."[128] Scholars surmise, in other words, that "perfidy" could have meant something akin to lack of perception and thus lack of faith, hence the "faithless Jews" translation above.[129] But it is also possible the term was quickly, if not immediately, associated with more damaging ones, such as "malevolent," "treacherous," or "hostile." This is due not only to the anti-Judaism of broader Christendom—the already common conflation of Jewish theology with Jewish treachery—but also the eventual practices surrounding the prayer itself. Congregants, for example, were taught not to say "amen" after the prayer or to kneel during its recitation so as to avoid showing any signs of adoration toward Christ's

127. For origins of this prayer and early meanings of the Latin *perfidias*, see Benjamin Leven, "The Good Friday Prayer for Jews: A 'Borderline Case' of Christian Prayer," *Studia Liturgica* 41, no. 1 (2011): 78–83.

128. 2 Corinthians 3:13–16. For more on this prayer and other early Catholic creeds and liturgies, see Michael, *A History of Catholic Antisemitism*, 17–21. See also Konrad Szocik and Philip L. Walden, "The Attitude of the Catholic Church Toward the Jews: An Outline of a Turbulent History," *Numen* 64, no. 2–3 (2017): 209–228.

129. See also Romans 11:20, in which Paul claims that most Jews do not believe.

killers.[130] The prayer was also paired with the Reproaches (*Improperia*), a collection of verses in which Jesus is imagined as chastising Jews for rejecting him. Good Friday participants were thus reminded of the divine repudiation of Jews even as they prayed for their salvation. Suffice it to say the prayer did not better relations between Jews and Christians. Even if the Reproaches or accompanying words and rituals were removed, praying for Jews to convert does not yield cross-cultural respect or understanding. Instead, it renders Christians the elite while assuming Jews must change who they are. In some instances, it incited further violence.[131]

Conversion was also often futile. Even when Jews were offered baptism, many Christians contended that Jews could never fully erase their ancestral ties.[132] In medieval England, for example, Jews were forced to add "convert" to their name so as to reveal their biological starting point.[133] Iberia enacted something similar in the fifteenth century. Jews who converted under inquisition and expulsion were called "New Christians" so as to demarcate them socially and legally from the "Clean" or "Natural" Christians.[134] Thus while

130. Michael, *A History of Catholic Antisemitism*, 18. See also George Demacopoulos's work on the *Idiomele*, Holy Week hymns dated to the reign of Emperor Justinian and adopted by the monks of the Mar Saba monastery in the mid-sixth century for Good Friday services, which addresses "the Jews" (*oi ioudaioi*) as collective killers of Christ. George Demacopoulos, "The Origins of Anti-Jewish Rhetoric in the Hymns of Good Friday," *Public Orthodoxy*, April 14, 2022, https://publicorthodoxy.org/2022/04/14/the-origins-of-anti-jewish-rhetoric-in-the-hymns-of-good-friday/. See also the late fourth-century interpolated Hellenistic *Synagogue Prayers* in the *Apostolic Constitutions*, which infer Jews as Christ-killers (2.61.1, 6.25.1, 7.38.7). Pieter Willem van der Horst, *Early Jewish Prayers in Greek*, Commentaries on Early Jewish Literature (Walter de Gruyter, 2008), 88, 92.

131. Michael, *A History of Catholic Antisemitism*, 18.

132. Already in the early centuries, some leaders denied the possibility of Jewish conversion to Christianity. See Leven, "The Good Friday Prayer for Jews," 82. For more on Jewish conversion across histories, see Paola Tartakoff, "Testing Boundaries: Jewish Conversion and Cultural Fluidity in Medieval Europe, c. 1200–1391," *Speculum* 90, no. 3 (July 2015): 728–762. Cf., *Constitutiones Sirmondianae* 4.

133. Heng, *The Invention of Race in the European Middle Ages*, 76. Generational tides also did not matter. Jewishness stuck to the offspring of converts as it did to the converts themselves. As Heng remarks, "*Four generations* after a conversion, the descendant of a once-Jew was still tagged as a Jew," 77, emphasis original.

134. *Cristianos limpios, Cristianos de natura*. Heng, *The Invention of Race in the European Middle Ages*, 74.

conversion may have saved Jews from death under the Inquisition, no baptismal water seemed to be enough to completely transform the medieval Jew.[135] Instead, Jews carried within them a genetic coding of Christ-killer, making their perfidy unconditional. That so many Christians were preoccupied with body purity and the lasting sinfulness of Jews is an interesting conundrum indeed, given the admiration frequently given to Paul "the convert" within both the Catholic and eventually Protestant traditions. Perhaps the idea was that he alone, in being chosen by God to bring the Christ movement to non-Jews, carried the unique ability to change his Jewish DNA.[136] One wonders how they justified the worshipping of Jesus, another first-century Jew.

Some, however, did celebrate the conversion of Jews, if only as proof of Christian supremacy (i.e., Christ is so glorious that even a Jew can see the light).[137] Others were likely relieved. And others still were likely indifferent. A glaring issue in the writing of ancient and medieval history is that most people couldn't read the polemics being circulated, let alone write down what they were actually thinking. Much was transmitted orally, and many of the specifics remain unknown. The fact that conversions were so ongoing, however, suggests that it is unlikely every single Jew and especially every single Jewish convert was forever established as morally and essentially Other.[138] That there even were Jews converting to Christianity alludes to some kind of Jewish-Christian acculturation. In fact, according to historian Jonathan Elukin, scholars have too often overlooked this kind of give-and-take. Yes, Christians and Jews fought with each other. But so did Christians and other Christians, as well as Jews and other Jews. Jews and Christians also worked together, lived together, and in many instances coexisted peacefully even in the

---

135. Robert C. Stacey, "The Conversion of Jews to Christianity in Thirteenth-Century England," *Speculum* 67, no. 2 (1992): 278.

136. Of course, this is almost the reverse situation that Paul faced. In Paul's context, it was the gentile believers who were second class.

137. See, for example, *Epistula Severi,* which is a story of mass Jewish conversion to Christianity in 418 CE. For some Christian thinkers, Jews converting to Christianity also signals to them the arrival of the eschaton, based in large part on interpretations of Romans 9–11. For more on the *Epistula Severi,* see Kraemer, *The Mediterranean Diaspora in Late Antiquity,* chapter 2.

138. Jonathan Elukin, *Living Together, Living Apart: Rethinking Jewish-Christian Relations in the Middle Ages* (Princeton University Press, 2007), 70.

face of anti-Jewish demonization. The fact that laws were created to prohibit Jewish and Christian interaction demonstrates, too, that Jews and Christians *were* interacting.[139] Jews, put simply, were not being attacked daily, and certainly not by every Christian neighbor. That there even were Jews who lived to see the modern era, Elukin asserts, is not something to dismiss.

To think that Jews were only ever oppressed, or that all Christians were only ever oppressors, is both inaccurate and naive.[140] Even throughout the Middle Ages, there were times in which Jews affiliated with the upper classes and held high-powered positions, especially through their work in finance and medicine.[141] The fact that Judaism survived into modernity shows that Jews did indeed persist. And some, I have no doubt, were those with questionable ethics; history is not a binary story of good victims versus bad oppressors. The physical survival and occasional success of Jews, however, cannot eradicate the psychic pain that comes from generations of cultural Othering and repeated instances of expulsion and extermination. That there existed Jewish-Christian socialization or that some Jews lived to see modernity must not be conceptualized as the sole effect of Christian tolerance. Human interaction and human persistence are profoundly complex; it would be unwise to reduce all Jews, all Christians, and all Jewish survival to simple singularities. But what can be said is this: Despite this complexity, humans are social. They make contact with other cultures and atmospheres and enter the global market of cultural and ideological exchange. One lasting exchange across gentile Christ-centered ideologies, from antiquity to modernity (albeit with different textures and localized framings), is that Jews were ugly, depraved, and not to be trusted.[142]

---

139. Fredriksen, *Ancient Christianities*, 28.

140. There are, of course, different types and levels of oppression too. For more on the "interfaith" socialization between Jews and Christians in late antiquity, see, for example, Fredriksen, *Ancient Christianities*, 27–29.

141. Although when kings owed Jewish moneylenders funds, they indulged in massacres as a way to erase the debt.

142. The points of this paragraph resonate with Elisabeth Schüssler Fiorenza's articulation of wo/men and kyriarchy. While some women can and do oppress some men, such does not disprove the endurance of sexism. See, for example, *Wisdom Ways: Introducing Feminist Biblical Interpretation* (Orbis Books, 2001), 107–109, which includes her proposal and understanding of the term "wo/men."

The point here is that just because early Christian supersessionism was grounded in theology, it was not devoid of essentialized or even racialized tendencies. For the vast majority of Christian history, anti-Jewish theology teetered into conceptions of ethnic essentialism and hereditary determinism. The intensity with which Christian ideological sparring against Jews attached to Christian perceptions of Jewish behavior, blood, and body cannot be overstated. While anti-Jewish violence and hatred remained particular to political, economic, and cultural contexts, Jews throughout the Christian world were to varying degrees and in various ways rendered "figures of absolute difference," often rejected for being "a lower order of creature manifesting bestiality, carnality, diabolism, vampirism, and uncontrollable effluxes of the body."[143] To put it otherwise, Jews were essentialized. They were racialized. And they were dehumanized.

The Old, Old Perspective on Paul

The hyperbole of the Old Perspective is that it is just that: old. For centuries, to be a good theologian was to be a good Christian, and to be a good Christian was to adhere to a gentile racialized sovereignty. The danger of the Old Perspective's more "enlightened" texture, however, was that it came with the added support of modern science. The culminating narrative for both the church and the academy was that Jews could not—and should not—be saved.

Having led us back to the Holocaust, readers will now see that, ironically for some, the left behind eventually included Paul, too.

The Nazi Deluge

What distinguished the Holocaust from previous anti-Jewish violence was the extent to which the Nazis utilized antisemitism to justify the creation of an industrialized killing machine.[144] The wholesale murder of six million Jews, substantiated first through widespread conceptions of a pure Germanic race, was then implemented by the use of shipping containers (trains) to deliver the Jewish products (Jews) to their on-site exterminations. The Reich and

143. Heng, *The Invention of Race in the European Middle Ages*, 55, 72.

144. Robert Rozett and Dan Michman, "The Unprecedented Nature of the Holocaust and Its Unique Features: Some Reflections Part I," January 3, 2021, https://www.yadvashem.org/blog/the-unprecedented-nature-of-the-holocaust.html.

its allies created more than forty-four thousand sites of terror across Europe, ranging from detention centers, to labor centers, to killing posts. Alongside other perceived enemies of the state (e.g., gay men, disabled persons, political dissenters, Roma),[145] more than 60 percent of the world's Jews were killed, with thousands more tortured until rescued.

The relationship between Christianity and the Reich is complicated. Adolf Hitler, for example, was not a practicing Christian, at least not in earnest, and did not become Führer on behalf of the church. Instead, he drew on imperial aspirations and modern race science to imagine a new world order for the hierarchically pure. But Christianity did play a major role in the economy of Nazi thought. Many Nazis did see their faith as part of the movement, and Hitler often spoke of his antisemitism bringing Christianity into full effect. Christianity, he said,

> points me to the man who once in loneliness, surrounded only by a few followers, recognized these Jews for what they were and summoned men to fight against them and who, God's truth! was greatest not as a sufferer but as a fighter . . . the Lord at last rose in His might and seized the scourge to drive out of the Temple the brood of vipers and adders. How terrific was his fight against the Jewish poison. Today, after two thousand years, with deepest emotion I recognize more profoundly than ever before the fact that it was for this that He had to shed his blood upon the Cross.[146]

Thus, he attested elsewhere, "the Catholic Church considered the Jews pestilent for fifteen hundred years, put them in ghettos, etc., because it recognized the Jews for what they were . . . I am thereby doing Christianity a great service by pushing them out of schools and public functions."[147]

It is important to keep in mind, however, that Nazi ideology extended beyond and was sustained by more than just Hitler. In other words, while

---

145. Due to its own racialized history, the term "Roma" for the Romani people is more frequently used than the more previously used "Gypsies" slur.

146. Adolf Hitler in a speech on April 12, 1922. See *The Speeches of Adolf Hitler, April 1922–August 1939*, trans. Norman Hepburn Baynes, vol. 1 (Oxford University Press, 1942), 19–20.

147. Cited in Richard Steigmann-Gall, *The Holy Reich: Nazi Conceptions of Christianity, 1919–1945* (Cambridge University Press, 2004), 117–118.

Hitler may have been the face of the Reich, he was not the only one steering it. But what can be said is this: Despite not adhering to any one faith doctrine—Hitler and other high-ranking Nazis also disparaged religion, brutally so—many proponents of the Reich relied on the centuries-long history of Christian anti-Judaism to better enforce its eschatological regime.[148] Some, in fact, argue that the Reich's invocation of traditional Christian hostility toward Jews, conjoined with the number of Christians in support of the regime (and the number of Nazis in support of Christianity), twisted the war into another holy one.[149] Historian Richard Steigmann-Gall makes a claim reminiscent of seventeenth- and eighteenth-century biblical studies: "For many of its leaders," he writes, just as for many of the early biblical scholars, "Nazism was not the result of a 'Death of God' in secularized society but rather a radicalized and singularly horrific attempt to preserve God *against* secularized society."[150]

With the vast majority of Germans identifying as Christian, it was good politics to not disgruntle the masses.[151] It was also good politics to make use of Christianity's already pervasive dehumanization of Jews. One of the Reich's most practical tools was Christianity's long-established accusation of Jews as demonic Christ-killers.[152] Nazi supporters made frequent use of anti-Jewish stereotypes and even passages from the Bible, including especially John 8:37–47, a pericope in which Jesus calls Jews children of the Devil and murderers "from the beginning." As seen in another tale from *The Poisonous Mushroom* (see figure 2.3):

---

148. Indeed, Hitler's views toward Christianity seem ambivalent at best. For example, in *Table Talk*, a collection of conversations Hitler had with his closest confidants throughout the war, Hitler allegedly connected Christianity with Judaism and therefore saw it as another downfall. He even said that the Lutheran Bible should be tossed aside so that Germans would not "become exposed to the whole of this Jewish mumbo-jumbo." At other moments, he praised Christianity, contending that it, alongside the Reich, was fighting for "pure morality." Steigmann-Gall, *The Holy Reich*, 117; for more on this ambivalence, see also 252–253. See also Doris L. Bergen, *Twisted Cross* (The University of North Carolina Press, 1996).

149. Richard L. Rubenstein, "Holocaust and Holy War," *The Annals of the American Academy of Political and Social Science* 548 (1996): 23–44; Steigmann-Gall, *The Holy Reich*.

150. Steigmann-Gall, *The Holy Reich*, 12.

151. Munson writes that 97 percent of Germany still identified as Christ-followers in some way. Henry Munson, "Christianity, Antisemitism, and the Holocaust," *Religions* 9, no. 1 (2018): 4.

152. Szocik and Walden, "The Attitude of the Catholic Church Toward the Jews," 215.

Figure 2.3. "When you see a Cross . . ." illustration by Philipp Rupprecht from "Der Giftpilz" by Julius Streicher. United States Holocaust Memorial Museum, courtesy of *Der Giftpilz: Erzahlungen* [*The Poisonous Mushroom*] - Hiemer, Ernst - Der Sturmer.

A peasant mother returning from field work, with her three children, pauses before a way-side Christ. The mother talks to them about the wickedness of the Jews.

She points to the Cross, which stands by the road:

"Children, look there! The Man who hangs on the Cross was one of the greatest enemies of the Jews of all time. He knew the Jews in all their corruption and meanness. Once He drove the Jews out with a whip, because they were carrying on their money-dealings in the Church. **He called the Jews: killers of men from the beginning.** By that He meant that the Jews in all times have been murderers. He said further to the Jews: Your father is the Devil! Do you know, children, what that means? It means that the Jews descend from the Devil. And because they descend from the Devil they can but live like devils. So they commit one crime after another."

The children look thoughtfully at the Cross. Mother continues:

"Because this Man knew the Jews, because He proclaimed the truth to the world, he had to die. Hence the Jews murdered Him. They drove nails through His hands and feet and let Him slowly bleed. In such a horrible way the Jews took their revenge. And in a similar way they have killed many others who had the courage to tell the truth about the Jews. Always remember these things, children. When you see the Cross, think of the terrible murder by the Jews on Golgotha. Remember that the **Jews are children of the Devil** and human murderers."[153]

Relying on Christian anti-Judaism worked. The Reich gained a variety of Christian support, with most German clergy and German professors of theology seeing God as acting through Germany to alleviate the world of its ultimate Jewish foe.[154] This was perhaps echoed most loudly in the Study and Eradication of Jewish Influence on German Church Life, an organization well-funded by the 600,000-member German Christian Movement.[155] According to its co-organizer Siegfried Leffler,[156] God sent both Martin Luther and Adolf Hitler to reform the world: "In Martin Luther we received the spiritual foundations of German Christianity. We should have eyes to see this and—in the hours of grace that the eternal Lord has granted us through Adolf Hitler—to

---

153. Emphases mine. See Hiemer, *Der Giftpilz*. Cf. John 8:37–47.

154. Steigmann-Gall, *The Holy Reich*, 15. See also Ericksen, *Complicity in the Holocaust*. Some of this was preconditioned, of course. Already in the 1884 issue of *La Civilità Cattolica*, a periodical published by Jesuits in Rome, the editors wrote that "Jews by religion are also Jews by race and nationality; they will never be Italians, or Spaniards, or Frenchmen but always Jews and nothing else but Jews."

155. Heschel, *The Aryan Jesus*, 3.

156. Leffler was the cofounder alongside Walter Grundmann, who, like Marcion, advised that the Old Testament be removed from the Christian canon. Heschel, *The Aryan Jesus*, 13.

meet the challenge Luther's redemptive act presents, but that could not be met during his own time."[157]

There was, however, an issue for some Aryan Christian supremacists, including members of the Study and Eradication of Jewish Influence on German Church Life. The issue was this: By Nazi logic, Jews were Jews, regardless of theological conviction. This means that Christians invested in Aryanism needed to dejudaize their Christian origins, including their messiah.[158] With a Marcionite zeal, Christians like Leffler interrogated the Christian use of Jewish texts and turned Jesus into the model Aryan man.[159]

Paul, interestingly, did not get the same treatment. Despite being the oft-praised herald to the gentiles—a man believed by many to have rightfully rejected Judaism—Paul's self-declared Jewish heritage made his Jewishness irreversible. Hitler himself agreed. In October 1941, the same month he determined to murder all Jews, Hitler announced in private conversation, "St. Paul transformed a local movement of Aryan opposition to Jewry . . . [causing] the death of the Roman Empire."[160] Being a "Hebrew born of Hebrews," Paul ruined the Jesus story, soiled the proper Christian message, and destroyed the Roman imperial system.[161] To put it otherwise, Christian supersessionism *did* continue to grow by way of Paul studies, but this time with an entirely different orientation toward Paul. Instead of serving the greater good by way

157. Emphasis in the original. Solberg, *A Church Undone*, 353; Munson, "Christianity, Antisemitism, and the Holocaust," 7–8. For more on the reception of Luther in Nazi Germany, see Christopher J. Probst, *Demonizing the Jews: Luther and the Protestant Church in Nazi Germany* (Indiana University Press, 2012); Probst, "Luther Scholars, Jews, and Judaism During the Third Reich."

158. For more on this, see Heschel, *The Aryan Jesus*; Susannah Heschel, "Reading Jesus as a Nazi," in *A Shadow of Glory: Reading the New Testament After the Holocaust*, ed. Tod Linafelt (Routledge, 2002), 27–41; Steigmann-Gall, *The Holy Reich*.

159. See especially the views of Ernest Renan, e.g., in Heschel, *The Aryan Jesus*, 33–38.

160. By this, he likely meant that Paul Judaized Jesus's message, or at least that's what others believed, which is supported by the fact that the New Testament refers to Paul as "a Hebrew of Hebrews." The German philologist Paul de Lagarde was another such believer, contending that the Aryan Jesus was robbed by Paul, who couldn't help but Judaize his message. See Martin Bormann, ed., *Hitler's Secret Conversations 1941–1944* (Farrar, Straus and Young, 1953), 64; Heschel, *The Aryan Jesus*, 8, 37, 42; Geoffrey G. Field, *Evangelist of Race: The Germanic Vision of Houston Stewart Chamberlain* (Columbia University Press, 1981), 307.

161. Philippians 3:5–6.

of his own conversion and anti-Jewish rhetoric, Paul's self-described biology proved his ultimate iniquity. Like the converts of England and Iberia, his perfidy was too much to undo.

Still, there are aspects of Paul that permeated the Reich. Nazis, like the apostle, saw themselves as setting the stage for a new world order—one that, à la the Old Perspective, was fundamentally devoid of Jews. And like Paul, they imagined this Jewish-free eschaton as arriving imminently. Traveling from city to city, pronouncing their views to the gentile masses, Nazi leaders made clear who and what needed to be left behind in order to guarantee future gentile success. For this, the left behind were clear: Jews.

No View from Nowhere

The Old Perspective as Anti-Jewish Introjection

Just as Luther was primed by Augustine, and Augustine by those who came before him, proponents of the Old Perspective were molded in the image of their predecessors and like-minded contemporaries. In the opening notes of this book, this was discussed in terms of social, cultural, and educational conditioning. Who we are—as well as where and when we are—impacts how we read. Studies in psychology offer a helpful additional framing, one that connects this "no view from nowhere" model to a process called "introjection." Its underlying theory is that humans unconsciously undergo an array of ideological assimilations and acculturations throughout their lives. The philosopher John Crosby explains it as a contrast to the more oft-discussed projection: "We know what it is to project our inner feelings on to another, as when we are irritated at someone and proceed to project something blameworthy onto him or her. Well, there is also the reverse movement—not projection but introjection—whereby we take some other into ourselves, identifying ourselves with that other." [162] A prime example of this comes from Hitler himself, who introjected an Old Perspective eschatology even as he raged against Paul and his theologies. Or from the anti-Pauline Leffler, who, through the process of Marcion-Luther-Reich introjection, imagined the Führer as fulfilling God's—and the Old Perspective Paul's—promises.

While there were some early objectors to these antisemitic mindsets, make no mistake: The origins of the biblical field were built on theologically

162. John F. Crosby, *Personalist Papers* (Lexington Books, 2016), 95.

supported anti-Jewish racist ideals. Such ideals, packaged into the Old Perspective, remained the norm in lay Christian settings and the adjacent academic field of biblical studies until the late twentieth century. The overwhelming majority of Christian biblical scholars, both Protestant and Catholic,[163] looked at the Old Perspective creation and saw that it, like Paul, was *good*.[164]

That is, until they didn't.

Newer Perspectives as Apology

The Old Perspective was rendered good—or, at the very least, standard—until it wasn't. The horrors of the Shoah pushed biblical scholars to reflect upon Christianity's role in the systematic murder of six million Jews.[165] Thinkers began to see the church's ongoing measures against Jews as a collective antisemitic prototype, one that increased throughout the centuries and supported, if not culminated in, the atrocities of the death camps. Theologian Gregory Baum summarized the issue rather distinctly as follows:

> While it would be historically untruthful to blame the Christian Church for Hitler's antisemitism and the monstrous crimes committed by him and his followers, what is true, alas, is that the Church has produced an abiding contempt among Christians for Jews and all things Jewish, a contempt that aided Hitler's purposes. The Church made the Jewish people a symbol of unredeemed humanity; it painted a picture of the Jews as a blind, stubborn, carnal, and perverse people, an image that was fundamental in Hitler's choice of the Jews as the

163. Again, beginning in 1943 with the papal encyclical *Divino Afflante Spiritu* and reiterated by the Second Vatican Council in 1962–1965, Roman Catholic scholars were encouraged to use modern methods for biblical analysis. Compare with the earlier twentieth-century Catholic Oath Against Modernism: https://www.papalencyclicals.net/pius10/p10moath.htm.

164. This phrasing is indeed a play on the first creation account in Genesis 1. See also Magnus Zetterholm, *Approaches to Paul: A Student's Guide to Recent Scholarship* (Fortress Press, 2009), 90. For more on Jewish interpretations prior to the New Perspective initiators, see Eisenbaum, *Paul Was Not a Christian*, as well as chapter 4.

165. Lloyd Gaston, "New Testament Theology After the Holocaust: Exegetical Responsibilities and Canonical Possibilities," in *A Shadow of Glory: Reading the New Testament After the Holocaust*, ed. Tod Linafelt (Routledge, 2002), 130.

> scapegoat. What the encounter of Auschwitz demands of Christian theologians [and biblical scholars], therefore, is that they submit Christian teaching to a radical ideological critique. Their task is to discern the trends in the Church's teaching that legitimate Christian power over others and have destructive effects on Jews (and other groups of men and women).[166]

Radical critiques did occur, but they did not occur overnight. For decades, the vast majority of biblical scholarship maintained its previous views.[167] It was not until the 1970s and 1980s that a handful of biblical scholars yearned to right Christianity's wrongs toward Jews. These scholars were not only questioning the role of Christianity in the making of modern antisemitism, but also questioning if alternative views toward Jews were possible. No longer wanting to uphold the Old Perspective status quo, for example, they brought with them a new set of good-book-making questions: Might Paul be saying something *different* from what was previously imagined? Might Paul actually be *supportive* of Jews and Judaism? Is there a way to show remorse for Christian anti-Judaism *and* reframe Christianity's relations to Jews with the support of modern historical methods? To put it otherwise, is there a way to make the New Testament good—dare one say *great*—again?

The answer, scholars eventually found, was "yes." By the late twentieth century, the contents of this chapter became the backbone of New Testament interpretation. Paul could no longer be studied without acknowledging his relations to Christian anti-Judaism and antisemitism, including especially how he could be used to legitimate the Holocaust. This made the shock of the Shoah, fueled by centuries of Christian anti-Judaism and the deluge of Third Reich race science, the collective turning point between Old and Newer Perspectives on Paul.[168]

---

166. Gregory Baum, "Introduction," in *Faith and Fratricide: The Theological Roots of Anti-Semitism*, ed. Rosemary Radford Ruether (Seabury, 1974), 7–8.

167. Into the 1950s, for example, Rudolf Bultmann maintained that Judaism was a sinful tradition of self-involved works that leads to death without salvation. See his *Theology of the New Testament* and *Primitive Christianity in Its Contemporary Setting* (Meridian, 1956).

168. It is important to remember, however, that anti-Jewish racism in the name of Christianity has not disappeared just because some biblical scholars have attempted to better Jewish-Christian relations in their scholarship.

scapegoat. What the encounter [illegible] demands of Christian theologians and biblical scholars, therefore, is that they submit Christian teaching to a radical theological critique. Their task is to uncover the extent to which the church's teaching has legitimated Christian power over others and [illegible] destructive effects on Jews (and other groups of men and women).[illegible]

Radical changes did occur, but they did not occur overnight. [illegible] the vast majority of biblical scholarship maintained its previous views.[15] It was not until the 1970s and 1980s that a handful of biblical scholars started to right Christianity's wrongs toward Jews. These scholars were not only questioning the role of Christianity in the making of modern antisemitism but [illegible] that alternative views of Paul and Jews were possible. No longer wanting to uphold the Old Perspective's status quo, for example, they brought with them a new set of ground-breaking questions: Might Paul be saying something different from what was previously thought? [illegible] of law and Judaism [illegible] Christian-Jewish relations [illegible] Jews [illegible] modern historical methods [illegible]

The [illegible] scholars [illegible] century [illegible] interpretation. Paul could no longer be [illegible] relations to Christian anti-Judaism and antisemitism, including especially how Paul could be used to [illegible] the Holocaust. This made the work of the Shoah [illegible] of Christians and Judaism and the [illegible] biblical [illegible] the [illegible] turning point between Old and New Perspectives on Paul.[16]

15. Gregory Baum, "Introduction," in [illegible] Rosemary Radford Ruether [illegible] (Seabury, 197[illegible]), 7–8.

16. [illegible] 1950s, for example, [illegible] that [illegible] Judaism was a [illegible] [illegible] and Protestant [illegible]

16[illegible]. It is important [illegible] that [illegible] Judaism [illegible] has not disappeared [illegible] to better Jewish-Christian relations in [illegible] scholarship.

CHAPTER THREE

A Good Jew

> *The finding that the traditional Christian attitude to Jews and Judaism helped make the Abomination possible and perhaps even inevitable has become a truism of recent historical scholarship.*
>
> —Arthur Roy Eckardt[1]

> *[Paul] the Jew serves as a way to reclaim Christianity from complicity in the Holocaust; even to insulate it from this complicity . . . [This] shows that what Christianity is not, at its core, is anti-Jewish or anti-Semitic.*
>
> —William Arnal[2]

---

1. Arthur Roy Eckardt, *Jews and Christians, the Contemporary Meeting* (Indiana University Press, 1986), 63.

2. Arnal makes this claim about Jesus, or really scholarship on Jesus, and I agree. In his words, "Jesus the Jew serves as a way to reclaim Christianity from complicity in the Holocaust; even to insulate it from this complicity. Intrinsically, then, Jesus—standing in for the whole of the 'true' and 'proper' Christian religion—shows that what Christianity is not, at its core, is anti-Jewish or anti-Semitic. How could it be, when its founder was a Jew? And not simply a Jew, but, apparently, a religious and identifiable Jew, a Jew of comparable kind to the Jews who have been so savagely persecuted in the last few centuries by Christians themselves?" Paul the Jew, this chapter shows, serves a similar, if not the same, purpose. William Arnal, "The Cipher 'Judaism' in Contemporary Historical Jesus Scholarship," in *Apocalypticism, Anti-Semitism and the Historical Jesus: Subtexts in Criticism*, ed. John S. Kloppenborg and John Marshall (T&T Clark International, 2005), 30. Arnal here is critiquing Paula Fredriksen's and Adele Reinhartz's, *Jesus, Judaism, and Christian Anti-Judaism*, which he sees as, despite discussing Christianity's anti-Jewish origins in various essays, on the whole "deny[ing] the anti-Jewish origins of the Christian religion, and so explain[ing] (later) Christian anti-Judaism as an aberration or deviation." See Paula Fredriksen and Adele Reinhartz, eds., *Jesus, Judaism, and Christian Anti-Judaism: Reading the New Testament After the Holocaust* (Westminster John Knox, 2002).

From the early church fathers through the Reformation and into modernity, Christianity declared itself the righteous heir of Judaism. This culminated in centuries of anti-Jewish racism, expulsions, and pogroms, all of which functioned as railways to the Nazi death camps. It was not until after World War II, however, that there was enough shifting cultural capital for Christian thinkers to address how traditional supersessionist views played a role in the centuries-long persecution of Jews. The guilt over the death camps in particular led to a number of reforms within both Protestantism and the Catholicism, as well as within the field of biblical studies. But shifting paradigms takes time.

After the War

Not much changed in the immediate postwar years. At least, this is what the scholarship used to suggest. Until recently, a consensus was established among historians that while the Holocaust was discussed in a brief burst from 1945 to 1946, relative silence ensued until the 1960s. Scholars are now asserting, however, that this does not align with evidence. People *were* talking. Councils *were* made. Trials *were* held. Insights *were* shared.[3] In other words, while there may have been a relative delay in culturally adapting new vocabulary to address new crimes against humanity, this should not be mistaken for silence.[4] Holocaust historian Andy Pearce suggests that we view post-Holocaust discussions as maintaining a "patchwork-quilt quality," which mirrors the complexities of memory, forgetting, and the transcultural dynamics of our modern world.[5] "The nature of the 'conundrum,'" he writes, "suggests that just as there was clearly not 'silence' in the sense of complete quiescence, so there was not an overwhelming wholesale cacophony of sound."[6]

What this points to, then, is something similar to what was discussed in chapter 2. Even as stronger ideological structures remained in place (e.g.,

3. See, for example, Lawrence Baron, "The Holocaust and American Public Memory, 1945–1960," *Holocaust and Genocide Studies* 17, no. 1 (2003): 62–88; David Cesarani and Eric J. Sundquist, eds., *After the Holocaust: Challenging the Myth of Silence* (Routledge, 2011).

4. Neil Levi and Michael Rothberg, "General Introduction: Theory and the Holocaust," in *The Holocaust: Theoretical Readings*, ed. Neil Levi and Michael Rothberg (Edinburgh University Press, 2003), 6–7.

5. He writes this of Britain, but I believe the metaphor can be applied elsewhere, too.

6. Pearce, *Holocaust Consciousness in Contemporary Britain*, 2, 12.

Christian anti-Judaism or Nazi antisemitism), voices to the contrary still existed. In other words, just as thinkers like Parkes, Geiger, Isaac, Montefiore, and Moore reflect upon anti-Jewish sentiment and protest the scholarship that privileged anti-Judaism, so, too, did thinkers reflect upon the Holocaust and protest the remaining supersessionist structures from the 1940s onward.

Already in 1942, for example, the Council of Christians and Jews (CCJ) in the United Kingdom was established and organized around the following four principles:

(a) To check and combat religious and racial intolerance
(b) To promote mutual understanding and goodwill between Christians and Jews in all sections of the community, especially in connection with problems arising from conditions created by the war
(c) To promote fellowship between Christian and Jewish youth organizations in educational and cultural activities
(d) To foster cooperation of Christians and Jews in study and service directed to postwar reconstruction[7]

In the same year, some Christians and Jews from Britain and America met for dinner in London. One of the Americans was Reverend Everett Clinchy, then-president of the National Conference of Christians and Jews (NCCJ). The conversation turned to the work of the CCJ and the NCCJ, and in the following year, a CCJ meeting was held to listen to Rabbi Dr. Israel Goldstein, who was a board member of the NCCJ. This meeting culminated in the overwhelming expression that international projects were necessary once the war was over. In 1946, over one hundred Jewish and Christian leaders from fifteen different countries met in Oxford as part of the new International Council of Christians and Jews (ICCJ) to discuss the urgent need for better Jewish-Christian relations.[8] The ICCJ met again in 1947; a collection of Jews, Catholics, and Protestants—some clergy and some scholastic, including Jules Isaac—worked together in Seelisberg to create an address that took seriously

7. Marcus Braybrooke, *Children of One God: A History of the Council of Christians and Jews* (Vallentine, Mitchell, 1991), 14. James Parkes was one of its Christian members.

8. This history is from Braybrooke, *Children of One God*, 118–119. This organization is now called the National Conference for Community and Justice.

the relationship between Christianity and antisemitism.[9] Titled *An Address to the Churches*, and influenced greatly by Isaac's 1948 book *Jésus et Israël*, it began as follows: "We have recently witnessed an outburst of antisemitism which has led to the persecution and extermination of millions of Jews. In spite of the catastrophe which has overtaken both the persecuted and the persecutors, and which has revealed the extent of the Jewish problem in all its alarming gravity and urgency, antisemitism has lost none of its force, but threatens to extend to other regions, to poison the minds of Christians and to involve humanity more and more in a grave guilt with disastrous consequences."[10]

This was followed by ten principles called the *Ten Points of Seelisberg*, which included statements such as "Remember that Jesus was born of a Jewish mother of the seed of David and the people of Israel," "Remember that the first disciples, the apostles and the first martyrs were Jews," and "Avoid distorting or misrepresenting biblical or post-biblical Judaism with the object of extolling Christianity."[11]

---

9. Also in 1948, the Protestant World Council of Churches met to discuss Christianity's role in antisemitism.

10. Isaac's book was translated into English in 1971. This was a time when, as discussed below, the American collective consciousness started to see Holocaust memory as American memory.

11. The full ten points were: "Remember that One God speaks to us all through the Old and the New Testaments; Remember that Jesus was born of a Jewish mother of the seed of David and the people of Israel, and that His everlasting love and forgiveness embraces His own people and the whole world; Remember that the first disciples, the apostles and the first martyrs were Jews; Remember that the fundamental commandment of Christianity, to love God and one's neighbour, proclaimed already in the Old Testament and confirmed by Jesus, is binding upon both Christians and Jews in all human relationship, without any exception; Avoid distorting or misrepresenting biblical or post-biblical Judaism with the object of extolling Christianity; Avoid using the word *Jews* in the exclusive sense of the enemies of Jesus and the words *The Enemies of Jesus* to designate the whole Jewish people; Avoid presenting the Passion in such a way as to bring the odium of the killing of Jesus upon all Jews or upon Jews alone. It was only a section of the Jews in Jerusalem who demanded the death of Jesus, and the Christian message has always been that it was the sins of mankind which were exemplified by those Jews and the sins in which all men share that brought Christ to the Cross; Avoid referring to the scriptural curses, or the cry of a raging mob: *His Blood be Upon Us and Our Children,* without remembering that this cry should not count against the infinitely more weighty words of our Lord: *Father Forgive Them, for They Know not What They Do;* Avoid promoting the superstitious notion that the Jewish people are reprobate, accursed, reserved for a destiny of suffering; Avoid speaking of the Jews as if the first members of the Church had not been Jews."

The problem, however, was that the address was scarcely publicized. It made such minimal impact, in fact, that many people remain unaware of its existence. Even in its own time, most people weren't listening. Looking to Germany, for example, historian Susanna Heschel argues that church and university leaders remained unequipped to confront Christianity's role in legitimating Nazi antisemitism.[12] Much of the blame, she adds, was positioned either back on Jews or on Germany's loss of a "proper" Christian faith. While various denazification efforts took place and some Nazis faced trial, clergy members sympathetic to the Reich were mostly pressed to confess their misguided loyalty to Hitler over their one true leader: Christ. Many also continued to repudiate Jews for their inability to worship Christ alongside them. For example, in the first official document about Jews by postwar German Protestants, the authors insinuate a "they asked for it" mentality: "By crucifying the Messiah, Israel rejected its election and intended purpose."[13]

This kind of victim blaming continued for decades and went beyond German borders. Even in 1961, nearly twenty years after the war ended, an article from the Vatican's *Osservatore Romano* newspaper attested that the "Jewish people had stained themselves with a horrible crime [deicide] deserving expiation."[14] This is all in addition to the more immediate postwar support of the ratlines, escape routes that funneled Nazis to countries mostly although not exclusively outside of Europe. The routes, constructed through fascist networking, the exploitation of connections, and bureaucratic lapses, used Rome as one of the key transit points, where Nazi sympathizers in the Vatican could provide more direct support. One of the most famous escapees was Adolf Eichmann, a German-Austrian SS officer who fled from Germany, to Italy, and then to Argentina with the help of an alias aided by a Catholic certificate of indulgence. While Eichmann was eventually captured and stood trial on numerous criminal charges, including crimes against humanity, his path to South America was made possible at least

12. Susannah Heschel, "Confronting the Past: Post-1945 German Protestant Theology and the Fate of the Jews," *Studies in Contemporary Jewry: An Annual* 24 (2010): 46.

13. Heschel, "Confronting the Past," 55.

14. Cited in Judith Herschcopf, "The Church and the Jews: The Struggle at Vatican Council II," *American Jewish Year Book* 66 (1965): 111. Cited also in Cohen, *Christ Killers*, 172.

in part by church leaders. What is also haunting about this story, at least for the present purpose, is that Eichmann's trial began airing publicly in 1961, just one month after the *Osservatore* published its own statement on what one might call—at least in the *Osservatore*'s view—the "Jewish crime" against its deity.[15]

Perhaps it is no surprise, then, that when it came to Paul studies, the traditional attitude toward Paul and Jews remained the same for much of the twentieth century: Paul converted from Judaism to Christianity and, in doing so, rendered Judaism *Spätjudentum* ("late" Judaism). Despite the efforts of Seelisberg and other councils, broad transformation was not yet happening. One might, in fact, describe these decades as a collective whiplash moment. Just as one group made strides toward bettering Jewish-Christian relations through the acknowledgment of unjust Christian antisemitism, others took two strides back. Even when members of the Council of Christians met to discuss this work, the Vatican, prior to Vatican II, instructed Catholics in England to not take part in it.

This in fact brings us to another whiplash moment: Vatican II. The Second Vatican Council *also* occurred in the 1960s, and is often credited as the first church council to make sustained world-shifting moves regarding Christianity's posture toward Jews.[16] Between 1962 and 1965, the Council met to discuss the changing tides of the Catholic Church and offer reforms. Pope John XXIII opened the council, and in 1963, contra the 1961 statement from *Osservatore Romano,* announced the following:

> We are conscious today that many centuries of blindness have cloaked our eyes so that we can no longer either see the beauty of Thy Chosen People nor recognize in their faces the features of our privileged brethren. We realize that the mark of Cain stands upon our foreheads. Across the centuries our brother Abel has lain in blood which we drew or shed the tears we caused by forgetting Thy Love. Forgive us for the curse we falsely attached to their name as Jews. Forgive

15. For insight into the ratline, including its connections to the Vatican, see, for example, Philippe Sands, *The Ratline: The Exalted Life and Mysterious Death of a Nazi Fugitive* (Knopf, 2021).

16. Still, it must be restated that previous thinkers set the stage, slowly but surely, for the Church's later cultural shift.

> us for crucifying Thee a second time in their flesh. For we knew not what we did.[17]

Pope Paul VI closed the council, and in 1965 promulgated *Nostra aetate* ("In Our Time"), an official declaration of Vatican II asserting that Jews are not rejected by God or collectively responsible for the death of Jesus.

This was not an easy process. The document was revised numerous times in response to much debate and pushback. Arab representatives at the Council asserted that it could be read as propaganda in favor of the modern state of Israel.[18] Spanish prelates circulated copies of the *Protocols of the Elders of Zion*.[19] Catholic leaders insisted that Jews *were* responsible for the death of Christ, and that to deny such would go against the holiness of God.[20] Even Pope Paul VI still argued that there was a "clash between Jesus and the Hebrew People, a people predestined to await the messiah but who . . . fought Him, abused Him, and finally killed Him."[21] The fourth and final version of *Nostra aetate* thus displays a sort of compromise. It states that first-century Jewish authorities (i.e., not all Jews) played an integral role in Jesus's crucifixion and affirms that the Church still holds the new people of God:

> Even though the Jewish authorities and those who followed their lead pressed for the death of Christ (see Jn 19:6), neither all Jews indiscriminately at that time, nor Jews today, can be charged with the crimes committed during his passion. It is true that the church is the

17. Cited in Robert Michael, *A Concise History of American Antisemitism* (Rowman & Littlefield, 2005), 207. In 1958, during the first year of his papacy, Pope John XXIII also removed references to Jews as "perfidious" in the Good Friday prayer in response to pleas from Jules Isaac. See Cohen, *Christ Killers*, 171. See also Baron, "The Holocaust and American Public Memory, 1945–1960," 75. Pope Pius XII before him added a genuflection to the ritual.

18. Cohen, *Christ Killers*, 172.

19. This document alleges to have knowledge of a Jewish plan for the destruction of Christianity and the establishment of Jewish global domination. Jeremy Cohen shows that the Spanish edition, published in 1963, connects this conspiracy with the charge of deicide through its cover art, which has Jesus nailed to a cross while devilish, animalistic Jews watch. Cohen, *Christ Killers*, 140–142.

20. See Cohen, *Christ Killers*, 172.

21. He argued this in 1965 in reference to the Passion. Cited in Michael, *A Concise History of American Antisemitism*, 207.

> new people of God, yet the Jews should not be spoken of as rejected or accursed as if this followed from holy scripture. Consequently, all must take care, lest in catechizing or in preaching the word of God, they teach anything which is not in accord with the truth of the Gospel message or the spirit of Christ.[22]

Despite *Nostra aetate's* continuing supersessionist tone and the mixed reaction from multiple communities, its effects on Jewish-Christian relations in the decades after its publication were monumental.[23] This is not to say that *Nostra aetate* rid Christianity of Christian anti-Judaism (it did not), but, rather, that it served as an internationally recognized example of how to wrestle with the past and modern social ethics.[24] It encouraged readers to not center their understanding of Jews and Judaism in deicide, and to not read the New Testament without recognition of its Jewish orientations. After all, it adds, "most of the early disciples who proclaimed Christ's Gospel to the world, sprang from the Jewish people."

Other Christian denominations eventually joined the conversation by crafting their own statements on the problem of Christian anti-Judaism and its role in the Nazi era. In 1980, the Synod of the Protestant Church in Rhineland produced a document naming Christianity's co-responsibility for the Holocaust. In 1984, the Evangelical Synod of Baden published a similar statement, contending a hope for new relations toward Jews and Judaism while naming Christian anti-Judaism as one of the roots of modern antisemitism. It was around the time of these synods that the Holocaust was being viewed more regularly, not by the few but by the many, as a "wound in the heart of Christian theology."[25]

Biblical Studies Moves to America and the United Kingdom

It was also around this time that the biblical field's intellectual center moved from Germany toward North America and the United Kingdom, which raises

22. Vatican Council II, *Nostra aetate:* Declaration on the Relationship of the Church to Non-Christian Religions, 1965, https://www.vatican.va/archive/hist_councils/ii_vatican_council/documents/vat-ii_decl_19651028_nostra-aetate_en.html.

23. For more on these reactions, see Cohen, *Christ Killers*, 174–178.

24. See Cohen, *Christ Killers*, 178–182.

25. Susannah Heschel, *The Aryan Jesus*, 289. For an earlier and deeply influential discussion of this wound, see Baum, "Introduction," 1–22.

additional contextualization concerns.[26] To be sure, these concerns encompass a wide spectrum. When analyzing post-Holocaust perspectives over various temporal and geographical contexts, numerous factors must be taken into account. These factors include, but are not limited to, the influence of popular culture, educational systems, and demographic considerations (e.g., the considerably larger Jewish population in the United States compared to the United Kingdom). Again, what follows is not a ground-up story of Holocaust responses in America and the United Kingdom but rather a summary of what secondary scholarship tells us about those responses.[27] My ultimate goal, as readers will see, is to use this scholarship to tell a deeper story of how Paul has been understood.

On the American front, several efforts were undertaken to address the trauma of the Holocaust. Alongside the work of the ICCJ, the United States played a significant role in the development of post-World War II Nazi trials, notably at Nuremberg. From November 1945 to October 1946, the International Military Tribunal, of which the United States was a part, prosecuted twenty-four of the highest-ranking Nazi leaders, aiming to convict them for war crimes. While this is generally remembered as a success, many

26. Writing on the Bible and America, Mark A. Noll notes that biblical studies was "decrepit" prior to 1976. In his words, "Since 1976 an almost entirely new situation has come into existence . . . Far and away the most important contribution to the history of Bible scholarship in America has come from the Centennial Publications series of the SBL. This venture began in 1975 when the Society established a Centennial Publications commission to propose means for highlighting specific American contributions to professional Bible scholarship and for tracing the more general history of the Bible in the culture as a whole." Mark A. Noll, "Review Essay: The Bible in America," *Journal of Biblical Literature* 106, no. 3 (1987): 496–498. See also Claudia Setzer and David A. Shefferman, "Introduction," in *The Bible in the American Experience*, ed. Claudia Setzer and David A. Shefferman (SBL Press, 2020), 1.

27. It is also important to note that there have been evaluations and reevaluations of how understandings of the Holocaust unfolded. There were generations of scholars thinking or not thinking about the Holocaust, and over time, there's been a more expansive sense of how memory politics circulated. In other words, we don't have one story of Holocaust memory; we have competing stories that have developed over time as methodologies and ways of telling history have shifted. Hasia Diner's *We Remember with Reverence*, for example, discusses why thinkers presumed people were silent even though they weren't, as well as how the "myth of silence" was even constructed. The examination of the construction of such a false yet adopted narrative could not have occurred two decades prior. See Hasia R. Diner, *We Remember with Reverence and Love: American Jews and the Myth of Silence After the Holocaust, 1945–1962* (New York University Press, 2009).

scholars criticize the tribunal for various shortcomings, including its failure to adequately address the specifically antisemitic nature of the genocide.[28] Another common critique is that the trials focused more on the perpetrators' narratives rather than those of the direct victims.[29]

Similar issues arose in broader documentation efforts. For instance, in April and May 1945, the US Army Signal Corps collaborated with the British Ministry of Information to film conditions in liberated concentration camps, but the footage lacked audio. Once again, survivors' stories were not being heard.[30] That said, American radio and television occasionally presented dramatic retellings, such as "The Battle of the Warsaw Ghetto." In 1947, Holocaust survivor Siegbert Freiberg shared his story on the radio show "Reunion," which included a now famous reunion with his father.[31]

A more radical shift occurred in American public consciousness in the 1960s and 1970s. Scholars suggest that one reason for this transformation was the 1961 global broadcast of the Adolf Eichmann trial, during which, unlike the trials at Nuremberg, a number of personal testimonies by Holocaust survivors were heard. As Jewish studies scholar Alan Mintz puts it, "The intense public nature of the trial not only communicated an enormous amount of information; it also transformed the status of the Holocaust in the American

---

28. Caroline Sharples writes, for example, that Jews being a systematically targeted race was left out of the conversation. She attributes this to the lack of a "conceptual and legal framework" for Holocaust crimes. Caroline Sharples, "'Where, Exactly, Is Auschwitz?' British Confrontation with the Holocaust Through the Medium of the 1945 'Belsen' Trial," in *The Palgrave Handbook of Britain and the Holocaust*, ed. Tom Lawson and Andy Pearce (Palgrave Macmillan, 2020), 192.

29. David Cesarani, *Final Solution: The Fate of the Jews 1933–1949* (Macmillan, 2016), 783; Jeffrey Shandler, *Holocaust Memory in the Digital Age: Survivors' Stories and New Media Practices*, Stanford Studies in Jewish History and Culture (Stanford University Press, 2017), 37; Sharples, "Where, Exactly, Is Auschwitz?," 184.

30. Shandler, *Holocaust Memory in the Digital Age*, 36. Shandler adds that American psychologist David Boder was an "outstanding exception" to this early issue. In the summer of 1946, Boder traveled to displaced persons camps across western Europe and used cutting-edge wire recording technology to conduct 119 interviews with survivors. These recordings were significant in that they offered some of the earliest and most extensive firsthand accounts of survivors discussing their wartime experiences during a time when the full extent of the Holocaust was still being comprehended.

31. This paragraph is indebted to the research and writing of Shandler, *Holocaust Memory in the Digital Age*, 36–37.

mind. It became, in a sense, 'registered' in American collective memory as a key event in the modern age and as a watershed in the definition of what humanity is capable of."[32]

Other watershed moments included viewings of *The Diary of Anne Frank* in film and on stage, the 1978 television miniseries *Holocaust*, and perhaps most especially President Jimmy Carter's very public move to make Holocaust memory part of American memory.[33] In 1978, Carter established a President's Commission on the Holocaust with Shoah survivor Elie Wiesel as chair. In 1979, the Commission presented to Carter its report, which included the recommendation of a Holocaust memorial on American soil. In 1980, the US Congress approved the memorial's construction by a unanimous vote.[34] Many scholars attest, in fact, that nowhere was the shift in American consciousness on the Holocaust seen more "dramatically" than the construction of the Holocaust museum on the National Mall.[35] Its building created a collective "salience," adds Mintz, one that centered the Holocaust in the hearts and minds of American citizens.[36] By the 1980s, Carter's goal became a reality: Holocaust memory became American memory.[37]

In the British context, it is argued that Bergen-Belsen entered collective memory first. British historian Caroline Sharples attributes this to Belsen

---

32. Alan Mintz, *Popular Culture and the Shaping of Holocaust Memory in America* (University of Washington Press, 2001), 11.

33. Mintz, *Popular Culture and the Shaping of Holocaust Memory in America*, 10.

34. Shandler adds that it was also during the 1970s and 1980s that the Center for Holocaust Studies, Documentation, and Research in Brooklyn, New York, among the earliest American institutions devoted to this topic, conducted 2,747 oral history interviews with Holocaust survivors and other witnesses. Yad Vashem also started writing down accounts from survivors in the late 1940s, shortly after the museum was established, with recordings on audiotape beginning in 1954 and on video in 1989. Shandler, *Holocaust Memory in the Digital Age*, 38.

35. See, for example, Mintz, *Popular Culture and the Shaping of Holocaust Memory in America*, 4.

36. Mintz, *Popular Culture and the Shaping of Holocaust Memory in America*, 4.

37. It is also worth noting that this time marked a particularly Jewish rise in consciousness, and that reckoning with the Holocaust's assault on other communities took longer. Although, for example, works like *The Producers* (1967) and *Cabaret* (1972) showed that while queer-related Holocaust trauma was being worked out, it wasn't seen as an influential measure by the masses.

being the only concentration camp liberated by British forces.[38] In her words, "So eager were the British population to see the [Belsen] Nazi perpetrators brought to account that the slightest delay generated impatience. Throughout the spring and summer of 1945, the UK press reported faithfully each new step on the road to establishing the Belsen trial."[39] In summary, Sharples writes, "'our camp' was dealt with through 'our trial.'"[40]

Britain also took part in establishing the International Tribunal at Nuremberg and, as noted above, played a role in creating film records of liberated concentration camps. However, much was going on behind the scenes. During this time, Britain faced significant labor shortages, leading to the development of several specialized programs aimed at recruiting European Volunteer Workers (EVW). And as the prominent work of historian David Cesarani has shown, EVW migrants underwent minimal vetting regarding potential involvement in war crimes.[41] In fact, not only was the vetting process minimal, but it was also marred by racial biases, including an anti-Jewish one, as Jewish displaced persons were frequently denied resettlement opportunities in Britain.[42] Not too unlike the effects of the ratlines, these oversights allowed numerous Nazi collaborators from both Central and Eastern Europe to start new lives in Britain without facing investigation.[43] In 1948, the British government even directed its commonwealth countries to cease investigations

---

38. Sharples, "Where, Exactly, Is Auschwitz?," 187. Proceedings against Josef Kramer (a.k.a. the "Beast of Belsen") opened in September 1945 in Lüneburg, Germany.

39. Sharples, "Where, Exactly, Is Auschwitz?," 187.

40. Sharples writes in full, "Although the victims of Belsen originated from at least ten different European nations, a multi-power tribunal was considered unwieldy. As British forces were already on the scene and held concentration camp staff in custody, Britain assumed full responsibility for the resultant 'Belsen' proceedings; 'our camp' was dealt with through 'our trial.'" Sharples, "Where, Exactly, Is Auschwitz?," 183.

41. See David Cesarani, *Justice Delayed: How Britain Became a Refuge for Nazi War Criminals* (Heinemann, 1992), 5, 79. See also Siobhán Hyland and Paul Jackson, "Campaigning for Justice: Anti-Fascist Campaigners, Nazi-Era Collaborator War Criminals and Britain's Failure to Prosecute, 1945–1999," in *The Palgrave Handbook of Britain and the Holocaust*, ed. Tom Lawson and Andy Pearce (Palgrave Macmillan, 2020), 202–206.

42. Cesarani, *Justice Delayed*, 79.

43. Hyland and Jackson, "Campaigning for Justice," 202.

into individuals potentially implicated in World War II atrocities.[44] This directive signaled a shift away from Britain's earlier leadership in postwar justice efforts.[45]

"Selective" is how scholars tend to describe the United Kingdom's collective memory of the Holocaust.[46] In fact, not too distant from the "good-book-making" assessments of *Wrestling with Paul*, historian Michelle Gordon suggests that this selectivity has much to do with British desires to maintain a sense of World War II benevolence. In her words, "Misperceptions that have long reigned in British history include representing the country as an unequivocally 'good' actor in World War II, not least fighting Adolf Hitler and the Nazis to 'save' European Jewry."[47] The conflicting goals of pursuing international justice through Nazi war crime trials and reconstructing postwar Britain without properly vetting its migrants highlight just some of the contradictions in Britain's postwar objectives.[48] Not even the global airing of the Eichmann trial changed this lackluster sentiment. While the trial contributed to a more public awareness of the Holocaust, especially through the airing of survivors' stories, it did not prompt the same cultural shift as seen in the United States.

This is not to say that Britain was isolated from the impact of the Holocaust following the liberation of Belsen. Major Hollywood films such as *Judgment at Nuremberg* (1961) and *The Pawnbroker* (1965), along with documentaries like the BBC's *Warsaw Ghetto* (1968), garnered significant audiences and addressed aspects of the Holocaust to varying extents. It is rather that maintaining and deepening public interest posed a distinct challenge. For decades, teaching about the Holocaust in classrooms remained "a Jewish

44. Hyland and Jackson, "Campaigning for Justice," 204.

45. Hyland and Jackson, "Campaigning for Justice," 205.

46. For exmaple, Cesarani, *Final Solution*; Michelle Gordon, "Selective Histories." See also Hyland and Jackson, "Campaigning for Justice," 202.

47. Gordon, "Selective Histories," 221. Or as Holocaust exhibits curator Paul Salmons put it, "Britain has failed to really discuss the Holocaust in a meaningful way in order to avoid asking difficult questions raised by considerations related to British history and identity." Cited in Gordon, "Selective Histories," 220–221.

48. Hyland and Jackson, "Campaigning for Justice," 206.

concern."[49] There was even talk of Britain becoming too "Americanized" when the BBC secured the rights to air the miniseries *Holocaust*.[50] Thus, while a considerable portion of the population might have been aware of the Holocaust and its significance, far fewer had acquired substantial knowledge and understanding or could articulate why these events were personally important and relevant.[51] Some might say the closest things to UK "watershed" moments were the 1991 implementation of Holocaust education into the British school system, the 1994 UK release of Steven Spielberg's film *Schindler's List*, and the 2001 establishment of a permanent Holocaust Memorial Day. Others might say there were no watershed moments but instead a long and complicated history that cannot be unknotted.

To be sure, the modern state of Israel was intricately intertwined in this history.[52] On one hand, the "decisive" Six-Day War of 1967 triggered a notable shift in attitudes within both the United States and the United Kingdom.[53]

49. Pearce, *Holocaust Consciousness in Contemporary Britain*, 27. Even after the Holocaust was added to British school curricula in 1991, it did not make a considerable impact upon the non-Jewish masses. Pearce, in studying the work of Christian brothers Stephen and James Smith, writes that their responses to visiting Yad Vashem in the 1990s highlight the issue well: "First, despite the advances of the 1980s, the Smiths' overriding impression was of 'ignorance' among 'the British public.' What they saw as one of its primary causes—'some kind of "victor's syndrome"'—is already familiar to us from the 1970s, but the Smith's citation of it points to the virulence of this cultural mood across the postwar decades. Second, there was the belief the Holocaust was not especially relevant to Britain at the end of the century; that in effect there was no 'need to address that Holocaust as a cause for concern, because it had not happened here.'" He quotes Smith further: "'It was all too easy for non-Jews . . . to feel sympathetic to the issue without it posing any real challenge to their lives, convictions or actions" (what they helped create was the Beth Shalom National Holocaust Centre and Museum). See Pearce, *Holocaust Consciousness in Contemporary Britain*, 96–97. See also Stephen D. Smith, *Making Memory: Creating Britain's First Holocaust Centre* (Quill Press, 2002), 38, 66.

50. Pearce, *Holocaust Consciousness in Contemporary Britain*, 170–171. "What was distinctive" about anti-Americanism in 1970s Britain, he adds, "was its filtering though concerns over Holocaust representation."

51. Pearce, *Holocaust Consciousness in Contemporary Britain*, 47–48. Even in the late 1980s, writes Pearce, Holocaust memory maintained a "distinctly jumbled, potpourri-like quality," 183.

52. Gaston, *Paul and the Torah*, 2; Gager, *Reinventing Paul*, 150.

53. For Americans, this was voiced "particularly in light of the contrast with perceived failures in Vietnam" James G. Crossley, "Other Problems from a British Perspective: 'Jewishness', Jesus, and the New Perspective on Paul," in *Ethnicity, Race, Religion: Identities and Ideologies*

On the other hand, there were underlying tensions accompanying this support.[54] For example, the backing for Israel was often linked with a rising tide of anti-Arab sentiment. In bleakest terms, more land for Jews meant less land for Arab Palestinians. Many Christian supporters also tied their allegiance to Israel to the belief that Jews would gather in the "Holy Land" in fulfillment of eschatological prophecies concerning Christ.[55] There was, in other words, support for Israel but not necessarily full or even genuine support for Jews or Israelis.[56]

Biblical scholar James Crossley links these tensions to a broader culture shift: the anti-racist and multicultural consciousness of postmodernity.[57] Emerging in the latter half of the twentieth century, postmodernity describes a period characterized by the rejection of universal truth claims in favor of diversity, plurality, and the acknowledgment of multiple perspectives. Scholars observe, however, that beneath the facade of liberal inclusiveness, racism and discrimination persist. Leaning on the insights of cultural theorist Slavoj Žižek, Crossley writes, "Liberal Western multicultural inclusiveness is

---

in Early Jewish and Christian Texts, and in Modern Biblical Interpretation, ed. David G. Horrell and Katherine M. Hockey (T&T Clark, 2018), 134. See also James G. Crossley, *Jesus in an Age of Terror: Scholarly Projects for a New American Century* (Routledge, 2008), 143–194.

54. Crossley, "Other Problems from a British Perspective," 134.

55. This is indeed related to conceptions of the rapture. Energized by British preacher John Nelson Darby in the late nineteenth century and his understanding of the world as being divided into dispensations, or ages, rapture theology asserts that human history will culminate in a final dispensation in which only the righteous-in-Christ will be rewarded. For many believers, the modern state of Israel plays an important role in this. To them, the Bible not only promises the Jews a homeland in Israel, but also asserts that the new world order would centralize it. While this may seem like support for Jewish self-determination in a Jewish state, the hope is still that a modern Israel will usher in the *Christian* end of days and, with it, a mass conversion of Jews (see Rom 9–11). Because Paul says that "all Israel will be saved" in Romans 11:26, many evangelicals believe that the left-behind Jews will eventually find their way to Christ and be restored in Jesus's new kingdom, often imagined as taking place in a New Israel. Such eschatological support for Israel is often referred to as "Christian Zionism." For more on modern rapture theology, see Frykholm, *Rapture Culture*. See also chapter 4 in this book.

56. Crossley, "Other Problems from a British Perspective," 135.

57. Crossley, "Other Problems from a British Perspective." See also David G. Horrell, *Ethnicity and Inclusion: Religion, Race, and Whiteness in Constructions of Jewish and Christian Identities* (Eerdmans, 2020), 36–37.

typically an acceptance of the Other without the Otherness."[58] Reminiscent of Jordan Peele's 2017 social horror film *Get Out*, Crossley highlights how philosemitism is often blurred with antisemitism. Just as the rich white characters in *Get Out* seek to (literally) inhabit black bodies while maintaining their white minds (thus showing a simultaneous fetishization and repulsion of blackness),[59] many thinkers in the Western postmodern era seek to engage the Jew on non-Jewish terms.

What This Means for Paul Studies

Some key insights to consider for moving forward are as follows: By the 1970s and 1980s, many biblical scholars, theologians, and public audiences were collectively haunted by the death camps and the role Christianity might have played in them. Similar to the impact of the Eichmann trial on American consciousness, the Holocaust "registered" in their minds as a key event linked to the history of the church. Recall, for example, the words of theologian Gregory Baum:

> The Church has produced an abiding contempt among Christians for Jews and all things Jewish, a contempt that aided Hitler's purposes . . . What the encounter of Auschwitz demands of Christian theologians [and biblical scholars], therefore, is that they submit Christian teaching to a radical ideological critique. Their task is to discern the trends in the Church's teaching that legitimate Christian power over others and have destructive effects on Jews (and other groups of men and women).[60]

---

58. Crossley, "Other Problems from a British Perspective," 136. See also, for example, Slavoj Žižek, *The Puppet and the Dwarf: The Perverse Core of Christianity*, Short Circuits (MIT Press, 2003).

59. As literary scholar Isiah Lavender III puts it, "Peele taps into racial science—pseudoscientific beliefs of a supposed black physical superiority measured against hypothetical white mental superiority—through the fictional and fiendish Coagula procedure, a brain transplant mixed with hypnotherapy, whereupon rich white folks inhabit black bodies and achieve a kind of immortality, deeply ironizing the United Negro College Fund slogan 'a mind is a terrible thing to waste'—that is, a white mind, not a black one." See Isiah Lavender III, "Getting All of It: On Jordan Peele's *Get Out*: Political Horror," *Science Fiction Film and Television* 15, no. 2 (2022): 220.

60. Baum, "Introduction," 7–8.

To put it another way, scholars were ready to explore the potential dangers of biblical interpretation and whether the ancient sources, including those we call Paul's, could be reexamined from new perspectives.

For some, however, the pursuit to read Paul differently remained limited. In Crossley's words, the perceived "difficult" and "strange" aspects of Paul's Jewishness—what Crossley describes as the "fully caffeinated" or fully round version of the apostle[61]—were dismissed, especially in British context.[62] In brief, while scholars in a post-Holocaust 1970s and 1980s world started to see Paul as a Jew instead of a Christian, some still, like the premise of *Get Out*, engaged Paul the Jew on non-Jewish—even antisemitic—terms.

Finally, I would be remiss to not name the import of the Dead Sea Scrolls for new attitudes toward Paul. From 1946 to 1956, a number of ancient sources—some known and many previously unknown—were found in caves on the northern shore of the Dead Sea at a site called Qumran. While I will delve deeper into the scrolls in the following chapter, it is important to note at this juncture that they did not necessarily unveil new insights about ancient Judaism. Rather, they affirmed and compelled readers to take more seriously Jewish texts that engaged in rigorous debate and diverse interpretations of eschatology. Still, as access to the Qumran materials became more widespread, many scholars—though not all—were eager (and perhaps hopeful) to grasp onto interpretations that could provide an alternative to Christian anti-Judaism.

In sum, our worlds do indeed shape how we read. Just as broader cultural perceptions of Jews and Judaism influenced biblical interpretation from Marcion through Bultmann, they also influenced subsequent biblical scholars. In various ways and to varying degrees, Holocaust memory became part of the biblical scholar's memory, which impacted scholarly readings of Paul.[63] To be sure, these new readings contained the kind of "patchwork-quilt quality"

61. A "round" character in literary studies refers to a character with depth and multidimensionality. For more on the multidimensionality of attraction and repulsion in contexts of hierarchy and hegemony, see Homi K. Bhabha, *The Location of Culture* (Routledge, 1994).

62. Crossley, "Other Problems from a British Perspective," 136. See also footnote 34.

63. The fact that so much about Paul has focused on the question of Paul and Jewish exclusion, as opposed to Paul and gentile exclusion, seems to advance this point. Simply stated, the real-world effects of Paul's exclusion of non-Christ-following gentiles have not been the same. The Holocaust made this abundantly clear.

discussed above. While the pursuit to render Paul "good" remained, the way in which scholars went about maintaining such "goodness" vis-à-vis Paul's Judaism took multiple if not contradictory turns, due at least in part to differing cultural dynamics and settings. The overall point, however, is that if the earliest biblical scholars (e.g., Baur, Weber, Bultmann) were trapped under their own social settings, as scholars tend to reveal, then it is important to consider how those discussed below were, too.[64] What follows is an overview of such "no view from nowhere" interpretive turns.

Toward a New Perspective on Paul

Krister Stendahl, a Swedish scholar who taught in an American academic milieu, is frequently recognized for his groundbreaking insights in biblical studies. In the 1960s, he gave a series of lectures in which he argued that both

64. I am not suggesting that post-Holocaust understandings of Jews exclusively shaped understandings of Paul during the last quarter of the twentieth century, but, rather, that it was a significant influence, especially given Christianity's relationship to both the Shoah and the biblical field. This is often acknowledged within the scholarly literature across schools of Pauline thought (for more on these schools or perspectives, see below). According to N. T. Wright, for example, "No-one who has followed the main movements of modern theology will need reminding how important these issues have been in the post-holocaust re-evaluation of the church's relationship to Judaism." Or John Gager: "For nearly twenty centuries Jews have suffered periodic episodes of hatred, discrimination, and genocide at the hands of Christians (and others) . . . My sense is that the Nazi Holocaust . . . account[s] for the possibility of reading Paul in a new way." Or Lloyd Gaston: "It is the task of exegesis after Auschwitz precisely to expose the explicit or implicit anti-Judaism inherent in the Christian tradition, including the New Testament itself . . . When I began I expected to find anti-Judaism particularly present in Paul. That is not, however, the conclusion to which my own studies have led me." Or Magnus Zetterholm: "The traditional anti-Jewish theology of the church and the Holocaust [has], in some case[, been] leading to a wish to contribute to the development of theological alternatives." See N. T. Wright, *The Climax of the Covenant: Christ and the Law in Pauline Theology* (T&T Clark, 1993), 233; Gager, *Reinventing Paul*, 150–151. (Within the ellipses above is Gager adding that the creation of the modern state of Israel also played a fundamental role. With its creation, he writes, "the story of Jews as a persecuted minority cane to an end. For many Jews, Christians were no longer the enemy in the castle." While I have no doubt the creation of modern Israel played a part, I find this reasoning a bit too simplistic.); Gaston, *Paul and the Torah*, 1987, 2; Zetterholm, *Approaches to Paul*, 233. Even Matthias Henze begins his book on the importance of the intertestamental period for New Testament contextualization with an evocation of the Holocaust. See Matthias Henze, *Mind the Gap: How the Jewish Writings Between the Old and New Testament Help Us Understand Jesus* (Fortress Press, 2017), 1–2.

the Christian church and the academic field of biblical studies had for centuries misunderstood Paul's message.[65] It was Augustine, he wrote, who set the stage for reading Paul through a bifurcated lens of justification by grace versus death by law, which "reached its climax" through Luther and was then inherited by the modern biblical field.[66] Stendahl added, however—akin indeed to the book of Acts—that this shows us more about Augustine's and Luther's views of Paul than it does about Paul himself.

Contra traditional Catholic and Protestant readings, Stendahl argued that Paul saw no problem with the law. After all, as Paul himself wrote, he was "blameless" before it (Phil 3:6). Stendahl also argued that Paul sought to bridge the divide between Jews and gentiles rather than widen it. He supported this view by suggesting that Paul never "converted" from Judaism to Christianity but rather that he, much like the prophets Isaiah (Isa 49:6) and Jeremiah (Jer 1:5) before him, turned his attention *as a Jew* to non-Jewish communities.[67] "Paul's ministry," Stendahl declared, "is based on the specific conviction that the *gentiles* will become part of the people of God without having to pass through the law. *This* is Paul's secret revelation and knowledge."[68]

Stendahl was ahead of his time, as readers will see. But what is often overlooked about his work are his seemingly paradoxical claims regarding the relationship between biblical interpretation and one's social location. On

65. Much of Stendahl's arguments from the 1960s are collected in Stendahl, *Paul Among Jews and Gentiles and Other Essays*.

66. Stendahl, *Paul Among Jews and Gentiles and Other Essays*, 85.

67. Paul was "called," he says, but did not "convert." See Stendahl, *Paul Among Jews and Gentiles and Other Essays*, 6–8. Cf. his earlier "Introspective Consciousness of the West," where Stendahl refers to Paul's turning to Christ as a conversion, albeit one that does not declare Judaism a sin and one that is not to a full-fledged "Christianity." *Paul Among Jews and Gentiles and Other Essays*, 78–96.

68. Stendahl, *Paul Among Jews and Gentiles and Other Essays*, 9; emphasis mine. Stendahl brought this perspective to his understanding of salvation. He contended that salvation for both Jews and non-Jews was integral to Paul's mission and that Paul made this clear in Romans 9–11. On Stendahl's reading, Paul says in Romans that Israel will fall so that gentiles may be saved, but then that all of Israel, too, will be saved (Stendahl, *Paul Among Jews and Gentiles and Other Essays*, 4). He also adds, however, that Paul does not talk about how Jews need to live prior to the eschaton; he only talks about how gentiles do. In Stendahl's words, "In none of his writings does he give us information about what he thought to be proper in these matters for Jewish Christians" (Stendahl, *Paul Among Jews and Gentiles and Other Essays*, 2). I counter these perspectives in chapter 4.

the one hand, as articulated above, he argued that biblical interpreters had for far too long imposed a Lutheran, and by extension Augustinian, perspective onto Paul's writings. This not only obscured Paul's original intentions, but also had devastating consequences, leading to violence against Jews in Luther's name and, ironically, in Augustine's.[69] On the other hand, Stendahl acknowledged that the American 1960s provided an opportunity to approach this understanding differently. In other words, the Lutheran social trappings for Stendahl were a problem, but the American 1960s ones were not. In his words:

> The United States of today is the first place in the modern world since Philo's Alexandria [20 BCE–40 CE] where Jews and Christians as people, as religious communities, and as learned communities, live together in a manner and in sufficient numbers to allow for open dialogue. It is the first time in recent history where there could be an open relation between Christians and Jews and where the conversation which Paul started in Romans 9–11, but which was broken off mainly by Christian expansion and superiority feelings, can start again. The pain of history and the same of the holocaust interfere with real dialogue, but the possibility really exists and, it is to be hoped, will increase.[70]

The conversation did increase, but not in immediate response to Stendahl. Too many biblical scholars still saw Judaism as a tradition of works-righteousness that could not be justified. A radical paradigm shift on Jewish legalism was needed in order for biblical scholars to take Stendahl's points (alongside those of Parkes, Moore, and the Seelisberg collective, etc.) seriously. It is to this shift we now turn.[71]

American professor Ed Parish Sanders's 1977 monograph, *Paul and Palestinian Judaism*, effected the paradigm shift in biblical studies.[72] Here,

---

69. I say "ironically" because of Augustine's "slay them not" contention.

70. Stendahl, *Paul Among Jews and Gentiles and Other Essays*, 37.

71. In doing so, we might do well to reflect upon Stendahl's observations regarding social locatedness—why some locations are "good", and others are not, and if or to what extent we can posit such adjectives onto a social moment with certainty—as we continue this story.

72. Contra the work of Seelisberg, however, Sanders was not grounding his scholarship in an ethical or theological pull to deconstruct Christian antisemitism. Instead, he writes, "The

Sanders argued that Israel's relationship with God was in fact always about grace. Countering the Judaism-as-legalism model, he contended that neither the Israelite God nor the people of Israel were ever expected to be perfect. God fails. Israel fails too. God, however, still accepts God's people, struggles and all. This idea, Sanders claimed, was made clear in at the beginning of the Bible: "I will make a great nation out of you," God says to Abram. "I will make your name great; you will be a blessing" (Gen 12:2–3). All Abram had to do was have faith, and God in return would transmit grace unto Abram's offspring, the Israelite people.[73]

---

history of the relationship between scholarly representations of Judaism and anti-Semitism is quite complex, but the present work is not a contribution to unraveling it. The charges of misunderstanding [of ancient Judaism and Paul's relations to it] should be read as simply that and no more." See Sanders, *Paul and Palestinian Judaism*, xiii. Sanders's work, however, paired with prior attempts to challenge traditional Christian interpretation (e.g., Stendahl, Parkes, and Isaac) eventually triggered a response in Paul studies, one that privileged an orientation toward post-Holocaust ethics, which is to say: *anti*-anti-Jewish ethics. Given his not-theological / not-ethical but instead historical focus, it is indeed interesting that Sanders's work is often credited as changing the theological and ethical discourse when others interested in both did similar work before him. This may also be complicated when taking into account his note in a later work, *Jesus and Judaism.* Here, he credits his upbringing: "I am a liberal, modern, secularized Protestant, brought up in a church dominated by low Christology and the social gospel." See E. P. Sanders, *Jesus and Judaism* (Fortress Press, 1985), 334. Also cited in Horrell, *Ethnicity and Inclusion*, 29–30, footnote 28.

73. Sanders, *Paul and Palestinian Judaism*, 19. Sanders does see an allegiance toward legalism, however, in *4 Ezra*. Richard Bauckham infamously argued against Sanders on this point. In Bauckham's view, even *4 Ezra* reflected a covenantal-nomistic logic and was not "legalistic." He writes, "To suppose that for *4 Ezra* God gives the righteous eschatological salvation not because they are members of his elect people but because, regardless of their corporate affiliation, they have individually merited salvation, is to pose a false alternative. God gives salvation to those members of his elect people who have kept the terms of the covenant and so merit the salvation promised in the covenant." See Richard Bauckham, "Apocalypses," in *Justification and Variegated Nomism: The Complexities of Second Temple Judaism*, vol. 1, ed. D. A. Carson, Peter T. O'Brien, and Mark A. Seifrid (Mohr Siebeck, 2001), 173. This volume is also a place in which Philip Alexander argued that ancient Judaism *was* "legalistic," and that, contra traditional Christian interpretation and traditional biblical studies, there is absolutely nothing wrong with that. He writes, for example, "Tannaitic Judaism *can* be seen as fundamentally a religion of works-righteousness, and it is none the worse for that. The superiority of grace over law is not self-evident and should not simply be assumed." Philip Alexander, "Torah and Salvation in Tannaitic Literature," in *Justification and Variegated Nomism: The Complexities of Second Temple Judaism*, ed. D. A. Carson, Peter T. O'Brien, and Mark A. Seifrid, vol. 1 (Mohr Siebeck, 2001), 300; emphasis mine. This volume is not without its drama. While one of the editors, D. A. Carson, in contrast to Sanders, argued that

Sanders coined the continuing relationship between God and Israelites "covenantal nomism." The idea was that, through God's love, God bestows a covenant to Abram, and in turn, to Israel. Then, through Israel's returned faith in God, Israel participates in God-gifted "works" or "laws."[74] To put it otherwise, God's promise to be Israel's God is made with grace, and the giving of codes is God's gift.

According to Sanders, then, the performance of these laws is not one of works-righteousness but instead one of conviction—an enactment that demonstrates to God the people of Israel's loyalty, gratitude, and ongoing navigation in the world. The laws also include means of atonement. To put it another way: Getting in is about grace; staying in is about relational ethics.[75] The important point, though, is that while observing God's laws adds depth, privilege, and import to the relationship between God and Israel, Israel is still offered relationship with God even when Israel falls short. In other words, while laws are instilled in Exodus—that is, many years after the Abram encounter in Genesis (Exod 19–24)—those laws are not the core of the covenantal relationship.[76] They are extra, they are often broken, and there are ways to continually establish and reestablish connection. God, through it all, remains.

Interestingly, despite deconstructing the notion that Judaism is a tradition of works without grace, Sanders still severed Paul from Judaism. On

---

ancient Judaism was too diverse to be simplified into a singular framework such as covenantal nomism, he, instead of promoting said diversity, went back to promoting ancient Judaism as a problematic religion of "legalism." See, for example, volume 2 of *Justification and Variegated Nomism* in comparison to volume 1.

74. Halakhic conduct (i.e., "works" or "law"; Deut 4:32–40; 6:10–12, 20–23; 7:6–8; 8:17–18). Many scholars also bring up Deuteronomy 30 as an extended example of covenantal nomist logic.

75. Or as Hebrew Bible scholar Jon Levenson puts it, "Election implies service, but service renews election." Jon D. Levenson, "The Universal Horizon of Biblical Particularism," in *Ethnicity and the Bible*, vol. 19, Biblical Interpretation Series, ed. Mark G. Brett (Brill, 1996), 156. Levenson understands election and service, however, as inherently equal (as opposed to the grace of election resting at the crux of the covenant and, therefore, perhaps of higher standing). In his words, "God's grace implies his law, but his law implies his grace. Neither takes precedent over the other; they are inextricable," 156–157.

76. There are earlier laws granted to Noah, but these are also not part of the Israelite covenant specifically, as *am-Israel* did not yet exist within the narrativized framework of the Torah.

his reading, Paul was in fact *not* a covenantal nomist, since Paul, in his view, still replaced participation in the law (the nomism part) with participation in Christ. Sanders arrived at this conclusion by arguing that Paul reasoned "from solution to plight," not plight to solution.[77] This means that Paul's logic did not run from "bad law" to "good gospel," as the Old Perspective maintained.[78] But it also means that God sent Jesus to save humanity (the solution), because humanity must have needed some kind of saving (the plight). In other words, Jesus for Sanders's Paul is still the solution—a solution that is not part of the Torah. Sanders's Paul thus still remained critical of the Torah and, in turn, Judaism. Neither could provide a means to salvation. Only Christ could.

For these reasons, Sanders is often considered more of an Old Perspective/Newer Perspectives "cusper."[79] While Sanders's Paul does not see the law as inherently "evil" or the ultimate reflection of Jewish self-righteousness,[80] he does see the law as missing the key ingredient: Jesus. Sanders, in fact, went as far as to say that Paul abandoned the laws of *kashrut* when preaching to gentiles and that he expected other Christ-followers from Jewish backgrounds to do the same (e.g., Peter).[81] In other words, while Jews could *technically* still follow the law for end-times inclusion as long as they also followed Christ, the law for Paul was not enough or even necessary. It could also detract from the goal at hand—the goal of finding "righteousness that comes from God

77. Sanders, *Paul and Palestinian Judaism*, 442–443. Cf. Frank Thielman, *From Plight to Solution: A Jewish Framework for Understanding Paul's View of the Law in Galatians and Romans* (E. J. Brill, 1989).

78. I.e., from plight (law) to solution (grace).

79. Zetterholm, *Approaches to Paul*, 12, 108.

80. Zetterholm, *Approaches to Paul*, 107.

81. Although Sanders imagines Paul eating non-kosher foods (and kosher foods when in Jewish spaces), he also writes that other Jewish Christ-followers may have "generally ke[pt] the law." Sanders references Romans 4:12 and 4:16 to make this claim, but does not expound upon what he means by "generally." The overarching point for the discussion here, however, is that the law, according to Sanders's Paul, was not required for end-times salvation, not even for those coming to Christ from a Jewish background. See E. P. Sanders, "Paul's Attitude Toward the Jewish People," *Union Seminary Quarterly Review* 33, no. 3–4 (1978): 176–177.

through Christ."[82] Sanders's Paul thus still distanced if not separated himself from Torah and, in turn, from contemporaneous Judaism.[83]

The Dunn-Wright "Get Out" Model

Still, Sanders's book is typically credited as changing the discourse on Paul.[84] British scholars James D. G. Dunn and N. T. Wright, for example, utilized Sanders's work to construct a similar approach to the Pauline material. Coining the term "New Perspective" to refer to this new orientation,[85] Dunn's basic thesis was this: Because Israel's theology of nationhood, including Israel's salvation, was always about grace, Paul could not be countering Israel via a works-versus-grace framework. God knows that humans cannot keep the law in full; humans are limited,[86] and God, through God's grace, lets Israel know that that is okay. The law, moreover, is not what saves Jews and never has been.

For the most part, Dunn agreed with Sanders. Where he differed was the extent to which he viewed Paul as situated within contemporaneous Judaism. Whereas Sanders's argument asserted that Paul's theology of Christ runs counter to first-century Jewish thinking—that Paul rejected Jewish covenantal nomism in favor something like a covenantal Christism—Dunn suggested that faith in Jesus was *part* of covenantal nomism and thus *part* of Judaism. To receive grace through faith in Jesus was a continuation of receiving grace through faith like Abram/Abraham (Gal 3; Rom 4). In other words, salvific grace granted unto humans by the Israelite God was a Jewish theology, *even as*

82. Sanders, "Paul's Attitude Toward the Jewish People," 184; emphasis in the original.

83. Sanders does add, however, that if he could vote against Paul on this—that is, against the exclusion of Jews in the eschaton who do not follow Christ—he would. Sanders, "Paul's Attitude Toward the Jewish People," 185.

84. While I will be going through the newer schools of thought in some detail now, know that there is a summary of them in the second-to-last paragraph of this chapter; if you are new to this material, it may help read that first, then come back and read the details.

85. "The New Perspective on Paul" was the title of Dunn's 1982 Manson Memorial Lecture at the University of Manchester. Some credit Wright, however, who wrote an article prior to Dunn's lecture in which he also offered "a new perspective" on Paul. See N. T. Wright, "The Paul of History and the Apostle of Faith," *Tyndale Bulletin* 29, no. 1 (1978): 61–88.

86. James D. G. Dunn, *The New Perspective on Paul*, rev. ed. (Eerdmans, 2008), 53. See also Romans 3:20; 4:15; 5:13; 7:13.

that theology extends to Jesus. While not everyone believed that Jesus was the messiah, those who *did* believe were still functioning within a Jewish understanding of God, grace, covenant, and salvation.

Still, Dunn added that Paul, ever the harsh presenter, must have been countering *something* about the law. He provided the following Pauline quotes as the basis of such assertion: "For we hold that a person is justified by faith apart from works of the law" (Rom 3:28); "We know that a person is righteous not by works of the law but by faith in Jesus" (Gal 2:16).[87] Dunn suggested that Paul's issue with the law is social.[88] On the one hand, Jewish law was too particular; it highlighted a relationship between Jews and their God by way of particular ethnic performance.[89] On the other hand, this very particularism created a hierarchical "Us-versus-Them" boundary between Jews and non-Jews. To say that only those who performed for God in the *right* way—the Jewish lawful way—was, for Dunn's Paul, wrong.[90] Jewish ethnic zeal and supremacy needed to go.[91] Gentiles also needed to know that they were invited into the Christ movement without needing to convert or take on Jewish law. According to Dunn, then, Paul was adamant that, through Jesus, there was no need for ethnic particularism or social distinction. God, through Jesus, was for *both* Jews and gentiles, *regardless* of one's bodily identifiers. The covenant was always about faith, and Jesus helped remind Paul of this understanding. In Dunn's words, "The perspective [Paul counters] is primarily of a status (covenant) given

87. Dunn provides a shortened version of these verses. *The New Perspective on Paul*, 1.

88. Dunn, *The New Perspective on Paul*, 1.

89. James D. G. Dunn, *Jesus, Paul, and the Law: Studies in Mark and Galatians* (Westminster John Knox, 1990), 129–240. In other words, the law for Dunn's Paul was nothing more than "an identity marker of covenantal status," not something that granted salvation. Zetterholm, *Approaches to Paul*, 116.

90. Dunn, *The New Perspective on Paul*, 177, 182. Here he is examining Galatians 6:12–13. In Dunn's words on these verses, "To limit participation in the promise to a relationship [according to the flesh] is to misunderstand the promise. Hence too the point of 6:12–13: the glorifying in the flesh which Paul condemns is a glory not in human exertion or in ritual action, but in ethnic identity."

91. Indeed, for Dunn and Wright in their 1980s and 1990s writings on ancient Judaism and also on Paul, "zeal" was a big key word. For them, and as Stephen Young reminded me in conversations about this book, references to zeal invoked an entire complex of ideas they claimed pervaded ancient Judaism. The word "zeal" comes up twelve times on page 68 alone, and also nine times on page 105, in Dunn's *Jesus, Paul, and the Law*.

exclusively to Israel, setting Israel apart from and privileging Israel over against the (other) nations, a status affirmed and maintained by the works of the law which demonstrated and constituted Israel's set-apartness to God; Paul now saw this attitude as a failure to grasp the character and 'to all-ness' of faith."[92] Paul, in other words, wanted to remind Jews of covenantal nomism and unite *all* believers in Christ, both Jew *and* gentile.

In a similar manner, N. T. Wright argued that Paul's theology was Jewish but also anti-ethnocentric, which countered the Jewish ethnic prejudice of Paul's time. According to Wright, Paul's main issue was that, instead of sharing the Torah as a light to the world, Israelites and later Jews kept their traditions to and for themselves; their connection to God was rendered an ethnic privilege unfit for non-Jews.[93] Wright contended that Paul took issue with such Jewish ethnic pride and thus declared any performance of it unjust. Wright also concluded that Paul saw circumcision and purity regulations as unnecessary for salvation, thus making the practice of circumcision and the following of purity regulations unnecessary, period.[94] For him, only the Jewish elect will be saved—the ones who rid themselves of ethnic pride and particularity and instead follow Christ—alongside the righteous Christ-following gentiles. "All Israel," he contends, akin to thinkers like Augustine before him, is a new True Israel: proper Jews and proper gentiles.[95]

The work of Dunn and Wright is often paired with Sanders's covenantal nomism to describe what is called the "New Perspective" on Paul.[96] This perspective maintains that Paul's theologies *are* Jewish *but* more eth(n)ically

92. Dunn, *The New Perspective on Paul*, 11. Dunn argues that this was an attitude also held by Jesus (Matt 11:19; Mark 2:17), 13.

93. Isaiah 2:2–4; Zechariah 8:21–23. See also Eisenbaum, *Paul Was Not a Christian*, 250–255.

94. See, for example, this work echoed in N. T. Wright, *Paul: In Fresh Perspective* (Fortress Press, 2009); N. T. Wright, *Paul and the Faithfulness of God* (Fortress Press, 2013).

95. It is unclear to me whether Wright believes that all Jews, many Jews, or just some Jews will find their way to Christ and thus become elect. Different sentences in Wright's writing, at least on my reading, seem to allude to different possibilities/conclusions. See especially Wright, *The Climax of the Covenant*, 250–251.

96. Although see Mark Chancey's introduction to the fortieth anniversary edition of *Paul and Palestinian Judaism*, where he discusses Sanders's opposition to the New Perspective.

sophisticated than his fellow Jewish contemporaries.[97] As N. T. Wright (in)famously put it, Paul cared about "grace not race," and thus created a more "perfected" anti-ethnocentric theology.[98] Overall, the New Perspective celebrates Paul as a *universalist* Paul—one who cares for *all* people in his theological orientations to Christ—while most Jews of his day cared for the *particulars*: their laws and themselves.[99]

For those interested in embracing a more ethnically diverse form of Christianity, a universalist Paul can feel like a good thing. As New Testament scholar Neil Elliot observes, "It is not surprising that this approach has proven popular in the United States and the United Kingdom, that is, in ethnically diverse, democratic societies where more liberal interpreters see a happy integration of different peoples as a paramount value."[100] But this is where we would do well to recall Crossley's evocation of Žižek: "Liberal Western multicultural inclusiveness is typically an acceptance of the Other without the Otherness."[101] As noted above, this perspective is starkly illuminated in the

97. Or as James Crossley famously quips, this perspective maintains a Paul who is "Jewish . . . but not that Jewish." See James Crossley, "The Multicultural Christ: Jesus and Jew and the New Perspective on Paul in an Age of Neoliberalism," *The Bible & Critical Theory* 7 (2011): 8–16.

98. Wright, *The Climax of the Covenant*, 194, 247. See also Wright, *Paul and the Faithfulness of God*, 415.

99. This is indeed different from the Old Perspective's legalistic model, in which Jews are depicted as earning salvation through works. Still, as David G. Horrell articulates, "there remains a structural similarity" between the Old Perspective and the New Perspective. Quoting Barry Matlock, he adds, "Substitute for 'legalism' in the traditional reading 'nationalism' in Dunn's [and Wright's], as the perverted attitude toward the law and its observance that is the real target of Paul's attack, and the old perspective fits Dun right down to the ground." See Horrell, *Ethnicity and Inclusion*, 35. See also R. Barry Matlock, "Sins of the Flesh and Suspicious Minds: Dunn's New Theology of Paul," *Journal for the Study of the New Testament* 21, no. 72 (1999): 86.

100. Neil Elliot, "The Question of Politics: Paul as a Diaspora Jew Under Roman Rule," in *Paul Within Judaism: Restoring the First-Century Context to the Apostle*, ed. Mark D. Nanos and Magnus Zetterholm (Fortress Press, 2015), 207. See also Daniel Boyarin, who agrees with the New Perspective reading and then both celebrates and problematizes this universal Paul. Boyarin, *A Radical Jew*. See also chapter 4.

101. Crossley, "Other Problems from a British Perspective," 135. Stephen Young's way of putting this with regard to N. T. Wright is that Wright turns Paul into a ventriloquist for the values that feel comfortable and prestigious to Wright's modern Christian readers (among whom values like being "countercultural" and "subversive" of empire are things they want to claim). Stephen L. Young, "So Radically Jewish That He's an Evangelical Christian: N. T. Wright's Judeophobic and Privileged Paul," *Interpretation* 76 (2022): 339–351.

double-sidedness of Jordan Peele's *Get Out* message. While, from the protagonist Chris Washington's perspective, the impetus is to "get out" of the situation in which he finds himself—that is, white people taking over his body but "leaving behind" his mind—it, from the antagonists' perspective, is to get the "right" amount of *black* out of Washington. Repeatedly, *Get Out* shows how an ideological move from conservative anti-black racism to liberal anti-black racism allows for a more concealed agenda of racialized fetishization and exploitation. Under the guise of "feel-good" progressivism, it is still only the "right" kind of black that is recognized as "good": in this example, black physicality without black culture. Similarly, the scholarly move from an Old Perspective to a New Perspective provided biblical scholars the opportunity to celebrate Paul the Jew with just the right—the *good*—amount of Jewishness: in this example, Jewish theology without Jewish ethnicity, as if the two could even be separated.[102] Under this expression, we might say that the New Perspective is how post-Holocaust scholars save Paul to save Jews *from Jews* to save themselves.

In sum, the traditional New Perspective showcases how Paul is a "good" Jew—a Jew, that is, who is not a full-fledged Protestant antisemite. The problem, however, is that the New Perspective's goal of having a universalist Paul not only overlooked much of Paul's own writing but also perpetuated an Old Perspective caricature. For Dunn and Wright, there was still something wrong with Judaism, which Paul sought to fix. Dunn and Wright concluded that Paul's answer was to renounce the particulars of Jewish ethnic identity (i.e., to renounce much of what made Jews Jewish). In other words, Paul, under the New Perspective, still opposed and superseded his Jewish contemporaries. He was just not *a* good Jew, but *the* good Jew, second perhaps to only Jesus, whereas other Jews—most Jews—needed to get out.[103]

Not Good Enough

There have been a number of pushbacks to the Dunn-Wright New Perspective, particularly by American or American-affiliated thinkers who recognize its

---

102. Crossley, "Other Problems from a British Perspective," 136.

103. See Neil Elliott for a similar synopsis, "The Question of Politics," 207–208. See also Young, "So Radically Jewish That He's an Evangelical Christian," for the weight of Wright's scholarship in New Testament and especially evangelical Christian circles.

Old Perspective undertones. Biblical scholar John Gager, for instance, asserts that Dunn's argument still positions Judaism in a negative light. In his words, Dunn's "emphasis on Jewish ethnic pride reverts to the outmoded, unhistorical dichotomy between Jewish particularism and Christian universalism."[104] Still, the work of these thinkers should not be entirely discounted. Each of them paved the way for a new understanding of Paul's relationship to Jews and Judaism, one that dismantled the impression that Judaism should die and Christianity should live.

Below are explications of various pushbacks to the Dunn-Wright model. Before continuing, however, I must insert a caveat: The following pushbacks—Radical New Perspective, *Sonderweg*, Paul within Judaism—are malleable. I could, for example, categorize them entirely differently, with an overarching heading of "New Perspective" and everything post-Luther included within it (i.e., this would make *all* the schools listed in this chapter part of the New Perspective). I could also flatten each of these schools into a *different* "old"-versus-"new" paradigm, in which Dunn and Wright—through such flattening—would become aligned, due to their Old Perspective allegiances and the extent to which so many scholars find their reasonings untenable, no longer with any sort of a "New Perspective," but instead the same "Old Perspective."[105] Effectively, this would make all of the pushbacks to Dunn and Wright part of the "New Perspective." In fact, in my experience, this is how many scholars outside of specific Paul-specialist circles refer to these approaches. Everything up to Dunn and Wright is "Old," and anything pushing back against them is "New."

In short, I have no doubt that some scholars will disagree with my reconstruction here. The fact of the matter remains that biblical scholars explain the perspectives differently and do different things with them.[106] All I can say is that this is how I understand them and will be using them.

---

104. Gager, *Reinventing Paul*, 49. See also Horrell's extended discussion of this issue in *Ethnicity and Inclusion*, 28–36.

105. But for a quick resource that works through the "Old Perspective" and tries to contrast it with the "New Perspective," see Stephen Westerholm, *Perspectives Old and New on Paul: The "Lutheran" Paul and His Critics* (Eerdmans, 2003).

106. See, for example, Scot McKnight and B. J. Oropeza, eds., *Perspectives on Paul: Five Views* (Baker Academic, 2020), which has five perspectives: Catholic, Protestant, New Perspective, Paul within Judaism, and the Gift Perspective.

The Radical New Perspective on Paul

Because of its Old Perspective undertones, many scholars have pushed back against the Dunn-Wright model, saying—and excuse the pun—it wasn't *done right*. A number of thinkers thus expanded aspects of the New Perspective to consider more fully the context within which Paul found himself. A focal point in this sense has become Paul's Jewishness in, as Stendhal himself had stressed, a non-Jewish environment.[107]

American Canadian thinker Lloyd Gaston made this clear in his 1987 book, *Paul and the Torah*.[108] In his view, readers must keep in mind that Paul's theology *is* Jewish, *and* that Paul was speaking to gentiles when writing his letters (Gal 1:15–16, 2:8–9; Rom 1:5, 11:13, 15:16). Taking Sanders as his starting point, Gaston affirms that God's relationship with the Jewish people is established through grace, but then adds that God's relationships with Jews and gentiles remain distinct. When Paul says that Christ-followers should not abide by Jewish law and practice, for example, he means that his implied readers—*gentiles*—should not abide by Jewish law and practice.[109] For Gaston, then, separation is still integral to Paul's mission, but not in terms of whether one group is better than another. For Gaston, Paul separates Jews from gentiles in how they are expected to show their righteousness. Jews follow one path; gentiles follow another.

107. Given the Radical New Perspective's focus on Paul's gentile audience, some may position Stendahl as a proto-Radical New Perspective thinker (or, as readers will see, a proto-Paul-within-Judaism thinker).

108. Gaston, *Paul and the Torah*, 33. See also page 66 of his 1979 essay "Paul and the Torah," which is reprinted in the 1987 monograph. Lloyd Gaston, "Paul and the Torah," in *Antisemitism and the Foundations of Christianity*, ed. Alan T. Davies (Paulist Press, 1979), 48–71. Gaston was eventually employed by the University of British Columbia, but grew up in the United States, taught in the United States, and was ordained in the United Presbyterian Church in the USA (UPCUSA).

109. Scholars in agreement with Gaston on Paul's audience, however, often note that gentiles are still required to follow a smaller set of laws, sometimes referred to as the Noahide laws. See Matthew Thiessen, *Paul and the Gentile Problem* (Oxford University Press, 2016), 11, 21. See more on this below and also in chapter 4.

Gaston's work evolved into what some thinkers called, at least for a time, the "Radical New Perspective" on Paul.[110] This perspective takes as its starting points Paul's Jewish context and his gentile audience. It argues that Paul's intended audience is in fact a gentile one, and that Paul's primary concern was ushering gentiles *as gentiles* into the Christ-following movement. This focus on gentiles moreover could be because of Paul's Jewish theological convictions. For most Jews, the messianic hope was that both Jews *and* gentiles would worship the God of Israel together in the end of days. According to the Radical New Perspective, then, Paul was saying what was necessary—including belittling Jewish law—in order to persuade gentiles to *stay* gentile (i.e., to *not* follow Jewish law, as doing so would make them Jewish), and thus prepare them for the messianic age.[111]

Paul, in short, was not trying to dismantle Judaism. He was simply trying to *stop gentiles* from converting to it. To put it another way, when Paul negates the import of the law, the Radical New Perspective says that he is negating it *solely* for gentiles. Jews, according to this model, can maintain the law without repercussion. The question from here becomes: Maintain the law in what? It is clear that gentiles, without the law, need to follow Christ. But do Jews, with the law, also need to follow Christ? The *Sonderweg* theory says no, and does so through Gaston's evocation of a two-pathed project: Jews follow one path toward salvation, and gentiles follow another.

110. Pamela Eisenbaum used the vocabulary of "radical" in "Paul, Polemics, and the Problem of Essentialism," *Biblical Interpretation* 13, no. 3 (2005): 232. At the time of writing, she situated scholars such as Mark Nanos, Neil Elliott, Paula Fredriksen, Lloyd Gaston, John Gager, Krister Stendahl, Stan Stowers and sometimes Nils Dahl and W. D. Davies within such "radical" orientation, and did so by engaging S. J. Gathercole's monograph *Where Is Boasting?* Here, Gathercole writes that he does not engage scholars such as Gaston and Stowers because they "have not been particularly influential with their theological conclusions because they are so *radical*." Emphasis Eisenbaum's, "Paul, Polemics, and the Problem of Essentialism," 232, note 18. See also Simon J. Gathercole, *Where Is Boasting?: Early Jewish Soteriology and Paul's Response in Romans 1–5* (Eerdmans, 2002), 18. Eisenbaum then repeated the use of "radical" terminology, and indeed situated her own work within what she called a "radical new perspective," in *Paul Was Not a Christian*, 250. She again lists scholars whom she believes are similarly (although not identically) "radical," who are "Krister Stendahl, Lloyd Gaston, John Gager, Stanley Stowers, Neil Elliott, and Mark Nanos."

111. Gaston, *Paul and the Torah*, 7–11. See also Stowers, *A Rereading of Romans*, 21–33, and even Stendahl, *Paul Among Jews and Gentiles and Other Essays*, 7–9.

The Magic of Sonderweg

While not all proponents of a Jewish Paul speaking to gentile audiences adhere to the two-path solution proposed by Gaston, several distinguished scholars do.[112] Influential thinkers such as John Gager, Stanley Stowers,[113] Pamela Eisenbaum, and Gabriele Boccaccini—all of whom have taught primarily in a US context—conclude in various ways and to various degrees that salvation for Jews is not predicated on an individual devotion to Jesus as the Christ. For Gaston and Gager in particular, Jews are granted access to the end-times through their relations to Abraham and Torah, whereas salvation for gentiles is granted through a "special way" (i.e., a *Sonderweg*): Christ.[114]

Gaston's work with the New Testament Greek helps further this point. For example, in Galatians 2:16, which is often cited in support of a grace-versus-works dichotomy (Christ-followers are for grace, while Jewish non–Christ-followers are for works), the Greek translates as follows: "We know that a person is justified not by the works of the law but through faith [or faithfulness] *of* Jesus Christ." In other words, whereas most English translations say "but through faith *in* Jesus Christ," the grammar is such that it is possible for

---

112. Some even connect the *Sonderweg* model back to a few sentences by Krister Stendahl on page 4 of *Paul Among Jews and Gentiles and Other Essays*. These sentences are in response to Romans 9–11, and in particular, to Paul's "all Israel will be saved" comment: "It should be noted that Paul does not say that when the time of God's kingdom, the consummation, comes Israel will accept to Jesus as the Messiah. He says only that the time will come when 'all Israel will be saved' (11:26). It is stunning to note that Paul writes this whole section of Romans (10:7–11:36) without using the name Jesus Christ." Terence Donaldson points to Mark Nanos and John Gager as two thinkers who connect the *Sonderweg* model to Stendahl, but then Donaldson adds that Stendahl himself does not agree with the approach in that it offers something more "concrete" than what Paul's texts "allow us to say." See Donaldson, "Jewish Christianity, Israel's Stumbling and the *Sonderweg* Reading of Paul," 29. See also Mark D. Nanos, *The Mystery of Romans: The Jewish Context of Paul's Letters*, 1st ed. (Fortress Press, 1996), 7; Gager, *Reinventing Paul*, 45. For Stendahl's rebuttal, see Krister Stendahl, *Final Account: Paul's Letter to the Romans* (Fortress Press, 1995), x.

113. I recognize that Stowers rejects readings of his work that affirm a "Jews don't need Christ" interpretation of Paul. I thus provide nuance on Stowers on pages 139–140.

114. *Sonderweg* was first used by Franz Mussner, albeit differently. See Franz Mussner, *Traktat über die Juden* (Kösel, 1979), 60. See also Donaldson, "Jewish Christianity, Israel's Stumbling and the *Sonderweg* Reading of Paul," 28, footnote 4.

it to be translated as "but through the faithfulness *of* Jesus Christ."[115] This is where further Jewish context is important. In Stowers's words, "A person must understand both the wider language and a specific practical context."[116] The "of" in this case is connected to that wider context.

The practical context of Galatians includes competing understandings of Abraham from the book of Genesis. Paul makes this clear throughout the letter. Whereas there appear to be other teachers of Christ invoking Abraham in a way that aligns Abraham either with a nomism different from covenantal nomism (i.e., with a law-keeping faith that not only sustains Abraham's relationship with his God but also creates it) or with a nomism that actually does mirror covenantal nomism (i.e., with a law-keeping faith that sustains Abraham's relationship with his God), Paul insists that his gentile audiences focus on the *beginning* of Abraham's story. In Galatians 3, for example, Paul recounts how the God of Israel first promised Abraham a great nation from his descendants in exchange for Abraham's *faith*, not law. In fact, if one follows the biblical canon, one sees that the laws of the Torah (Exodus) were gifted hundreds of years *after* such a promise was even made to Abraham (Genesis). This, for Paul, shows that the entire premise of God's promise to Abraham is bound up in the faith *of* Abraham.[117] If Abraham *has faith*, God will protect his people and make a nation out of them. To put it otherwise, Paul seems to be in agreement with the starting point of Sanders's covenantal nomism.

---

115. In Greek, the phrase "faith in Jesus Christ" simply appears as a word for faith (*pistis*) and words for Jesus Christ, which occur in what is called the genitive case. It is possible for this pairing of *pistis* with the genitive for Christ to be translated in the traditional way as "faith in Jesus Christ." But it is also possible for it to be translated as "through the faith [or faithfulness] of Jesus Christ." For a quick overview of this debate, see Simon Gathercole, "Justification by Faith," in *The Oxford Handbook of Pauline Studies*, ed. Matthew V. Novenson and R. Barry Matlock (Oxford University Press, 2022), 433–439. See also Jimmy Hoke, "The Letter of Paul to the Romans," in *The Westminster Study Bible*, ed. Emerson B. Powery et al. (Westminster John Knox, 2024), 1938, which engages this debate in relation to Romans 3:21–26—verses that have the same language—and *Sonderweg*. Note, too, that the New Revised Standard Version Updated Edition translates the verse(s) as "faith of Jesus Christ," thus marking a shift from almost every other mainstream translation.

116. Stowers, *A Rereading of Romans*, 7.

117. See, for example, Stephen L. Young, "Paul's Ethnic Discourse on 'Faith': Christ's Faithfulness and Gentile Access to the Judean God in Romans," *Harvard Theological Review* 108 (2015): 30–51, at 37–50.

This starting point, in fact, is particularly important for Paul's gentile audiences. For, on the one hand, it seems to be the case that Paul, like the teachers he opposes, presumes that God's promises are ethnically specific to Israel, which means that gentiles need to become affiliated with Abraham's descent in order to inherit God's promises. But on the other hand, Paul does not want gentiles to become affiliated with God's promises by following the law. Paul thus invokes Abraham in a way that, counter to the teachers who *do* want gentiles to follow the law in their faith for Christ, *dissociates* Abraham's God-given promises from the law. Abraham received the promises because he believed. Thus, says Paul, believing gentiles (in Christ, and thus also in Abraham) will receive the promises as well. The law for them is not needed.

Although Pamela Eisenbaum differs from Gaston on certain points, she agrees with him on the import of Abraham's faith and how it relates to later Jesus followers and the meaning of Galatians 2:16. She explains that just as Abraham's faithfulness in God put right his Israelite and later Jewish descendants, "it is *Jesus'* faithfulness [that] puts right gentiles and incorporates them into the family of God."[118] In other words, like New Perspectivers, Eisenbaum reads Galatians 2:16 in light of Paul's Jewish background and his Jewish understanding of ancient Israelite texts. Then, like a Radical New Perspectiver with a *Sonderweg* bend, she adds, "Just as Abraham and the patriarchs' great acts of faithfulness enabled Israel to enjoy God's grace through the merit of the fathers, so, too, Jesus' faithfulness [to the point of death] means that God will look favorably upon the nations and not hold them accountable for their accumulated sin. It was not Israel's faith *in* Abraham that allowed her to enjoy God's favor, but the faith *of* Abraham. The same kind of theological system is at work with Jesus and the Gentiles."[119]

This does not mean that gentiles should act however they please. Just as Israelites and later Jews are asked to emulate Abraham's faithfulness through a faithful response to Torah, so, too, are gentiles asked to live faithfully.[120] This means reflecting Jesus's faithfulness, participating in ritual washing

118. Eisenbaum, *Paul Was Not a Christian*, 240; emphasis mine.

119. Eisenbaum, *Paul Was Not a Christian*, 241. This is also Richard Hays's reading in "'Have We Found Abraham to Be Our Forefather According to the Flesh?': A Reconsideration of Rom 4:1," *Novum Testamentum* 27 (1985): 76–98.

120. Eisenbaum, *Paul Was Not a Christian*, 241–242.

(*baptize*),[121] and abstaining from a life of excess. Paul even lists half of the Ten Commandments in his letter to the Romans for gentiles to follow. In his words, "you" (as in "you gentiles") "shall not commit adultery, shall not murder, shall not steal, and shall not covet." Adding that these laws can be summed up in the Leviticus commandment to "love your neighbor as yourself" does not eradicate these laws but rather further supports them (Rom 13:8–9; Lev 19:18). To put it simply, this is not a law-free message. It is just not a *the* law, or a fully Jewish law, message.

This does not mean that Jews following *the* law are wrong, however. According to Stowers, in fact, it is the gentiles who need the most help. Whereas Jews can atone for their wrongdoings through the law, gentiles have nothing. Moreover, if readers take seriously the argument that Paul is speaking not to Jews but to gentiles, they see how much Paul thinks gentiles are indeed the inferior group.[122] The entire opening in Romans, for example, is about how much more gentiles are impure compared to Jews. Unable to control their urges—control being a virtue in first-century Greco-Roman thinking—they are instead enslaved to their passions. But because, says Stowers, the law was set aside for Jews, following the Torah will not help gentiles in these matters. God has thus provided them a *different* way to obtain forgiveness and salvation: Christ.

There is a nuance to this, however, that should not be overlooked. Despite seeing different relations to God for Jews and gentiles (e.g., through a reading of Rom 4:16b), Stowers and Eisenbaum do still see Jesus as part of God's overarching eschatological plan for *both* Jews and gentiles. Whereas Jews do not need to have faith *in* Jesus or require the faith *of* Jesus for salvation, they are still granted access to God's eschatological kingdom because Jesus shows up for gentiles. To put it otherwise, it is still Jesus's work with gentiles that brings about salvation, in that the original promise was always about everyone (i.e., "nations"). Without Jesus, there is no "everyone."

---

121. Baptism stems from Jewish ritual immersion practiced, for example, at the mikveh. For an accessible introduction to this, see Robert R. Cargill, "Origins of Baptism," *Bible Odyssey*, https://thesacredpage.bibleodyssey.org/video-gallery/origins-of-baptism/.

122. See also Brian Rainey, *Religion, Ethnicity and Xenophobia in the Bible: A Theoretical, Exegetical and Theological Survey* (Routledge, 2020), 229–238; Joseph Marchal, *Appalling Bodies: Queer Figures Before and After Paul's Letters* (Oxford University Press, 2020), 164–171; Stowers, *A Rereading of Romans*, 42–82; Young, "Ethnic Ethics," 236–238.

Without everyone, there is no end-times. Without end-times, there is no eschatological salvation.[123] On the one hand, one could argue that this is not *Sonderweg*, which is a two-covenant model: Torah for Jews and Christ for gentiles. On the other hand, one could argue that it is at the very least *Sonderweg*-like, in that Jews can stay Jewish while not focusing their individual beliefs toward Christ. Eisenbaum notes herself how her interpretation can at times read as both *Sonderweg* and not. She closes her *Paul Was Not a Christian*, for example, by suggesting that if one reads Romans 9–11 as a roadmap to individual salvation, then yes, her reading is that of a "two way." But if one understands Romans 9–11 as how to participate in a redemption that will happen no matter what, then no, her reading is not *Sonderweg*. Jews and gentiles must act faithfully, but at the end of time, she says that it is really "the big sins of the world that need to be accounted for."[124] In other words, a Jew not blamelessly following Torah and a gentile not blamelessly following Christ won't mean they are left behind. In her view, all will still be saved—the "full number" of Jews and gentiles—which she sees as not merely good but rather great: "I think everyone can agree that Paul's message was about grace. Why is it necessary to put limits on this grace? Let's let Paul's message of grace stand as it is. It seems to me a great start for thinking about religious pluralism," a pluralism she may find personally valuable as one of the few Jews within the field of New Testament studies.[125]

* * *

I was trained in the *Sonderweg* school. Equipped with Gaston, Gager, and a *Sonderweg*-like understanding of Eisenbaum, my doctoral seminars focused on how only gentiles needed Christ in order to be saved in Paul's imagined end of days.[126] The conclusion was often that Jews were fine; they don't need

---

123. Eisenbaum, *Paul Was Not a Christian*, 241–242, 250–255; Stowers, *A Rereading of Romans*, 202–206.

124. Eisenbaum, *Paul Was Not a Christian*, 253.

125. Eisenbaum, *Paul Was Not a Christian*, 255. These in fact are the final sentences of her book, which seems to be a common way to end books and articles about Paul. For more, see the final paragraphs of this book's chapter 4.

126. This is based only on my memory, of course. I do not seek to speak on behalf of others in my doctoral program who may have experienced class conversations about Paul differently.

Jesus. Only gentiles do. I so internalized this expression of Pauline thought that I came to believe it was scholarly consensus. Reader, it is not.

Important to the intellectual history of biblical interpretation, however, is the context in which biblical scholars are trained. Perhaps it will be no surprise to hear my fourth confession, which is that my doctoral training took place in a liberal Protestant setting, a setting in which *Sonderweg* has the potential to make liberal Christianity feel better about its anti-Jewish past. It was also a setting in which certain "New" Perspectives on Paul were deemed "Old." In particular, Dunn and Wright were, along with Baur, Weber, and Bultmann, "Old," whereas pushbacks to them were rendered "New."[127] The New Perspective under these terms—a Newer New Perspective—was thus celebrated, and the *Sonderweg* model was seen as an integral part of it.

Even in graduate school, I disagreed firmly with the *Sonderweg* premise. In my view, Paul *was* an exclusivist thinker: He was a Jewish man whose understanding of the end of days left many Jews, no less than gentiles, behind. In my first year of coursework, I wanted to write a term paper on this, but an interlocutor warned me that promoting such a view could result in promoting Christian anti-Judaism. The logic was that because the New Testament has been used throughout Christian history to justify the demonization of Jews and Judaism, reading Paul as excluding non-Christ-following Jews (note: nobody seems to bother much about those excluded gentiles!) amounted to an extension of this dangerous thinking. In other words, with *Sonderweg*, Jews are safe. They are also saved. Christians do not need to change, convert, or kill Jews simply because they are Jewish.

I get the magic of the *Sonderweg* model. Suffice it to say that the research required for this book was at times devastating. I had to steep myself *so intensely* and *so sustainably* in centuries of anti-Jewish vitriol, which, in effect, generated night terrors of colleagues sending me to Auschwitz. "Everybody hates us," I cried to a Jewish colleague one day. "They've hated us for so long. What if they are right?" By the time I revisited Stendahl, I was desperate to hear his words anew. And by the time I revisited *Sonderweg*, I could understand why scholars desiring to better Jewish-Christian relations might especially want its premise to be true. The more distance I got from the extremes of the anti-Jewish past, however, the more convinced I became that the *Sonderweg* theory was wrong. Hebrew Bible scholar Ethan Schwartz reminded me, however, that

127. As noted above, this is also a common reconstruction within New Testament scholarship.

my pushbacks to *Sonderweg* may be animated at least in part because I am not being actively persecuted.[128] I suspect he is right.

I now see the horns of the *Sonderweg* dilemma as follows: On the one hand, if Christians believed in *Sonderweg's* two-path premise, the "goodness" of converting or killing Jews would be irrelevant. Claims like Luther's or Baur's or Bultmann's—or even the following, published on Good Friday 2024—would be illogical: "If one truly loves Jewish people, then a call for their conversion would be true evidence of that. Simply put, there is no salvation outside the Church, and Christ *is* King and always will be. To hold fast to those truths is *not* antisemitic; it is, instead, orthodox Catholic belief."[129] On the other hand, the *Sonderweg* model spares Christianity from its own inherent antisemitism. With the two paths, Paul, both *as* a Jew and as a thinker *of* Jews, is still *good*. No Jews are left behind. Moreover, if Paul *is indeed good*, then Christianity at its core can *also* be good. In other words, with *Sonderweg*, it is interpretive history that is the problem. Not Paul. Not Christianity properly understood.

I understand the desire to have one's scripture match one's ethics. It is not an easy feeling when aspects of one's culture go against the grain of one's moral compass. My mother, in fact, alluded to this conflict on our recent trip to northern Italy. "What does it feel like, Sarah, to know that your heritage is both?" This is the question she asked me after visiting a concentration camp in her city of origin, Trieste. It is one that simultaneously haunts me and leads to my fifth confession, which is that my heritage is Jewish, yes, but it is also gentile Austrian.

My mother was born on May 8, 1955, exactly ten years after Germany surrendered and nearly a decade after the war ended. Her mother's family arrived in Trieste by way of Venice, Sardinia, and Iberia. Her father's family arrived by way of Venice, Austria, and Pazin. Rotter, an Austrian surname, is my mother's maiden name. She converted from Catholicism to Judaism in her twenties, and soon after took my father's Jewish last name: Lieberman.

---

128. This was at a roundtable conference at Villanova University in which *Wrestling with Paul*, in one of its earliest stages, was being discussed.

129. Kennedy Hall, "Good Friday 'Antisemitism' and the Conversion of the Jews," *Crisis Magazine*, March 29, 2024, https://crisismagazine.com/opinion/good-friday-antisemitism-and-the-conversion-of-the-jews. I extend gratitude to Ethan Schwartz for alerting me to this publication. See also Riley-Smith, "Crusading as an Act of Love"; and chapter 2, page 85 and its accompanying footnotes 104 and 105.

For the first five years of her life, my mother lived with her family in an apartment around the corner from Piazza Unità, the square in which Benito Mussolini enacted the anti-Jewish racial laws of 1938. Facing the Adriatic Sea and addressing a roaring crown, Mussolini announced:

> Dear men and women of Trieste! . . . World Jewry has been, for sixteen years, despite our policy, an irreconcilable enemy of Fascism [loud cheers]. In Italy our policy has led, in the Semitic elements, to what can today be called a true rush to board the ship. However, Jews of Italian citizenship who have unquestionable military or civil merit towards Italy and the Regime will find understanding and justice. As for the others, a policy of separation awaits them. When all is said and done, the world will perhaps be surprised more by our generosity than by our severity; that is, unless the Semites beyond your borders and within our country and above all their powerful friends and defenders force us to radically harshen our policy.[130]

Trieste also housed Italy's only concentration camp with a crematorium. Called Risiera di San Saba, it functioned as both a transit station and a detention center, primarily for political dissenters but also for Jews, many of whom were sent from San Saba to larger camps like Auschwitz and Dachau.

My family wasn't sympathetic to Mussolini or to the Reich but wasn't filled with vocal dissenters either. I'm told that, in many instances, family members played the role of "trickster" in order to survive. My mother's aunt, for example, was once placed in a train line controlled by Nazis—she was in the wrong place at the wrong time—and shared in an interview that she "played the flirt" to help her escape. A Nazi officer found her attractive, and so she flirted with him until he let her go free.[131] She did not name the train station at which she found herself, but it is likely it was San Saba. My mother's father also used the tools available to him to avoid fighting in the army. A concert pianist, he played Chopin's "Ballade No. 1" for a high-ranking officer, who, in response, enlisted

---

130. Benito Mussolini, "Speech in Trieste, September 18, 1938," trans. *Biblioteca Fascista*, March 4, 2012, https://bibliotecafascista.blogspot.com/2012/03/speech-in-trieste-september-18-1938.html.

131. When she recalled this event in the interview, she switched from speaking in English to speaking in her native language of Italian, suggesting a reexperiencing of the event as she retold it, which is a common response to trauma and trauma recall.

him to be his secretary and teach his daughter how to play the piano during the war. These, however, are just the stories I have been told. I would not be surprised if the past happened differently. I would also not be surprised if more distant relatives did fight in the war, and not on the side of Jews.

My mother and her immediate family immigrated to the United States in 1960, when she was still a child, but she remembers life in Trieste, including seeing swastikas painted on the walls of the city. She even recalls drawing a swastika in art class when she started school in the United States. When I asked her why she did this, she said, "I was five years old. I couldn't speak any English. I didn't know what a swastika was. But I saw it everywhere, and it was one of the only things I knew how to draw." She also shares what she learned about Jews in Catholic settings. Her parents sometimes took her to catechism classes, and it was there, over fifteen years after the war ended and on another continent, that American nuns taught her that God does not hear the prayers of Jews. She also tells me that members of her family, even though not supporters of Mussolini or the Third Reich, were still shaped by antisemitic stereotype; tropes of Jews as ugly, cheap, and socially inept circulated widely. She even shares that she still stores her baptism certificate in a safe deposit box, just in case she needs it to protect her children from the kind of theologized race science that permeated much of her childhood. The logic is that if she can prove she's not "really" Jewish according to such race science, then maybe she can prove her children are not "fully" Jewish either, if ever needed.

I think about this a lot. I think about the fear my mother has in being Jewish—a fear instilled within her because of her experiences with antisemitism as a non-Jew. I think about how she knows what people say about us behind closed doors. I think about the antisemitism still common in churches today. I think about the antisemitism in my mother's family. I think about what it means to be a Jew today, a time in which there exists a modern Jewish state that people seem to either love or hate. Growing up, my attitudes toward Israel were not strong—Italy was my family's second home. The modern state of Israel was also not a regular topic of discussion in my Hebrew School classes. Still, when Israel *was* discussed, I was encouraged to think of it as a fair and democratic country. I was never taught about the relationship between Israel and Palestine, let alone the suffering of the Palestinian people. As an adult today, writing in the midst of a growing global anti-Jewish hatred related to the actions of the state of Israel in Gaza, I very much want the state—for the sake of all its citizens and neighboring peoples—to be *good*. I even want to tell myself it *is* and *always has been* a fair and nondiscriminatory country; if people believe this, then maybe people will stop hating Jews. This is striking to me, as it reminds me of the *Sonderweg* model. It reminds me of how it can indeed feel easier to bend or ignore history than to face reality—a reality in which Triestini gassed Jews, a reality in which a Nakba and Palestinian suffering very much exists (as, of course, do two intifadas and October 7), and a reality in which Paul theologically consigned "unbelieving" Jews and gentiles to damnation.

I say all this to explain that I fully understand why people want their history and culture to be "good." This very phenomenon is in fact currently dominating public discussions and political fights over US history. There are many who need an American exceptionalist version of US history in which the United States has always been a "force for good" and "source of liberty" overall, even though such a history requires colossal special pleading: Africans enslaved Africans too; Indigenous Americans fought and killed each other too; "we" didn't commit genocide against Indigenous Americans—it was just accidental transmission of diseases for which they weren't ready, and so on. Or to return to the Israel-Hamas war, the propaganda that Hamas *alone* is responsible for the loss of Palestinian lives because Hamas uses civilians as human shields is, in some circles, a means by which to maintain a benign image of Israel's moral standing. To ignore Paul's ethnocentric exclusivism—or to somehow make his ethnocentric exclusivism everlastingly "good"—similarly requires a bending of history and a bending of text. It also requires making Paul's conception of "good" fit our conceptions of "good."

I have been asked throughout the course of writing this book why I have a problem with manipulating Paul's ideas if doing so could mean a better life for Jews. My answer is this: While it's understandable to want one's culture, not least one's religious culture, to be perceived as inherently moral, I'd rather struggle with Paul—radically *refute* him, in fact—than radically sanitize what he had to say. New Testament scholar Luke Timothy Johnson had it right: "Not much is left over when every sensibility is assuaged."[132]

* * *

132. He adds, "Censorship always finds itself in a baby-and-bathwater situation, texts that offend one way can build positive identity in another. The premise that sacred texts must always confirm and never challenge contemporary ideology is perhaps the most problematic

Paul within Judaism

The most recent movement is called "Paul within Judaism" and seems to have, at least in my research, the broadest geographical and intellectual reach.[133] Led

---

aspect of this approach." Johnson, "The New Testament's Anti-Jewish Slander and the Conventions of Ancient Polemic," 421.

133. According to the Society of Biblical Literature program books, there was a meeting to discuss a new unit on "Paul and Judaism" in 2010. This new unit, first titled "Paul and Judaism," was featured at the national conference for the first time in 2012. The unit had a panel with Magnus Zetterholm presiding and Mark Nanos, Christine Hayes, Karin Hedner Zetterholm, George Carras, and Anders Runesson presenting. All papers were from scholars affiliated exclusively with American institutions. The unit was then labeled "Paul and Judaism / Paul within Judaism" in 2014 and then took off as "Paul within Judaism" from 2015 onward. In 2023, the unit devoted a panel to "open questions and unresolved issues" related to the Paul within Judaism perspective and featured scholars affiliated with institutions in the United States, Canada, Germany, Norway, Sweden, and the United Kingdom (Scotland). At the same time, some have noted that the "Paul within Judaism" SBL group has also, despite its geographical reach, still been insular in the making of its panels in that conveners typically invite/accept presenters from an already established scholarly circle. For more on the Paul within Judaism approach, see, for example, Mark Nanos, "Paul and Judaism: Why Not Paul's Judaism?," in *Paul Unbound: Other Perspectives on the Apostle*, ed. Mark D. Given (Hendrickson, 2010), 117–160; Mark Nanos, "A Jewish View," in *Four Views on the Apostle Paul*, ed. Michael F. Bird, Counterpoints: Bible and Theology (Zondervan, 2012), 159–193; Mark D. Nanos, *Reading Paul Within Judaism: Collected Essays of Mark D. Nanos, Vol. 1* (Wipf and Stock, 2017); Mark D. Nanos and Magnus Zetterholm, eds., *Paul Within Judaism: Restoring the First-Century Context to the Apostle* (Fortress Press, 2015); Magnus Zetterholm, "The Paul Within Judaism Perspective," in *Perspectives on Paul: Five Views*, ed. Scot McKnight and B. J. Oropeza (Baker Academic, 2020), chapter 4; Michael Bird, "An Introduction to the Paul Within Judaism Debate," in *Paul Within Judaism: Perspectives on Paul and Jewish Identity*, ed. Michael Bird et al. (Mohr Siebeck, 2023), 1–28.

"Within Judaism" as a category of analysis has also been applied to New Testament texts beyond Paul's and has received some pushback. Adele Reinhartz, for example, has recently argued that a "within Judaism" framework does not necessarily lead to new insights (this can even be thought of in relation to the Gager quote in the next footnote). To study the Jewishness of the New Testament or the relationship between Jews and the New Testament, she asserts, does not require this specific, and often flattening, category of classification (flattening in the sense that it can oversimplify the New Testament and even bifurcate Jewishness from other classifications). I have pushbacks to the "within Judaism" movement too, at least when it comes to reading non-Pauline New Testament texts. In brief, while a "within Judaism" approach in Paul studies responds to categories *already set* in Paul studies (i.e., Old Perspective/New Perspective/Radical New Perspective), these categories do not exist in other areas of New Testament studies. In short, I think a "within Judaism" approach is useful when it can help counter other frameworks or categories. To add a "within Judaism" approach to non-Pauline texts, however, could create frameworks that are not needed. It could, in fact,

by New Testament scholars Marc Nanos and Magnus Zetterholm, it tasks interpreters to analyze Paul's writings *within* ancient Judaism, not against it.[134] This means taking seriously the theologies of other ancient Jewish writings and recognizing Paul's as conversing with them. This includes Pauline verses that centralize a gentile Christ-following populace. In other words, even when Paul urges gentiles to stay gentile, the Paul within Judaism approach urges readers to consider Paul as a Jewish teacher trying to bring about the eschatological inclusion of the gentiles, as opposed to as a Christian teacher with some uniquely non-Jewish concern for gentiles.

This may sound familiar. For many thinkers, a Paul within Judaism approach is the newer term for the Radical New Perspective.[135] Whereas scholars such as Gaston, Gager, and Stowers, for example, may have previously been categorized under the heading of the Radical New Perspective, many now understand them as Paul within Judaism thinkers. For others, however, the Paul within Judaism school is its own variant.[136] Certainly, the Paul within Judaism approach is informed by previous perspectives, regardless of how distinct one views it to be. I tend to understand it as a more expansive version of

even backfire by creating "without Judaism" categories akin to the Old and traditional New Perspective. See Adele Reinhartz's presentation in the section, "What Are the Implications of the Within Judaism Perspective for the Study of the New Testament? And What are the Implications of the Study of the New Testament for the Within Judaism Perspective?," at The New Testament Within Judaism conference, The Enoch Seminar, January 7, 2025, https://enochseminar.org/ntwithinjud/.

134. Although see also the earlier work of Gager, *The Origins of Anti-Semitism*, 113. Here he writes, "The very earliest groups of those who confessed Jesus as the Christ (Messiah) are now generally seen and studied as religious movements *within* Judaism" (emphasis in the original). Gager is not necessarily naming or creating a "within Judaism" framework, but his thinking showcases how the eventual "within Judaism" school was shaped by preceding conversations. It also showcases the malleability of these frameworks. Gager may indeed identify his *Sonderweg* reading as part of what has now been named a "within Judaism" approach. And others still might draw the line differently, contending that non–Paul within Judaism scholars hold that Paul ceased to keep Jewish law (which includes Gaston and Gager!), whereas Paul within Judaism scholars maintain otherwise.

135. Magnus Zetterholm, "Paul Within Judaism: The State of the Questions," in *Paul Within Judaism: Restoring the First-Century Context to the Apostle*, ed. Mark D. Nanos and Magnus Zetterholm (Fortress Press, 2015), 34.

136. For example, one may still refer to Eisenbaum's work as "radical," given her own evocations of the term. See *Paul Was Not a Christian*, 250.

the Radical New Perspective in that it leaves room, at least on my reading, for more pushback to the Bible benevolence project than other schools. Of course, this is not an entirely fair assessment; if we were to still use the terminology of Radical New Perspective to describe the developing views of a Jewish Paul talking to gentile audiences, then it would have likely grown to include these more expansive ventures, too.

Regardless of how one makes sense of the Radical New Perspective in relation to Paul within Judaism, the fact of the matter remains that ancient Judaism was complex, and proponents of the Paul within Judaism perspective affirm that interpreters must understand Paul from within that complexity. This includes recognizing the parts of Paul's Jewish theology that *were* nationalistic and ethnocentric. Matthew Thiessen, for example, argues against traditional aspects of the "good" Paul model by studying Paul's views about gentiles from within Judaism. In doing so, he in fact claims that Paul was never "above" particularity or ethnocentrism. Paul, he says, *was* ethnocentric: "Paul's own thinking was stressing, for instance, that the gospel was for the Jew first, and then for the Greek (e.g., Rom 1:16). *Even something as basic as Paul's frequent use of the term 'gentile' to refer to all non-Jews demonstrates the ethnocentric nature of this thought*—dissolving all non-Jewish ethnicities and cultures into one catch-all-word."[137] Thiessen thus starts with a different premise by arguing that Paul *is* particularistic in his focus on the Israelite God via the particularly ethnic Jewish Jesus, regardless of whether Paul is talking about how to follow Jesus as a Jew or a gentile.[138] For Thiessen, all are eventually saved—that is, both Jews and gentiles—but all are saved in the *particular* Christ.[139]

Not everyone has taken this route, however. The Paul within Judaism approach is filled with diversity, and some proponents rely on it to *maintain* a Bible-benevolent view. For example, Michael Bird writes in his introduction to the Paul within Judaism framework that the approach necessitates "avoiding the anachronism of thinking of Paul as a 'Christian' theologian, stripping away caricatures of Judaism as a 'religion' of 'legalism' or 'ethnocentrism,' undermining the presupposition that sets Paul's discourse against Jews

137. Thiessen, *Paul and the Gentile Problem*, 7; emphasis mine.

138. See also chapter 4, page 182 and accompanying footnote 91.

139. A Christ who, on the topic of particulars, is a Jewish male, just like Paul. For more on this, see chapter 4.

and Judaism, and exposing anti-Jewish perspectives in Pauline scholarship."[140] For some, in other words, the Paul within Judaism project assumes Paul *is* a "good" anti-ethnocentrist and that his anti-ethnocentrism stems from his own "good" Judaism.

Many also rely on the Paul within Judaism approach to make "good"—or at least make better—Jewish-Christian relations. This isn't limited to the work of Christian scholars, either. Mark Nanos, in fact, a forerunner of the approach and, like Eisenbaum, a Jewish scholar of the New Testament, introduces his understanding of the method as follows:

> [A Paul within Judaism approach] involves investigating ways to read Paul's letters "within Judaism" during the mid-first century, an effort I share with others involved in exploring this way to re-conceptualize how to interpret Paul. Together, we strive for historical probability within the New Testament discipline of exegesis. At the same time, this project is especially appealing because the historical reading proposed appears (to me, at least) to hold special promise for advancing better Christian-Jewish relations in the years to come. "I am not ashamed" to express that these two interrelated "interests" drive my research and communication objectives.[141]

Such interrelated interests continue to drive the work of much post-Holocaust biblical scholarship. Early Judaism scholar Gabriele Boccaccini, for example, has recently relied on the Paul within Judaism approach to say that Paul was so anti-ethnocentric that he promoted *three* paths to salvation: righteous Jews through Torah, righteous gentiles through natural law (what Boccaccini describes as "universal unwritten law" or "wisdom"), and sinning Jews and gentiles through Christ.[142] According to Boccaccini, in other words, the answer is *Sonderweg*+. For Paul, *everyone* gets a chance, regardless of their ethnic standing. Boccaccini also maintains that Paul was speaking to both

140. Bird, "An Introduction to the Paul Within Judaism Debate," 3.

141. This is from his personal and public-facing website, https://marknanos.com/about/.

142. Gabriele Boccaccini, *Paul's Three Paths to Salvation* (Eerdmans, 2020), 108, 162. He, in conversation with Romans 5:13–14 ("there is no law . . . from Adam to Moses"), does not see the gentile law as the Noahide laws, but rather as a natural knowing through divine nature / what God has made (he gathers this latter conclusion from Romans 1:20 and his understanding of Hellenistic Judaism). Boccaccini, *Paul's Three Paths to Salvation*, 108.

Jews and gentiles, even if his primary audience was the latter. Relying also on Romans 2:6, in which Paul says that God "will repay according to each one's deeds," Boccaccini concludes that works remain important for everyone; all humans will be judged by their deeds.[143] To put it otherwise, "Everyone is under the power of grace, but not all will be saved."[144] Because of evil's hold in the world, many will still sin, even if they follow God's gifts of Torah and natural law. Christ thus offers a third path to eschatological glory. For Jewish and gentile sinners alike—the ones who cannot maintain righteousness through Torah or good consciousness—Christ is there to offer forgiveness and eschatological acceptance in the final days for those who believe in his glory and repent of their wrongdoings. "Only the unrepentant," he concludes, will be condemned.[145]

Interestingly, despite Boccaccini wanting his theology to better Jewish-Christian relations today, I suspect many Christians, if they were to follow Boccaccini's theory, would continue to hand out Bibles with the assumption that most people, including Jews with the Torah, are still sinning and thus need Christ as their way to salvation.[146] Boccaccini's theory is also still tied to ethnic thinking, even if it is not hierarchically imagined. Righteous Jews, an *ethnos*, are to act one way, and righteous gentiles, another *ethnos*, are to act another way. Perhaps the sinners can even become a distinct ethnic community in Christ, too.

Where We've Been and Where We're Going

If you are new to Paul studies and your head is spinning with interpretative possibility, *welcome*. If you are having trouble distinguishing certain arguments from others, you are not alone. In academia, there is a running joke that to fill a "gap" in scholarship is to fill a space the size of a grain of rice. Scholarship

143. Boccaccini is also in conversation with Sanders, who similarly argues that works remain integral to Paul's doctrine. Sanders, *Paul and Palestinian Judaism*, 517. He is also in conversation with Kent L. Yinger, who writes that works "will not so much determine as reveal one's character and status as righteous or wicked." Yinger, *Paul, Judaism, and Judgment According to Deeds* (Cambridge University Press, 1999), 16.

144. Boccaccini, *Paul's Three Paths to Salvation*, 116.

145. Boccaccini, *Paul's Three Paths to Salvation*, 160.

146. Boccaccini, *Paul's Three Paths to Salvation*, 161.

is informed by other scholarship, and it can be difficult to navigate who is in conversation with whom, who differs from whom, or what is new or nuanced within a particular school of thought.

The approaches covered thus far have been the Old Perspective, New Perspective, Radical New Perspective, *Sonderweg* model, and the Paul within Judaism approach. Based on my reconstruction (and again, there are other reconstructions!), the Old Perspective claims that Paul converted from Judaism to Christianity in his belief in Jesus as the Christ and was anti-ethnocentric. The New Perspective claims that Paul became a rare "good" Jew in his belief in Jesus and was anti-ethnocentric. The Radical New Perspective, *Sonderweg* model, and Paul within Judaism schools each see Paul as a Jew among gentiles. While the *Sonderweg* model sees gentiles as the only ones in need of saving, the Paul within Judaism approach leaves room—at least in some cases—for a particularistic ethnocentric Paul.

In the next chapter, I offer my own analysis of Paul in conversation with ongoing scholarly insights. While my overall argument is informed by each school of thought, it is grounded most acutely in a Paul within Judaism variant, albeit without a "let's save Paul" mentality. My thesis is that Paul—*as a Jew*—was a hierarchical, exclusivist, and ethnonationalist thinker. Jews and gentiles who did not fall in line were left behind from his Israel-centered end of days. Jews and gentiles who did were not valued equally.

CHAPTER FOUR

An Average Jew

From a methodological point of view, the Christian ideological perspectives that continue to characterize much of the ostensibly historical work done in New Testament studies is problematic.

—Magnus Zetterholm[1]

If the Church wants to clear itself of the anti-Jewish trends built into its teaching, a few marginal correctives will not do. It must examine the very center of its proclamation and reinterpret the meaning of the gospel of our times. Is such a reinterpretation possible?

—Gregory Baum[2]

Back to Paul and Paul's Letters

Paul's first known letter was written to a community in Thessaloniki, a Greek port city off the Aegean Sea. In it, Paul shared his belief that Jesus died, was raised, and would return to earth in order to inaugurate the end of days. Paul's apocalyptic eschatology here is direct. Christ-followers are suffering but will be rewarded soon:

> We . . . told you beforehand that we were to suffer persecution . . . [But] the Lord himself, with a cry of command, with the archangel's

1. Zetterholm, "Paul Within Judaism: The State of the Questions," 32 and reasserted on 42. Reading this quote was akin to rereading Stendahl for me. I am grateful for Zetterholm's scholarship and allyship when it comes to naming the remaining Christian-centrism of biblical studies.

2. Baum, "Introduction," 6.

> call and with the sound of God's trumpet, will descend from heaven, and the dead in Christ will rise first. Then we who are alive, who are left, will be caught up in the clouds together with them to meet the Lord in the air, and we will be with the Lord forever. (1 Thess 3:1–4; 4:13–18)

First Thessalonians sets Paul up as a fundamentally Jewish thinker. He, like many fellow Jews of the late centuries BCE and into the early centuries CE, thought apocalyptically, eschatologically, and soteriologically—which is to say, he thought about good and evil and about how such forces would be overcome by God and God's subordinates. Like other Jewish thinkers, he also thought that only the righteous would be saved in the end-times. For Paul, the righteous constituted not the many but the few: proper Jewish and proper gentile believers in Jesus as the messiah.

All this was typical of a first-century Jew.[3] It was also steeped in typical ethnonationalist orientations. I must add, however, that when I say "typical" or "average" here, what I really mean is "typical" or "average" based on the literary evidence we have available to us. As early Judaism scholar Shayna Sheinfeld has importantly noted, it is only "with a superficial reading" of the ancient sources that one can "walk away with the impression that all Jews awaited a Messiah."[4] It is much more likely, she adds, that many Jews "lived their lives without much thought to these topics."[5] In other words, when taking into account the *many Jews* who did not have the ability to write or dictate their own worldviews, it is possible that ideas of messianism and eschatology were more peripheral. Implementing a "Paul within Judaism" approach thus means recognizing our limited perspective: We simply do not have enough evidence to have a full understanding of what "within Judaism" meant for most people. Indeed, as biblical scholar Matthew Novenson rhetorically probes, "What evidence do we modern historians have for the

3. Cf., for example, Michael F. Bird, *An Anomalous Jew: Paul Among Jews, Greeks, and Romans* (Eerdmans, 2016); Boyarin, *A Radical Jew.*

4. Shayna Sheinfeld, "Messianism," in *End of Days: An Encyclopedia of the Apocalypse in World Religions*, ed. Wendell G. Johnson (Bloomsbury USA, 2017), 236.

5. Sheinfeld, "Messianism," 236.

messianism of the ancient ninety-nine percent?"[6] In short, while my thesis here is that Paul from a "within Judaism" approach is *not* exceptional or radical but rather typical, it must be clear that this thesis works only within the bounds of the material available to us. Paul, *based on the limited sources*, was an average Jew who left behind non-Christ-confessing Others in his understanding of the end of days. All explanations below must be taken with this understanding of limits in mind.

An Average Jewish Context

Judaism in the ancient world, much like Judaism today, was not a singularity. There were too many differing ideas for us to arrive at a uniformed conception of ancient Jewish belief or practice. While many scholars envision Jews as constructing a sense of collective self in and around the Jewish God, Temple, and Torah (i.e., the God of Israel, the Temple in Jerusalem, and sacred texts and practices), the ancient sources also point to numerous subgroups or "sects" developing with nuanced views of this tripart system.[7] Pharisees, Sadducees,

6. Matthew V. Novenson, *The Grammar of Messianism: An Ancient Jewish Political Idiom and Its Users* (Oxford University Press, 2017), 20.

7. This "tripart" system comes from Seth Schwartz, *Imperialism and Jewish Society: 200 BCE to 640 CE* (Princeton University Press, 2001), 8–10, 49–74, 91–92. But even this could be nuanced further. For example, we don't generally know what Paul or Josephus or Philo (or 4 Ezra, etc.) meant when they talk about the law/Torah, and when they do specify, they do not agree. See Shayna Sheinfeld, "From Nomos to Logos: Torah in First-Century Jewish Texts," in *The Message of Paul the Apostle Within Second Temple Judaism*, ed. František Ábel (Lexington Books/Fortress Academic, 2020). On the definition of "sects," I follow Cohen's understanding of "sect" in a neutral sense. In his words, "The English words 'sect' or 'heresy' usually convey a negative meaning . . . In their original usage, however, the Latin word *secta* and its equivalent Greek word, *hairesis*, lacked any negative connotation and were neutral terms for 'school' (a group of people) or 'school of thought' (a group of ideas)." Cohen, in other words, values the original meaning of these terms. He adds, however, that when he sees a sect combat other groups in the ancient literature (e.g., the Halakhic Letter and *Pesher Habakkuk*), the sect can be rendered "a small, organized group that separates itself from the larger religious body and asserts that it alone embodies the ideals of the larger group because it alone understands God's will." Even when reading these texts—that is, the Halakhic Letter and *Pesher Habakkuk*—I maintain a neutral understanding of "sect" or "school of thought." In my view, "normative" Judaism was multifarious Judaism. Leadership or privilege does not negate that for me (e.g., if someone or someones in Temple leadership value one perspective, that doesn't make that perspective more "normative"). See also Shaye J. D. Cohen, *From the Maccabees to the Mishnah*, 3rd ed. (Westminster John Knox, 2014), 124. I explain my

Essenes, and Zealots are some of the most noted ancient Jewish groups, but there were likely many more. It is also possible that many Jews did not identify with any of them.

Ancient Jews also interacted with non-Jews, otherwise known as "nations" or "gentiles" by most Jewish authors. Archaeological evidence points to acculturation if not collaboration between these groups. Some gentiles, in fact, were so intrigued by Jewish rite and ritual that they, in addition to maintaining connection with their own deities, frequented Jewish worship spaces. Sometimes called "Godfearers," these gentiles were engaged in Jewish thought and practice without having to profess full ideological or ritual commitment. In other words, they did not need to convert to Judaism (although some did) in order to take part in aspects of Jewish culture.[8] The same can be said in the reverse. As much as Jews were rendered collectively inferior by the broader Greco-Roman world, many Jews still participated in civic life—which is to say Hellenistic life—received Hellenistic education, and funded Hellenistic cultural spaces.

Hellenization was so pervasive, in fact, that many scholars contend that all Judaism in the Greco-Roman period is Hellenistic Judaism, regardless of whether one's community attempted to draw strong borders over and against Hellenization.[9] Greek language and Greek philosophy seeped into the minds of the common folk, so much so that Jews eventually wrote their sacred texts in Greek and at times connected their own worldviews to those of the Greek

understanding also in Emanuel, *Humor, Resistance, and Jewish Cultural Persistence in the Book of Revelation*, 4, footnote 9; and 27, footnote 20.

8. It is a contested position that "Godfearers" had a stable and specific meaning, however. As Ross Kraemer has argued, sometimes the term simply seems to mean "pious," and the specifics of that piety then depend on what the writer in question would have in mind for a gentile. In other words, the term on its own, according to Kraemer, need not be affiliated with Jewish association specifically (although it *can* be, depending on the writer and context). See Ross Kraemer, "Giving up the Godfearers," *Journal of Ancient Judaism* 5 (2014): 61–87. For an engagement with Kraemer's thesis—one that concludes that, despite the ambiguities, "Godfearer" remains a usable term for gentiles with interest in Jewish ethnic/cultic practices—see Paula Fredriksen, "'If It Looks like a Duck, and It Quacks like a Duck . . .': On Not Giving Up the Godfearer," in *A Most Reliable Witness: Essays in Honor of Ross Shepard Kraemer*, ed. Susan Ashbrook Harvey et al. (Brown Judaic Studies, 2015), 25–33.

9. See Schwartz, *Imperialism and Jewish Society*, 12. As he puts it, "Hellenization was so pervasive and fundamental that it has little utility as an analytical category."

philosophical tradition.[10] Plato in particular was influential in this regard. Middle Platonism posited a hierarchical divine realm, with the ultimate One at the pinnacle, followed by gradations of being, including daemons and lower-level gods. The God of Israel was the ultimate One for first-century Jews, followed by that God's divine helpers (e.g., angels and possibly divine-like messiahs).[11] This heavenly mapping, generally speaking, was a concept gentiles could understand, and with which they could converse. The Jewish Temple in Jerusalem even had a courtyard reserved for gentile participation, mirroring what first-century historian Josephus calls access for "all nations" (*Antiq* 8:116–117). Of course, even Josephus knew that access for "all" has its qualifications. Admission was tiered and conditional, with purity requirements governing entry into each area of the Temple, including the outer gentile court (*Against Apion* 2:103). Still, the fact that certain gentiles were admitted into the outer courtyard—even when, for example, menstruating Jewish women were not—underscores the potential and even support for cross-cultural exchange.

This is not to say that everyone got along. Diversity existed within such cultural give-and-takes. Jews, for example, were mocked regularly by the wider culture for their "odd" ways of honoring their God. This included but was not limited to the Jewish practice of circumcision, dietary restrictions, resting on the Sabbath, and the prohibition on statues of the Jewish God—even in the Temple.[12]

Diversity also existed within Judaism and had the habit of spinning into harsh debate. The apocryphal *Psalms of Solomon*, a collection of eighteen psalms written by different Jewish authors around the first century BCE,

10. The Septuagint is the earliest Greek translation of the Hebrew Bible, beginning in the third century BCE.

11. For nuances on the idea of ancient Jewish monotheism, see, for example, Daniel Boyarin, *Border Lines: The Partition of Judaeo-Christianity* (University of Pennsylvania Press, 2004), chapter 4; Emanuel, *Humor, Resistance, and Jewish Cultural Persistence in the Book of Revelation*, 29–30; Paula Fredriksen, "Philo, Herod, Paul, and the Many Gods of Ancient Jewish 'Monotheism,'" *Harvard Theological Review* 115, no. 1 (2022): 23–45. For more on Middle Platonism and Hellenistic Judaism, including Platonist relations to Paul, see Young, "So Radically Jewish That He's an Evangelical Christian."

12. For a more recent exposition of mockery of circumcision, see Michael Peppard, "Bearing a 'Jewish Weight': A New Interpretation of a Greek Comedic Papyrus About Athletics (CPJ 3.519)," *Journal for Interdisciplinary Biblical Studies* 5, no. 2 (2024): 21–41.

illustrates just one example of how Jews in antiquity disagreed with each other. Antagonizing the Jerusalem leaders, the psalmists write:

> And the daughters of Jerusalem were profane according to your judgment, because they had defiled themselves with a confusion of mingling. I am troubled in my entrails and my inward parts over these things . . . I will justify you, O God, in uprightness of heart, for in your judgements is your righteousness, O God. For you have repaid the sinners according to their works, and according to their sins, which were very wicked. You have exposed their sins, that your judgment might be evident; you have wiped out their memorial from the earth. (Ps 2:13–17)

Texts from the Dead Sea Scrolls also provide insight into the kinds of intra-Jewish debates taking place around Paul's time. Qumran's *Pesher Habakkuk* (1QpHab),[13] for example, also a first-century BCE text, targets figures known as the "Wicked Priest" and the "Liar," whom scholars believe represented Jewish leaders in Jerusalem.[14] According to the (Jewish) pesherist, his Jewish enemies have "buil[t] a city in blood" and wronged the virtuous, among them being his own leader, the "Teacher of Righteousness." Not much is known about this teacher, but the pesherist believed he received divine revelation from the Israelite God, unlike his enemies. The pesherist even leans into the same "mystery" language that Paul does in Romans to explain this: His teacher is the "one whom God made known all the mysteries of the words of

13. *Pesher Habakkuk* (or *Habakkuk Pesher*) is a first-century BCE commentary on the Hebrew Bible's prophecy of Habakkuk. The pesherist provides commentary and interpretation (*pesher* means "interpretation") by providing quotes from the prophetic source material of Habakkuk and then commenting on those quotes. None of the Qumran sources has original titles. Like other Qumran sources, *Pesher Habakkuk* is abbreviated as "1QpHab," with the "1" and the "Q" having to do with the cave in which it was found (cave 1 at Qumran).

14. By "wronging the righteous," most scholars believe the pesherist saw the Jerusalem leaders as taking unjust possession of the high priesthood in the Temple. John J. Collins, *The Apocalyptic Imagination: An Introduction to Jewish Apocalyptic Literature*, 3rd ed. (Eerdmans, 2016), 185–186. For more on this text, see also Timothy H. Lim, *The Earliest Commentary on the Prophecy of Habakkuk* (Oxford University Press, 2020). There are also scholars who contend that the Wicked Priest and the Liar are two names for the same figure.

his servants the prophets" (1QpHab 7:5).[15] This includes the mysteries of the end-times. As the pesherist continues, "There shall be yet another vision concerning the appointed time. It shall tell of the end and shall not lie" (1QpHab 7:6; Hab 2:3). The fortitude of the Teacher is contrasted with the Wicked Priest and his allies; they are the ones who "shall double their guilt upon themselves" (1QpHab7:15).[16]

The *Halakhic Letter* (4QMMT) from Qumran, a text that discusses various points of Jewish practice, also demonstrates intra-Jewish hostility.[17] Like Paul, its author relies on terminology like "things of instruction" or "things of the law" to discuss proper Jewish action.[18] Its author also maintains that only those who acted properly—properly, that is, from his perspective—were granted access to the end-times.[19] While the letter's "you will be left behind" warnings may not be as harsh as the pesherist's, they are certainly polemical. After listing what he considers to be proper Jewish purity, the author writes: "Understand these (matters) and ask him to straighten your counsel and put you far away from thoughts of evil and the counsel of Belial. Consequently, you will rejoice at the end of time when you discover that some of our sayings are true. And it will be reckoned for you as righteousness when you perform what is right and good before him, for your own good and for that of Israel" (C 28–30).[20] Jews who obey are "in." Jews who do not are "out."[21]

---

15. See also Qumran's and Cairo Geniza's *Damascus Document* for more on the Teacher of Righteousness.

16. See also 1QpHab 11:17–12:10; cf. Hab 2:17, 1:2, 5–6. See also Lim, *The Earliest Commentary on the Prophecy of Habakkuk*, 12.

17. Collins, *The Apocalyptic Imagination*, 64–65. See also Steven D. Fraade, "To Whom It May Concern: 4QMMT and Its Addressee(s)," *Revue de Qumran* 76 (2000): 507–526, which argues that 4QMMT attempts to induct initiates into its own contested views, including making its teachers' enemies inductees' enemies.

18. The terminology used is *Ma-ase ha-torah*, which Paul writes as "works of the law" or "convention" (*erga nomou*) in Greek.

19. C 13–15, C 25–32.

20. See Geza Vermes, trans., *The Complete Dead Sea Scrolls in English* (Penguin Books, 2011), 229.

21. The relationship between the Dead Sea Scrolls and biblical studies is certainly an interesting one. The fact that the sources were discovered just after the war only adds to the drama. Readers must remember that, while the majority of mid-twentieth-century biblical scholars

All of this is to say: It was *typical* of Jews to debate with one another about Jewish belief, practice, and politics.[22] And it was *typical* of Jews to Other, ostracize, and oppose other Jews. Just as gentile Christ-followers relied on rhetorical antagonism so as to Other those with whom they disagreed (recall Marcion), so, too, did Jews from *within* Judaism. Reading Paul from a "within Judaism" perspective thus means recognizing the kinds of intra-Jewish debate and rhetorical punches that existed within it. When Paul writes in 1 Thessalonians that Jews are displeasers and opposers to everyone (2:15), one does not necessarily have to interpret it as a post-Pauline antisemitic interpolation; it is possible that Paul's words here illustrate his polemic against competing Jews.[23]

---

were still making sense of Paul as a separatist from Judaism, they were on their way to wanting alternative views. How great would it be, some scholars wondered, if we could conclude that, instead of overturning the entirety of Judaism, thinkers like Paul were simply debating from *within* Judaism? The texts at Qumran helped make this wish come true. The sources pushed scholars to take more seriously the use of slander *by Jews against Jews* as a method of persuasion and rhetorical takedown in the ancient world. I do find it intriguing, however, that it took the discovery of the scrolls to better attend to anti-Jewish polemic. The Bible itself, paired with numerous noncanonical sources, already showcased the diversity of thought among ancient Jews. As Hebrew Bible scholar Cynthia Chapman has so succinctly remarked, "Within the biblical text itself, we see an ongoing conversation and negotiation of truth that is contentious." Thus, perhaps once again, it was the broader cultural structures of the late twentieth century that shaped how scholars viewed the sources. See "Liberationist Hermeneutics: Interview with Cynthia Chapman and Traci West [podcast episode]," *Feminists Talk Religion*, season 1, episode 3, April 10, 2020, Feminist Studies in Religion.

22. For more examples, especially when it came to Jewish law, see Cohen, *From the Maccabees to the Mishnah*, chapter 5.

23. The primary difficulty about this polemical passage is that Paul here also accuses "the Jews" (2:14) of killing Jesus, which he pairs with the accusation that "the Jews" kill their own prophets. Such internal charges, however, are not new to Jewish sources (see, e.g., Neh 9:26; Jer 26:20–23). Paul's insistence that Jews killed Jesus could indeed be a way of spotlighting Paul's distaste for *some* Jews, including some Temple elite. Given the fact that Jesus was killed by way of Roman crucifixion, however, despite the real possibility that *some* Temple elite assisted in handing Jesus to Roman officials, complicates this passage. That said, it is also possible that someone inserted these lines into the text as a way to promote an anti-Jewish Jesus movement and the anti-Jewish charge of deicide. That Paul here uses the infamous definite article—"*the* Jews"—gives it an uncomfortable Johannine flair, one that is not seen elsewhere in 1 Thessalonians. Still, given the reality of ancient intra-Jewish debate, including charges of killing or at the very least persecuting prophets (e.g., 2 Chron 36:16; Jer 20:1–2), it remains possible that the historical Paul wrote these lines. To assume that Paul didn't write them could also, writes Melanie Johnson-DeBaufre, "smac[k] of apologetic." For more on this conversation, see, for example, Abraham J. Malherbe, *The Letters to the Thessalonians: A*

His following comment about God's wrath being enacted upon these Jews (2:16) can also be read as mirroring the standard domino effect of ancient Jewish eschatological schemes wherein there is an imaged climactic period of sin or wickedness (even among God's own people), followed by God's wrath upon the wicked, followed by the final rescue of the righteous (e.g., the entire book of Revelation). Such harshness wasn't limited to Paul or other apocalyptic narratives, either. Even Josephus utilized rhetorical hardball in historical writings: "For Judas and Sadducus [two Jews] . . . filled our civil government with tumults at present, and laid the foundations of our future miseries, by this system of philosophy, which we before were unacquainted withal."[24] Or of Justus of Tiberias, a Jewish reviewer of Josephus's book *Jewish War*, Josephus attests he was "a charlatan and a demagogue and a deceiver" who was "full of 'knavish tricks,' 'fraudulent practice,' and impudence."[25]

As much as the discovery of the Dead Sea Scrolls demonstrated the use of the rhetorical punch among ancient Jews, it also revealed how common it was for Jews to think apocalyptically, eschatologically, and soteriologically.[26] It must be emphasized, however, that the Qumran sources were not the only ancient Jewish texts to reflect these imaginings. Instead, they aligned with the other Jewish texts that did. Most of the apocalyptic sources from Jewish antiquity, whether at Qumran or elsewhere, are not apocalypses by genre, but instead by theology. What I mean by this is that many of them are not texts of revelatory report—ones bestowed to a human being by a cosmic force like

New Translation with Introduction and Commentary (Yale University Press, 2007). Melanie Johnson-DeBaufre, "A Monument to Suffering: 1 Thessalonians 2: 14–6, Dangerous Memory, and Christian Identity," *Journal of Early Christian History* 1, no. 2 (2011): 94.

24. *Antiquities of the Jews* 18.1.

25. Cited as such in Johnson, "The New Testament's Anti-Jewish Slander and the Conventions of Ancient Polemic," 436. It is also important to note, however, that while Jews did indeed debate regularly *about* their God, Temple, and Torah—which included but were not limited to issues of theology, liturgy, and law—they nevertheless all cared about the answers. Ancient Jewish difference and debate was not a situation of fixed borders but instead of theological multiplicity with a shared goal of determining how best to practice Judaism. Even when one group "left behind" another group, they were all still understanding themselves as Jewish. See Emanuel, *Humor, Resistance, and Jewish Cultural Persistence in the Book of Revelation*, 28.

26. Among other things, of course. We have texts that are not apocalyptic in outlook or genre, too. But again, this is all based on the limited information we have. It is possible some Jews (many Jews?) did not consider these topics at all in their daily lives.

we see in the Hebrew Bible's book of Daniel or the New Testament's book of Revelation—but instead ones that uphold the broader apocalyptic themes of good versus evil and the hope of a future cosmic restoration.

While not all of the apocalyptic sources mention ideas of a messiah, many of them do. Many also connect ideas of soteriology with ones of ethnonationalism. Before turning to Paul specifically, below are some brief remarks to help make sense of these concepts.

Messianism

Messianism revolved around three themes: hope, fear, and ethnonationalism. In the face of suffering, many Jewish writers of the late Second Temple period hoped for a messiah—a term that translates in English to "anointed"—who would help establish and/or rule over a new and immutable Israel-centered kingdom.[27] The overall hope was that, in this messianic kingdom, the righteous would be delivered. The particulars beyond this hope, however, including who the messiah would be, when the messiah would arrive, and if or to what extent the messiah would be divine or human or both, differed depending on one's perspective.[28] Even the ideas of "righteous" and "deliverance" were contested. Authors influenced by messianic ideals thus worked to not only reassure implied readers that their understanding of the messiah was the "right" one—that if they continued to believe and act "rightly," they would be delivered in the end-times—but to also persuade others, sometimes by way of fear, to believe and act as the authors saw fit.[29]

27. While the kingdom itself was often imagined or inferred as immutable, the reign of its messianic figure may be temporary (e.g., 4 Ezra).

28. As Peter Schäfer put it, "It is tempting to view the various facets of the Messianic expectation as stages of a certain historical development, and I confess that I couldn't resist this temptation completely. However, I should like to re-emphasize that the different Messianic figures cannot be reduced to a uniform underlying pattern; they are to be described adequately only as the dynamic interaction of various and changing configurations within different historical constellations." Peter Schäfer, "Diversity and Interaction: Messiahs in Early Judaism," in *Toward the Millennium: Messianic Expectations from the Bible to Waco*, SHR 77, ed. Peter Schäfer and Mark R. Cohen (Brill, 1998), 35.

29. For an excellent study of messianism, see Novenson, *The Grammar of Messianism*. Here, Novenson studies messianism as a language game, and claims that what he calls "the grammar of messianism" constitutes "the rules of the game: The way messiah language worked for the

It is unclear when and where ideas of messianism originated, but some of the earliest hints of a messianic expectation—or at the very least a discursive reservoir for later ideas—come from the Hebrew Bible's prophetic books of Isaiah, Jeremiah, and Ezekiel.[30] Biblical prophets are generally understood by scholars as social commentators—those who saw pain in the world, spoke about that pain, attempted to express reason for that pain, and in some instances hoped for better futures. The types of social pains experienced by ancient Israelites and later Jews are vast. As biblical scholar David Carr puts it in his recent work on the Bible and trauma, "Suffering, and survival of it, was written into the Bible."[31] From the Assyrian onslaught in 722 BCE, to the Babylonian exile beginning in 597 BCE, to the Roman conquest of Judea in 63 BCE, ancient Israelites and later Jews fought repeatedly for cultural persistence, and often used narrative as a means of doing so.[32] In some of the more comforting chapters of the books of Isaiah and Jeremiah, for example, the authors imagine a reconciliation between God and the Israelite people after the Babylonian exile. They even imagine a restored Davidic line: "A shoot will spring from the stem of Jesse," Isaiah 11:1 proclaims. "From his roots a branch will bear fruit."[33] And in Jeremiah, the author writes, "The days are surely coming . . . when [the Lord] will raise up from David a righteous Branch, and he shall reign as king" (Jer 23:5). The book of Ezekiel also imagines a Davidic king or prince who will oversee a restored Israel: "I will take the Israelites out of the nations [diaspora and/or exile] where they have gone and will gather them

---

ancient authors who chose to use it, the discursive possibilities it opened up, as well as the discursive constraints it entailed." Novenson, *The Grammar of Messianism*, 14.

30. For more on the framing of discursive reservoir, or discursive resources, see Novenson, *The Grammar of Messianism*.

31. David M. Carr, *Holy Resilience: The Bible's Traumatic Origins* (Yale University Press, 2014), 4.

32. By narrating moments of suffering, apocalyptic writers gave voice to collective grief and in turn provided solace to readers in the face of pain. It also gave readers the hope that their God was still listening—still providing—at least for those who followed the same conception of righteousness a particular text did. Scholars typically refer to the apocalyptic ability to both narrate grief and console readers in it—and sometimes even distract them from their pain through visions of new worlds—as the "apocalyptic cure." Collins, *The Apocalyptic Imagination*, 250.

33. Some date this verse, along with the larger poem of which it is a part (Isa 11:1–9), to an earlier period.

from every quarter and bring them to their own land . . . My servant David shall be king over them" (Ezek 37:21–28; 40–48).[34] It is less likely these texts intended to convey a David-centered messianic hope as opposed to a desire for the continuation of an idealized past of Davidic rule, but they were certainly read through the lens of messianism by Jewish readers in Paul's own time.[35]

The book of Daniel was read especially through the lens of later messianism and, given its second-century BCE codification, may have already been relaying some kind of messianic hope. Instead of associating with King David, however, its messianic figure is connected with the divine realm: He is "one like a Son of Man," and is given authority by the "Ancient of Days" (i.e., the high God/God of Israel) to rule over a new world order.[36] A variety of Jewish writings from the Roman period, and thus the general time of Paul, adapted Daniel 7's "one like a son of man" precisely in an active messianic manner, even if they didn't use that specific terminology (e.g., 4 Ezra, the Parables of Enoch, Paul, Mark/Matthew, and Revelation).[37] Interestingly, while the Son of Man is more of a passive figure in Daniel 7—he doesn't do much within the narrative; instead, the high God vindicates him and gives judgment for him—these later adaptations of Daniel 7 transform the figure into an active warrior and/or judge. Not much else is said about this being in Daniel, but many interpreters understand him to be a divine subordinate, perhaps even the angel Michael, who is given glory and dominion of the eschaton by the high God.[38]

---

34. Outside of the prophetic texts, see, for example, 2 Samuel 7:11–16.

35. David was king of the unified Israelite monarchy in the tenth century BCE, and many Jews in the later centuries imagined the messiah as being connected to him in some way.

36. Rather than adhering to modern conceptions of sons of men or even other contemporaneous understandings—that is, sons of human males—Daniel's Son of Man arrives with the clouds of heaven and sits on the right-hand side of God in the heavenly realm. Cf., for example, Genesis 11:5; Deuteronomy 32:8; Ezekiel 2:1.

37. The book of Enoch is an ancient Jewish apocalyptic text with sections written at different times. The parables are found in 1 Enoch 37–41 and are likely dated to ca. 100 BCE. Though he's mostly focused on 4 Ezra and the Parables of Enoch, see the following for more on how Jewish writings around Paul's time were similarly invoking Daniel 7. John J. Collins, "The Son of Man in First-Century Judaism," *New Testament Studies* 38 (1992): 448–466.

38. See Daniel 7–12. The angel Michael also appears as a messianic figure in Qumran's *War Scroll*. For more on how Daniel's one like a Son of Man is a subordinate divine figure,

Another example comes from the second- to first-century BCE *Psalms of Solomon*. Like Isaiah, Jeremiah, and Ezekiel, the text anticipates a Davidic ruler who will usher in the righteous for the world to come. This ruler also has divine-like qualities. He is described as "pure of sin"—that is, *above* human imperfection—and we are told his divine-like gifts will enable him to uphold everlasting justice in the new age.[39] An even greater variety of messiahs are seen in the Dead Sea Scrolls. The author of what is known as *The Pierced Messiah* (4Q285), for example, imagines a future military leader called the "Prince of the Congregation," who leads in battle against the *kittim*, the author's Roman enemies.[40] He is again understood as a Davidic ruler—a "shoot from the stump of Jesse"—who builds on King David's earlier military conquests. Another human-like messiah comes from Qumran's *Messianic Apocalypse* (4Q521), but this one is not described as Davidic. Of this leader, the author writes:

> [. . . For the hea]vens and the earth shall listen to his messiah . . . For he will honor the pious upon the th[ro]ne of eternal kingdom, setting prisoners free, opening the eyes of the blind, straightening out those who are bent . . . and the Lord shall do glorious things which have not been done, just as he sa[id]. For he shall heal the terminally ill, he shall

---

specifically the high "angel" over Israel, see John J. Collins, "The Son of Man and the Saints of the Most High in the Book of Daniel," *Journal of Biblical Literature* 93 (1974): 50–66.

39. Kenneth Atkinson, "Enduring the Lord's Discipline: Soteriology in the Psalms of Solomon," in *This World and the World to Come*, ed. Daniel M. Gurtner (T&T Clark, 2013), 160.

40. Some scholars think that the fragmentary texts of 4Q285 and 11Q14 (found with *The Pierced Messiah*) are conclusions to the *War Scroll* (1QM), which also has Michael (a.k.a. "The Prince of Light") appearing as a messianic figure. The pierced messiah's Prince is mentioned in other sources from Qumran, including the *Scroll of Blessings* (1QSb), in which the following blessing is bestowed upon the Prince: "He may establish the kingdom of his people forever." It should be noted, though, that the pierced messiah fragment could be translated differently; it is possible that rather than saying the Prince will kill, it could be read as the Prince *being* killed. This alternative reading could turn upside down the triumphant one posed in the prose above. It could also be read in tandem with ideas of Jesus as a pierced messiah. Most scholars read with the former (triumphant) possibility. See Collins, *The Apocalyptic Imagination*, 197, 205. See also Martin G. Abegg, "Messianic Hope and 4Q285: A Reassessment," *Journal of Biblical Literature* 113, no. 1 (1994): 81–91.

> revive the dead, he shall send good news to the poor/downtrodden, he shall [ ], guide the uprooted, he shall make the hungry rich.[41]

Many scholars connect this messiah to a prophetic-type figure, perhaps even Elijah from the Hebrew Bible, who, in 1 Kings 17:17–24, helped revive a child back to life and, in Malachi 4:5–6, is promised by God to be sent ahead of the end-times. Even though human, this messiah seems to have contact with and assistance from the divine realm.

Other texts allude to the belief in multiple messiahs: one from the line of David who functions as a restored king, and another from the line of Aaron who functions as a restored priest. In the *Community Rule* from Qumran (1QS), members are told to abide by the *Rule's* guidelines "until there shall come the prophet and the messiahs of Aaron and Israel."[42] The *Damascus Document*, a rule book found at both Qumran and in the Cairo Geniza, also references these two messiahs.[43] And *Jubilees*, a work canonical within the Ethiopic Tewahedo Church but apocryphal to Jews and most Christians (with many copies found at Qumran), imagines the same. While the role of the Davidic messiah, generally speaking, was to usher in the end of days and serve as king of the new community, the Aaronite priest was to perform sacrifices, teach the community, and even serve as a "check" on full Davidic authority. Some writers even depicted the Aaronite priest as having more authority than the Davidic king once the new age started.[44] The only constant, it seems, was imagining the messiah(s) as Jewish males.

Messianism as It Relates to Apocalypticism, Resurrection, and Eschatology

As discussed, apocalypticism is a theological framework that refers to the ways ancient Jews made sense of good and evil. In many of the ancient apocalyptic

41. Cited in Menahem Kister, "The Dead Sea Scrolls," in *The Jewish Annotated New Testament*, 2nd ed., ed. Amy-Jill Levine and Marc Z. Brettler (Oxford University Press, 2017), 712.

42. 1QS 9:11. A number of fragments of this document with variants were also found at Qumran in caves 4 and 5.

43. The Cairo Geniza is a library of Jewish texts and documents from the Fatimid administration that were kept in a storeroom in Cairo, Egypt.

44. See, for example, John J. Collins, "'He Shall Not Judge by What His Eyes See': Messianic Authority in the Dead Sea Scrolls," *Dead Sea Discoveries: A Journal of Current Research on the Scrolls and Related Literature* 2, no. 2 (1995): 145–164. From Qumran, see also 4Q541.

writings, authors envisioned an overthrowing of global evil, often, although not always, with the help of a messiah, followed by the inauguration of a new world order, otherwise known as the "eschaton." While these texts sometimes differed on when the eschaton would appear, where it would be located, and who would be included in it, many instilled a sense of hope in implied readers (or fear, on the flip side, if one was not operating in the way a particular text demanded). By the late centuries BCE and early centuries CE, hopes of an immutable end of days paired with hopes of a messiah ushering it in were widespread. For some, resurrection was a part of this.[45] The general idea was that, in the end-times, the righteous deceased would be raised from the dead and welcomed into the new world order.

This idea likely started as a metaphor. Already in the books of Isaiah and Ezekiel, the authors included images of deceased Israelites being revived at the start of a new God-centered age.[46] In both sources, the Babylonian enemies do not rise from the dead, but the righteous Israelites do. Here is a verse from Isaiah:

> Your dead shall live, their courses shall rise.
> O dwellers in the dust, awake and sing for joy!
> For your dew is a radiant dew,
> And the earth will give birth to those long dead.[47]

---

45. Not everyone believed in the possibility of resurrection. Josephus, for example, writes of Pharisees believing in resurrection but not Sadducees. See *Antiquities of the Jews* XVIII.1. Additionally, for those who did believe in a resurrection, the expectation of a resurrection of the *flesh* body may have been the minority position. Most ancient Jewish sources with resurrection eschatology tend to stress resurrection to angelic deification (2 Baruch; Daniel) and/or resurrection of the spirit. Paul's resurrection is a *pneumatic* bodily resurrection and explicitly not-flesh. For an accessible overview of Paul and *pneuma*, see Thiessen, *A Jewish Paul.*

46. Some scholars refer to these earlier sources as "proto-apocalyptic," but given their focus on good, evil, and the hope of restoration, I think an apocalyptic designation (even if not fully of the apocalypse genre) still works. For more on resurrection in ancient Israelite/Jewish sources, see Jon D. Levenson, *Resurrection and the Restoration of Israel: The Ultimate Victory of the God of Life* (Yale University Press, 2006).

47. Isaiah 26:19. This verse is part of a passage known as the "apocalyptic psalm." Early Judaism scholar Benjamin Wright adds that the very interpersonal nature of these sources heightens the psychic repair: These texts "reestablish intimacy with the divine that was lost in [exile]." Benjamin Givens Wright, *Praise Israel for Wisdom and Instruction: Essays on Ben Sira and Wisdom, the Letter of Aristeas and the Septuagint* (Brill, 2008), 167. Here, Wright is in conversation with Hindy Najman's conference paper titled "Reconsidering *Jubilees*:

In other words, while it is unlikely Isaiah or Ezekiel imagined a new world order at the end of human-centered time in the way later Jewish sources did, they were still leaning into resurrection as a metaphor to instill hope for survival—a rebuilt Jerusalem, even—in the face of the Babylonian exile. Salvation is possible, says these sources. Both declare that God has not forgotten God's people. The implied righteous will find solace—their hearts and minds will see life anew—in a postexilic age.[48] Even if life is terrible now, it won't be forever.

By the first century CE, we see this metaphor of survival converge with actual theologies of end-times and bodily resurrection. The apocalypses of Revelation, 2 Baruch, and 4 Ezra provide just a few examples of how early Jewish thinkers not only mourned Jewish loss, but also imagined a future in which the God of Israel would send a messiah, restore Jerusalem, resurrect the dead, and repair the damage imposed upon the collective Jewish psyche.[49] The overarching idea was that, through these moves, God would end human-centered history and create a new and immutable God-centered world. For many, this hope extended beyond mortality; even if one had already died, there was hope for life anew (e.g., Rev 20:4–6; 2 Baruch 50:2, 4 Ezra 2:16–23). This, in fact, is exactly what Paul says in 1 Thessalonians: "We . . . told you beforehand that we were to suffer persecution . . . [But] the Lord himself, with a cry of command, with the archangel's call and with the sound of God's trumpet, will descend from heaven, and the dead in Christ will rise first. Then we who are alive, who are left, will be caught up in the clouds together with them to meet the Lord in the air, and so we will be with the Lord forever.

Prophecy and Exemplarity," from the Fourth International Enoch Seminar that was published later in Hindy Najman, *Past Renewals: Interpretative Authority, Renewed Revelation and the Quest for Perfection in Jewish Antiquity*, Supplements to the *Journal for the Study of Judaism*, vol. 53 (Brill, 2010), 193.

48. See Henze, *Mind the Gap*, 154–156.

49. 2 Baruch and 4 Ezra lament specifically the destruction of the Second Temple in 70 CE. The focus of Revelation's lament is less clear, as it remains unknown whether Revelation was written before or after the fall of the Second Temple. For more on this, see Emanuel, *Humor, Resistance, and Jewish Cultural Persistence in the Book of Revelation*, 9–11, and for more on Revelation as a Jewish text, see that book in full, as well as David Frankfurter, "Revelation," in *The Jewish Annotated New Testament*, 2nd ed., ed. Amy-Jill Levine and Marc Zvi Brettler (Oxford University Press, 2017), 536–575; Frankfurter, "Jews or Not?"; John W. Marshall, *Parables of War: Reading John's Jewish Apocalypse* (Wilfrid Laurier University Press, 2001).

Therefore encourage one another with these words" (1 Thess 4:15–18). This image aligns with the order of 4 Ezra. Paul believes that the righteous dead will be "caught up" *first* (4 Ezra 2:23; 1 Thess 4:16–17).

Salvation, Ethnonationalism, and the Role of the Gentiles

This is where soteriology and ethnonationalism meet. For many of these sources, even if imagined with differing nuance, salvation was thought to occur at the hands of an Israel-centered God and/or Israel-centered messiah, and to come to fruition in an Israel-centered space. Early Christianity scholar Paula Fredriksen relates this to conceptions of human and divine ethnicity. Not only did humans have ethnic boundaries, but their gods were also understood as being bound to them.

In order to understand this claim, it is first important to understand ethnicity. Like race, ethnicity is a term used to discuss human boundaries and human difference.[50] Biblical scholar Caroline Johnson Hodge unpacks this by way of two opposing approaches: the essentialist and the constructivist. "In the essential approach," Johnson Hodge writes, "ethnic identity is understood to be based on something perceived to be inherent and immutable, like biological relationship. In the constructivist approach, ethnic identity is understood as something that can be created and adapted, and can be based on a variety of factors, including shared culture."[51] Hodge goes on to say that ethnic identity is usually a combination of these two understandings. On the one hand, it tends to be self-made; it is a construct based on the boundaries one creates and the various "'cultural stuff[s]' enclosed by the boundar[ies]."[52] On the other hand, it is often given power through the evocation of immutable blood ties.[53]

---

50. Denise Kimber Buell coined the term "ethnic reasoning" to show how rhetorics of ethnicity work to persuade and create/change ideas of identity. See, for example, "Rethinking the Relevance of Race for Early Christian Self-Definition," *Harvard Theological Review* 94, no. 4 (2001): 449–476.

51. Hodge, "Paul and Ethnicity," 552.

52. Shaye J. D. Cohen, *The Beginnings of Jewishness: Boundaries, Varieties, Uncertainties* (University of California Press, 1999), 5. See also Fredrik Barth, ed., *Ethnic Groups and Boundaries: The Social Organization of Culture Difference* (George Allen & Unwin, 1969).

53. I use the word "evocation" here to denote that the very attachment to blood ties is in itself a mutable choice.

We see this combination at play in ancient Jewish self-understandings. Many Jews in antiquity embodied their Jewishness ethnically through their self-made relations to Jewish story, heritage, and practice, including the practice of Jewish law and cultural debate. They also embodied it through conceptions of seed and kin: Jews understood themselves as descendants of Abraham; thus, the promises bestowed to him belonged to them.

This gets us back to Fredriksen. Part of the way Jews understood themselves was through heaven-earth or deity-human relations. In utter contrast to the later Christian conception of the Israelite God as a distant deity, this God was perceived by ancient Jews as a hands-on, close-knit being. Throughout many ancient Jewish sources, we see that God talks with humans. We also see humans talk with God. We see God intervening, interjecting, and even making ethnic-orientated, kinship-making vows to God's people. In Exodus 4:22–23, God refers to Israel as God's firstborn son: "Israel is my firstborn son . . . Let my son go so he may worship me." God then repeats this sentiment in Exodus 6:7: "I will take you [Israel] as my own people. Then you will know that am the Lord your God."[54] King Solomon and King David are also described as God's sons in more specific terms. In Psalm 2:7, the psalmist writes, "I will proclaim the Lord's decree: He said to me, 'You are my son; today I have become your father.'" And in 2 Samuel 7:14, God promises to be a father to Solomon and to establish his kingdom: "I will be his father, and he will be my son. When he does wrong, I will punish him with a rod wielded by men, with floggings inflicted by human hands." Such understandings of kinship extended to understandings of ethnicity. In Deuteronomy, for example, the author reminds the people of Israel: "You have declared this day that the Lord is your God and that you will walk in obedience to him, that you will keep his decrees, commands and laws—that you will listen to him. And the Lord has declared this day that you are his people, his treasured possession as he promised, and that you are to keep all his commands."[55] The Israelites, in short, are being described as agreeing to the boundaries created by their ethnic group, a group that saw itself as connected to God as God's own kin.

God was understood through these boundaries too. As Fredriksen adds, God from an ancient Jewish perspective "keeps a premier Jewish practice.

54. See also 2 Samuel 7:23.

55. Deuteronomy 26:17–18.

According to Gen 2:2–3, God rested on the Sabbath, a privilege and a responsibility that he will share uniquely with his own people, Israel. In Jubilees, we find out that God kept not only the first Shabbat: he continues to keep Shabbat weekly" (see Jub 2:17–20).[56] Even God's divine realm in *Jubilees* is filled with circumcised beings:

> And every one that is born, the flesh of whose foreskin is not circumcised on the eighth day, belongs not to the children of the covenant which the Lord made with Abraham, but to the children of destruction; nor is there, moreover, any sign on him that he is the Lord's, but (he is destined) to be destroyed and slain from the earth, and to be rooted out of the earth, for he has broken the covenant of the Lord our God. For all the angels of the presence and all the angels of sanctification have been so created from the day of their creation, and before the angels of the presence and the angels of sanctification He hath sanctified Israel, that they should be with him and with his holy angels (Jub 15:26–27).

Israelites, in other words, were not just the people of Israel, but also the people of the Israelite God. This made God, in turn, the ethnic head of an ethnic people.[57]

Jews were not the only people who imagined ethnic kinship between themselves and their God. This was common practice in Greco-Roman antiquity. Alexander the Great was considered a descendent of Heracles, Julius Caesar of Venus, and the Seleucids of Apollo.[58] Greek and Roman gods had

---

56. Fredriksen, "How Jewish Is God?," 198.

57. In Fredriksen's words, "If he is the father of the people Israel and of Israel's rulers, referring to each as his 'son,' then God is 'Jewish.' If, of all the places on the earth, his glorious presence dwells most particularly in Judea, within Jerusalem's temple, then God is 'Jewish.' And if, ultimately, at the end of time, all other humans and their gods will acknowledge him by conforming to two fundamental protocols of Jewish worship—that is to say, with no other gods and without images (see Exod 20:3–4, Deut 5:7–8)—while they gather together with a reunified Israel in Judea . . . ('the mountain of the Lord's house,' Isa 2:2–4), then God is 'Jewish.'" Fredriksen, "How Jewish Is God?," 199. Note, though, that it is not that Fredriksen is making the overarching argument that God is Jewish, but rather that by ancient criteria of ethnicity (e.g., land, language, kinship, cult, ancestral practices) ancient people, including Jews, *thought* of God as an ethnic god.

58. Fredriksen, "How Jewish Is God?," 195, footnote 2.

sex with humans, sometimes by force, and even procreated with humans, showcasing all the more the extent to which the crevices between heaven and earth were spread.[59] What "*was* odd," Fredriksen adds, at least for non-Jews, "was the Jews' insistence that their particular god was also the universal god, the highest god, the supreme god. Even odder was the claim of some Jews of apocalyptic bent: the Jewish god, they said, would ultimately be worshiped by ethnic others, both human and divine."[60]

Some of God's eschatological promises, in other words, were understood as also belonging to gentiles *as gentiles*. As usual, this was expressed in a variety of ways across ancient Jewish texts. In some instances, gentiles were imagined as offering willful submission to God in the new world (e.g., in conversation with Isa 2:2–4: "In days to come, the mountain of Yahweh's house shall be established as the highest of the mountains and . . . all gentiles shall stream to it. Many peoples shall come and say, 'Come, let us go up to the mountain of Yahweh.'"). In other places, gentiles were seen as forced into submission (e.g., Isa 49:22–26: "Thus says the god Yahweh, 'I will soon lift up my hand to the gentiles and raise my signal to the peoples . . . with their faces to the ground they shall bow down to you and lick the dust of your feet . . . I will make your oppressors eat their own flesh, and they shall be drunk with their own blood as with wine, then all flesh shall know that I am Yahweh, your savior and redeemer, the mighty one of Jacob.'").[61] And in other places still, gentile

---

59. I use this sexualized language purposefully. Gods were imagined as sexual beings who at times forced their sexuality onto humans. Just as I refuse to wipe clean Paul's exclusivism, I also refuse to wipe clean the sexualized and even rapist imagery of the gods. For more on this conversation, see, for example, James N. Hoke, "'Behold, the Lord's Whore'? Slavery, Prostitution, and Luke 1:38," *Biblical Interpretation* 26, no. 1 (2018): 43–67.

60. Fredriksen, "How Jewish Is God?," 193–194; Sarah Emanuel, "When Women of the Bible Say #MeToo," *Feminist Studies in Religion*, January 26, 2018, https://www.fsrinc.org/women-of-the-bible-say-metoo/; Emanuel, *Humor, Resistance, and Jewish Cultural Persistence in the Book of Revelation*, chapter 3.

61. In Revelation, too, the author seems to include at least some enslaved gentiles in its imagined New Jerusalem. Emanuel, *Humor, Resistance, and Jewish Cultural Persistence in the Book of Revelation*, 190–191. For examples of both forced and willful submission of gentiles (or even a mix of both), see Sanders, *Jesus and Judaism*, 212–218. See also Emanuel, *Humor, Resistance, and Jewish Cultural Persistence in the Book of Revelation*, 190, footnote 81. Sometimes, however, gentiles were imagined as being annihilated. It has also been argued that Revelation's faithful, regardless of ethnic standing, carry the mark of those enslaved (e.g., Rev 7:3, 14:1, 22:3–4). See, for example, Lynn R. Huber, "Reading Enslavement in Revelation 1,"

gods were imagined as bowing down to the God of Israel (e.g., Ps 97:7: "Every god must bow down to [Yahweh]"). Paul seemed to take part in the typical Jewish understanding that gentiles would—or at least should—be a part of the eschatological movement: "In the name of Jesus, *every* knee should bend (*kampsē*) in heaven and on earth and under the earth and every tongue should confess that Jesus Christ is Lord" (Phil 2:10–11).[62]

The point, then, at least for the present purpose, is that in many Jewish eschatological expectations, gentiles played a key role. They were not imagined as renouncing their ethnic status as gentiles in the end of days but were instead enlisted *as gentiles* in it.[63] Despite the diversity of members, however—that is, both Jews and gentiles—the eschaton was still an Israel-centered world. It was imagined as an ethnocratic ethnonation, one in which the Jewish God reigned alongside that God's Jewish angels, Jewish messiah(s), and chosen humans: righteous Jews first, and selected gentiles second (see, e.g., Rom 1:16).[64]

The idea of the righteous, however, requires further unpacking. Even if Jews were imagined as ushered in *first*, that does not mean *all* Jews were welcome. Texts like Isaiah, the *Damascus Document*, and 4 Ezra talk about how only a "remnant" of Jews will be saved. In Isaiah, this remnant refers to a select group of Israelites who will be delivered from Babylonian exile

---

in *Revelation and Material Religion in the Roman East: Essays in Honor of Steven J. Friesen*, ed. Nathan Leach, Daniel Charles Smith, and Tony Keddie (Routledge, 2023), 32–51; Lynn R. Huber and Gail R. O'Day, *Wisdom Commentary: Revelation* (Liturgical Press, 2023), 342. See also Jennifer A. Glancy and Stephen D Moore, "How Typical a Roman Prostitute Is Revelation's 'Great Whore'?," *Journal of Biblical Literature* 130, no. 3 (2011): 551–569; C. P. Jones, "Tattooing and Branding in Graeco-Roman Antiquity," *Journal of Roman Studies* 77 (1987): 139–155; Shanell T. Smith, *The Woman Babylon and the Marks of Empire: Reading Revelation with a Postcolonial Womanist Hermeneutics of Ambi*veil*ence* (Fortress Press, 2014).

62. Emphasis mine. See also Fredriksen, "How Jewish Is God?," 194. Also note that many scholars argue/assume in this passage that Paul is quoting from a hymn.

63. For a pivotal article on this matter, see Paula Fredriksen, "Judaism, the Circumcision of Gentiles, and Apocalyptic Hope: Another Look at Galatians 1 and 2," *Journal of Theological Studies* 42, no. 2 (1991): 532–564.

64. This, too, relates to the malleability of ethnicity. As Hodge explains, "Ethnic identity does not exist in isolation and is not permanent, but it exists always in relation to others and changes as relationships and circumstances change." Hodge, "Paul and Ethnicity," 552. For a thoughtful take on how gentile ethnicity relates to Israelite ethnicity in the end-times by way of Paul and Jesus, see Thiessen, *A Jewish Paul*, chapter 8.

(Isa 10:21–23).[65] But in the *Damascus Document*, a text likely relying on Isaiah to construct its claims, the remnant refers to select Israelites who will be delivered in the end of days. Shayna Sheinfeld, in fact, contends that the Damascus remnant is meant to be a continuation of Isaiah's. In her words, the *Damascus Document* "provides a clear connection between membership in [its] community and the exilic remnant [of Isaiah], thus alluding positively to a continuation of the [first] remnant community . . . The documents from Qumran indicate a community that clings to the idea that they represented the true Israel, the elect, and they use remnant language in order to express this idea."[66] The Jewish text known as 4 Ezra imagines something similar. In considering the relationship between this world and the next, Ezra laments that "the Most High made this world for the sake of the many, but the world to come for the sake of the few" (8:1). The few, he adds, are the "remnant" (12:34).[67] As an angel says to Ezra, "[The messiah] will deliver in mercy the remnant of my people, those who have been saved throughout my borders, and he will make them joyful until the end comes, the day of judgment, of which I spoke to you at the beginning" (12:34).[68]

---

65. While the remnant will be saved, Isaiah posits that the wicked are "like the tossing sea, which cannot rest, whose waves cast up mire and mud." For them, "there is no peace" (Isa 57:16–21). According to Markus Vinzent, this is exactly the kind of material Marcion wanted to change; he "[sought] to replace this carrot and stick approach with a new Torah that is free of fear and condemnation." Vinzent, *Christ's Torah*, 323. For more on the relationship between earlier passages of Isaiah and those that appear in the later chapters, see, for example, Ethan Schwartz, "Mirrors of Moses in Isaiah 1–12," in *The History of Isaiah: The Formation of the Book and Its Presentation of the Past*, ed. Jacob Stromberg and James Todd Hibbard (Mohr Siebeck, 2021), 269–295.

66. Shayna Sheinfeld, "Who Is the Righteous Remnant in Romans 9–11?: The Concept of Remnant in Early Jewish Literature and Paul's Letter to the Romans," in *Paul the Jew: Rereading the Apostle as a Figure of Second Temple Judaism*, ed. Gabriele Boccaccini and Carlos A. Segovia (Fortress Press, 2016), 36, 38. See also John J. Collins, "The Idea of Election in 4 Ezra," *Jewish Studies Quarterly* 16, no. 1 (2009): 83–96.

67. Sheinfeld adds that the remnant may for this author be only Jews who live within certain borders. Sheinfeld, "Who Is the Righteous Remnant in Romans 9–11?," 39.

68. This, too, is part of communal ethnic-making. The text, by instilling a sense of "who is in" and "who is out," encourages readers to act in a way that constitutes an "in." See also Sheinfeld, "Who Is the Righteous Remnant in Romans 9–11?," 40. Again, Denise Kimber Buell coined the term "ethnic reasoning" to allude to this kind of community-making.

The overall takeaways are these: Many ancient Jewish authors, especially in the late centuries BCE and early centuries CE, made sense of the world through the lens of apocalypticism. The hope was that God, and perhaps a God-related ruler or rulers, would establish a new world order at the end of human-centered history. This new world order was ethnocratic and ethnonationalist: Ethnic pride, loyalty, and devotion to the Israelite God were required. This God's righteous kin would be granted access first, followed by some elect gentiles. Thinkers who abided by this mindset, however, often disagreed on the details. This included what was righteous, who was righteous, and who the messiah(s) would be, as well as whether bodily resurrection would be a part of it, and where that resurrected body would dwell.

Paul within an Average Jewish Context

Paul asserted himself as a Jew. He quoted the Torah and the Prophets, engaged matters of Jewish faith and practice, observed Jewish commandments, believed in the God of Israel, and focused on Jewish ethnic lore through his writings on figures such as Adam, Moses, Abraham, David, and Jesus. Paul shows this across his letters. Here are just a few examples from 1 and 2 Corinthians, Romans, and Philippians:

> For since death came through a human, the resurrection of the dead has also come through a human, for as all die in Adam, so all will be made alive in Christ. (1 Cor 15:21–22)

> Are they Hebrews? So am I. Are they Israelites? So am I. Are the descendants of Abraham? So am I. (2 Cor 11:22)

> My kindred, according to the flesh. They are Israelites, and to them belong the adoption of sons, the glory, the covenants, the giving of the law, the cult, the promises; to them belong the patriarchs, and from them, according to the flesh, comes the Messiah. God who is over all be blessed forever. (Rom 9:3–5)

> If anyone else has reason to be confident in the flesh, I have more: circumcised on the eighth day, a member of the people of Israel, of the tribe of Benjamin, a Hebrew born of Hebrews; as to the law, a

> Pharisee [recall Josephus!]; as to zeal, a persecutor of the church; as to righteousness under the law, blameless. (Phil 3:4–6)

Paul was also an apocalyptic thinker. That he received cosmic truths from a resurrected being—one who resided in the divine realm (1 Thess 1:9–10)—positions his theology within an apocalyptic frame: "Have I not seen Jesus our Lord?" he asks in 1 Corinthians 9:1. "He appeared also to me," he confirms in 1 Corinthians 15:8. While the historical Paul did not disclose in narrative form the full experience of this unveiling moment, he does share with readers the eschatological message he received: Jesus is the long-awaited Christ, the end of days is near, and gentiles need to be ready. Like many other apocalyptic writers, Paul throughout his letters also acts as a Jewish exemplar figure: He writes as if he has divine speech because Jesus gave it to him.[69]

For Paul, Jesus fulfilled the role of his Jewish messiah. He is "from the root of Jesse," said Paul, and like David, he is the son of God (Rom 15:12; Rom 1:3–4; 2 Cor. 1:19; Gal 2:20; 1 Thess 1:9–10).[70] Like the divine-like messiah of the *Psalm of Solomon*, however, Paul writes that Jesus, even in earthly form, was above humanity. He "knew no sin so that in him we might become the righteousness of God" (2 Cor. 5:21). Even the belief that Jesus was raised maps onto Paul's Hellenistic Pharisaic worldview. As Josephus explains, Pharisees "believe that souls have an immortal vigor in them: and that under the earth there will be rewards, or punishments; according as they have lived virtuously or viciously in this life: and the latter are to be detained in an everlasting prison; but that the former shall have power to revive and live again" (*Ant.* 18.1; see also *J.W.* 2.163). And many Greeks, influenced by Plato's philosophy, believed in the immortality of the soul. Again, this confluence with Greeks did not diminish Paul's Jewishness; it simply showed that his Jewishness—like that of many other Jews—interacted with the

69. This is the work of Wright, *Praise Israel for Wisdom and Instruction*, 166–168. Najman, *Past Renewals*, 201. I extend gratitude to Heather Macumber for guiding me to this resource and intertextual understanding of Paul with former exemplar figures.

70. Unlike David, however, it is possible Jesus was appointed the status of "son" at his resurrection, thus making Jesus less of an earthly son of God and more of a heavenly one. This at least is a common interpretation of Romans 1:3–4, which was likely quoting an earlier Christ-following creed. It is unclear to what extent Paul agreed with it. This idea also connects with a Hellenistic one. The Roman emperor Julius Caesar, for example, was thought to be divinized at death, thereby making his son also a "son of God."

broader culture.[71] Related to these Jewish-Greek encounters, Paul believed that Jesus would "rule over the gentiles" in the messianic age: "The root of Jesse will spring up as one who will rise to rule over the gentiles. In him the gentiles will hope" (Rom 15:12). In other words, it is in the *Jewish* Davidic messiah, said Paul, that gentiles could finally see their beliefs in the immortality of the soul come to fruition.[72]

Contra the Old Perspective, Paul did not "convert" from Judaism to anything *not* Judaism.[73] He simply had a change of mind *within* his own Judaism: Whereas he once believed that Jesus was not the Jewish messiah, he eventually believed he was. Not even Paul's harsh rhetoric against other Jews negated his Jewish outlook.[74] Like the author of *Pesher Habakkuk,* who accuses his Jewish enemies of being blood-spillers, Paul charges his own Jewish enemies of killing Jesus and the prophets, contending that "God's wrath [will] come upon them at last" (1 Thess 2:15–16).[75] But it is still only a *part* of Israel, like a *part* of Israel in the *Pesher Habakkuk* and other ancient Jewish texts, that are "enemies of God" (Rom 11:28). Paul's own letters, in fact, akin to the pesher, attest to the ideological polemics circulating throughout Paul's ministry. The entire book

---

71. This is not a "Judaism-versus-Hellenism" situation, as New Testament scholar Stephen L. Young has phrased it. As much as Paul interacted with the diversities of the Greco-Roman world, his overarching understanding of Jesus was still influenced by Jewish principles. See Young, "Let's Take the Text Seriously"; Young, "So Radically Jewish That He's an Evangelical Christian."

72. For a pivotal source that helped normalize or at least establish taking seriously that Paul's messiah language for Christ (i.e., *Christos*) should, in fact, be interpreted as Jewish messiah language as opposed to a title distinct from Jewish messianism, see Matthew V. Novenson, *Christ Among the Messiahs: Christ Language in Paul and Messiah Language in Ancient Judaism* (Oxford University Press, 2012). See also John G. Gager, "Messiahs and Their Followers," in *Toward the Millennium: Messianic Expectations from the Bible to Waco,* ed. Peter Schäfer and Mark R. Cohen (Brill, 1998), 38.

73. For more on the problematics of relying on "conversion" as a term for ancient Judaism and Christianity, see Sara Parks, Shayna Sheinfeld, and Meredith J. C. Warren, *Jewish and Christian Women in the Ancient Mediterranean* (Routledge, 2021), 265–267. See also Zeba A. Crook, *Reconceptualising Conversion: Patronage, Loyalty, and Conversion in the Religions of the Ancient Mediterranean* (Walter de Gruyter, 2004).

74. Just as his harsh rhetoric against gentiles does not erase his work with gentiles (see, e.g., Galatians and Romans 1).

75. Stephen L. Young similarly argues that Paul was writing about the sins of other Jews precisely *as a Jew*. See Young, "Ethnic Ethics."

of Galatians, for example, is about how, from Paul's point of view, certain Christ-followers, both Jewish and gentile, lost their way. While some gentile Galatians wanted to convert to Judaism in order to better follow Jesus (a man who, after all, was Jewish!), Paul insisted they stay gentile. Paul in fact goes as far as to say that the messengers convincing gentiles to convert to Judaism—messengers who were quite possibly also Jewish—will "pay the penalty" (Gal 5:10). This polemic not only shows Paul's own views about conversion, but also that his views were not the only ones being circulated. In another text, Paul even sarcastically nicknames a group of Christ-following missionaries "super-apostles"—a jab he makes in response to their own mockeries toward *him*—which demonstrates once again that there were apostles with whom Paul disagreed *and vice versa* (2 Cor 11–12).[76]

All of this is to say: When taking Paul's self-disclosures seriously, readers see quickly that neither Paul's belief in Jesus nor his harsh rhetoric against his adversaries diminished his Jewishness, but rather functioned as nuanced views *within* Judaism. He, like fellow ancient Jews, believed that evil existed in the world, and that one day the goodness of God would be restored in a new world order.

What, then, of salvation? If Paul is Jewish, does he think all Jews will be saved in the end of days?

Paul and the Fate of the Jews

Again, the set of verses most often analyzed to study Paul's eschatological soteriology is from Romans 9–11, in which Paul explains what he calls "the mystery" of God's soteriological plans. In these verses, Paul argues that, aside from sparing a *remnant* of Israel, God has temporarily disabled Israel from recognizing Jesus as the messiah. As a result, many Jews have lost their invitation to the new world order in the end of days. As noted previously, in Paul's view, such hardening is for the gentiles: "Through [Israel's] stumbling, salvation

76. In fact, from a "super-apostle" perspective, Christ-followers have been giving Paul too much credit. He was never the only apostle; his views were never the only outlooks. Some fourth-century leaders may have even advocated for additional letter writers to be included within the canon so as to offset Paul as the only Christ-following influencer (see the letters of James, Peter, John, and Jude). See also Arminta M. Fox, *Paul Decentered: Reading 2 Corinthians with the Corinthian Women*, Paul in Critical Contexts (Lexington Books / Fortress Academic, 2019).

has come to the gentiles" (Rom 11:11). Paul then adds that those of Israel who come to believe that Jesus is the Christ may be grafted back into God's saving grace (to repeat, this is presumably when God is no longer disabling them, although the subject of Jewish free will here is unclear). Using an olive tree as a metaphor for the new world order, including who is saved and how, Paul says that Jewish and gentile believers in Christ represent the tree's (i.e., the new nation's) lasting branches. A remnant of believing Jewish branches have stayed; unbelieving Jewish branches have fallen / been cut off;[77] believing gentile branches have been grafted in, and Jewish branches can be grafted *back* in through a stopping of unbelief. Paul then concludes with a summary and added note: "I want you to understand this mystery: a hardening has come upon part of Israel until the full number of the gentiles has come in [this is the summary]. And so all Israel will be saved [this is the addition]."

As we have seen, the traditional Old Perspective on Paul claims that "all Israel" for Paul meant all Christ-followers, predominantly if not exclusively gentiles.[78] If Jews *were saved*, and it was a big *if*, they had to believe in Christ. After the Holocaust, however, it became increasingly clear that this traditional view played a role in the centuries-long persecution of Jews and could no longer be tolerated. Alongside the discovery of the Dead Sea Scrolls, E. P. Sanders's argument on covenantal nomism enabled a new reading of Paul. In fact, most post-Sanders evaluations of Paul and Judaism begin with acknowledging the change the Holocaust necessitated, and then build on Sanders's thesis with the

77. Again, Paul uses both images but culminates in the latter. See Romans 11:20–22.

78. Rabbinic scholar Daniel Boyarin leans into the terminology of "particular universalism" to explain this view. Whereas Paul is described by Dunn and Wright as a universalist thinker counter to Judaism's particularistic ideologies, Boyarin asserts that even when scholars characterize Paul as a universalist thinker—as someone who ushers in "all" people to Christ—he is still bringing particularity into his universal reach because the focus is still on Christ. Christianity, in other words, is open to "everyone," *as long as* Christ is followed. We can showcase this even further. From a traditional New Perspective mindset, Paul claims that Christianity is open to "everyone," as long as the "outdated" modes of Jewishness and the "idolatrous" modes of gentileness are no longer practiced in the name of Jesus and the Israelite God. It is, in other words, remarkably particular. See Boyarin, *A Radical Jew*, 201–216, especially 216. See also Levenson, "The Universal Horizon of Biblical Particularism," 143–69. Indeed, as Levenson writes, it's not just that Christ-following orientations, including Paul's and also later Nicene Christianity's, are *not* universal, but that "the all-too-common contrast between 'universal' and 'particularistic' religion is, in every instance, simplistic, grossly misleading, and even dangerous," 144.

help of the Dead Sea Scrolls. Here are some examples of the Holocaust starting point: In the words of Lloyd Gaston, "The horrors of the Holocaust impelled Christians to take responsibility for their past exegesis and historiography and preaching and liturgy."[79] Or John Gager: "The Nazi Holocaust . . . account[s] for the possibility of reading Paul in a new way."[80] Or Gabriele Boccaccini: "The Holocaust forced Christians to rethink their relations with the Jews and Judaism."[81] Or Magnus Zetterholm: "I am quite aware that recognizing the connection between the traditional Christian teaching on Paul and the crimes committed against the Jewish people throughout history has led me to take a [Paul within Judaism] approach."[82] Or Mark Nanos, who writes that his scholarship is "a product of many factors, not least the long shadow of the Holocaust."[83] Or Matthew Thiessen, who contends that "where uncertainty [in Paul's letters] persists, we have a moral obligation to choose against readings that harm others."[84] With Christian supersessionism and the Holocaust in mind, he reads Paul in a way that "is not dependent on the denigration of ancient Jews and Judaism."[85]

As we have also seen, a key factor in the pursuit to no longer see Paul as denigrating Jews and Judaism is to consider more fully the context within which Paul found himself. Paul was a Jew, says the New Perspective. He was a Jew among gentiles, replies the Radical New Perspective / Paul within Judaism approach, and as a Jew among gentiles, he was trying to establish a distinct, *gentile* Christ-following movement, perhaps even as a way to fulfill the *Jewish* hope that all people, both Jews *and* non-Jews, would honor the God of Israel in the end of days. The *Sonderweg* way takes this premise to the highest courts. Pioneered by Gaston and Gager, it claims that only gentiles need Christ in

79. Lloyd Gaston, "New Testament Theology After the Holocaust: Exegetical Responsibilities and Canonical Possibilities," in *A Shadow of Glory: Reading the New Testament After the Holocaust*, ed. Tod Linafelt (Routledge, 2002), 130.

80. Gager, *Reinventing Paul*, 150–151.

81. Boccaccini, *Paul's Three Paths to Salvation*, 6.

82. Zetterholm, *Approaches to Paul*, x.

83. Mark D. Nanos, *The Irony of Galatians: Paul's Letter in First-Century Context* (Fortress Press, 2002), 4.

84. Thiessen, *A Jewish Paul*, 21.

85. Thiessen, *A Jewish Paul*, 21.

order to be saved in Paul's imagined end of days. Because gentiles do not have the Torah, they are the ones who need a separate, special path: Christ. The overall point regarding Jews, then, is that they are fine. They don't need Christ. Thus, Paul, both *as* a Jew and in his thinking *of* fellow Jews, is still *good*.

From this angle, the New Perspective and the *Sonderweg* variant may actually not be so different. As noted previously, the Dunn-Wright New Perspective takes issue with the very idea that Jews don't "get" the universality of Paul's theology. Jews who continued to celebrate their exceptional relationship with God failed to grasp the character and "the all-ness of faith."[86] Jews, according to Paul—or, really, according to Dunn's and Wright's Paul—must see that God is not ethnocentric, and that God's grace is for *everyone*. The *Sonderweg* model replies in the affirmative, at least when it comes to salvation: Yes, *everyone* is saved—Jews by way of the Torah, gentiles by way of Christ. As discussed, Boccaccini goes as far as to suggest that Christ is a *third* gift: Righteous Jews are saved by the Torah, righteous gentiles by natural law, and sinning Jews and gentiles by Christ. *All* can be ushered into the end-times because God is *good* and God has *grace*.

Again, there are pushbacks. Scholars such as Caroline Johnson Hodge, Sze-kar Wan, Matthew Thiessen, Matthew Novenson, Paula Fredriksen, Stephen Young, Shayna Sheinfeld, and Jason Staples, to name a few, argue against traditional aspects of the universalist model by claiming that Paul was not "above" particularism or ethnocentrism.[87] Paul is "strikingly" ethnocentric, writes Staples.[88] "It seems difficult to escape the conclusion that Paul was

---

86. Dunn, *The New Perspective on Paul*, 11, 13.

87. See, for example, Hodge, "Paul and Ethnicity"; Hodge, *If Sons, Then Heirs*; Sze-kar Wan, "Does Diaspora Identity Imply Some Sort of Universality? An Asian-American Reading of Galatians," in *Interpreting Beyond Borders*, ed. Fernando F. Segovia, The Bible and Postcolonialism (Sheffield Academic Press, 2000), 107–131; Thiessen, *Paul and the Gentile Problem*; Thiessen, *A Jewish Paul*; Matthew Novenson, *Paul and Judaism at the End of History* (Cambridge University Press, 2024); Fredriksen, *Paul: The Pagans' Apostle*; Fredriksen, "How Jewish Is God?"; Young, "Ethnic Ethics"; Sheinfeld, "Who Is the Righteous Remnant in Romans 9–11?"; Jason A. Staples, *Paul and the Resurrection of Israel: Jews, Former Gentiles, Israelites* (Cambridge University Press, 2024). See also Concannon, *Profaning Paul*; Denise Kimber Buell, *Why This New Race: Ethnic Reasoning in Early Christianity* (Columbia University Press, 2005); Horrell, *Ethnicity and Inclusion*; Rainey, *Religion, Ethnicity and Xenophobia in the Bible*, 229–238.

88. Staples, *Paul and the Resurrection of Israel*, 6.

ethnocentric," writes Wan.[89] He was so ethnocentric, attests Thiessen, that "even something as basic as Paul's frequent use of the term 'gentile' to refer to all non-Jews demonstrates the ethnocentric nature of this thought—dissolving all non-Jewish ethnicities and cultures into one catch-all-word."[90] These scholars thus start with a different premise—one mirrored in Fredriksen's work above on the ethnic particularity of the Israelite God—by arguing that Paul *is* particularistic in his focus on the Israelite God via the particularly ethnic Jewish Jesus. For Thiessen, all are eventually saved, but all are eventually saved in the particular Christ.[91]

This brings us to another fundamental question: *Why gentiles?* I find Pamela Eisenbaum's answer to be a productive one. In her view, Paul writes to gentiles so as to maintain a core tenant of most messianic expectations, which is that a messiah would inaugurate a messianic age in which the God of Israel would be the God of *all* people (Rom 15:12; Isa 11:10). The "all," Eisenbaum argues, is imperative, so much so that Paul is desperate to bring gentiles into the fold before the messianic age arrives (which he thinks will be imminent). If Paul has gentiles on board with Jesus and therefore with the God of Israel, then the messianic age can more easily come to fruition.[92] To put it another way, one can imagine Paul's eschatological ideas functioning like a series of dominoes that fall down in a line. As New Testament scholar Stephen Young explains it, the obedience of some gentiles was, for Paul, an end-times domino that *had* to fall before the final pieces could.[93] Bringing gentiles into the fold was thus Paul's way of getting the "final" piece to eventually move.

---

89. Wan, "Does Diaspora Identity Imply Some Sort of Universality?," 126.

90. Thiessen, *Paul and the Gentile Problem*, 7. See also Hodge, "The Question of Identity," 155–156.

91. This may sound like Boyarin's version of "particular universalism," but it is not. Thiessen firmly disagrees with Boyarin's understanding of Paul as seeking to erase ethnic and social distinction in Christ. See footnote 78 in this chapter.

92. Pamela Eisenbaum, "Jewish Perspectives: A Jewish Apostle to the Gentiles," in *Studying Paul's Letters: Contemporary Perspectives and Methods*, ed. Joseph A. Marchal (Fortress Press, 2012), 141. See also Nanos, *The Mystery of Romans*, 10; Nanos, "A Jewish View," 183–188 (here, Nanos discusses practical issues of gentile Christ-followers converting to Judaism, including those having to do with Roman policy); Sanders, *Jesus and Judaism*, 212–218.

93. In conversation, November 21, 2024.

Gentiles also needed to *act* in a particular manner. As Thiessen explains further, "Paul emphasizes that participating in [the eschaton] requires [gentiles] living according to its [particular] rules."[94] These rules are outlined in multiple places, including but not limited to 1 Thessalonians 4:3–5, 1 Corinthians 7:19, Romans 1, Romans 6:15–19, Romans 13:8–10, and the entirety of Galatians, which, contra the Old Perspective indeed, includes the call for gentiles to "do good works" (e.g., Gal 5:19–23 and 6:9–10).[95] Eisenbaum stresses this too: "It is not as if a follower of Jesus has nothing to do in response to God's grace . . . the gift of Jesus required a faithful response from Gentiles."[96] Such a faithful response may not be easy, but at least it seems clear: Gentiles need to transform their unrighteous condition and, in doing so, join forces with Abraham's seed through faith in and of Christ (Gal 2:16). "For this is the will of God," he writes in 1 Thessalonians and echoes in Romans. "You [must] abstain from sexual immorality [which is to say, at least in modern parlance, queer immorality, especially the lesbian kind].[97] You must know how to control your own body in holiness and honor as opposed to the lustful

94. Thiessen, *A Jewish Paul*, 75.

95. Notably, the list in Galatians 5:19–23 concludes with *enkrateia*, a signature way ancient moralists wrote about the mastery of the passions that encapsulates virtue.

96. Eisenbaum, *Paul Was Not a Christian*, 241. Although note that Eisenbaum softens this, highlighting that faithful action is not necessary about one's personal salvation but rather personal participation in inevitable redemption. See also 253–255.

97. In the words of New Testament scholar Jimmy Hoke, "Paul cannot bear to describe women's unnatural sexuality—or, just as likely, he (like most men) cannot imagine what women might do outside of male dominance." But as Hoke helpfully adds, Paul is not clear on the specifics. In addition to female-female sexual love, Paul may have also taken issue with "women [who] were taking an active role when having sex with men" (another queer act from Paul's perspective, I would say, at least in modern parlance). While Paul was most disgusted with women, male sexual immorality was also an issue. In what ways beyond what we might call "queerness," however, we cannot know. In Hoke's words, Paul in Romans "specifies neither the exact sexual activities in which these men engaged nor what would make these acts unnatural [with the accompanying footnote: 'Edging? Fisting? Sucking? Rimming? Anal sex? Mutual masturbation? Piss play? All of the above?']." For more on this conversation, see Jimmy Hoke, *Feminism, Queerness, Affect, and Romans: Under God?* Early Christianity and Its Literature 30 (SBL Press, 2021), 85. For more on sexuality and 1 Thessalonians, see James N. Hoke, "Be Even Better Subjects, Worthy of Rehabilitation: Homonationalism and 1 Thessalonians 4–5," in *Bodies on the Verge: Queering Pauline Epistles*, Semeia Studies, no. 93, ed. Joseph A. Marchal (SBL Press, 2019), 84–114, which looks at the racialized/ethnocentric ideas about gentile sexuality as a form of homonationalism.

passion of the gentiles who do not know God" or the "good news" that comes with belonging to Christ (1 Thess 4:3–5; Rom 1). For a lesbian like me, this life seems pretty terrible, but for gentile Stoics who sought to control the urges, it may have had some appeal, at least enough for it to impact the later creation of a Christian Orthodox movement.[98] "Be modest. Don't engage in queer sex. Be properly masculine. Remember the penis. Follow the God of Israel. Connect with Jesus as the Christ. Do these 'good' things, fair gentiles, and you will not only help usher in the eschaton, but you will be included in it."[99]

To think about proper gentile action in addition to proper Jewish action was also typical. The early rabbis, for example, believed that a set of seven "Noahide Laws" were given to gentiles in the book of Genesis: no worshipping idols, no cursing God, no murdering, no engaging in sexual immorality, no thieving, no eating living animals, no living without a court of justice. Those who follow these laws, said the rabbis, were "righteous" and granted access to the world to come. The major difference for Paul was that believing in Jesus as the messiah was a necessary part of proper gentile action. All this adds an interesting nuance to the discussion, one that readers may already be noticing. Yes, gentiles *are* to remain gentile—but not *too* gentile. For Paul, gentile eschatological salvation requires renouncing pagan gods in favor of the Jewish one. It also requires accepting the Jewish God's chosen messiah, all alongside a host of laws heralded with Jewish sacred texts. In other words, Dunn and Wright may have been on to something, just with the wrong ethnic group. For Paul, *gentiles* must not be *Jew*-ish. Instead, they must be Jew-*ish*.[100]

---

98. Again, Paul's audience, like Paul himself, is simultaneously immersed in a wider Hellenistic culture, including Hellenistic philosophical thinking (e.g., Stoicism). For an accessible overview of this, including how certain Platonist ideas were combined with Stoic ones, see Young, "So Radically Jewish That He's an Evangelical Christian."

99. This, of course, is my own rendering. It is worth noting, too, that advocates of both "faith of Jesus" translations and "faith in Jesus" translations emphasize that Paul repeatedly writes about his expectation or demand that gentiles themselves maintain faithfulness, loyalty, belief, and proper action. Moral belonging, in short, is still required, regardless of how one translates *pistis Christou*. Many exponents of the "faithfulness of Christ" approach argue, in fact, that since Paul's point is that gentiles participate in Christ and are conformed to him, it is imperative that they are characterized by Christ's faithfulness or loyalty to God and his norms. For more on this conversation, see Young, "Paul's Ethnic Discourse on 'Faith.'" See also chapter 3, footnote 115.

100. For this reason, Caroline Johnson Hodge understands gentile Christ-followers as gentiles of a "special sort," perhaps even ethnically hybrid. She writes, "Think about the differences

But what about *Jews* and Christ? Is the *Sonderweg* school correct that "all Jews will be saved" solely through their allegiance to Abraham and Torah—that is, without belief in Christ?

Contra the Old Perspective, it certainly seems to be the case that Jews are to remain Jews. After all, Paul never says that they need to stop being Jewish and even argues against the surgical (re)making of foreskin (1 Cor 7:18).[101] He says twice that followers need to live the ethnic life God assigned to them (1 Cor 7:17, 7:20), and also declares that Christ-following Jews need to keep upholding the law (Rom 3:31). In Thiessen's words, "One of the consistent maxims is that believers are to remain as they are."[102] Paul also applauds his own remaining connections to Jewish law, boasting that he is blameless before it (Phil 3:6).[103] The eschaton, moreover, *was* to contain *both* Jews and gentiles—that is, both gentiles *and Jews*. The *Sonderweg* school thus seems to be right on at least one thing: Jews are meant to *stay* ethnically Jewish. As Fredriksen similarly concludes, "Not only must eschatological gentiles remain gentiles: so too Israel must remain Israel, that family group, God's 'sons' and Paul's blood brothers, united by the covenants, the Law, the temple cult, the

---

of being 'in-Christ' for gentiles and Jews. Jews do not cross ethnic boundaries by virtue of their commitment to Christ; they do not change their God, their ancestry, or their ancestral customs. Gentiles do . . . To be in Christ, gentiles give up their gods and religious practices, profess loyalty to the God of Israel, accept Israel's messiah, Scriptures, and ancestry. All of these are Jewish ethnic markers, yet the gentiles do not become Jews. They are tucked into the seed of Abraham as gentiles, and they remain gentiles, of a special sort." Hodge, "The Question of Identity," 172.

101. Acts 18:18 and 21:23–24 show that early Jesus followers understood Paul as similarly advocating for such ethnic maintenance and distinction. For more on these passages and how they at the very least show *Luke's* understanding of Paul as Jewish, see Thiessen, *Paul and the Gentile Problem*, 24–28.

102. Thiessen, *Paul and the Gentile Problem*, 30. Some readers may look to certain translations of 1 Cor 7:21 to refute this claim, at least when it comes to enslaved status (e.g., the NIV). This is because the verb *chrēsai*, or "make use of," lacks a direct object in the Greek. Based on the surrounding verses, it makes the most sense for Paul to be saying enslaved persons should "make use of" their current, enslaved status as opposed to "make use of" emancipation or freedom, even if emancipation were to become available to them, which is an argument counter to the oft-cited NIV. The NRSV, for example, translations the verse as follows: "Even if you [as in an enslaved person] gain your freedom, make use of your present condition now more than ever."

103. Fredriksen, *Paul: The Pagans' Apostle*, 113.

promises, the patriarchs, and—again the family, 'flesh' connection—by the Christ, the son of David (Rom 9.4–5; cf. 1.3, 15.9)."[104]

Paul *adds*, however, that Jews cannot be saved apart from Jesus. He insists that Jews, in staying Jews, obey the good news (Rom 10:14–16). He supports Peter's mission to Jews (Gal 2:7–9) and focuses his own beliefs on Abraham, the law, *and* Jesus.[105] He even invokes the image of the remnant in Isaiah, contending that "not all those from Israel are Israelites [true Israel?]. . . . only a remnant of them will be saved" (see Rom 9:6–7 and 9:27). Contra Fredriksen, as readers will see in more detail below, I do not envision the remnant turning into the entire nation of Israel at Romans 11:26. Like other Jewish writers, the remnant for Paul stays a remnant.[106]

Jesus, in short, is just as necessary for Jewish salvation as he is for gentile salvation; the only difference is that Jews are to remain *Jews*, while gentiles are to remain for-the-most-part *gentile*. I thus agree with rabbinic scholar Daniel Boyarin when he writes that the post-Holocaust *Sonderweg* theory is not persuasive.[107] Instead, he asserts, it is "a moving attempt to rescue Paul from charges of anti-Judaism and save him from modern Christians."[108] I'd

104. Fredriksen, *Paul: The Pagans' Apostle*, 165. Matthew Thiessen contends similarly, although, at least on my reading, he has a slightly different view regarding the import of such ethnic differences for the oncoming of the eschaton. He writes, "God's commandments, *distinct* for Jews and for gentiles, still matter . . . Being Jewish or being gentile, belonging to the circumcision or to the foreskin, is important but only incidental to God's deliverance. God saves both" (emphasis added). Yes, God saves both (who are in Christ), but their differences, I maintain, are integral to the messianic age. That is why, again in my view, Paul is so adamant that gentiles join the movement. See Thiessen, *A Jewish Paul*, 33.

105. In Terence L. Donaldson's words, "If all Israel had followed Paul's *example*, we would have had a company of Israelites who, whatever their degree of loyalty to 'the righteousness of God expressed in the Torah', were very 'loyal to the righteous of God expressed in Jesus Christ.'" Emphasis original. Donaldson, "Jewish Christianity, Israel's Stumbling and the *Sonderweg* Reading of Paul," 30. See also Thiessen, *A Jewish Paul*, 151.

106. See Fredriksen, *Paul: The Pagans' Apostle*, 114 and accompanying footnote 72.

107. Still, though, I disagree firmly with his erasure of Paul's need for ethnic difference. See footnote 108 below. For other pushbacks to *Sonderweg*, see, for example, Donaldson, "Jewish Christianity, Israel's Stumbling and the *Sonderweg* Reading of Paul"; Matthew V. Novenson, "Anti-Judaism and Philo-Judaism in Pauline Studies, Then and Now," especially 117–118. Again, akin to this book, Novenson here is thinking metacritically.

108. See Boyarin, *A Radical Jew*, 14. Contra *Sonderweg*, Boyarin contends that Paul believed both Jews and gentiles needed Christ for the end of days. The very need to believe in Christ,

take this point even further, however. The *Sonderweg* model may not just be an effort to make Paul a good Jew *for Jews*, but rather—and perhaps even more so—a good Jew for good-book-making interpreters.[109] To borrow again from Hicks-Keeton, it may be another attempt to save Paul to save *themselves.*[110] To read Paul as a good Jew *for Jews* makes Paul ethically palatable for readers haunted by the centuries-long anti-Jewish interpretive history. It means that the long-standing anti-Jewish history in the name of Paul can be countered as a product of faulty interpretation. This is all especially helpful for those who seek to dismantle Christian anti-Judaism—including conceptions of Jews being "left behind"—yet who still want to render Paul's letters authoritative. As Jewish New Testament scholar Adele Reinhartz has put it, it means that "contemporary values that *condemn* both anti-Judaism and antisemitism" can persist.[111] A good book, in short, means a good modernity.

---

on his reading, and as noted in footnote 78 in this chapter, still made the salvation "particular" (i.e., it is "particular" to Christ). Beyond this, in conversation with the traditional New Perspective (chapter 3) and perhaps even reminiscent of thinkers like Baur (chapter 2), Boyarin sees Paul as influenced by Platonic thought and therefore reaching for a ridding of ethnic particularity in the end-times. He writes that Paul was "motivated by a Hellenistic desire for the One, which among other things produced an ideal of a universal human essence, beyond difference and hierarchy. This universal humanity, however, was predicated (and still is) on the dualism of the flesh and the spirit, such that while the body is particular, marked through practice as Jew or Greek, and through anatomy as male or female, the spirit is universal." Boyarin, *A Radical Jew*, 14. Boyarin seems to suggest further that the time to be rid of such ethnic particularity has arrived for Paul: "The Law was rather given to the Jews, as a temporary measure for specific historical reasons, meant to be superseded by its spiritual referent, faith, when the time would come, which, of course, it has . . . Paul dreamed of a day in which all human distinctions that led to hierarchy would be erased." Boyarin, *A Radical Jew*, 156, 216. This is, of course, a part of Boyarin's argument with which I firmly disagree. In fact, as readers will soon see, I see Paul as sustaining hierarchical difference *even in* the eschatological age. But where we do align, beyond this, is the extent to which we see Christian readers using ideas of Paul to support their own ideas of goodness. Contra other New Perspective thinkers, Boyarin asserts that Paul's universalism (i.e., what he and the New Perspective see as Paul's universalism) has, in the long run, contributed to profound Christian anti-Judaism.

109. To cite from the introduction of this book, many readers of the Bible "have found it easier to maintain that the Bible is not just a good book, but a great book, carrying within its good-God clutches a lasting cultural relevance that must be good, or at the very least *made* good, for humanity."

110. Hicks-Keeton, *Good Book*.

111. Emphasis mine. Here, Reinhartz is speaking about interpretations of John's Gospel, but the argument remains the same. Reinhartz, *Cast Out of the Covenant*, 163. In doing so,

Interestingly, even some proponents of the Paul within Judaism school or those for whom the New Testament is not authoritative lean into this kind of thinking. Recall the quotes above: "Where uncertainty persists, we have a moral obligation to choose against readings that harm others."[112] With the pains of Christian anti-Judaism in mind, we must read Paul in a way that "is not dependent on the denigration of ancient Jews and Judaism."[113] This interpretive move is not limited to solely Christian readers, either. As Sheinfeld remarks in response to *Wrestling with Paul* in the next chapter, "In the case of Emanuel's argument, then, I would have taken another step: to provide a justice-informed reading of Paul, readings that not only state the harm done, but also highlight interpretations that work against supersessionism and other forms of hatred."[114] Even Boyarin seems to lean into a good-book, good-modernity model. Instead of using Paul to help Jewish-Christian relations, however, he uses his interpretation of Paul to justify his own views toward Israel—that is, he makes Paul good *for him*.[115]

I do think the traditional New Perspective is correct that Paul is countering something. Rather than countering ethnic particularity, however, I

Reinhartz also affirms that her own positionality at least in part shapes her reading. She writes that her resistance to John's anti-Judaism and apologetic interpretation of it are "no doubt . . . grounded in my own Jewish identity and my knowledge of how this Gospel was used to justify anti-Semitism, as recently as in the Nazi era." Reinhartz, *Cast Out of the Covenant*, 163. Again, our contemporary relations to Jews shape our readings. With Reinhartz, I, too, no doubt at least in part because of my Jewishness, am seeking to "resist efforts to explain away or other[wise] justify [Paul's] problematic statements." Reinhartz, *Cast Out of the Covenant*, 164.

112. Thiessen, *A Jewish Paul*, 21.

113. Thiessen, *A Jewish Paul*, 21. Novenson connects these interpretive moves to a particular form of philosemitism. Engaging Gaston, who writes, "A Christian church with an antisemitic New Testament is abominable, but a Christian church without a New Testament is inconceivable. . . . a fresh reading of the letters of Paul can save us," Novenson adds, "Philo-Judaic exegesis of the New Testament becomes a moral imperative, and Paul is the canon within the canon who will admit of such an exegesis." See Novenson, "Anti-Judaism and Philo-Judaism in Pauline Studies, Then and Now," 118. For more on the relationship between antisemitism, philosemitism, and the fetishization of Jews, see chapter 5 of *Wrestling with Paul*.

114. Sheinfeld in *Wrestling with Paul*, page 228. This of course does not mean that Sheinfeld is necessarily on board to make the Bible "good." But she does seem to at least want to highlight how readers can engage Paul and interpretations of him in ways that can lead people toward a sense of "good" and "goodness."

115. To put it another way, Boyarin uses his pushback to what he sees as Christian anti-Judaism in the name of Pauline universalism to support his own "good" politics about the modern state of Israel.

suggest that Paul is countering a particular *version* of ethnic particularity (i.e., a lack of Christ), thereby creating a *different* form of ethnic particularity (i.e., communities for Christ).[116] Paul's "all Israel will be saved" from the oft-praised Romans 9–11 diatribe refers to a particular "all"—a *True* Israel—not just of ethnic Jews, but also of grafted-in ethnic gentiles, the lot of whom must worship the Israelite God and believe in the theological power of that God's heirs: Abraham first, followed by Abraham's long-awaited kin, Jesus of Nazareth, God's chosen messiah.[117]

In short, Paul was *not* a universalist.[118] Instead, he, *as a Jew*, was ethnocentric in his ideology, including his theology, which spanned into his assertions of eschatological supremacy for *Christ-following* Jews and gentiles. For him, Jews needed to maintain the law in Christ, including that which kept them ethnically distinct, and gentiles needed to abstain from the law in Christ, especially that which kept Jews ethnically distinct. Both groups, in other words, needed to maintain particular ethnic difference in their ethnocentric Christ-following orientations so as to be saved in Paul's imagined, *Jewish* end of days. While Sanders's covenantal nomism is not necessarily dismissed here—it is not individual human action that grants one a starting relationship with God, at least not for Jews—humans *were* still required to act according to their ethnicity in order to be granted access to the eschaton. This in fact seems to be a point of covenantal nomism that gets quickly overlooked. Action, overall, was still important. Works-righteousness was *still a model* for salvation.[119] Paul believed this—not just for Jews, but also for gentiles, perhaps even more so, as they were not part of God's original covenantal deal. For Jews, in other words, action was required for maintenance. For gentiles, action was required

---

116. I see Christ as representative of a particular version of cultic particularity, and thus, in turn, of ethnic particularity.

117. So again, gentiles must *not* become Jewish. But they must still, *as gentiles*, must become theologically and (to a limited extent) also ethnically Jew-*ish*. This limited extent is not because Jewishness was the problem. It is because gentileness was. For Paul, gentiles needed to change their ways—but *just enough* (maintained gentileness was still key)—to bring about the *Jewish* messianic age.

118. See also Terence Donaldson for patterns of universalism in ancient Judaism that show Paul is "less universalistic" than many ancient Jews. Terence L. Donaldson, *The Gentiles: Jewish Patterns of Universalism (to 135 CE)* (Baylor University Press, 2007).

119. See also Alexander, "Torah and Salvation in Tannaitic Literature."

for maintenance *and* eleventh-hour entry.[120] None of this made Paul special. It made him normal.

What Abouts: Then and Now

Biblical scholars often include in their work a nod to the academic *what abouts*—What about this or that passage? this or that claim? this or that possibility? this or that interpretive stake?[121] A common factor to arise in these considerations is the symbiotic relationship between the ancient "thens" and the present "nows," as discussed at the beginning of this book. Biblical scholars J. Cheryl Exum and Stephen Moore summarize this symbiosis well. Biblical interpretation, they write, is not just about "the Bible influencing culture or culture reappropriating the Bible, but a process of unceasing mutual redefinition in which cultural appropriations constantly reinvent the Bible, which in turn constantly impels new appropriations."[122] Paul, I have argued, has been repeatedly appropriated for changing good-book-making needs. By charting the interpretations of Paul as a good anti-Jew, a good anti-Semite, *the* good Jew, and a good Jew for Jews, we can see how social mores have consistently shaped interpretations of Paul and ancient Judaism. But *what about* passages that *do* seem to comply with modern ideas of Paul as a good Jew for Jews? *What about* the dangers of reading Paul as a particularistic ethnocentric Jew, given the anti-Judaism surrounding this interpretation?

I will focus here on three pushbacks to the average Paul that relate to such "what abouts." These three are the potential dangers of my reading, Galatians 3:28, and more on Paul's "all Israel."

What About Hate in the Name of Paul?

I remain aware of the dangers of my own argument. I fear indeed that my reading will be used as justification for the denigration of non-Christ-

120. At least entry in any sustained or interpersonal way. In other words, the rabbinic Noahide codes may imply that, for some ancient Jews, there was the belief that God was also "always there" for gentiles, even if at a distance. For more on this use of "eleventh-hour" terminology, see the evocation of Stendahl below and Matthew 20:1–16.

121. Thiessen, *A Jewish Paul*, 161; Eisenbaum, *Paul Was Not a Christian*, 250.

122. Stephen D. Moore and J. Cheryl Exum, "Biblical Studies / Cultural Studies," in *Biblical Studies / Cultural Studies: The Third Sheffield Colloquium*, ed. Stephen D. Moore and J. Cheryl Exum (Sheffield Academic Press, 1998), 35.

following Jews (i.e., most Jews) in modern Christian imagination, let alone non-Christ-following gentiles. I also fear that my argument will be used to separate Paul from Jesus, as Hitler himself did. I can hear the possibilities now: "Paul may have been ethnocentric, but the real hero, Jesus, was not." Or in Hitler's own words, "St. Paul transformed a local movement of Aryan opposition to Jewry . . . [causing] the death of the Roman Empire."[123] My reading can also be interpreted as blaming Paul's Judaism for his ethnocentrism and ethnonationalism, two attacks antisemitism has made repeatedly on Jews and Judaism, including in our current "now."[124]

These attacks, however, are part of the problem. The historical Jesus was *also* an average Jew, perhaps even more so: He, like most Jews, did not have the means to travel across the ancient Mediterranean and spread his understanding of Judaism to a vast number of people.[125] The attacks above also imply that all Jews and Judaism, from antiquity to today, support Jewish ethnocentrism at the expense of others. This implication is simply inaccurate. Neither ancient Judaism nor Rabbinic Judaism contains creeds, but instead, they maintain the right to think in multitudes. Again, Paul is only "average" in his ethnonationalist ideals based on the *limited* evidence we have; it is quite possible the actual "average" Jew rarely thought about messianism or apocalypticism or an eschatological age. Jews in modernity have certainly ushered in a wide range of possibilities. The Reconstructionist movement, for example, rejects the notion of Jews as ethnically "chosen" in its ideology, and the Humanistic movement does not focus on having any sort of relationship with any kind of god.[126]

---

123. See Bormann, *Hitler's Secret Conversations 1941–1944*, 64; as well as page 100 of this book and accompanying footnote 160.

124. Indeed, libels of Jews as monstrous ethnonationalists by way of "Zionism" have been thrown across the United States in the 2023–2024 "now" in which I write this sentence, as if there is only one definition of Zionism (there is not), and as if all Jews fit into all or any definition (they do not). Not all Jews identify as Zionists, either.

125. See Paula Fredriksen, "The Question of Worship: Gods, Pagans, and the Redemption of Israel," in *Paul Within Judaism: Restoring the First-Century Context to the Apostle*, ed. Mark D. Nanos and Magnus Zetterholm (Fortress Press, 2015), 175–176.

126. For an accessible overview, see Richard A. Hirsh, "Reconstructionist Judaism and the Rejection of Chosen People," *My Jewish Learning*, Republished from *The Reconstructionist*, September 1984, https://www.myjewishlearning.com/article/reconstructionist-judaism-and-the-rejection-of-chosen-people/; and Paul Golin, "What Is Secular Humanistic Judaism?," My Jewish Learning, accessed March 6, 2025, https://www.myjewishlearning.com/article/judaism-with-no-god/.

Many Jews today do not even consider ideas of an end of days, messianism, or an afterlife, but instead focus their attention on *tikkun olam b'olam ha-ze*: human efforts to help the world in the here and now.[127]

Additionally, while the purpose of this book is to wrestle with the relationship among Paul, his readers, and Jews, it must be said that my analysis of Paul might also be used to harm additional persons, including women, queer folks, and those enslaved, historically or otherwise. Suffice it to say, I fundamentally disagree with Paul on his views here. Rather than pretending his views don't exist, however, I urge readers to recall the many ways in which the ancient sources invite readers into a world of diversity, difference, and contestation. Paul disagreed with others. Others disagreed with Paul. The texts *themselves* wrestle with this contestation, as do many of their interpreters. Even though Paul, as a product of his time, seemed to not take issue with slavery or gendered hierarchy, there are many modern readers—including those who read Paul's letters as scripture—who have *already* found ways to wrestle with Paul's texts and indeed *think differently* from Paul.

What About Galatians 3:28?

I am also well aware that many readers of Paul point to Galatians 3:28 as proof of an anti-ethnocentric apostle and, to the points above, an antislavery and anti-gendered-hierarchy one. This verse proclaims, "There is no Jew or Greek; there is no slave or free; there is no male or female. For you are all one in Christ Jesus."[128]

This declaration has been invoked repeatedly to redeem Paul from charges of Jewish particularism. As biblical scholar Sze-kar Wan notes, "[It] is the very

127. In fact, as Levenson asserts, while "anti-Semitism has historically focused on the alleged Jewish clannishness and has charged that Jews' absorption with their own group leads to lack of concern for others. . . . [O]ne of the reasons for absence of a missionary thrust in rabbinic theology is the doctrine of human dignity in general, whether Israelite or not." See Levenson, "The Universal Horizon of Biblical Particularism," 143 and 148, respectively.

128. It is possible that Galatians 3:28 is a recitation of an existing liturgy, rather than Paul's original words. Cf. 1 Corinthians 12:13. Also, my translation here is debatable. Technically, the last clause translates as "there is no male and female," which has led many scholars to think that Paul is thinking intertextually with Genesis 1:27–28. Grammatically, however, the Greek *kai* or "and" in English could function as an emphasized "or."

foundation, the very basis, for Christian universalism."[129] Moreover, it has served as a recurring touchstone for notions of a Pauline-driven Christian equality. Even Mark Nanos, a pioneer of the Paul within Judaism approach, interprets Galatians 3:28 as Paul supporting a new world order in which discrimination is erased. The verse, Nanos contends, shows that equality is a cornerstone of Paul's "utopian" vision, where unity in Christ transcends social hierarchies.[130]

I'll be blunt here. Galatians 3:28 is not about erasing particularism, difference, or inequality, but rather reinforcing them. As Paul emphasizes, Christ remains the central axis of his thought: "There is no Jew or Greek" *in Christ*.[131] Paul, moreover, is not trying to collapse those who are "in Christ" into some kind of "oneness" or "sameness."[132] Nor is he trying to create space for equality

---

129. Indeed, as biblical scholar Sheila Briggs explains, New Testament readers tend to interpret Paul's authentic letters with an "appeal to a normative emancipatory core." Galatians 3:28 is the hallmark appealed-to passage, with other authentic texts "read in its light and subordinated to it in interpretation." See Wan, "Does Diaspora Identity Imply Some Sort of Universality?," 115; Briggs, "Slavery and Gender," 173.

130. In other words, although Nanos does not see Paul as a universalist, he does see him, by way of Galatians 3:28 (and Romans 11:26, in which "all Israel" is saved), as an egalitarian. See Nanos, "A Jewish View," 187–188, 193.

131. See, among others, Hodge, "Paul and Ethnicity," 556; Concannon, *Profaning Paul*, 3; Levenson, "The Universal Horizon of Biblical Particularism," 166. Elisabeth Schüssler Fiorenza also asks "whether the expressions 'Jew/Greek, slave/free' mean only men or whether they include wo/men." Elisabeth Schüssler Fiorenza, *Rhetoric and Ethic: The Politics of Biblical Studies* (Fortress Press, 1999), 155–156.

132. As Daniel Boyarin has now famously argued. In other words, as alluded to in footnote 108 in this chapter, while Boyarin's overarching thesis is that a Platonist-inspired Paul was dissatisfied with Jewish ethnic particularism, I argue that Jewish ethnic particularism, along with class and gender hierarchy, was integral to Paul's Christ-following mission, so much so that, for Paul, ethnic distinction was required for eschatological deliverance. I do agree with Boyarin, however, when he argues that sameness does not mean equality. Often, he asserts, when difference is squashed into sameness, the culturally established "norm" (e.g., maleness over females) subsumes the whole (e.g., everything becomes male). Boyarin thus reads his understanding of Paul—as one urging for sameness—as overarchingly problematic. In his view, in fact, it is the start of a male-centered and even gentile Christian worldview over and against women and the particularity of Jews. There is a problem with the last part of his argument, however (the part where Boyarin contends that Paul is responsible for sparking a gentile Christian worldview). I agree with Pamela Eisenbaum when she writes that "Boyarin is absolutely right that there is no such thing as a human essence that is truly universal, because such essences are always envisioned with some particular template of what constitutes a human being, but he projects back upon Paul the wrong template. Boyarin works with essentialized

among and across identities in Christ.[133] Instead, Paul is simply saying that persons from each of the above identities—Jews, gentiles, the enslaved, free persons, males, females—have shared *access* to participation in Jesus as the messiah and thus an inheritance in the Jewish deity's blessings and rescue, including salvation in the end of days.[134] In other words, it is not Jew *or* Greek, but rather both. Separate identities and even statuses are not erased, nor, in Paul's view, should be erased. Paul *himself* maintained Jewish difference in Christ, and perhaps even used an enslaved scribe to write down the verse now known as Galatians 3:28.[135]

It is Paul's surrounding verses that make this interpretation clear. For example, immediately after reciting the liturgical lines, Paul remarks that those who belong *to Christ* will inherit the promises *of Abraham*: "And if you belong in Christ, then you are Abraham's offspring, heirs according to the promise." Particularism thus remains through his Christ-centered worldview *and* his acknowledgment of Abrahamic/Jewish supremacy. In order to be "in" for Paul, one has to be "in" in the *right* way. One must have faith in Jesus as the Christ and abide by an overarching Abrahamic (i.e., Jewish) framework. Those who

notions of 'Jews' and 'Christians' that are anachronistic. For Paul, the prototypical human ideal is best represented by the free Jewish man. When Paul juxtaposes 'Jew' and 'Greek,' he means that the *Jew* possesses the preferred condition." In other words, Paul, contra Boyarin, did not set up the world to be a gentile Christian world "free" of Jewish particularism (or any particularism, for that matter, as gentiles *are also* particular). That came from later interpreters asserting their own idea of Christianness onto Paul. See Pamela Eisenbaum, "Is Paul the Father of Misogyny and Antisemitism?," *CrossCurrents* 50, no. 4 (2000): 514, emphasis hers.

133. As Sze-kar Wan has attested as a nuanced response to Boyarin's view on Paul and sameness. Wan, for example, still sees Paul as thinking ethnically, but also as "attempt[ing] to erase the *power differential* . . . [and] by *combining these differences into a hybrid existence*." In the end, for Wan, ethnocentrism is upheld, but so in fact is universality: "Universality is upheld, but it is universality that is predicated on, requires, and erected on the foundation of cultural and ethnic particularities." Wan, "Does Diaspora Identity Imply Some Sort of Universality?," 126; emphasis in the original.

134. The same can be said for 1 Corinthians 12:13. Regarding Galatians 3:28, Sanders expresses a similar view about Paul referring to shared access (as opposed to erasure of difference); he references Krister Stendahl and W. D. Davies as being in agreement in his summary. See Sanders, "Paul's Attitude Toward the Jewish People," 176.

135. Candida Moss seems to suggest this especially for Galatians, as language of scribal work permeates the text in a way that is missing from his other letters. Moss, *God's Ghostwriters*, 85–86. See also chapter 1 of this book, pages 17 and 20–21, and accompanying footnotes 2 and 12.

do not abide by these particulars are left out of Paul's eschatological plan. And while these particularisms alone illustrate a hierarchical view of insiders versus outsiders, Paul also maintains difference and hierarchy for those on the inside of his eschatological overview. For example, after Paul says that "in Christ" there is "neither slave nor free," he retells the story of Sarah and Hagar from the book of Genesis. In doing so, he emphasizes how Hagar, the non-Israelite enslaved woman, is inferior to Sarah, the Israelite free woman (Gal 4:21–31).[136] In other words, Paul, even "in Christ," maintains and perpetuates a slave/free dichotomy.

Paul also maintains a hierarchy in Christ for Jews and gentiles.[137] One must remember that the entire framework here is a Jewish one—the "right" one, according to Paul. But we also see evidence of Paul's Jewish superiority across texts. That he consistently refers to different groups of non-Jews under the single heading of "gentile" demonstrates this point well. Generally speaking, while some non-Jews referred to other non-Jews as *ethnē*, or "gentiles," they more often referred to themselves with more regional specificity. Depending on the context, the use of the word "gentile" could bring with it a connotation of "foreignness" or even "barbarity," such as we see in Aristotle's *Politics* (7.1324b5–10). For many Jews, the use of the word "gentile" is a way to clump all non-Jews into this flattening and sometimes belittling category (akin to "goy" or "shiksa" in modernity).[138] Paul, moreover, did not seek to override the separation between Jews and gentiles or this derision of non-Jews. In Galatians, in fact, just before the infamous 3:28, he explicitly reasons in

136. Briggs, "Slavery and Gender," 184. See also Christy Cobb, "Enslaved Women, Women Enslavers: Kyriarchy and Intersectionality in the New Testament," *Journal of Feminist Studies in Religion* 40, no. 1 (2024): 43–60. To bring this in conversation with Paul's letter to Philemon, a text that discusses the enslaved Onesimus, see, for example, Marchal, *Appalling Bodies*, chapter 4. To bring this in conversation with 1 Cor 7:21, a text sometimes translated as Paul advocating for enslaved persons' freedom, see footnote 102 in this chapter.

137. There was also hierarchy between women and men. Repeatedly, Paul asserts that Christ-followers must perform proper masculinity, as seen above in Romans 1. For more on Paul and privileging masculinity, see Young, "Make Rome Great Again." For more on Paul and sexual ideals, see Bernadette J. Brooten, *Love Between Women: Early Christian Responses to Female Homoeroticism* (University of Chicago Press, 1996); Hoke, *Feminism, Queerness, Affect, and Romans*; Joseph A. Marchal, "The Exceptional Proves Who Rules: Imperial Sexual Exceptionalism in and Around Paul's Letters," *Journal of Early Christian History* 5, no. 1 (2015): 87–115.

138. Thiessen, *A Jewish Paul*, 84. See also Hodge, "The Question of Identity," 156, including footnote 6.

these xenophobic, Jewish supremacist ways about gentiles. The non-Jews, he says, are "sinners" (*harmatōloi*); they exist in contrast to those who are Jews "by nature" (*phusei*, Gal 2:15). He then repeats this in Romans. The power of salvation, he affirms, is for "the Jew first" (Rom 1:16, 2:9–10), whereas gentiles are disparaged for being "against nature" (*para physin*, Rom 1:26). As if this wasn't enough, he then reminds readers of such Jewish supremacy by asking and answering, "What advantage has the Jew? Or what is the value of circumcision? Much in every way" (Rom 3:1–2). Indeed, for Paul, it is the gentile who is the problem. And it is the Jew (Paul) who provides the guiding light.[139]

Again, this does not mean that gentiles are to become Jewish. As we have seen, he makes clear that Jews and gentiles are to "*remain* in the condition in which [they] were called" (1 Cor 7:17, 7:20).[140] Such conditions are also to remain hierarchical ones. Pamela Eisenbaum, for example, connects these verses to Galatians 3:28, stating that "one term in each pair [Jew/Greek, slave/free, male/female] represents the ideal, the desired status for the believer."[141] When Paul, a Jew, "juxtaposes 'Jew' and 'Greek,' he means that the *Jew* possesses the preferred condition . . . It is the Greeks who are underprivileged. Being 'in Christ' allows Gentiles to be part of the people of God, a privilege Jews already hold."[142] The only thing I'd add to this—or really emphasize—is that it is *Christ-following* Jews, for Paul, who are held in highest regard and to whom the Israelite God bestows highest privileges.[143] As Paul himself remarks,

139. Brian Rainey also makes an argument that Paul's xenophobic polemic about gentiles portrays them as sinners by nature or heritage. See Rainey, *Religion, Ethnicity and Xenophobia in the Bible*, 229–235. See also Young, "Ethnic Ethics," 237.

140. Emphasis mine.

141. Eisenbaum, "Is Paul the Father of Misogyny and Antisemitism?," 514.

142. Eisenbaum, "Is Paul the Father of Misogyny and Antisemitism?," 514; emphasis in the original. In this way, one could argue that the various "freedoms" Paul says Christ-following gentiles will receive are those from their sinful gentile ways and the gentile ways of the broader, non-Jewish world that have, thus far, at least in Paul's mind, not only made the world suffer but have also prohibited gentiles from being part of the people of God (e.g., Rom 6:18–22, 8:2, 8:20–21). Such "freedoms," however, do not negate gentiles' lesser-than status or the fact that Paul still sees them, even in Christ, as being in some sense against nature (Rom 11:24). The freedom, in other words, is from the *fullness* of their sins/abhorrence.

143. This, for example, is a point at which I disagree with both Pamela Eisenbaum and Mark Nanos, albeit for different reasons. For Eisenbaum's Paul, Jews don't need to believe in Jesus as the Christ in order to achieve salvation, with which I disagree. She, for example, reads Paul's

it is the grafted-in gentiles who will always remain in some sense "against nature" (*para physin*, Rom 11:24).[144]

---

understanding of Jewish lack of faith as "not a lack of faith in God but a failure to recognize that God has initiated the process of redemption [by bringing Jesus to the gentiles]." While this is likely part of the problem for Paul, I do not think it is all of it. And in Nanos' view, Paul thought that Jews *did* need Christ, but that "non-Jews should be regarded as if they had equal standing with Jews," with which I also disagree. In other words, I see Paul as needing both Jews and gentiles to believe in Christ (contra Eisenbaum), and that in such belief Jews for Christ were superior to gentiles for Christ (contra Nanos). See Eisenbaum, *Paul Was Not a Christian*, chapter 14 (p. 253 for the quotation); and Nanos, "A Jewish View," 191–193. Nanos adds to this idea, too, in a more recent essay. He writes:

> As I understand Paul, he confessed Jesus as Messiah and upheld that his fellow Jews should do the same, but not in order to be saved in evangelical salvation-based terms by any mechanism, period. For Paul, that was a truth claim made within Judaism; it did not involve Jews being saved in evangelical soteriological terms because they were never lost in the logical way that paradigm requires. What he promoted was a chronometrically based propositional claim that an awaited event, when the reign of God would arrive to rescue those who were already in a living covenant relationship from sinfulness, from sinners, from enemies, and so on—so that they could complete their calling to bring the gospel announcement to the nations—had begun. That premise, central to the gospel, should shape the thoughts and lives of the non-Israelites he addressed toward humble concern for the well-being of those Israelites who were not persuaded that was the case yet: they remained the "beloved" because of the promises made to their fathers, not least to Jacob/Israel. To argue that Israelites were being *protected* during this anomalous period of alienation while retaining continued covenant standing is not the same as the later evangelical concept that Jews need to believe in Jesus Christ to become saved, which empties their historical covenantal standing as "irrevocable" of the substance that Paul labors to explain.
>
> Paul's conviction that Jews should profess a Jewish Messiah was conceptualized within Jewish communal life; the calling of Israel was to announce this news to the nations. Israelites who were doubtful of the claims made by the gospel and thus that it was the appropriate time to herald this news to the nations needed "to be kept safe" until they were persuaded.

In other words, Nanos argues that all Jews "will be kept safe" until they are persuaded that Jesus is the Christ. This means that, contra the traditional evangelical salvation-based terms, Jews, for Paul, retain their covenantal relationship with God *even when* they are not yet persuaded by the Jesus movement. I remain curious if Nanos sees gentiles as receiving the same protections, and if not—which is my suspected reading of his work—whether that might alter his view that Paul believed "non-Jews should be regarded as if they had equal standing with Jews," as cited above. See Mark Nanos, "All Israel Will Be *Saved* or *Kept Safe*? (Rom 11:26): Israel's *Conversion* or *Irrevocable Calling to Gospel the Nations*?," in *Israel and the Nations: Paul's Gospel in the Context of Jewish Expectation*, ed. František Ábel (Lexington Books/Fortress Academic, 2021), 254–255; emphasis original.

144. Whereas the righteous Jews entering the end of days are "of nature" (Gal 2:15).

Paul also privileges men above women and, relatedly, masculinity above femininity. Going back to 1 Thessalonians, for example, it is perhaps worth noting that Paul never addresses women within the letter. He speaks only to "brothers," leaving some scholars to question if he, at least in his early ministry, hoped for the Christ movement to be a male-only fraternity, one that would adopt the Jewish god and Jewish Christ as their patron male superiors.[145] In fact, even when he includes women in later instructions (e.g., 1 Cor 7, 9:5, 11–14), perhaps indicating a change in his ideas for the movement or simply him writing to a different kind of social formation, he still addresses his recipients in overarching male terms.[146] "Greetings brothers (*adelphoi*)," he writes, never "greetings brothers and sisters (*adelphoi kai adelphē*)." In other words, although English translations often interpret Paul's use of *adelphoi* as a "generic masculine" that encompassed both men and women (akin to "mankind" in English), it is clear that Paul is not trying to override this patriarchal practice, as egalitarian interpretations of Galatians 3:28 would suggest. To be "against nature," in his view, includes the forgetting of proper masculine action. As seen in Romans 1, he makes clear that even sex must revolve around the penis and proper (i.e., "topping") masculine use of it (Rom 1).[147] Considering all that is

145. See Richard Ascough, "The Thessalonian Christian Community as a Professional Voluntary Association," *Journal of Biblical Literature* 119 (2000): 311–328. Although Paul writes about women's experiences and uses feminine imagery a few times in 1 Thessalonians (e.g., 2:7), there is a difference between writing about women and Paul actually addressing women within the letter. Abraham Malherbe also makes the argument that such feminine language was common in moral-philosophical texts to stress how a good (male) teacher should be gentle and adaptable. See Abraham J. Malherbe, *Paul and the Popular Philosophers* (Fortress Press, 1989). Looking beyond solely the rhetorical, however, Melanie Johnson-DeBaufre argues that women were indeed part of the community to whom Paul writes in 1 Thessalonians. In her words, "Despite the uneven and accidental nature of ancient remains, archaeology often provides a visible and material confirmation of a basic dictum of feminist historians: *wo/men were there*." Emphasis original. Melanie Johnson-DeBaufre, "'Gazing Upon the Invisible': Archaeology, Historiography, and the Elusive Women of 1 Thessalonians," in *From Roman to Early Christian Thessalonikē: Studies in Religion and Archaeology*, ed. Laura Nasrallah, Charalambos Bakirtzis, and Steven J. Friesen, Harvard Theological Studies 64 (Harvard University Press, 2010), 73–108. Again, "wo/men" is from Elisabeth Schüssler Fiorenza; see *Wisdom Ways*, 107–109.

146. See also Jorunn Økland, *Women in Their Place: Paul and the Corinthian Discourse of Gender and Sanctuary Space* (T&T Clark, 2004).

147. Again, see Young, "Make Rome Great Again." For a reading of Paul that identifies him with the conquered and thus does *not* see him as modeling Roman masculinity, see Davina

at stake for Paul on gender, sex, class, and ethnicity elsewhere, it is difficult to imagine he was erasing his hierarchical ideologies in a single verse.[148]

Some scholars have even linked Galatians 3:28 to discussions of masculine androgyny in Christ. For example, in an almost factual manner, New Testament scholar Diana Swancutt writes that Galatians 3:28 refers directly to the primal androgyne myth of Genesis 1–3, whereby God creates the first human as an androgynous being: "And God created the earth creature [*adam*] in his image, in the image of God he created him, male and female he created them" (Gen 1:26–27).[149] Interestingly, for some thinkers, the androgyny of the first human is less male *and* female (or, alternatively, and to get to some renderings of Galatians 3:28, less of a "neither male nor female" quality) and more a subsuming of the female into the perfect male: "And God created the earth creature in *his* image, in the image of God he created *him*, male and female he created them" (Gen 1:26–27).[150] The "them" in this case, given the surrounding information, is with maleness. Such reading is heightened when combined with what happens in the next story: *Adam*, the earth creature, is distinguished as a man (*ish*, counter to *ishah*; Gen 2:22–24). When reading the two stories together, one notices that the androgynous *adam* is consistently

---

C. Lopez, *The Apostle to the Conquered: Reimagining Paul's Mission* (Fortress Press, 2010).

148. Or a single quotation of a circulating liturgy, if one believes Paul is quoting or borrowing from a preexisting liturgical formula in Galatians 3:28.

149. In Swancutt's words, "Paul's Christ is the eschatological recreation of the original androgyne, a distinct sex within whose body believers are materially, collectively remade. By 'putting on' Christ's body . . . they became 'no longer male and female.'" See Diana M. Swancutt, "Sexing the Pauline Body of Christ: Scriptural Sex in the Context of the American Christian Culture War," in *Toward a Theology of Eros: Transfiguring Passion at the Limits of Discipline*, ed. Virginia Burrus and Catherine Keller (Fordham University Press, 2006), 67. As for the translation of Genesis, I, like many scholars, am following Phyllis Trible's play on words by referring to *adam*—"the thing of the earth"—as an earthling and/or earth creature. See Phyllis Trible, "Not a Jot, Not a Tittle: Genesis 2–3 After Twenty Years," in *Eve and Adam: Jewish, Christian, and Muslim Readings on Genesis and Gender*, 1st ed., ed. Kristen E. Kvam, Linda S. Schearing, and Valarie H. Ziegler (Indiana University Press, 1999), 431–443.

150. For a brief exposition of the masculinized androgyne, see Marchal, *Appalling Bodies*, 34–36. For a related exposition of gender mixing/fluidity as privileging maleness, see also Virginia Burrus, "Mapping a Metamorphosis: Initial Reflections on Gender and Ancient Religious Discourses," in *Mapping Gender in Ancient Religious Discourses*, ed. Todd C. Penner and Caroline Vander Stichele (Brill, 2007), 1–10.

linked with dominant maleness, so much so that both the earth creature and the first man share the same designation: *Adam*.[151]

The relevant point for interpreting Galatians, then, is that Paul, if indeed influenced by the androgyne myth, may have been presuming an additional kind of masculine hierarchy. Indeed, comparable discourses on androgyny have it as a decidedly *masculine* androgyny, with the weak/inferior femininity eliminated or assimilated to the masculine. An oft-cited verse to support this male-centered discourse comes from the extracanonical Gospel of Thomas, where Simon Peter says of Mary of Magdala, "Let Mary leave us, for women are not worthy of life." Jesus then responds to this by saying, "I myself shall lead her in order to make her male, so that she too may become a living spirit resembling you males. For every woman who will make herself male will enter the kingdom of heaven" (Thom 114). A problem with this citation, however, at least when trying to decipher Paul, is that it was written after Paul's own time.[152] In other words, while this gospel seems to understand perfection in male terms—and while it may indeed be doing so in reference to a perfect, masculinized primal androgyne—it is unclear how much we can interpret Paul's thought as something reflected in this story.

Regardless of whether one thinks Paul was influenced by masculinized androgyny myths, I see no reason to think that Paul's eschaton functioned without the aforementioned social hierarchies and privileges in place. Akin to contemporaneous Jewish imaginings of the end-times, Paul imagined resurrected bodies maintaining their pre-resurrected shape and form. Biblical scholar Isaac Soon demonstrates this well through his reading of 1 Corinthians 15:36–49. In his words,

> Nowhere does [Paul] say openly that the form or shape of the resurrected body will be different from the one that believers have presently. He does speak about difference in quality (pneumatic, luminous, etc.), which scholars have often mistakenly conflated, but this is not the same thing as the form and physical shape of the body . . . The same body sown is also the same body raised . . . Paul argues it is "this body" ([*to phtharton touto*], i.e. the present body) that will take

151. This reading, of course, requires interpreting the two creation accounts together, the first being Genesis 1:1–2:3 and the second being 2:4–3:24.

152. Marchal, *Appalling Bodies*, 34–35.

> on immortality in 15:53–4, suggesting structural continuity with regard to shape and form.[153]

What this means, among other things, is that in Paul's imagined end of days, Jewish males retained their circumcision, and gentile males retained their foreskin. This retained set of bodily markers—and bodily differences—is one that highlighted for Paul the long-standing Jewish relationship with God that gentiles do not have. Reflecting the circumcised angels of *Jubilees* discussed above, Jewish males are closer to perfection—closer to God—than Jewish females or any gentile in the eschaton. To put it another way, Paul provides another example of how people prior to the advent of modern race science conceptualized ethnic identity as a marker of one's overall worth. While the focus of this book's chapter 2 was on gentile Christ-following ethnocentrism and hierarchy, Jews were not immune to thinking through a framework of social domination. Paul, like other ancient Jewish messianists, may have inverted the Jewish-gentile hierarchy of the broader Greco-Roman world by placing Jews (or, in his case, Jewish Christ-followers) at the top of his social hierarchy, but the overall concept of ethnicity determining value stays the same.[154]

Thus, to summarize, even in Galatians 3:28, Paul's messianism adheres to the common Jewish hope that ethnically and hierarchically distinct Jews and gentiles would follow the God of Israel in the end of days. For Paul, eschatological deliverance was bestowed first to the ethnically righteous Jewish Christ-confessor—the remnant—followed by the ethnically gentile Christ-confessor. Jewish males would continue to be treated as first in the end of days.

153. For an overview of Paul's multistage understanding of the resurrection process, including the retainment of body—and thus bodily differences—see Isaac T. Soon, *A Disabled Apostle: Impairment and Disability in the Letters of Paul* (Oxford University Press, 2023), 165–166.

154. Indeed, when thinking in this way, Paul and John of Revelation start to not look so different. Whereas most scholars contend that John stands directly against Paul's views, I see them as far closer in outlook than is often suggested. Another similarity between Paul and Revelation is Revelation's strong masculine over feminine hierarchy, such that Revelation (14:1–5) seems even to imply an absence of women or at least of defiling femininity in the eschaton. For more on Revelation's simultaneous mimicry and mockery of the gendered Greco-Roman social system, see Emanuel, *Humor, Resistance, and Jewish Cultural Persistence in the Book of Revelation*.

What About "All Israel"?

Finally, I am aware of the well-established argument that "Israel" for Paul, including his line that "all Israel will be saved," never includes gentiles but rather refers solely to Jews. Matthew Thiessen and Paula Fredriksen argue this, for example, writing, "For Paul, consistently, Jews are Israel, and Israel, his own family, is the Jews."[155] But as they also note, Paul is super "weird."[156] Much of his rhetoric is "awkward."[157] The fact that Paul imagines a new tree featuring Christ-believing Jews and Christ-believing gentiles as representing God's true people shows that the culminating "all Israel will be saved" verse could indeed be, even if unusual—even if awkward—a reflection of this tree's new Israel: Christ-believing Jews *and* grafted-in Christ-believing gentiles. Let me be clear: This is not about gentiles changing ethnicities. Going back to the fluidity of ethnic identity, for example, it *was* considered possible in the ancient world for genealogies to be changed and/or updated. People could be added to—and taken out of—an ethnic boundary, including genealogically.[158] But while gentiles *could* undergo a full ethnic adhesion to Judaism, that is not what I am suggesting is happening here. Instead, I am suggesting that Paul is simply making sense of "all Israel" in a new, ethnonationalist, *eschatological* way. *Both* distinct ethnic Jews and distinct ethnic gentiles will serve as the "true-but-different populaces" of the "new Christ-centered nation" that is the "new true Israel."[159] In other words, the tree is a metaphor for the new messianic nation and its saved, Christ-centered inhabitants. Christ-following

155. Thiessen and Fredriksen, "Paul and Israel," 384. Interestingly, Sanders contends that "Israel" means both Christ-following Jews and gentiles only in Gal 6:16 (thus not in Rom 11:26, as I am claiming in this chapter). In Sanders's note on Romans, he writes, "In [Rom] 9:6, [Paul] seems to be headed toward a distinction of two 'Israels': those who are descended from Israel and those who belong to Israel, but the terminology is not carried through." Sanders does, however, agree that Paul understands certain people as "True Israel" and others as not. See E. P. Sanders, *Paul, the Law, and the Jewish People* (Fortress Press, 1983), 174, 207.

156. Thiessen, *A Jewish Paul*, chapter 1.

157. Thiessen and Fredriksen, "Paul and Israel," 371.

158. Hodge, "Paul and Ethnicity," 553. See Fredriksen, "The Question of Worship," 183.

159. Paul's "True Israel" is indeed a particular universalist model—an *ethnically particular* "all" of *distinct* Jews and gentiles for Christ—but not in the way Daniel Boyarin suggests. Cf. Boyarin, *A Radical Jew*, 201–206. Also cf. Garroway, *Paul's Gentile-Jews*.

Jews will still be first as members of this new "True Israel." Christ-following gentiles will still be second.[160]

But even if we don't agree that "all Israel" of Romans 9–11 refers to a "True Israel" of Christ-following Jews *and* gentiles, it still refers to, at the very least, contra *Sonderweg, Christ-following* Jews: "Only those who do not persist in unbelief will be grafted back in" (Rom 11:23). Given this qualification, paired with the fact that Paul sees the eschaton as arriving imminently, it is hard to imagine that Paul believed *every single Jew* would all of a sudden follow Jesus and thus be saved in the eschaton. Paul, in fact, appears to be nothing short of flummoxed. This whole thing is a "mystery," he writes, perhaps indicating his own supposition that *of course* some Jews won't buy in—*of course* "all" can't really mean "all"—*of course* non-Christ-confessing Jews, alongside non-Christ-confessing gentiles, will be left behind. Again, as even he remarks earlier in reference to Isaiah, "only a remnant of them will be saved" (Rom 9:27).[161]

But what if it *does* mean all Jews? What if, for Paul, it *is* true, as many theologians and biblical scholars have indeed surmised, including those who interpret from a Paul within Judaism approach, that a hardening has come upon unbelieving Jews. Such unbelieving Jews *will* be abandoned by the Israelite God as seen in the olive tree metaphor. But *then,* the mystery: After a number of gentiles believe, the Jews who were abandoned—the ones who were *just* left behind—*will* all be saved because God will make it so. God will harden their hearts from Christ so the gentiles can join in. And then all Jews will somehow unharden. *Every* Jew in this scenario *will* be saved in the messianic age—in Christ, of course. But have no fear. This for Paul is the "merc[iful]"

160. This is similar to what we see in Revelation's New Jerusalem, although Paul imagines a higher status for gentiles. See Emanuel, *Humor, Resistance, and Jewish Cultural Persistence in the Book of Revelation*, chapter 5. It is also similar to Roman populaces. Not all civilians of the Roman Empire were Roman or even Roman citizens, but they still lived under Rome. Thus, not all civilians of Paul's eschaton are Jews (or from the Israelite nation), but all live under Israel.

161. Cf., for example, Nanos, "A Jewish View," 192–193; Sheinfeld, "Who Is the Righteous Remnant in Romans 9–11?," 43; Young, "Ethnic Ethics," 241; Fredriksen, *Paul: The Pagans' Apostle*, 114.

part, writes Thiessen.[162] It is Paul's "utopian" vision, writes Mark Nanos.[163] Or as Paul might put it, it is the "*good* news" (emphasis mine; see 1 Cor. 15:1; 1 Thess 4:3–5; Rom 1:16, 10:14–16).

Is It?

What often differentiates my scholarship from traditional Paul in/and Judaism—including Paul within Judaism—scholarship is the extent to which I implement a "no view from nowhere" or a "then *and* now" approach. As seen throughout this book, I insert into my work the knowing that emotion and position motivate our inquiry. Even facts, as early Christianity scholar Maia Kotrosits reminds us, are charged by "the indefinite electricity of interpersonal moments; the temperature of mood of a given room; the hyper-particular situation in which something is said or the way in which something unfolds, the historical and cultural force fields and unconscious desires that coalesce people, give ideas traction, or sweep possibilities away."[164] Thinking effectively, in other words, means thinking affectively—recognizing the many texts and contexts that make us think and feel the way we do. Interestingly, many New and Newer Perspectivers start with this understanding by naming the Old Perspective's biased Protestant motivations or the pain of the Holocaust as they quest for new orientations. "No exegesis is without presuppositions," writes Lloyd Gaston of the Old Perspective.[165] "The crimes committed against the Jewish people throughout history has led me to take a [Paul within Judaism] approach," writes Magnus Zetterholm, as cited earlier.[166] This "no view from nowhere" lens, however, seems to stop here. In Newer Perspective work, it rarely goes beyond addressing how and why the Old and Newer Perspectives got their legs.

162. Thiessen, *A Jewish Paul*, 156. See also Romans 11:30–32.

163. Nanos, "A Jewish View," 193. See also Amy-Jill Levine, "Supersessionism: Admit and Address Rather than Debate or Deny," *Religions* 13, no. 2 (2022): 155–166, esp. 157 and 164. Here Levine argues that while she finds Christian supersessionism to be inevitable, "a promotion of Romans 11 over [texts like] Galatians and 1 Thessalonians would be of enormous help" for Jewish-Christian relations.

164. Kotrosits, *How Things Feel*, 2.

165. Gaston, "New Testament Theology After the Holocaust," 129.

166. Zetterholm, *Approaches to Paul*, x.

I'd like to do it differently. With affect and intertext in mind, I should say that I came to Paul studies by way of Revelation studies. My first book is on John's Apocalypse, a text of affective terror, especially for women.[167] When reading Romans 9–11, however, I cannot help but imagine the walls between it and Revelation crumble. I am not making a claim of authorial intent, imagining that either Paul or John of Patmos had access to each other's writings. But I do see Revelation as opening an unsettling vista on Romans 9–11. Reading with the grain of Revelation, for example, means celebrating the demise of those who do not follow God in the "right" way. Revelation's Others, depicted often with feminine imagery, are pawns for the eschaton, examples of who *not* to be while on the road to eternal salvation.

For Paul, non-Christ-confessing *Jews* are these pawns—they are clay vessels with whom God can do what God wants (Rom 9:21–23, 11:8)—and their stumbling is required for the ushering in of gentiles and thus for the eschaton. Gentiles, in fact, have the quickest path of all: "Do you know who the eleventh-hour folks are?" Krister Stendahl asks. "They are we, the Gentiles. It was Israel who worked through the whole long heat of sacred history and we lazy Gentiles came in at the last moment and got the same pay."[168] Sure, law-abiding (i.e., ethnic) Jews who follow Jesus are a glorious remnant—they are included in the tree and thus the end of days. And sure, maybe *all* the Jews who were once disabled *will*, all of a sudden, also be saved in the end-times. But even if they are—and I am not convinced this is how Paul sees it—every one of these once-left-behind Jews will ostensibly be "cared for" *only after* having been manipulated, used, and abused by God for the sake of gentiles and a Christ-centered eschaton.[169] As Paul himself writes, it is God's severity [*apotomia*],

167. See, as just a few examples, Pippin, *Death and Desire*; Amy-Jill Levine and Maria Mayo Robbins, eds., *A Feminist Companion to the Apocalypse of John*, illustrated ed. (T&T Clark, 2010); Lynn R. Huber, *Thinking and Seeing with Women in Revelation* (T&T Clark, 2013); Emanuel, *Humor, Resistance, and Jewish Cultural Persistence in the Book of Revelation*.

168. Stendahl is paraphrasing what he remembers the preacher, Rev. Henry Horn, saying at his home parish. Stendahl, *Paul Among Jews and Gentiles and Other Essays*, 38. Note, however, that I do not think Christ-following gentiles get the same pay (cf. Matthew 20: 1–16). I still, as noted above, think that Paul envisions Christ-following Jews as ranked above Christ-following gentiles in the eschaton.

169. Cf. Mark Nanos, who, as alluded to in footnote 143 above, asserts that "all Israel will be saved" is best translated as "all Israel will be kept safe." According to Nanos, this means that God will protect Jews while the gentiles join the movement, in part because gentiles need the

in direct contradistinction to God's kindness—indeed, God's "goodness" [*chrēstotēs*]—that will be cast toward the Jewish fallen (Rom 11:22).[170] But behold!: "If their transgression means riches for the *world*, and if their defeat [*hēttēma*] means riches for *gentiles*, how much more will their [grafted back in] full inclusion mean!" (Rom 11:12).

Paul's entire eschatological project, in fact, seems manipulative, as I do not think "riches for Christ-following gentiles" will be the same as "riches for Christ-following Jews" in the eschatological age. Jews, for Paul, will always reign supreme. What is interesting, however, is that this is the opposite of how Romans 11 has been read for much of interpretive history. Instead, it's been read for gentile supremacy. According to traditional Old Perspective theology—and to flip the script of the August 2017 "Unite the Right" rally in Charlottesville—*gentiles* will replace us. And by *us*, I mean Jews. But again, going back to the idea that all Jews *will* be saved (i.e., that gentiles will *not* replace us), Romans 9–11 still functions as a blueprint for an Old Perspective condescension to Jews and Judaism: We are simply too blind to recognize the truths of our own tradition. And what a perfect setup for later gentile Christ-followers—including modern Christians—to reaffirm their eleventh-hour evangelism, their attempts to get the "let's help the Jews find their way to Christ" ball rolling.[171] I know these phone calls. I know these letters. One, in fact, comes from a Christian friend in my adolescence, which is to say, relatively speaking, back to the now: "Sarah, this book [the Bible with the New Testament] is the most important thing in my life . . . I hope with all my heart that you will read and pray about it. . . . Jesus Christ is our

---

insight of Jews in order to do so. Given the surrounding verses, however (e.g., Rom 11:22), I find "*all* Jews will be kept safe" (i.e., even the non-Christ-following ones) to be unconvincing. See Nanos, "All Israel Will Be *Saved* or *Kept Safe*? (Rom 11:26)."

170. Paul is playing with words here, as *apotomas* can mean a "split piece of wood" (remember this is all bound up in a tree metaphor), something "severe," and "in the strictest sense." The image Paul presents here is also quite drastic. There are those who are "in" and those who are "out"—not just regarding the tree and thus the end of days, but also God's very goodness (*chrēstotēs*).

171. As Ben Merkle remarks on even a remnant of ethnic Israel being saved, "This interpretation fuels evangelistic efforts, since we have the promise that God will always have a remnant of Jewish people who will be saved by grace through faith in the Messiah." Ben L. Merkle, "Romans 11 and the Future of Ethnic Israel," *Journal of the Evangelical Theological Society* 43, no. 4 (December 2000): 721.

savior. . . . He knows us and loves us. . . . He knows your name and everything about you. . . . I hope with all my heart that you will read it."[172] "Gross, not grace!" was my affective response then—and still is. I will never be "good" enough for the many who think I'm lacking without Christ. Indeed, playing "what about" with the "all Israel = no Jews left behind" theory can actually *not* feel good, but instead quite terrible. Not everything, it seems, can be made good for *everyone*.

The problem, at least to my mind, is that much of the Newer Perspectives still fall prey to a gross-to-grace thinking, or what Dara Horn describes as the Christian need for a happy ending.[173]

The traditional New Perspective makes Paul *good* from the perspective of Dunn and Wright, the *Sonderweg* Newer Perspective makes Paul *good* from the perspective of Gaston and Gager, and many (other) Paul within Judaism readings also find ways to make Paul ethically palatable for readers who need Paul's words to remain, in some way, shape, or form, *good*. Stendahl, one of the movers and shakers of what became known as this Newer Perspective work, performed this move quite well: Paul, he wrote, "was a pretty *good* [Christ-follower]. He may not really have been attractive; he was not a sympathetic sort of fellow; he was certainly arrogant. But he was *great*!"[174] Or Mark Nanos, who ends his chapter on Paul saying, "I, for one, really appreciate [Paul's] utopian ideals and the vision of a day when differences among us can be respected

---

172. This is from a letter I received upon graduating high school.

173. Or what Jill Hicks-Keeton calls the "Bible benevolence project." See Horn, *People Love Dead Jews*, 78–79; Hicks-Keeton, *Good Book*, 8. This also relates to what Stephen L. Young calls "protectionism." He sees it as "the privileging of a source's own claims to such an extent that interpreters let them dictate academic analysis . . . If the New Testament gospels depict Jesus's teachings as profound and shocking to audiences, then scholars may interpret them as radically distinctive and present Jesus as, historically, a profound teacher. The idea of interrogating what the rhetoric of esotericism, profundity, and shock may be doing for the text is bypassed in favor of taking it at face value. If Paul claims that he began teaching gentiles because of his encounter with the risen Jesus (Gal 1:11–17) and that some Galatian gentiles initially accepted his instruction because of their 'spirit' wrought experience (Gal 3:2–5), scholars may then overwhelmingly attend to Paul's and the Galatians' 'religious experience' in their own historical explanations." Young, "Let's Take the Text Seriously," 328–329. This move isn't limited to Paul studies, either. Again, see Reinhartz, *Cast Out of the Covenant*. See also Graybill, *Texts After Terror*; Myles, "The Fetish for a Subversive Jesus," 52–70.

174. Stendahl, *Paul Among Jews and Gentiles and Other Essays*, 38; emphases mine (but exclamation his).

without discrimination."[175] Or Paula Fredriksen, who ends her monograph on Paul by remarking that the Paul she wishes readers to see is still "the *brilliant* student of Jewish law. The *expert* interpreter of his people's ancient scriptures. The *charismatic* worker of *mighty* deeds."[176]

But what if Paul isn't so good, after all? What if the above statements are ultimately products of the Christian-made guild of which we are a part—a guild that *says* it is past the assumption of a moral core in the New Testament, or the imposition of such a core on it, but really isn't? What if bettering Jewish-Christian relations requires doing so on Christian terms? What if situating Paul within a first-century Jewish framework—the agreed-upon tenet of post-Holocaust New and Newer Perspective work—simply reveals that Paul is an *average* first-century ethnocentric Jew, a non-brilliant Saul with a deficient moral imagination who is fine with discrimination in the end of days? Or worse: what if he's nothing more than terrible PR for all the Jews born after him?

Instead of offering a happy ending, I'm going to end this chapter here.

---

175. Nanos writes this in response to his contention that Paul's end of days indeed includes "all" Jews and is an age without inequality. See Nanos, "A Jewish View," 193.

176. Fredriksen, *Paul*, 174; emphases mine. Eisenbaum also ends her monograph on Paul by saying that Paul offers "a great start for thinking about religious pluralism." While I have situated Eisenbaum within the Radical New Perspective model in chapter 3, many scholars, as noted, consider the Radical New Perspective to have been renamed Paul within Judaism, which is indeed a wide-ranging approach. See Eisenbaum, *Paul Was Not a Christian*, 255.

CHAPTER FIVE

In Our Time[1]

As part of a Louisville Institute Grant for Researchers, I conducted a multisite research tour to test and reflect upon *Wrestling with Paul*'s three-part thesis. I spent most of my time gathering feedback from communities in California, Michigan, and New Jersey, not because I think these places fully represent human difference or complexity, but rather because I thought each was unique *enough* to help me (and us) start thinking about the potential impact of a potential not-good Paul.

In each of these settings, I spoke primarily with Jews, Catholics, and Protestants (i.e., those who may have a particular stake in this conversation), although I spent time with persons from other backgrounds, too. Some talks occurred in congregational settings, others in classrooms, others in lecture halls, and others in more relaxed conversational spaces. Sometimes the ethos of the space was religious. Sometimes it was academic. Sometimes it was both.

My goal in doing this work was not to search for patterns between or across communities (that would take much more time, with many more communities) but rather to foster a space for reflection on who Paul is for these communities and how Paul functions. I asked each group whether they think the theses within this book are too dangerous for modern Jews or, relatedly, too dangerous for modern Christians who may want Paul, or the Bible writ large, to promote a particular kind of "good."

Responses differed widely—not just across communities but also within.

1. The quotations in this chapter are sometimes based on my personal notes, so they may not always be exact. All quotations from private communications are used with permission; when correspondents are named, that is also with permission.

California

Avocet Playa Vista, Los Angeles

My first talk was at a Jewish retirement home in Los Angeles, California, where I encountered diverse perspectives on Paul's relationship with Judaism.[2] Respondents' reactions fell into three primary categories:

1. Paul's legacy is inextricably linked with antisemitism; nothing can or should change that.
2. Paul *did* abandon his Judaism.
3. Paul was a "good salesman"; by promoting access to the God of Israel without the law, the gentile Christ movement would inevitably gain more followers than a law-focused Judaism.

Many of the respondents actually agreed with at least part of the Old Perspective, believing that Paul renounced his Jewishness in the name of Christ. What made their views distinct from thinkers like Luther and Baur and Weber, however, was that they viewed such renouncement as morally harmful.

One respondent stood out in that he refused to consider Paul's Jewishness. To him, a Jewish Paul was contradictory to all he had learned before. Such framework also felt like an attempt to erase the harm caused by the Old Perspective. This respondent in fact *wanted* Paul to be the Old Perspective Paul. And he wanted the right to hate him.

When the talk was over, other community members shared additional perspectives. A few even seemed convinced that Paul remained Jewish throughout his ministry. But for the majority with whom I spoke, the idea that Paul was a Jew from birth until death was a foreign one; it would take more time for them to think through the possibility that Paul stayed Jewish, even as he preached to gentiles.

Loyola Marymount University, Los Angeles

My next destination was Loyola Marymount University, my home institution, where I engaged with a dynamic group of graduate students in a summer intensive course on the apostle Paul. I shared draft chapters of *Wrestling with Paul*

2. For this visit, my work on Paul was situated within a larger talk on anti-Judaism and the New Testament.

with this diverse cohort, comprised of five Catholic students, one Protestant student, and me. Notably, the students defied typical demographics. Whiteness was not dominant. Nor was early adulthood. Nor was a US upbringing.

Toward the end of the term, one student revealed that the course had fundamentally shifted his perspective on Paul. He described a Pauline-like "turn" of his own: Initially, he had accepted the traditional Old Perspective as historically accurate, but through our explorations, he came to firmly believe that Paul remained a devoted Jew through his life and ministry. He also, like many others in the class, believed that Paul wanted both Jews and gentiles to have faith in Jesus as the Christ. In other words, he was not *Sonderweg*—he believed that, for Paul, Jews needed Christ in order to be saved—but he also did not have a moral problem with this message.

Others, however, grappled with profound moral discomfort. One student was moved to tears as she confronted the antisemitic legacy of Pauline interpretation in Catholic and Protestant traditions. The staggering extent to which Paul's teachings had been used to justify the racialization, demonization, and extermination of Jews left her visibly shaken. Another student confessed that she couldn't bring herself to finish reading Luther's infamous tract *On the Jews and Their Lies*. The rhetoric was too much to bear. Interestingly, these same students responded differently to the *Sonderweg* thesis. One acknowledged her attraction to the thesis, candidly admitting it was driven by personal preference. She wanted Paul's ethics to match her own. The other student remained suspended in uncertainty.

Another student's experiences as a black child in segregated America informed her perspective on Paul. Throughout the course, she shared how witnessing anti-black racism, especially among otherwise well-intentioned individuals, allowed her to imagine Paul as a hierarchical thinker without difficulty. She not only acknowledged Paul's Jewish identity alongside his ethnocentric, ethnonationalist, and ethnocratic tendencies, but also found this version of Paul to be productively humanizing. Paul was a human, she noted. And humans have flaws.

Crucially, our classroom approach—examining Paul's letters without assuming readers must agree with his views—enabled her acceptance of this image of the apostle. Had I presented him as a figure to emulate, particularly in light of his support of enslavement, I wouldn't have been surprised if she and others had walked out of the classroom. This, in fact, is what Rev. J. Colcock

Jones recounts of his experience in 1833, preaching to a large congregation of enslaved persons on Paul's letter to Philemon. When he "insisted on fidelity and obedience as Christian virtues in servants, and upon the authority of Paul, condemned the practice of *running away*, one-half of [his] audience deliberately rose up and walked off with themselves."[3] I would have walked off in response to such preaching, too.

Preaching, in fact, is where another student found herself asking the most questions. "So much about Paul," she said, "depends on the social location of the recipient. Sometimes afflicting the comfortable is important, especially in preaching. But what about the people who will respond with pitchforks saying, 'What are you doing to my Paul?'"

To her, I said, "I don't know."

Michigan

Blue Ocean Faith and St. Clare of Assisi Episcopal Church, Ann Arbor

My third stop was with two Protestant communities in Ann Arbor, Michigan, which share a partnership with each other and a Reform synagogue. Given their commitments to Jewish-Christian dialogue, the congregants were already well-versed in Paul's anti-Jewish interpretive history. They were also familiar with scholarly efforts to recontextualize Paul within an ancient Jewish context. Because of this, much of my presentation seemed to resonate as a confirmation of their existing knowledge. One congregant even posed the question, cutting to the heart of this project: "What are you so afraid of?"

In that moment, I recognized a shift in my concerns. Among these two communities—ones dedicated to confronting and combating Christian antisemitism—I did not fear Paul's letters being used as a tool for anti-Judaism. Instead, I shared a different apprehension, one related to how I often feel in the classroom: I was afraid of being "the Jew" disrupting Christian sacred texts.

3. Quoted in Melanie Johnson-DeBaufre and Laura S. Nasrallah, "Beyond the Heroic Paul: Toward a Feminist and Decolonizing Approach to the Letters of Paul," in *The Colonized Apostle, Paul Through Postcolonial Eyes*, ed. Christopher D. Stanley (Fortress Press, 2011), 161. They also write, "In her chapter on postcolonial and feminist biblical interpretation, Kwok Pui-lan tells a similar story about an early-twentieth-century Chinese woman who could barely read, yet who nonetheless 'used a pin to cut from the Bible verses where Paul instructed women to be submissive and remain silent in the church.'" Johnson-DeBaufre and Nasrallah, "Beyond the Heroic Paul," 161.

I was afraid of being "the Jew" turning the New Testament into something potentially "not good." I was afraid of a pitchforked "What are you doing to my Paul?" interrogation.

With unguarded sincerity, I shared this fear with the group. One individual, acquainted with the weight of marginalized identity, grasped the depth of my concern. They shared that while they can indeed imagine other communities raising such pitchforks, it should not be my responsibility to travel around and teach them how to be uncomfortable with uncomfortable texts. It is my responsibility to do this work when students take my classes, however, and I must be honest: It can be extremely hard to do when students know that I am Jewish. Recently, one of my students bought a book about how to combat Jewish thinking as a way to survive learning about the New Testament from a Jewish professor (as if, for example, the difficult passages are only difficult because I, a Jew, manipulate them to be so). Another even wrote a letter to my university's president to make sure he knew a Jew was teaching his Introduction to New Testament course. I will thus be honest and say that I indeed played it "safe" by meeting with these communities in Ann Arbor; I knew that they were already primed to learn about the New Testament from a Jewish professor, and to also think about Paul in difficult ways. But members of these groups knew, and shared with me, that they understood why I was too afraid to go elsewhere.

I received a number of email responses after my time in Ann Arbor, one with great self-awareness regarding an interpretive want. A church leader wrote to me, in pseudo-*Sonderweg* fashion,

> I read Paul as saying, "Come as you are." Jews remain Jews. Non-Jews remain non-Jews, and so on. God our God is One. Love your neighbor as yourself. We do not need to change our identity or "fully convert" in order to belong. Our *enmity* is abolished, but not our differences. I also see him as celebrating the repentance of the oppressors (i.e., Rome/the nations) who have received mercy, while also affirming and confirming God's promises to the Jewish people/to Israel and also to other oppressed groups.
>
> In this way, there is hope for the oppressors of our own time to repent of their harm and receive God's mercy, while the oppressed people of our world will (finally, one day, hopefully soon) be free and fully affirmed!

Then in parenthesis, she reflected, "(Oh wow. This is such an idealistic vision.)"

That is not where her email ended, however. Instead, she took the conversation to the book of Revelation, sharing:

> A friend once said, "Some people feel victimized when they're asked to take their boot off your neck." This was in the context of race relations, but I think it applies to other areas of our (human) relationships as well. So, I wonder if some people will feel put off by your reading of Paul in the same sense . . . I [also] see the same pattern from *Roasting Rome* playing out in your understanding of Paul. Clearly, the Jewish people were among the most harshly oppressed at the time the New Testament books were written. What I hear you saying is that these particular Jews (Paul and in the book of Revelation) recreated, imitated, or even framed themselves as now being the ones on top. Now the oppressed have become the oppressor. The supremacists. The ethnocentrists. The one who was oppressed by Rome has now recreated "Rome" in their eschatological vision.
>
> So, my last question is this: If the boot of the oppressor is taken off the neck of the vulnerable, and the vulnerable now stand eye-to-eye and face-to-face, no longer enemies but as equals (justified/confirmed/affirmed), does their relationship remain problematic? Does the vulnerable underdog now become the "oppressor," because now perhaps they're "on top" / does someone necessarily need to be "under the boot"?[4]

By way of background, *Roasting Rome* was my first book. In it, I argue that the implied author of Revelation, John, uses satiric humor to undermine Rome, the empire responsible for systemically Othering him and his fellow Jewish Christ-following community. Like other Jewish eschatological thinkers, John's end of days looks much like Paul's: Righteous Jewish Christ-followers—or at least John's idea of righteous Jewish Christ-followers—reign supreme.

Something about *Roasting Rome* that has thus far been missing from *Wrestling with Paul* is the extent to which I tried to make sense of John's emotions. Although Jews experienced various levels of autonomy in the Jerusalem city center, Judea, and in the diaspora, they were nevertheless a minority group

4. Private communication, September 9, 2024; emphasis original.

who had to live under Roman imperial rule and cultural dominance. Even for those who did not practice Jewish customs, life in the Roman world was not easy. As biblical scholar and trauma researcher David Carr puts it, "Even more than today, every day people yearned for 'salvation' from basic threats to their lives, health, and livelihood."[5] Jews of the first century also carried within them a collective cultural consciousness of anti-Jewish suffering. From the Assyrian onslaught in 722 BCE, to the Babylonian exile in 597 BCE, to the destruction of the first Temple in 586 BCE, to the Roman conquest of Judea in 63 BCE, to the destruction of the second Temple in 70 CE, Israelites and later Jews fought repeatedly for cultural persistence and often used narrative—including a narrativized fantasy of eschatological salvation—as a means of doing so. That the Jews could survive in eschatological narrative, and even take the upper hand, helped preserve the hope that survival in real life was possible.[6]

So *does* someone necessarily need to be "under the boot"? I certainly hope not. But I do understand the human impulse to fantasize in response to repeated imperial oppression. Paul, as far as we know (and John, for that matter), never actually created a world in which Jews reigned supreme; he merely imagined one. Paul's gentile Christian readers, however, eventually did build a world in which, in many respects, their ideologies held sway. In a stark twist, parts of Paul's fantasies did become reality, just in a different packaging. Rather than Jews reigning supreme, it has been gentile Christians. Paul's visions of a transformed world, in other words, did influence the course of history. His imaginings of the eschaton, paired with ahistorical interpretations of him as an anti-Jewish leader, ultimately shaped the gentile Christian empires that would later claim his legacy.

It is important to keep in mind, however, that even if interpretations had more regularly maintained Paul's Jewish outlook, Paul would likely be surprised to see his letters having such wide-reaching social capital. As a Jew living under Roman occupation, Paul's ideas were not part of centers of power. In fact, Roman officials would have likely met Paul's ideas of eschatological supremacy with scorn and ridicule. The notion of Jewish dominance would have been laughable to those who wielded imperial authority. Roman leaders already mocked Jews simply for their identity, and early

5. Carr, *Holy Resilience*, 240.

6. See also Melissa Jackson, *Comedy and Feminist Interpretation of the Hebrew Bible: A Subversive Collaboration* (Oxford University Press, 2012), 28.

Christ-followers—Jewish or gentile—faced similar disdain, at least until Nicene Christianity's fourth-century ascendancy. In other words, it is not as if Paul wrote his letters at a time when his ideas were widespread or believable to most groups. While it may be easy for modern readers to blame Paul for later Christian inheritances, we have to take his status as a Jew into consideration. Jews did *not* reign supreme. To imagine that they would—or could—was against the grain of the imperial norm. Like Pamela Eisenbaum, we might do well "to regard Paul as a Jew who wrestled with an issue with which many modern American Jews wrestle: how to reconcile living as a Jew with living in and among the rest of the non-Jewish world."[7]

There is a difference, however, between wrestling as a Jew in non-Jewish antiquity versus wrestling as a Jew in non-Jewish modernity. The notion of Jewish dominance, although absurd to first-century Roman thinking, has taken hold in modern popular imagination. Antisemitic conspiracy theories perpetuate the claim that Jews, despite comprising 0.2 percent of the global population, exert disproportionate control over governments, finance, and media.[8] This pernicious narrative often relates to an additional—and indeed paradoxical—dynamic: Antisemitism and philosemitism are often intertwined. For example, even as some bemoan the idea of Jewish global domination, they simultaneously fetishize Jewish success, attributing it to exceptional industriousness. As Donald Trump infamously remarked, "The only guys I want counting my money are short guys that wear yarmulkes all day."[9] This statement exemplifies the complex, often contradictory attitudes toward Jews: Admiration for perceived business acumen coexists with sinister insinuations of undue influence.

Beyond overt conspiracy theories, the fetishization of Jews permeates subtler aspects of modern non-Jewish society. Journalist Mairav Zonszein recounts a striking example of this at the Jewish Heritage Museum in New York City:

> I was recently in New York City and decided to visit the Jewish Heritage Museum in Battery Park (a Holocaust museum), as I had

---

7. Eisenbaum, *Paul Was Not a Christian*, 3.

8. Indeed, the fact that the global population size of Jews is so small adds to the claim that Jews have disproportionate power.

9. *USA Today*, May 20, 1991.

> never been there, though I have been to a fair share of Holocaust museums in the world. As I entered the beginning of the permanent exhibit, I overheard a guide talking to a group of high school students. First she asked them: "Does anyone here know a Jew?" Only a few raised their hands, among them one of the grown-ups. Then she said: "Jews come in all shapes and sizes," right as I walked by them and I had to hold back my combination of laughter and dismay.
>
> Obviously such a statement is disconcerting, as it should be obvious that Jews are just people. But in the setting of a Holocaust museum, it is expected that Jews will be talked about in this manner. This is part of what I see as so tragic about the Holocaust's effect on Jewish identity and life: it necessarily places the Jew in a special role as mystified victim of an offense of epic proportions. It allows the Jew to be fetishized, as indeed Nazism's obsession with exterminating Jews reflected an excessive compulsion that can be seen as a fetish. And just as hating the Jews is a fetish, so is loving them, singling them out for greatness—a condition sometimes called philosemitism.[10]

This is indeed similar to what Dara Horn expresses in *People Love Dead Jews.* Jewish things—their scrolls, their shofars, their tallitot, their stars, their kippot—can indeed be fascinating. But they tend to be *especially* fascinating, even beloved, Horn argues, when kept at a distance (e.g., when they are secured behind museum glass, away from living Jews using or wearing them).

While I wouldn't call this an instance of philosemitism, one respondent from Ann Arbor asked if there was anything I wanted from Paul, including perhaps his own love (*philos* in Greek). Referencing Hebrew Bible scholar Phillis Trible, known for confronting the painful aspects of biblical narratives, they asked if I, like Trible—and indeed like Jacob in Genesis—sought to wrestle with challenging texts until they yielded their blessings (Gen 32:22–32).[11]

---

10. Mairav Zonszein, "The 'Israel Fetish': Singling Out Jews and Israelis for Hate and Love," *+972 Magazine*, March 15, 2011, https://www.972mag.co m/the-israel-fetish/.

11. See Phyllis Trible, "Biblical Views: Wrestling with Faith," *Biblical Archeology Review*, September/October 2014, https://library.biblicalarchaeology.org/department/biblical-views-wrestling-with-faith/. See also Trible, *Texts of Terror*, 4–5.

"I don't seek their blessing," I replied. "I don't *want* their blessing. But I recognize there are many who do."

The gathering concluded with an effective remark from another congregant: "Christians have done enough," he said. "I think you and other Jewish readers have the right to engage Paul on your own terms. Maybe we Christians need to learn to step back and listen." With sincerity, this person questioned whether I would be open to letting the conversation about Paul remain a Jewish one. As readers will soon see, I am.

New Jersey

Bnai Keshet, Montclair

My fourth engagement took me to Bnai Keshet, a Reconstructionist synagogue in Montclair, New Jersey, where notions of Jewish "chosenness" are reexamined, and language of election is absent from the liturgy. Bnai Keshet's prayer books even list the names of ancestors who were not Israelite as a way to deconstruct the idea that Israelites and Jews are the only important figures in Jewish communal memory. I say this to remind readers that Judaism isn't a monolith. Many Jews—despite assumptions of the contrary—are not as insular or hierarchically ethnocentric as many anti-Jewish stereotypes seem to purport.

In fact, in the spirit of "two Jews, three opinions," there was hardly any view from this community that was repeated twice. One person said, "You know what? If making Paul 'good' will make readers of Paul 'good,' then I say go for it." Another said, "You have a choice here. You can say what might be dangerous or you can what might be helpful. Sometimes, the two are the same. Sometimes, they are not. But the choice is yours." And another said, "What scares me though about a 'good' *Jewish* Paul is how quickly it can lean into a fetishizing of ancient Jews—and in turn modern ones." This concern resonates deeply, as some scholars of Paul and Judaism risk overcorrecting the anti-Jewish history to the point of perpetuating philosemitic stereotypes. Like Mairav, I experience a haunting sensation when watching colleagues enthusiastically highlight ancient Jewish diversity when, often, I am the only living Jew in sight.[12]

12. There are, of course, as seen in this book, other Jewish scholars of the New Testament. Outside of our field's major annual conference, however, it is rare to be in the same room.

The rabbis at Bnai Keshet also offered differing insights. One said, "I *do* find your thesis to be dangerous. It scares me. Jews, for some, have not only become white; they have become the whitest of white. This book can complement that." I agreed and said this is a fear I have, too. As expressed in previous chapters, never could I have anticipated writing a book about the Jewish Paul's ethnocratic tendencies at the same time as the Israel-Hamas war, a war that has sometimes fostered the conflation of all Jews with the actions of the Israeli government or, even, the ideologies of ethnocentric, ethnonationalist, white settler-colonialism.

The other rabbi, however, emphasized that some ethnocentric, ethnonationalist Jews *do* exist, and that something needs to be done about it. "Paul feels like the entire book of Isaiah to me," this rabbi shared. "I have no interest in modeling either one of them." This is actually quite similar to what another congregant wrote to me, making this rabbi's viewpoint the only one to have been noticeably repeated. This congregant shared, "I too feel awful about bringing out Jewish supremacy and ethnonationalism at this point in time particularly. But you know what? Ben Gvir [an Israeli far-right politician] and his minions are claiming biblical authority for their ethnonationalism."[13] For these respondents, wrestling with Jewish figures like Paul means wrestling with the parts of our own communities we may not like. Sometimes, in fact, it can mean more than wrestling; it can mean contesting, countering, and participating in our own form of "leaving behind."

Drew University, Madison

My final engagement took me full circle to Drew University, where the ideas for this book first took shape. Instead of warning me about the project's dangers, however, I was challenged to critically examine my underlying frameworks.

"What do you mean by your terms?" one scholar asked. "What constitutes the particular, the universal, the ethnocentric? Where are these words coming from?"

My response traced their use to the history of biblical interpretation. The Old Perspective, influenced by Martin Luther, relies on the "goodness" of Christ-centered universalism—a particular universalism, to be sure, one that assumed the wretchedness of Jews and Judaism. The New Perspective agrees

13. Private communication, September 28, 2024.

with this overarching conception of "goodness," whereas the Paul within Judaism approach seeks to redeem Paul from such "bad" forms of anti-Jewish interpretation. These terms also help highlight the bridging between the academy and the laity. For many, regardless of academic or lay status, the Bible must remain the Good Bible, despite social changes of good and goodness, as Jill Hicks-Keeton has shown.[14] Like the godhead of Genesis, there is a common impulse to read each verse and say, "Indeed, it [is] very good" (Gen 1:31).

By answering in this way, it became clear just how much this book is not about the historical Paul, but rather ways of reading Paul. In fact, "it can't be about finding Paul," one scholar said. "You will never find *the* Paul. Nobody will."

This observation highlights an inherent challenge of most Paul and Judaism scholarship. All of the aforementioned approaches—the Old Perspective, the New Perspective, the Radical New Perspective, and the Paul within Judaism approach—create a systematic Paul from nonsystematic sources. We can't even confirm which verses are from the historical Paul and which are from later writers.[15] This ambiguity prompts another important "what about": What about the fact that we *don't know Paul*?

As expressed in chapter 1, Paul's historical ambiguity presents a formidable challenge. To navigate this complexity, this book positions Paul more as an interpretive foil—as a case study to examine our relations to the biblical material—than a historical figure to be definitively explicated. This metacritical approach exposes two key issues. First, we don't know Paul, and yet we often act as if we do. Second, my interpretation of the apostle as an ethnocentric, hierarchical, even ethnocratic thinker relies on conventions of the biblical discipline, including the privileging of the seven letters over the thirteen, and even of Romans over the other undisputed six. In other words, *Wrestling with Paul* demonstrates how our methodological choices shape our understanding of Paul. But it also demonstrates that even when using the tools and rules of the biblical discipline, close readings do not necessarily reveal the "good" universalist that many readers make Paul out to be.

In fact, it may not even matter if my reconstruction of Paul is about the historical Paul. It is still the Paul that is mirrored in the sources to which we

14. Again, see Hicks-Keeton, *Good Book*.

15. Early Christianity scholar Markus Vincent, for example, has recently made the claim that most of what we think of as Pauline, even within the seven undisputed letters, was actually added in by second-century Christ-followers.

have access. And it is still the Paul who has shaped later Christian understandings of Jews and Judaism. In other words, if it is the New Testament's Paul (which again may not reflect the historical Paul) who has shaped history, then that is the Paul with whom I choose to struggle.

Another question I received was why I insisted on a continued language of "goodness." My response, akin to my response about terminology above, was because I was seeking to engage conceptions of the Good Book, which required the use of "good-book, good-Paul" language. Respondents pushed me on to consider if relying on this language implied that the Paul I have been describing is inherently "bad." While I certainly don't agree with much of what I see in Paul's letters, that doesn't mean I think everything about the New Testament's Paul is bad. As the title of chapter 4 suggests, he is neither good nor bad. He is simply a Jew. And a complicated one at that.

"Why, then, not title your last chapter 'A Jew'?" one scholar asked. "Why do you need the 'average' qualifier?"

I suppose I don't. Paul, which again is to say the New Testament's Paul, was a Jew. And like other Jews—like other *humans*—he was multifaceted. But this gets us back to another metacritical aspect of this project: Many scholars freely label morally difficult passages within the Hebrew Bible "Texts of Terror" (e.g., the imagined conquest of Canaan in Joshua 10–12).[16] Why, I wonder, is there an impulse to take away a less-than-good qualifier from a figure within the New Testament—a figure who images an even greater global conquest? I contend, in fact, that calling Paul "average" can assist readers in recognizing that Paul was not the only person shaping the early Christ movement. He relied on many other texts and contexts to sustain his perspective—something that did not necessarily make him "special," but that simply shaped him as a first-century Jew—and he did not necessarily excel or struggle in his apostleship more than those around him. The New Testament's Paul is just one Christ-follower, among other Christ-followers, who had things to say.[17]

16. I say "imagined" because there is no historical evidence that this happened. Akin to the fantasies of Paul and John of Revelation, Joshua 10–12 represents fictive imagining by a marginalized community.

17. This interacts with feminist and womanist decentering approaches to Paul that place Paul as one among many. See, for example, Johnson-DeBaufre and Nasrallah, "Beyond the Heroic Paul," which also engages Paul as neither a hero nor a villain; Schüssler Fiorenza, *Rhetoric and Ethic*, especially 187; Fox, *Paul Decentered*; Mitzi J. Smith, *Chloe and Her People: A Womanist Critical Dialogue with First Corinthians* (Wipf and Stock, 2023). For expansions of a decentering approach toward the New Testament and traditional historical-critical biblical interpretation,

Finally, I was pushed to consider if everything about my reconstruction is necessarily less-than-good. In other words, as one scholar asked plainly, "Is ethnocentrism necessarily *not* good?"

---

see, as just a few examples, Mitzi J. Smith, Yung Suk Kim, and Michael Willett Newheart, *Toward Decentering the New Testament* (Wipf and Stock, 2018); Mary F. Foskett and Jeffrey Kah-Jin Kuan, eds., *Ways of Being, Ways of Reading: Asian American Biblical Interpretation* (Chalice Press, 2006); Adele Reinhartz, "The Hermeneutics of Chutzpah: A Disquisition on the Value/s of 'Critical Investigation of the Bible,'" *Journal of Biblical Literature* 140, no. 1 (2021): 8–30; pages xvi-xx of *Wrestling with Paul*'s Author's Note, including the works cited in the accompanying footnotes. In line with the purpose of this chapter—that is, to invite others to join me "on that mat"—I also include an example of expanded decentering here, from biblical studies doctoral student YoungHak Lee, who shared the following in response to *Wrestling with Paul* in conversation with other readings of Paul as an ethnocentric Jew:

> I have a concern related to the ethnocentrism of the argument that Paul was not interested in gentiles becoming Jews. Paul did not want them to become Jews. Although I was initially convinced, I needed more time to process this as a minoritized reader who is often neglected to participate in leadership and perpetually portrayed as a foreigner.
>
> At the same time, I also worked on tackling some of the anti-Jewish reading within the minjung theology. For example, *laos* is used twice in Mark, referring to "the Pharisees and the scribes." Ahn Byung-Mu, a minjung theologian and biblical scholar, perceived *laos* as the oppressor while *oxlos* are the oppressed. Speaking from the Korean historical context, where religious elites aligned themselves with government officials in power rather than the oppressed, minjung theologians frequently referred to these Korean religious elites as Pharisees. I contend that this approach runs the risk of falling prey to supersessionist or anti-Jewish readings.
>
> So, I read *Wrestling with Paul* with these questions in mind. [The book] talk[s] about how our understanding of Paul's view on Jews shaped our understanding of Jews [and vice versa]. This is an important work for sure. I wanted to explore further how our understanding of Paul's view on Jews shapes our understanding of minjung. Drawing from minjung theology's perspective, I'm particularly hoping to read the Jews as a part of minjung rather than the oppressor or religious elites as some minjung theologians have argued. However, I'm still working on it.
>
> One possibility is to think of a nationalist movement in Korea that was a very ethnocentric movement that resisted Japanese colonial rule. However, whether we can consider the Korean nationalist movement a genuine anti-colonial movement is a matter of debate. In late nineteenth-century Korea, nationalism emerged as a resistance movement against foreign colonial powers. Key South Korean political events, including colonial experiences, national division, Korean War, authoritarian rule, democratization, and globalization, have interacted with evolving discourses of nationalism in society. However, Korean nationalism has encountered obstacles as democracy progresses and globalization intensifies, particularly concerning the rise of racism and xenophobia. I would argue that Korean nationalism was a form of anti-colonial resistance against colonialism, but not entirely against coloniality. How does our new understanding of Paul's perspectives on the Jews resonate with the minjung movement today? I will need more time to reflect on this. (YoungHak Lee, private communication, December 19, 2024)

The consensus in the room was no, not necessarily.[18] In many instances, it is simply inevitable. Even supersessionism, writes Jewish New Testament scholar Amy-Jill Levine, is inevitable. "All religions," she writes, "have supersessionist tendencies. All propose, albeit in various ways, that they have improved upon an anterior or rival tradition, and most argue that if they are right, then rival groups must be wrong or at least lacking."[19] The problem, she adds, is when this enables abuse. Did Paul ever think—or hope—his fantasy of a Jewish ethnonational age would *actually* become a reality? And if so, would he seek to *sustain* such a reality? We cannot know.

Talmudic Thoughts on Paul

What, then, is the point of this chapter, this collection of disparate feedback?

As noted in the introduction, what I have tried to do here is simply gather responses to the notion of Paul as an ethnocentric, hierarchical Jew, including the fear that such a Paul might be difficult for some readers or even misused. My hope is that this can help us start a conversation about how and why we relate to Paul in the ways that we do, whether as scholars or as public readers.[20] To put in another way, I am indeed interested in the then and the now. I remain haunted by the centuries-long use and abuse of biblical texts to justify a Christian fueled anti-Judaism and antisemitism. I want to work with others on this, but I also want to invite them to wrestle with the possibility that

18. I would say the same for other forms of particularism and, relatedly, for works-righteousness. In other words, I agree with Philip Alexander when he writes that "the superiority of grace over law is not self-evident and should not simply be assumed." Alexander, "Torah and Salvation in Tannaitic Literature," 300.

19. Levine, "Supersessionism," 158. And indeed, I have been arguing that Paul maintained a type of *Jewish* Christ-following supersessionist lens. He was a *Jewish* Christ-follower who presumed that *Jewish* Christ-followers were at the top of the new, True Israel. Those without Christ, including non-Christ-following Jews, were not entitled to his eschaton. Levine's understanding of supersessionist tendencies being inevitable can also, in a way, be put into conversation with Jon Levenson on universalism and particularism. As he puts it, "Although some religious traditions may on occasion conceive of themselves as representing or answering to a universal human condition, as a matter of historical fact all religious traditions are particular, since no includes everyone." See Jon D. Levenson, "The Universal Horizon of Biblical Particularism," 144–145.

20. This is also part of *Wrestling with Paul's* double-crossover intentions. I have tried to write in a way that can bring scholarship on Paul to a more public audience (crossover one), and to then bring public responses back to academia (crossover two).

contemporary movements in biblical studies against antisemitism—the radical re-readings of Paul, for example, that seek to counter the Old Perspective's anti-Judaism and Christian supersessionism—aren't necessarily working. Post-Holocaust biblical analyses, akin to other analyses inspired by dead Jews, may seem inspirational but in fact remain bound to broader "good book" making patterns, ones that have led not only to ahistorical readings of Paul, but also ones that aren't necessarily "good" for, to borrow from Paul, "all."

An additional point of this chapter, then, is to engage the value of such type of self- and social reflection. As another scholar wrote to me:

> Your book promotes a readerly subjectivity of wrestling both with the New Testament and your argument. It tackles a most salient set of questions, not just about reading the Bible, but about reading in general: What is the value of "wrestling" if, indeed, you/no one can "win"? How might broader audiences, who are conditioned to read for lessons and messages, be encouraged to re-envision the act of reading someone like Paul as a more dynamic experience? How can meaning/insight be produced when a reader isn't in alignment with the dominant/dominating voice of the text? Your exploration is not an academic exercise attempting to snatch the text away from devoted readers, but a model for reading that leads to critical self- and social-reflection.[21]

So, in a response to the point made in Ann Arbor—that maybe Jews should respond as Jews—and the suggestion that ethnocentrism is not inherently "bad," I offer a Jewish wrestling with Paul. Mimicking the style of the Talmud, an ancient Jewish text that inserts multiple interpretations onto a single page, below are four Jewish (i.e., ethnocentric) responses to Paul and also this book. As readers will see, Jewish tradition often resists tidy resolutions by embracing the liminal, the complex, and the polyphonic instead. Here is just one way, among many ways, we do this.

---

21. Danna Nolan Fewell, private communication, October 2, 2024.

***Ethan Schwartz* says:** In *Wrestling with Paul*, Sarah Emanuel argues that New Testament scholars—especially in the so-called New Perspective but also sometimes in the "within Judaism" approach—have often downplayed Paul's Jewish "ethnocentrism" in favor of a more palatable universalism. While readers of various backgrounds (including Jews) have participated in this, it originated with mid-twentieth-century Christian scholars who were aghast at Christianity's contribution to the Holocaust. The move goes something like this: Paul is Jewish and therefore must be good because being Jewish must be good—but ethnocentrism is bad, so Paul can't be ethnocentric. However, Emanuel argues that Paul *is* ethnocentric—so we need to acknowledge that maybe he's "bad" too. In thinking through her claim, I'd like to address a question that arose in the discussion of her book at Drew University: Are we so sure that ethnocentrism is bad?

Asking this might seem absurd, even reprehensible. Isn't ethnocentrism to blame for history's worst crimes (including the Holocaust)? Yes—if by "ethnocentrism" we mean the idea that one ethnic group is *superior* to others. However, I would suggest that this is better described as ethno*supemacism*. I'm inclined to see ethno*centrism*, by contrast, as broader and, at least potentially, less malign

> Circumcised on the eighth day, of the stock of Israel, of the tribe of Benjamin, a Hebrew of the Hebrews; according to the law, a Pharisee.

Sarah Emanuel says: Paul was a Jew, but not a universalist. Instead, he was ethnocentric in his ideology, including his theology, which spanned into his assertions of eschatological supremacy for Christ-following Jews and gentiles. Jews needed to maintain the law in Christ, and gentiles needed to abstain from the law in Christ. Both groups, in other words, needed to maintain particular ethnic differences in allegiance to Christ lest they be "left behind" from Paul's end of days. Paul, moreover, understood these groups through ethnocentric, ethnonationalist, and hierarchical means.

Shayna Sheinfeld says: Paul was a Jew. Paul's understanding of Christ and of salvation were understandings of a Jewish Christ and of Jewish salvation. The gentiles to whom he preached, to whom he sought to turn to Christ, were, according to Paul, special: They were lucky enough to be brought into this Jewish salvation *as gentiles*. I came to these conclusions as a scholar of Second Temple Judaism. Sarah Emanuel identifies this as Paul's ethnocentrism, ethnonationalism, and hierarchy.

Paul's own positionality is complicated. We who read Paul, regardless of where we are coming from, cannot really know what Paul meant. We can only interpret Paul's letters based on sociohistorical clues and evidence. While we know more about Paul than we do about many people in antiquity, we still do not have, nor can we gain, extensive knowledge, and thus we understand Paul through our own experiences as well as centuries of scholarship and theology. This is what Emanuel means when she argues that scholars cannot be objective. That Paul is not systematic—despite the centuries of theological interpretations that try to

Rabbi Ariann Weitzman says: It challenges me to think of Paul as a lifelong Jew when my own understanding of Christianity has always required a clear separation between Jesus and Paul. Jesus was Jewish, his message was Jewish, and his message is familiar to me. I can point to our own rabbinic sages who seem to be having the same conversations in the same milieu. Jesus preaches to Jews about Jewish concerns. It is easy for me to therefore "rescue" Jesus, to not conflate him with the history of Christian antisemitism. In fact, when Christians ask me, "What do Jews think about Jesus?" I can honestly answer, "We don't, but we know he was a Jew who suffered under Roman occupation like so many other Jews." In that way, Jesus is part of *our* Jewish story. Paul, who I know to have

than ethnosupremacism. *Ethnocentrism* means focusing on one's own group, "centering" them in one's worldview, feeling uniquely close to them and being grateful for being among them, perhaps even regarding them as privileged—but not necessarily considering them inherently superior.

Non-supremacist ethnocentrism is what Judaism endorses in the form of "chosenness," i.e., God's unique covenantal relationship with Israel. In the Bible, God loves Israel irrespective of their merits (Deut 7:6–7) and accordingly makes things harder on them, not easier (Amos 3:2). He allows non-Israelites to worship their (false) gods, effectively telling Israel to mind their own business (Deut 4:19–20). Rabbinic Judaism took these ideas and ran with them. The Mishnah stresses that humanity was created from one person so as to invalidate pretenses to superiority (m. Sanh. 4:5). Maimonides clarifies that righteous non-Jews merit salvation (Mishneh Torah, Repentance 3:5). The most frequent Jewish blessing says that God "sanctified [i.e., distinguished] us *through his commandments*," not through ethnic essence.

Is this to suggest that chosenness is impervious to ethnosupremacism? "Certainly not!" (*mē genoito*), as Paul would say. Dangerous ideologies of Jewish superiority appear, for instance, in Judah Halevi's *Kuzari* (Spain,

> Circumcised on the eighth day, of the stock of Israel, of the tribe of Benjamin, a Hebrew of the Hebrews; according to the law, a Pharisee.

Although both were important for his messianic age (i.e., his imagined new nation), Paul saw Jewish Christ-followers as the superior assemblage in Christ and gentile Christ-followers as the inferior assemblage in Christ.

Scholarly readings in a post-Holocaust world have often "left behind" Paul's ethnonational exclusivism in order to make him "good" for modern Jews and guilt-ridden interpreters. To play on Hicks-Keeton's most recent metacritical project, *Good Book: How White Evangelicals Save the Bible to Save Themselves*, this one might well be called—in

show otherwise—should also be a given: Paul writes letters that are situational for himself and for the people to whom he wrote. All of this, I think, Emanuel and I agree on, although we do not always agree on how to interpret some of Paul's writings. Disagreements on interpretation are to be expected considering the complexity and paucity of our sources.

That scholars and theologians interpret verses that support an outcome they want is also, in my opinion, a given. We hope, as scholars, that we do so critically and constructively, but that we all examine subjectively is without a doubt. Emanuel highlights how these subjective interpretations were produced (she would say "manipulated") toward specific outcomes. My own understandings of Paul, as noted above, come from my positionality as a Jewish scholar of ancient Judaism, with a focus on the first century CE. As a Jew, it makes sense for me to understand Paul as a Jew. I see Paul wrestling with his own ideas, with how to share and explain them to people with diverse identities living in different cities and circumstances, and how to adapt them when

turned outward, to have rejected Jews and Judaism, who formulated a message that was distinctive from Judaism and cannot be included within Judaism, can bear the brunt of my suspicions about Christianity, Christians, and modern interfaith relations. Beyond this, the central theology of Christianity, the need for a salvific sacrifice in the person of Jesus, onto whom we need to heap our sins, which marks it as irreconcilably different from and mysterious to Judaism, feels like an entirely Pauline invention. Paul is as far away from Jewish as one can be.

If Paul was a Jew who did not abandon Jews or Judaism, but was acting out of an ethnocentric pro-Jewish worldview, I am challenged to figure out how he fits into *my* Jewish

twelfth century) and in Kabbalah. Today, when Jews have newfound state power, the ramifications of these odious ideas are painstakingly clear. However, in the overall context of the Jewish tradition, such views are marginal. In principle and, indeed, usually in practice, Jewish chosenness is ethnocentric but not ethnosupremacist. In fact, by focusing on one group, it facilitates a surprising degree of pluralism: Provided that other groups maintain basic human ethics, Jews should respect their religious practices—"mind your own business"—and may even pursue coexistence with them. As such, Christians who think that Judaism is ethnocentric are not wrong about Judaism. But if they think that Judaism is *bad* because it's ethnocentric, they might well be wrong about *ethnocentrism*—at least, as Jews have typically understood it.

Although she doesn't put it exactly this way, Emanuel argues that Paul transforms Jewish ethno*centrism* into Jewish ethno*supremacism* by creating a secondary space for non-Jews within Jewish chosenness. Through believing in Christ, non-Jews may partially access the covenantal promise that Jews may fully access through both believing in Christ and keeping the Torah. Emanuel focuses on how this claim reinforces Jewish superiority. However, I'm just as struck by how it simultaneously eliminates the pluralism of

> Circumcised on the eighth day, of the stock of Israel, of the tribe of Benjamin, a Hebrew of the Hebrews; according to the law, a Pharisee.

lieu of *Wrestling with Paul—Good Paul: How Post-Holocaust Scholars Save Paul to Save Jews to Save Themselves.* This book, in short, attempts to highlight that there are indeed Pauline materials that create Us-versus-Them dialectics—ones that, ironically (given Paul's own privileging of Jewish Christ-following views), have become fodder for gentile Christian exceptionalism, supersessionism, and the fetishizing of proselytizing to modern Jews. It argues that Paul "leaves behind" most Jews (not to mention most gentiles) in his theology and that the biblical field has "left behind"

things don't work the way he imagines they will, such as the delayed return of Christ. I see this wrestling as inherent in Judaism, so how could we see Paul as anything but Jewish? But since most Pauline interpreters are Christian or Christian-adjacent, my identity as a Jew understanding Paul as a Jew is rare.

Emanuel moves beyond the argument of subjectivity, noting how interpretations have shifted dramatically to the Paul within Judaism framework as a response to post-Holocaust guilt. Embedded in (many of) these interpretations are the glosses of Paul's difficulties, such as the ethnocentrist Paul and the supersessionist understandings of his work that have reigned in Christian interpretation of Paul from very early on. Again, I think Emanuel is spot on, but following this is where we differ: While I agree that wrestling with Paul's exceptionalism and with Christian supersessionist interpretation is an important *first step*, I also support following this work with the feminist praxis of reading toward justice. Take, as a brief example, the quote from Philippians 3:5 centered on this page. Paul is clearly

story and the story of my own community. In fundamentally important ways, the "Paul" of the New Testament is not a real person and cannot be rescued as a real person. He is a myth, an idea, a malleable character to make sense of in whatever way Christians may choose to make sense of him. In most ways, Paul is simply not my business. But as a data point, he can be connected to a religious heritage that makes room for ethnocentrism to this very day, and not just by obvious supremacists whose thinking is out of line with the bulk of contemporary Jewish religious attitudes. In the wake of October 7th, even liberal Jews have felt alone in the world, misunderstood and mischaracterized, subject to increasing antisemitism. Ethnocentrism, even if subtly expressed, is one unsurprising

Jewish chosenness. By saying that non-Jews are no longer ethnically disqualified from the covenant, Paul forecloses the possibility of valid alternatives: "join us—or else." Paradoxically, Paul's *in*clusivity becomes the motor of an even more radical exclusivity. In this relief, I would say that Paul *is* a universalist—just not the tolerant, anodyne kind that many Christians imagine.

If Paul is "bad," it's not because he's too ethnocentric. It's because he's not ethnocentric *enough*. He interweaves the wool of ethnocentrism with the linen of universalism, producing an illicit mixture that maintains the privileged status of the Jewish people's covenant while demanding that the entire non-Jewish world play by its rules.

> Circumcised on the eighth day, of the stock of Israel, of the tribe of Benjamin, a Hebrew of the Hebrews; according to the law, a Pharisee.

Paul's seemingly capacious interest in all people, not his seemingly narrow interest in his own people, is actually what most directly enabled two millennia of Christian (or Christian-inspired) atrocities: exploitative proselytizing, forced conversion, violent colonialism, and, eventually, gas chambers—all of which, in their own ways, engage the universal only to subject it to the particular. Until Paul's Christian defenders come to terms with this, no amount of reading him "within Judaism" will ever clear their conscience of the Jewish blood that reading him "without Judaism" has shed.

difficult analyses in favor of tidier, more comforting narratives.

The Bible's lasting cultural relevance—the many ways it has been used to justify anti-Judaism and antisemitism—has not only made scholarly "objectivity" unattainable, but has also led interpreters to consistently manipulate its verses so as to make it subjectively and ahistorically "good." To put it another way, the way we think about Jews has—for millennia—impacted the way we think about Paul. The changing "goodness" of Paul's perspective on Jews wrests from our own changing social consciousnesses, not from Paul's.

self-identifying as a Jew. What comes next, however, is also important: "As to zeal, a persecutor of the assembly; as to righteousness under the law, blameless. Yet whatever gains I had, these I have come to regard as loss because of Christ" (Phil 3:6–7). Here scholars and theologians have identified these statements as Paul turning away from a legalistic Judaism to embrace his new religion, Christianity. This reading *is* a possible reading, one that promotes an anti-Jewish perspective. A justice-informed reading would align with readings, which are also possible, that in this pericope Paul is not *leaving* Judaism, but is considering how his understanding of his Judaism has been changed since his turn to Christ: Paul is still a Jew, no longer persecuting but among those who are persecuted. His loss, then, is of his self-assuredness in his positionality, *not* of his Jewishness. In the case of Emanuel's argument, then, I would have taken another step: to provide a justice-informed reading of Paul, readings that not only state the harm done, but also highlight interpretations that work against supersessionism and other forms of hatred.

reaction to this sense of increasing marginalization. Dr. Emanuel's work underscores for me the importance of this cross-religious critique—it means something different for a Jewish scholar to interrogate Paul than for a Christian, and the identity of the scholars in this work is an essential part of the work itself. This work, and Dr. Emanuel's gracious sharing of it, allows Jews to show up fully to the conversation of what Christian anti-Judaism has meant for both Christianity and Judaism over the last two thousand years.

Conclusion

What's Left?

As I make my way off the mat, my legs trembling beneath me, I don't feel as if I'm leaving with relief or elation or triumph. I end this match with muscle fibers shaking, and I'm almost surprised I made it. To date, *Wrestling with Paul* is the hardest project I've ever written. The biblical field, as we have seen, has centuries of anti-Jewish interpretation with which to struggle.

As we have also seen, scholars of the Bible will never implement a fully objective optic. As humans, we can't. And as appreciative as I am for such recognition of human subjectivity—and as content as I am to have closed the fifth chapter with an embrace of a Jewish subjectivity, an ethnocentric subjectivity, even—I remain acutely aware that the biblical field, in most instances, will remain a Christian one. That is a particularity to which I cannot acquiesce, at least not consciously, and for that reason, I fear, my muscles will continue to twitch with exertion. That said, the word "consciously" is important here, as I am also a product of the field, and thus likely take on certain Christian interpretive modalities without realizing it. Even my focus on Romans throughout this book may demonstrate some kind of acquiescence to a Christian sensibility, even if unintentional.[1]

In *Wrestling with Paul*, I have tried to reveal what is known about Paul's historical context while also inviting readers to consider their own relations to text, history, and epistemology. Meaning is made relationally and contextually, and meaning can change. Meaning *has* changed. To put it otherwise, and to get back to that aforementioned pathology of the biblical field, a goal of this book has been to interrogate the discipline's "then *not* now" but also "then *and* now" scholarly norm while also being honest about the contexts, feelings, and interpretive subjectivities that shape such a multilayered approach. Indeed, Paul is not just a figure in history but also a figure of history, with a legacy that has impacted how we relate to him and his writings. As New Testament

1. See chapter 1, footnote 24.

scholar Melanie Johnson-DeBaufre puts it, "What you see depends on where you stand."[2]

From where I stand, it seems clear to me that scholars have analyzed Paul through their own contextual and relational understandings of Jews and Judaism, which include their own conceptions of "good" and "goodness." It also seems clear to me that interpretations of Paul have always been shaped by a changing yet symbiotic relationship between the present and the past. In other words, as much as traditional readings of Paul and Judaism may assert otherwise, the "then" and the "now" cannot escape each other. Social, cultural, and personal understandings of Jews and Judaism have—*for millennia*—impacted the ways Paul has been reconstructed. That is what this book has tried to consider. That is what it has tried to explore.

So, what's left? In a way, everything. Perhaps to Paul's chagrin, the messianic age he seemed to imagine did not arrive. The "end," as he envisioned it, did not happen. Such lack of ending, however, reminds me of a different "now," a now that Paul, in all likelihood, would not find "good," as its starring figure lives a life—an authentic life—that goes against the grain of Paul's own sexual ethics.

This now is the story of Harper Steele, a modern writer who recently transitioned from male to female. She and her friend, actor Will Ferrell, recently shared in documentary form their New York-to-California road trip that took place shortly after Harper's transition.[3] At the end of the documentary—or perhaps at its not-end—Will and Harper sit together on the beach in Santa Monica, just a few miles from where I wrote this book. Here, Will says to his friend, "I'm going to think of something tomorrow that I forgot to ask you."

"Me too," Harper replies. "I'm going to think of a bunch of stuff I should have said that I wanted to tell you."

"We have time."

"We have time."

I, too, am going to think of a bunch of things to add to this book—this match with Paul and his readers, as it were—tomorrow. And the day after that. And the day after that. But even when these pages are published—and apologies to Paul—it is not the end. I may still shake from exertion, but we do have time.

Yes. We have time.

2. Johnson-DeBaufre, "Historical Approaches," 16.

3. Josh Greenbaum, *Will & Harper* (Netflix, 2024).

BIBLIOGRAPHY

Abegg, Martin G. "Messianic Hope and 4Q285: A Reassessment." *Journal of Biblical Literature* 113, no. 1 (1994): 81–91.

Adelman, Janet. *Blood Relations: Christian and Jew in the Merchant of Venice.* University of Chicago Press, 2010.

Alexander, Philip. "Torah and Salvation in Tannaitic Literature." In *Justification and Variegated Nomism: The Complexities of Second Temple Judaism*, vol. 1, edited by D. A. Carson, Peter T. O'Brien, and Mark A. Seifrid. Mohr Siebeck, 2001.

Anderson, Janice Capel, and Jeffrey L. Staley, eds. *Taking It Personally: Autobiographical Biblical Criticism.* Semeia 72. Scholars Press, 1995.

Arnal, William. "The Cipher 'Judaism' in Contemporary Historical Jesus Scholarship." In *Apocalypticism, Anti-Semitism and the Historical Jesus: Subtexts in Criticism*, edited by John S. Kloppenborg and John Marshall. T&T Clark International, 2005.

Ascough, Richard. "The Thessalonian Christian Community as a Professional Voluntary Association." *Journal of Biblical Literature* 119 (2000): 311–328.

Atkinson, Kenneth. "Enduring the Lord's Discipline: Soteriology in the Psalms of Solomon." In *This World and the World to Come*, edited by Daniel M. Gurtner. T&T Clark, 2013.

Augustine. *Confessions.* Translated by Henry Chadwick. Oxford University Press, 2008.

Augustine. *Confessions. Letters, Volume 3 (131–164).* Translated by Wilfrid Parsons. Catholic University of America Press, 1953.

Baynes, Norman Hepburn, trans. *The Speeches of Adolf Hitler, April 1922–August 1939*, vol. 1. Oxford University Press, 1942.

Baddiel, David. *Jews Don't Count.* HarperCollins, 2021.

Baden, Joel S. *Source Criticism.* Wipf and Stock, 2024.

Baron, Lawrence. "The Holocaust and American Public Memory, 1945–1960." *Holocaust and Genocide Studies* 17, no. 1 (2003): 62–88.

Barth, Fredrik, ed. *Ethnic Groups and Boundaries: The Social Organization of Culture Difference.* George Allen & Unwin, 1969.

Bauckham, Richard. "Apocalypses." In *Justification and Variegated Nomism: The Complexities of Second Temple Judaism*, vol. 1, edited by D. A. Carson, Peter T. O'Brien, and Mark A. Seifrid. Mohr Siebeck, 2001.

Baum, Gregory. "Introduction." In *Faith and Fratricide: The Theological Roots of Anti-Semitism*, edited by Rosemary Radford Ruether. Seabury, 1974.

Baur, Ferdinand Christian. *Paul, the Apostle of Jesus Christ*. "Preface to the First Edition." Translated by Robert F. Brown and Peter C. Hodgson. Wipf and Stock, 2021.

Beck, Evelyn Torton. "The Politics of Jewish Invisibility." *NWSA Journal* 1, no. 1 (1988): 93–102.

Becker, Adam H., and Annette Yoshiko Reed. "Introduction." In *The Ways That Never Parted: Jews and Christians in Late Antiquity and the Early Middle Ages*, edited by Adam H. Becker and Annette Yoshiko Reed. Fortress Press, 2007.

BeDuhn, Jason D. *The First New Testament: Marcion's Scriptural Canon*. Polebridge Press, 2013.

Bergen, Doris L. *Twisted Cross*. The University of North Carolina Press, 1996.

Bhabha, Homi K. *The Location of Culture*. Routledge, 1994.

Bird, Michael F. *An Anomalous Jew: Paul Among Jews, Greeks, and Romans*. Eerdmans, 2016.

Bird, Michael F. "An Introduction to the Paul Within Judaism Debate." In *Paul Within Judaism: Perspectives on Paul and Jewish Identity*, edited by Michael Bird, Ruben A. Bühner, Jörg Frey, and Brian Rosner. Mohr Siebeck, 2023.

Boccaccini, Gabriele. *Paul's Three Paths to Salvation*. Eerdmans, 2020.

Bonar, Chance. "Myth: 'The Name Palestine Is a Roman Invention.'" *Everyday Orientalism*. September 23, 2024. https://everydayorientalism.wordpress.com/2024/09/23/myth-the-name-palestine-is-a-roman-invention-eopalestine-06/.

Borchardt, Francis. "CSTT and Gender #2: A Gender Theory Critique of the Historical-Critical Method." *Changes in Sacred Texts and Traditions*. July 6, 2017. https://blogs.helsinki.fi/sacredtexts/2017/07/06/cstt-and-gender-a-gender-theory-critique-of-the-historical-critical-method/.

Bormann, Martin, ed. *Hitler's Secret Conversations 1941–1944*. Farrar, Straus and Young, 1953.

Bouie, Jamelle. "On Whoopi Goldberg's Comments and the Origins of Racism." *New York Times*, February 5, 2022. https://www.nytimes.com/2022/02/05/opinion/whoopi-goldberg-race-history.html.

Bowens, Lisa M. *African American Readings of Paul: Reception, Resistance, and Transformation*. Eerdmans, 2020.

Boyarin, Daniel. *Border Lines: The Partition of Judaeo-Christianity*. University of Pennsylvania Press, 2004.

Boyarin, Daniel. *A Radical Jew: Paul and the Politics of Identity*. University of California Press, 1997.

Boyarin, Daniel. *Unheroic Conduct: The Rise of Heterosexuality and the Invention of the Jewish Man*. University of California Press, 1997.

Braybrooke, Marcus. *Children of One God: A History of the Council of Christians and Jews*. Vallentine, Mitchell, 1991.

Brake, Deborah. "Wrestling with Gender: Constructing Masculinity by Refusing to Wrestle Women." *Nevada Law Journal* 13 (2013): 486–532.

Branfman, Jonathan. "Teaching for Coalition: Dismantling 'Jewish-Progressive Conflict' Through Feminist and Queer Pedagogy." *Frontiers (Boulder)* 40, no. 2 (2019): 126–166.

Brettler, Marc. "Monopoly and Biblical Studies." *Ancient Jew Review*, August 9, 2023. https://www.ancientjewreview.com/read/2023/8/3/monopoly-and-biblical-studies.

Briggs, Sheila. "Slavery and Gender." In *On the Cutting Edge: The Study of Women in the Biblical World: Essays in Honor of Elisabeth Schüssler Fiorenza*, 1st ed., edited by Jane Schaberg, Alice Bach, and Esther Fuchs. Continuum, 2003.

Britton, Dennis Austin. "Definitions and Representations of Race." In *A Cultural History of Race in the Reformation and Enlightenment*, edited by Nicholas Hudson. Bloomsbury Academic, 2023.

Brodkin, Karen. *How Jews Became White Folks and What That Says About Race in America*. Rutgers University Press, 2002.

Brooten, Bernadette J. *Love Between Women: Early Christian Responses to Female Homoeroticism*. University of Chicago Press, 1996.

Buell, Denise Kimber. "Rethinking the Relevance of Race for Early Christian Self-Definition." *Harvard Theological Review* 94, no. 4 (2001): 449–476.

Buell, Denise Kimber. *Why This New Race: Ethnic Reasoning in Early Christianity*. Columbia University Press, 2005.

Bultmann, Rudolf. *Essays Philosophical and Theological*. Translated by J. C. N. Greig. SCM Press, 1955.

Bultmann, Rudolf. *Primitive Christianity in Its Contemporary Setting*. Meridian, 1956.

Bultmann, Rudolf. *Theology of the New Testament*. Translated by Kendrick Grobel. Charles Scribner's Sons, 1951.

Burrus, Virginia. "Mapping a Metamorphosis: Initial Reflections on Gender and Ancient Religious Discourses." In *Mapping Gender in Ancient Religious Discourses*, edited by Todd C. Penner and Caroline Vander Stichele. Brill, 2007.

Caplan, Jennifer. *Funny, You Don't Look Funny: Judaism and Humor from the Silent Generation to Millennials*. Wayne State University Press, 2023.

Cargill, Robert R. "Origins of Baptism." Bible Odyssey. Accessed March 10, 2025, https://thesacredpage.bibleodyssey.org/video-gallery/origins-of-baptism/.

Carr, David M. *The Formation of the Hebrew Bible: A New Reconstruction*. Oxford University Press, 2011.

Carr, David M. *Holy Resilience: The Bible's Traumatic Origins*. Yale University Press, 2014.

Carter, J. Kameron. *Race: A Theological Account*. Oxford University Press, 2008.

Cesarani, David. *Final Solution: The Fate of the Jews 1933–1949*. Macmillan, 2016.

Cesarani, David. *Justice Delayed: How Britain Became a Refuge for Nazi War Criminals*. Heinemann, 1992.

Cesarani, David, and Eric J. Sundquist, eds. *After the Holocaust: Challenging the Myth of Silence.* Routledge, 2011.

Cobb, Christy. "Enslaved Women, Women Enslavers: Kyriarchy and Intersectionality in the New Testament." *Journal of Feminist Studies in Religion* 40, no. 1 (2024): 43–60.

Cohen, Jeremy. *Christ Killers: The Jews and the Passion from the Bible to the Big Screen.* Oxford University Press, 2007.

Cohen, Jeremy. *Living Letters of the Law: Ideas of the Jew in Medieval Christianity.* University of California Press, 1999.

Cohen, Jeremy. *The Salvation of Israel: Jews in Christian Eschatology from Paul to the Puritans.* Cornell University Press, 2022.

Cohen, Shaye J. D. *The Beginnings of Jewishness: Boundaries, Varieties, Uncertainties.* University of California Press, 1999.

Cohen, Shaye J. D. *From the Maccabees to the Mishnah.* 3rd ed. Westminster John Knox, 2014.

Collins, John J. *The Apocalyptic Imagination: An Introduction to Jewish Apocalyptic Literature,* 3rd ed. Eerdmans, 2016.

Collins, John J. "'He Shall Not Judge by What His Eyes See': Messianic Authority in the Dead Sea Scrolls." *Dead Sea Discoveries: A Journal of Current Research on the Scrolls and Related Literature* 2, no. 2 (1995): 145–164.

Collins, John J. "The Idea of Election in 4 Ezra." *Jewish Studies Quarterly* 16, no. 1 (2009): 83–96.

Collins, John J. "The Son of Man and the Saints of the Most High in the Book of Daniel." *Journal of Biblical Literature* 93 (1974): 50–66.

Collins, John J. "The Son of Man in First-Century Judaism." *New Testament Studies* 38 (1992): 448–466.

Concannon, Cavan W. *Profaning Paul.* University of Chicago Press, 2021.

Connelly, John. "Catholic Racism and Its Opponents." *Journal of Modern History* 79, no. 4 (2007): 813–847.

Cousin, Glynis, and Robert Fine. "Brothers in Misery: Reconnecting Sociologies of Racism and Anti-Semitism." In *Race, Color, Identity: Rethinking Discourses About "Jews" in the Twenty-First Century,* edited by Efraim Sicher. Berghahn Books, 2013.

Cowan, Brian. *The Social Life of Coffee: The Emergence of the British Coffeehouse.* Yale University Press, 2011.

Critchley, Simon. *The Faith of the Faithless: Experiments in Political Theology.* Verso Books, 2012.

Crook, Zeba A. *Reconceptualising Conversion: Patronage, Loyalty, and Conversion in the Religions of the Ancient Mediterranean.* Walter de Gruyter, 2004.

Crosby, John F. *Personalist Papers.* Lexington Books, 2016.

Crossley, James G. *Jesus in an Age of Terror: Scholarly Projects for a New American Century.* Routledge, 2008.

Crossley, James G. "The Multicultural Christ: Jesus and Jew and the New Perspective on Paul in an Age of Neoliberalism." *The Bible & Critical Theory* 7 (2011): 8–16.

Crossley, James G. "Other Problems from a British Perspective: 'Jewishness', Jesus, and the New Perspective on Paul." In *Ethnicity, Race, Religion: Identities and Ideologies in Early Jewish and Christian Texts, and in Modern Biblical Interpretation*, edited by David G. Horrell and Katherine M. Hockey. T&T Clark, 2018.

Daniel, Drew. "Early Modern Affect Theory, Racialized Aversion, and the Strange Case of Foetor Judaicus." In *Race & Affect in Early Modern English Literature*, edited by Carol Meija LaPerle. ACMRS Press, 2022.

Dauber, Jeremy. *Jewish Comedy: A Serious History*. W. W. Norton, 2017.

Demacopoulos, George. "The Origins of Anti-Jewish Rhetoric in the Hymns of Good Friday." *Public Orthodoxy*, April 14, 2022. https://publicorthodoxy.org/2022/04/14/the-origins-of-anti-jewish-rhetoric-in-the-hymns-of-good-friday.

Derrida, Jacques. *Of Spirit: Heidegger and the Question*. Translated by Geoffrey Bennington and Rachel Bowlby. University of Chicago Press, 1989.

Diner, Hasia R. *We Remember with Reverence and Love: American Jews and the Myth of Silence After the Holocaust, 1945–1962*. New York University Press, 2009.

Donaldson, Terence L. "Jewish Christianity, Israel's Stumbling and the *Sonderweg* Reading of Paul." *Journal for the Study of the New Testament* 29, no. 1 (2006): 27–54.

Donaldson, Terence L. *Judaism and the Gentiles: Jewish Patterns of Universalism (to 135 CE)*. Baylor University Press, 2007.

Drake, Susanna. *Slandering the Jew: Sexuality and Difference in Early Christian Texts*. Divinations: Rereading Late Ancient Religion. University of Pennsylvania Press, 2013.

Du Bois, W. E. B. "The Negro and the Warsaw Ghetto [1952]." In *The Social Theory of W. E. B. Du Bois*, edited by Phil Zuckerman. Pine Forge Press, 2004.

Du Bois, W. E. B. *The Souls of Black Folk*. Jubilee ed. Blue Heron Press, 1953.

Dunn, James D. G. *Jesus, Paul, and the Law: Studies in Mark and Galatians*. Westminster John Knox, 1990.

Dunn, James D. G. *The New Perspective on Paul*, rev. ed. Eerdmans, 2008.

Duran, Eduardo. *Healing the Soul Wound: Trauma-Informed Counseling for Indigenous Communities*. Teachers College Press, 2019.

Eckardt, Arthur Roy. *Jews and Christians, the Contemporary Meeting*. Indiana University Press, 1986.

Edwards, J. Christopher. *Crucified: The Christian Invention of the Jewish Executioners of Jesus*. Fortress Press, 2023.

Efron, John M. *Defenders of the Race: Jewish Doctors and Race Science in Fin-de-Siècle Europe*. Yale University Press, 1994.

Efroymson, David Patrick. "Tertullian's Anti-Judaism and Its Role in His Theology." PhD diss., Temple University, 1975.

Ehrman, Bart D., trans. *The Apostolic Fathers*. Harvard University Press, 2003.

Eisenbaum, Pamela. "Is Paul the Father of Misogyny and Antisemitism?" *CrossCurrents* 50, no. 4 (2000): 506–524.

Eisenbaum, Pamela. "Jewish Perspectives: A Jewish Apostle to the Gentiles." In *Studying Paul's Letters: Contemporary Perspectives and Methods*, edited by Joseph A. Marchal. Fortress Press, 2012.

Eisenbaum, Pamela. "Paul, Polemics, and the Problem of Essentialism." *Biblical Interpretation* 13, no. 3 (2005): 224–238.

Eisenbaum, Pamela. *Paul Was Not a Christian: The Original Message of a Misunderstood Apostle*. HarperOne, 2009.

Elkins, Kathleen Gallagher. "The Jews as 'Children of the Devil' (John 8:44) in Nazi Children's Literature." *Biblical Interpretation* 31, no. 3 (2022): 374–390.

Elliot, Neil. "The Question of Politics: Paul as a Diaspora Jew Under Roman Rule." In *Paul Within Judaism: Restoring the First-Century Context to the Apostle*, edited by Mark D. Nanos and Magnus Zetterholm. Fortress Press, 2015.

Elukin, Jonathan. *Living Together, Living Apart: Rethinking Jewish-Christian Relations in the Middle Ages*. Princeton University Press, 2007.

Emanuel, Sarah. "Down the Rabbit Hole . . . to the Humor of Apocalypse and the End of the World, LOL." In *Apocalypses in Context: Apocalyptic Currents Through History*, edited by Kelly J. Murphy and Justin Jeffcoat Schedtler, 2nd ed. Fortress Press, 2025.

Emanuel, Sarah. *Humor, Resistance, and Jewish Cultural Persistence in the Book of Revelation: Roasting Rome*. Cambridge University Press, 2020.

Emanuel, Sarah. *Trauma Theory, Trauma Story: A Narration of Biblical Studies and the World of Trauma*, Brill Research Perspectives in Biblical Interpretation 4. Brill, 2021.

Emanuel, Sarah. "When Women of the Bible Say #MeToo." *Feminist Studies in Religion*. January 26, 2018. https://www.fsrinc.org/women-of-the-bible-say-metoo/.

Ericksen, Robert. *Complicity in the Holocaust: Churches and Universities in Nazi Germany*. Cambridge University Press, 2012.

Eva, Richard. "Wrestling with Philosophy." *Public Discourse*, August 8, 2021. https://www.thepublicdiscourse.com/2021/08/77088/.

Falk, Gerhard. *The Jew in Christian Theology: Martin Luther's Anti-Jewish Vom Schem Hamphoras*. McFarland and Company, 1992.

Fanon, Frantz. *Black Skin, White Masks*. Translated by Richard Philcox. Grove Press, 2008.

Favret-Saada, Jeanne. "A Fuzzy Distinction: Anti-Judaism and Anti-Semitism (an Excerpt from Le Judaisme et Ses Juifs)." *HAU: Journal of Ethnographic Theory* 4, no. 3 (2014): 335–340.

Feldman, Daniel. "Reading Poison: Science and Story in Nazi Children's Propaganda." *Children's Literature in Education* 53, no. 2 (2022): 199–220.

Feminists Talk Religion. Season 1, episode 3, "Liberationist Hermeneutics: Interview with Cynthia Chapman and Traci West." Feminist Studies in Religion, April 10, 2020. Podcast. https://podcasts.apple.com/us/podcast/liberationist-hermeneutics-interview-with-cynthia/id1500952459?i=1000471191525.

Field, Geoffrey G. *Evangelist of Race: The Germanic Vision of Houston Stewart Chamberlain*. Columbia University Press, 1981.

Fine, Michelle, Lois Weis, Linda Powell Pruitt, and April Burns, eds. *Off White: Readings on Power, Privilege, and Resistance*. 2nd ed. Routledge, 2004.

Foskett, Mary F., and Jeffrey Kah-Jin Kuan, eds. *Ways of Being, Ways of Reading: Asian American Biblical Interpretation*. Chalice Press, 2006.

Fox, Arminta M. *Paul Decentered: Reading 2 Corinthians with the Corinthian Women*. Paul in Critical Contexts. Lexington Books / Fortress Academic, 2019.

Fraade, Steven D. "To Whom It May Concern: 4QMMT and Its Addressee(s)." *Revue de Qumran* 76 (2000): 507–526.

Frankfurter, David. "The Fiction of the Seven Letters in the Apocalypse: Representing Heavenly Authority in the Shadow of Paul." *Harvard Theological Review* 117 (2024): 79–98.

Frankfurter, David. "Jews or Not?: Reconstructing the 'Other' in Rev 2:9 and 3:9." *Harvard Theological Review* 94 (2001): 403–425.

Frankfurter, David. "The Letter of James as a Document of Paulinism?" In *Reading James with New Eyes: Methodological Reassessments of the Letter of James*, edited by R. L. Webb and J. S. Kloppenborg. T&T Clark, 2007.

Frankfurter, David. "Revelation." In *The Jewish Annotated New Testament*. 2nd ed., edited by Amy-Jill Levine and Marc Zvi Brettler. Oxford University Press, 2017.

Fredriksen, Paula. *Ancient Christianities: The First Five Hundred Years*. Princeton University Press, 2024.

Fredriksen, Paula. *Augustine and the Jews: A Christian Defense of Jews and Judaism*. Yale University Press, 2010.

Fredriksen, Paula. "The Birth of Christianity and the Origins of Christian Anti-Judaism." In *Jesus, Judaism, and Christian Anti-Judaism: Reading the New Testament After the Holocaust*, edited by Paula Fredriksen and Adele Reinhartz. Westminster John Knox, 2002.

Fredriksen, Paula. "How Jewish Is God?: Divine Ethnicity in Paul's Theology." *Journal of Biblical Literature* 137, no. 1 (2018): 193–212.

Fredriksen, Paula. "'If It Looks Like a Duck, and It Quacks Like a Duck . . .': On Not 'Giving Up the Godfearer.'" In *A Most Reliable Witness: Essays in Honor of Ross Shepard Kraemer*, edited by Susan Ashbrook Harvey, Nathaniel P. DesRosiers, Shira L. Lander, Jacqueline Z. Pastis, and Daniel Ullucci. Brown Judaic Studies, 2015.

Fredriksen, Paula. "Judaism, the Circumcision of Gentiles, and Apocalyptic Hope: Another Look at Galatians 1 and 2." *Journal of Theological Studies* 42, no. 2 (1991): 532–564.

Fredriksen, Paula. "Original Sin." Bible Odyssey. Accessed March 9, 2025. https://short-question.bibleodyssey.com/articles/original-sin/.

Fredriksen, Paula. "Paul and Augustine: Conversion Narratives, Orthodox Traditions, and the Retrospective Self." *Journal of Theological Studies* 37, no. 1 (1986): 3–34.

Fredriksen, Paula. *Paul: The Pagans' Apostle*. Yale University Press, 2017.

Fredriksen, Paula. "Philo, Herod, Paul, and the Many Gods of Ancient Jewish 'Monotheism.'" *Harvard Theological Review* 115, no. 1 (2022): 23–45.

Fredriksen, Paula. "The Question of Worship: Gods, Pagans, and the Redemption of Israel." In *Paul Within Judaism: Restoring the First-Century Context to the Apostle*, edited by Mark D. Nanos and Magnus Zetterholm. Fortress Press, 2015.

Fredriksen, Paula. *Sin: The Early History of an Idea*. Princeton University Press, 2012.

Fredriksen, Paula, and Adele Reinhartz, eds. *Jesus, Judaism, and Christian Anti-Judaism: Reading the New Testament After the Holocaust*. Westminster John Knox, 2002.

Fredriksen, Paula Landes, trans. *Augustine on Romans: Propositions from the Epistle to the Romans and Unfinished Commentary on the Epistles to the Romans*. Society of Biblical Literature, 1982.

Frykholm, Amy Johnson. *Rapture Culture: Left Behind in Evangelical America*. 1st ed. Oxford University Press, 2004.

Gafney, Wilda C. "White Supremacy in Biblical Interpretation." 2020. https://www.youtube.com/watch?v=7hemIaya_Ic.

Gager, John G. "Messiahs and Their Followers." In *Toward the Millennium: Messianic Expectations from the Bible to Waco*, edited by Peter Schäfer and Mark R. Cohen. Brill, 1998.

Gager, John G. *The Origins of Anti-Semitism: Attitudes Toward Judaism in Pagan and Christian Antiquity*. Oxford University Press, 1985.

Gager, John G. *Reinventing Paul*. Oxford University Press, 2002.

Gallagher, Edmon L., and John D. Meade. *The Biblical Canon Lists from Early Christianity: Texts and Analysis*. 1st ed. Oxford University Press, 2018.

Garroway, Josh. *Paul's Gentile-Jews: Neither Jew nor Gentile, but Both*. Palgrave Macmillan, 2012.

Gaston, Lloyd. "New Testament Theology After the Holocaust: Exegetical Responsibilities and Canonical Possibilities." In *A Shadow of Glory: Reading the New Testament After the Holocaust*, edited by Tod Linafelt. Routledge, 2002.

Gaston, Lloyd. "Paul and the Torah." In *Antisemitism and the Foundations of Christianity*, edited by Alan T. Davies. Paulist Press, 1979.

Gaston, Lloyd. *Paul and the Torah* [monograph]. University of British Columbia Press, 1987.

Gathercole, Simon J. "Justification by Faith." In *The Oxford Handbook of Pauline Studies*, edited by Matthew V. Novenson and R. Barry Matlock. Oxford University Press, 2022.

Gathercole, Simon J. *Where Is Boasting?: Early Jewish Soteriology and Paul's Response in Romans 1–5*. Eerdmans, 2002.

Gerdmar, Anders. "Jewish Studies in the Service of Nazi Ideology: Tübingen's Faculty of Theology as a Center for Antisemitic Research." In *The Betrayal of the Humanities: The University During the Third Reich*, edited by Bernard M. Levinson and Robert P. Ericksen. Indiana University Press, 2022.

Gerdmar, Anders. *Roots of Theological Anti-Semitism: German Biblical Interpretation and the Jews, from Herder and Semler to Kittel and Bultmann*. Brill, 2009.

Gilman, Sander L. "Foreword." In *Race, Color, Identity: Rethinking Discourses About "Jews" in the Twenty-First Century*, edited by Efraim Sicher. Berghahn Books, 2013.

Gilman, Sander L. *The Jew's Body*. Routledge, 1991.

Glancy, Jennifer A., and Stephen D. Moore. "How Typical a Roman Prostitute Is Revelation's 'Great Whore'?" *Journal of Biblical Literature* 130, no. 3 (2011): 551–569.

Goldberg, David Theo. *Racist Culture: Philosophy and the Politics of Meaning*. Blackwell, 1993.

Golin, Paul. "What Is Secular Humanistic Judaism?" My Jewish Learning. Accessed March 6, 2025, https://www.myjewishlearning.com/article/judaism-with-no-god/.

Goodblatt, David M. *Elements of Ancient Jewish Nationalism*. Cambridge University Press, 2006.

Goodman, Alan. "Race Is Real, But It's Not Genetic." *SAPIENS*, March 13, 2020. https://www.sapiens.org/biology/is-race-real/.

Gordon, Michelle. "Selective Histories: Britain, the Empire and the Holocaust." In *The Palgrave Handbook of Britain and the Holocaust*, edited by Tom Lawson and Andy Pearce. Palgrave Macmillan, 2020.

Graybill, Rhiannon. *Texts After Terror: Rape, Sexual Violence, and the Hebrew Bible*. Oxford University Press, 2021.

Greenbaum, Josh. *Will & Harper* [film]. Netflix, 2024.

Greenberg, Cheryl. "'I'm Not White—I'm Jewish': The Racial Politics of American Jews." In *Race, Color, Identity: Rethinking Discourses About "Jews" in the Twenty-First Century*, edited by Efraim Sicher. Berghahn Books, 2013.

Gritsch, Eric W. *Martin Luther's Anti-Semitism: Against His Better Judgment*. Eerdmans, 2012.

Hall, Kennedy. "Good Friday 'Antisemitism' and the Conversion of the Jews." *Crisis Magazine*, March 29, 2024. https://crisismagazine.com/opinion/good-friday-antisemitism-and-the-conversion-of-the-jews.

Harvey, Richard S. *Luther and the Jews*. Wipf and Stock, 2017.

Hays, Richard. "'Have We Found Abraham to Be Our Forefather According to the Flesh?': A Reconsideration of Rom 4:1." *Novum Testamentum* 27 (1985): 76–98.

Heng, Geraldine. *The Invention of Race in the European Middle Ages*. Cambridge University Press, 2018.

Henze, Matthias. *Mind the Gap: How the Jewish Writings Between the Old and New Testament Help Us Understand Jesus*. Fortress Press, 2017.

Herschcopf, Judith. "The Church and the Jews: The Struggle at Vatican Council II." *American Jewish Year Book* 66 (1965): 99–136.

Heschel, Susannah. *Abraham Geiger and the Jewish Jesus*. University of Chicago Press, 1998.

Heschel, Susannah. *The Aryan Jesus: Christian Theologians and the Bible in Nazi Germany*. Princeton University Press, 2008.

Heschel, Susannah. "Confronting the Past: Post-1945 German Protestant Theology and the Fate of the Jews." *Studies in Contemporary Jewry: An Annual* 24 (2010): 46–70.

Heschel, Susannah. "Reading Jesus as a Nazi." In *A Shadow of Glory: Reading the New Testament After the Holocaust*, edited by Tod Linafelt. Routledge, 2002.

Hicks-Keeton, Jill. *Good Book: How White Evangelicals Save the Bible to Save Themselves*. Fortress Press, 2023.

Hiemer, Ernst. *Der Giftpilz [The Poisonous Mushroom]*. Illustrated by Philipp Rupprecht. Stürmerverlag, 1938.

Hirsh, Richard A. "Reconstructionist Judaism and the Rejection of Chosen People." *My Jewish Learning*. Republished from *The Reconstructionist*, September 1984. https://www.myjewishlearning.com/article/reconstructionist-judaism-and-the-rejection-of-chosen-people/.

Hodge, Caroline Johnson. *If Sons, Then Heirs: A Study of Kinship and Ethnicity in the Letters of Paul*. Oxford University Press, 2007.

Hodge, Caroline Johnson. "Paul and Ethnicity." In *The Oxford Handbook of Pauline Studies*, edited by Matthew V. Novenson and R. Barry Matlock. Oxford University Press, 2022.

Hodge, Caroline Johnson. "The Question of Identity: Gentiles as Gentiles—but also Not—in Pauline Communities." In *Paul Within Judaism: Restoring the First-Century Context to the Apostle*, edited by Mark D. Nanos and Magnus Zetterholm. Fortress Press, 2015.

Hoke, James N. "Be Even Better Subjects, Worthy of Rehabilitation: Homonationalism and 1 Thessalonians 4–5." In *Bodies on the Verge: Queering Pauline Epistles*, edited by Joseph A. Marchal. Semeia Studies 93. SBL Press, 2019.

Hoke, James N. "'Behold, the Lord's Whore'? Slavery, Prostitution, and Luke 1:38." *Biblical Interpretation* 26, no. 1 (2018): 43–67.

Hoke, Jimmy. *Feminism, Queerness, Affect, and Romans: Under God?* Early Christianity and Its Literature 30. SBL Press, 2021.

Hoke, Jimmy. "The Letter of Paul to the Romans." In *The Westminster Study Bible*, edited by Emerson B. Powery, Stacy Davis, Mary F. Foskett, and Brent A. Strawn. Westminster John Knox, 2024.

Hood, John Y. B. "Did Augustine Abandon His Doctrine of Jewish Witness in Aduersus Iudaeos?" *Augustinian Studies* 50, no. 2 (2019): 171–195.

Horrell, David G. *Ethnicity and Inclusion: Religion, Race, and Whiteness in Constructions of Jewish and Christian Identities*. Eerdmans, 2020.

Horn, Dara. *People Love Dead Jews: Reports From a Haunted Present*. W. W. Norton, 2021.

Huber, Lynn R. "Reading Enslavement in Revelation 1." In *Revelation and Material Religion in the Roman East: Essays in Honor of Steven J. Friesen*, edited by Nathan Leach, Daniel Charles Smith, and Tony Keddie. Routledge, 2023.

Huber, Lynn R. *Thinking and Seeing with Women in Revelation*. Bloomsbury T&T Clark, 2013.

Huber, Lynn R., and Gail R. O'Day. *Wisdom Commentary: Revelation*. Liturgical Press, 2023.

Hudson, Nicholas. "Introduction." In *A Cultural History of Race in the Reformation and Enlightenment*, edited by Nicholas Hudson. Bloomsbury Academic, 2023.

Hyland, Siobhán, and Paul Jackson. "Campaigning for Justice: Anti-Fascist Campaigners, Nazi-Era Collaborator War Criminals and Britain's Failure to Prosecute, 1945–1999." In *The Palgrave Handbook of Britain and the Holocaust*, edited by Tom Lawson and Andy Pearce. Palgrave Macmillan, 2020.

Isaac, Benjamin. *The Invention of Racism in Classical Antiquity*. Princeton University Press, 2004.

Isaac, Jules. *Genèse de l'Antisémitisme*. Calmann Lévy, 2014.

Jackson, Melissa. *Comedy and Feminist Interpretation of the Hebrew Bible: A Subversive Collaboration*. Oxford University Press, 2012.

Jacobs, Andrew S. "Christianizing the Roman Empire: Jews and the Law from Constantine to Justinian, 300–600 CE." In *The Cambridge Companion to Antisemitism*, edited by Steven Katz. Cambridge Companions to Religion. Cambridge University Press, 2022.

Jacobson, Matthew Frye. *Whiteness of a Different Color: European Immigrants and the Alchemy of Race*. Harvard University Press, 1998.

Jervis, L. Ann. "Paul the Theologian." In *The Oxford Handbook of Pauline Studies*, edited by Matthew V. Novenson and R. Barry Matlock. Oxford University Press, 2022.

Johnson, Luke T. "The New Testament's Anti-Jewish Slander and the Conventions of Ancient Polemic." *Journal of Biblical Literature* 108, no. 3 (1989): 425–426.

Johnson-DeBaufre, Melanie. "'Gazing Upon the Invisible': Archaeology, Historiography, and the Elusive Women of 1 Thessalonians." In *From Roman to Early Christian Thessalonikē: Studies in Religion and Archaeology*, edited by Laura Nasrallah, Charalambos Bakirtzis, and Steven J. Friesen. Harvard Theological Studies 64. Harvard University Press, 2010.

Johnson-DeBaufre, Melanie. "Historical Approaches: Which Past? Whose Past?" In *Studying Paul's Letters: Contemporary Perspectives and Methods*, edited by Joseph A. Marchal. Fortress Press, 2012.

Johnson-DeBaufre, Melanie. "A Monument to Suffering: 1 Thessalonians 2: 14–6, Dangerous Memory, and Christian Identity." *Journal of Early Christian History* 1, no. 2 (2011): 91–118.

Johnson-DeBaufre, Melanie, and Laura S. Nasrallah. "Beyond the Heroic Paul: Toward a Feminist and Decolonizing Approach to the Letters of Paul." In *The Colonized Apostle, Paul Through Postcolonial Eyes*, edited by Christopher D. Stanley. Fortress Press, 2011.

Jones, C. P. "Tattooing and Branding in Graeco-Roman Antiquity." *Journal of Roman Studies* 77 (1987): 139–155.

Jütte, Robert. *The Jewish Body: A History*. University of Pennsylvania Press, 2020.

Kalmanofsky, Amy. *Sexual Violence and Sacred Texts*. FSR Books, 2017.

Kartzow, Marianne Bjelland. "'Asking the Other Question': An Intersectional Approach to Galatians 3:28 and the Colossian Household Codes." *Biblical Interpretation* 18, no. 4–5 (2010): 364–389.

Kelley, Shawn. *Racializing Jesus: Race, Ideology and the Formation of Modern Biblical Scholarship*. Routledge, 2013.

Kister, Menahem. "The Dead Sea Scrolls." In *The Jewish Annotated New Testament*, 2nd ed., edited by Amy-Jill Levine and Marc Z. Brettler. Oxford University Press, 2017.

Knox, Robert. *The Races of Men: A Fragment*. Forgotten Books, 2018.

Kohler, Noa Sophie, and Dan Mishmar. "Genes as Jewish History? Human Population Genetics in the Service of Historians." In *Race, Color, Identity: Rethinking Discourses About "Jews" in the Twenty-First Century*, edited by Efraim Sicher. Berghahn Books, 2013.

Kotrosits, Maia. *How Things Feel: Affect Theory, Biblical Studies, and the (Im)Personal*. Research Perspectives in Biblical Interpretation 1. Brill, 2016.

Kraemer, Ross. "Giving up the Godfearers." *Journal of Ancient Judaism* 5 (2014): 61–87.

Kraemer, Ross. *The Mediterranean Diaspora in Late Antiquity: What Christianity Cost the Jews*. Oxford University Press, 2020.

Lavender, Isiah III. "Getting All of It: On Jordan Peele's Get Out: Political Horror." *Science Fiction Film and Television* 15, no. 2 (2022): 219–226.

Lawson, Tom. "Coming to Terms with the Past: Reading and Writing Colonial Genocide in the Shadow of the Holocaust." *Holocaust Studies: A Journal of Culture and History* 20, no. 1–2 (2014): 129–156.

Legaspi, Michael. *The Death of Scripture and the Rise of Biblical Studies*. Oxford University Press, 2010.

Leven, Benjamin. "The Good Friday Prayer for Jews: A 'Borderline Case' of Christian Prayer." *Studia Liturgica* 41, no. 1 (2011): 78–83.

Levenson, Jon D. *Resurrection and the Restoration of Israel: The Ultimate Victory of the God of Life*. Yale University Press, 2006.

Levenson, Jon D. "The Universal Horizon of Biblical Particularism." In *Ethnicity and the Bible*, edited by Mark G. Brett. Biblical Interpretation Series 19. Brill, 1996.

Levi, Neil, and Michael Rothberg. "General Introduction: Theory and the Holocaust." In *The Holocaust: Theoretical Readings*, edited by Neil Levi and Michael Rothberg. Edinburgh University Press, 2003.

Levine, Amy-Jill. "Supersessionism: Admit and Address Rather than Debate or Deny." *Religions* 13, no. 2 (2022): 155–166.

Levine, Amy-Jill, and Maria Mayo Robbins, eds. *A Feminist Companion to the Apocalypse of John*, illustrated ed. T&T Clark, 2010.

Levinson, Bernard M. "Gerhard von Rad's Struggle Against the Nazification of the Old Testament." In *The Betrayal of the Humanities: The University During the Third Reich*, edited by Bernard M. Levinson and Robert P. Ericksen. Indiana University Press, 2022.

Levinson, Bernard M. "The Impact of Johann Wolfgang von Goethe's Discovery of the 'Original' Version of the Ten Commandments upon Biblical Scholarship: The Myth of Jewish Particularism and German Universalism." In *Confronting Antisemitism in Christianity, Islam, and Judaism*, vol. 2 of *An End to Antisemitism!*, edited by Armin Lange, Kerstin Mayerhofer, Dina Porat, and Lawrence H. Schiffman. Walter de Gruyter, 2020.

Lieu, Judith M. *Marcion and the Making of a Heretic: God and Scripture in the Second Century*. Cambridge University Press, 2015.

Lim, Timothy H. *The Earliest Commentary on the Prophecy of Habakkuk*. Oxford University Press, 2020.

Lin, Yii-Jan. "Junia: An Apostle Before Paul." *Journal of Biblical Literature* 139, no. 1 (2020): 191–209.

Lindemann, Albert S. *Anti-Semitism Before the Holocaust*. 2nd ed. Routledge, 2014.

Livesey, Nina E. *The Letters of Paul in Their Roman Literary Context: Reassessing Apostolic Authorship*. Cambridge University Press, 2024.

Lopez, Davina C. *The Apostle to the Conquered: Reimagining Paul's Mission*. Fortress Press, 2010.

Luther, Martin. *Lectures on Romans*. Translated by Wilhelm Pauck. Westminster John Knox, 1961.

Luther, Martin. "On the Jews and Their Lies, 1543." In *Luther's Works*, vol. 47, *The Christian in Society IV*, edited by Franklin Sherman. Translated by Martin H. Bertram. Fortress Press, 1971.

Magid, Shaul. "Judeopessimism: Antisemitism, History, and Critical Race Theory." *Harvard Theological Review* 117, no. 2 (2024): 368–390.

Magid, Shaul. "The Price of (Non) Whiteness." *Contending Modernities*, September 18, 2020. https://contendingmodernities.nd.edu/theorizing-modernities/the-price-of-non-whiteness/.

Malherbe, Abraham J. *Paul and the Popular Philosophers*. Fortress Press, 1989.

Malherbe, Abraham J. *The Letters to the Thessalonians: A New Translation with Introduction and Commentary*. Yale University Press, 2007.

Matthews, Shelly. "Teaching Fiction, Teaching Acts: Introducing the Linguistic Turn in the Biblical Studies Classroom." In *Reading and Teaching Ancient Fiction: Jewish, Christian, and Greco-Roman Narratives*, edited by Sara R. Johnson, Rubén R. Dupertuis, and Christine Shea. Society of Biblical Literature, 2017.

Marchal, Joseph A. *Appalling Bodies: Queer Figures Before and After Paul's Letters*. Oxford University Press, 2020.

Marchal, Joseph A. "The Exceptional Proves Who Rules: Imperial Sexual Exceptionalism in and Around Paul's Letters." *Journal of Early Christian History* 5, no. 1 (2015): 87–115.

Marshall, John W. *Parables of War: Reading John's Jewish Apocalypse*. Wilfrid Laurier University Press, 2001.

Matlock, R. Barry. "Sins of the Flesh and Suspicious Minds: Dunn's New Theology of Paul." *Journal for the Study of the New Testament* 21, no. 72 (1999): 67–90.

McDonald, Lee M. *The Biblical Canon: Its Origin, Transmission, and Authority*. 3rd ed. Baker Academic, 2007.

McKnight, Scot, and B. J. Oropeza, eds. *Perspectives on Paul: Five Views*. Baker Academic, 2020.

Mell, Julie. "Jews and Money: The Medieval Origins of a Modern Stereotype." In *The Cambridge Companion to Antisemitism*, edited by Steven Katz. Cambridge Companions to Religion. Cambridge University Press, 2022.

Mendez, Hugo. "Did the Johannine Community Exist?" *Journal for the Study of the New Testament* 42 (2020): 350–374.

Merkle, Ben L. "Romans 11 and the Future of Ethnic Israel." *Journal of the Evangelical Theological Society* 43, no. 4 (2000): 709–721.

Michael, Robert. *A Concise History of American Antisemitism*. Rowman & Littlefield, 2005.

Michael, Robert. *A History of Catholic Antisemitism: The Dark Side of the Church*. Palgrave Macmillan, 2011.

Mintz, Alan. *Popular Culture and the Shaping of Holocaust Memory in America*. University of Washington Press, 2001.

Mussner, Franz. *Traktat Über die Juden*. Kösel, 1979.

Montefiore, Claude Goldsmid. *Judaism and St. Paul: Two Essays*. Max Goschen, 1914.

Moore, George Foot. "Christian Writers on Judaism." *Harvard Theological Review* 14, no. 3 (1921): 197–254.

Moore, Stephen D., and J. Cheryl Exum. "Biblical Studies/Cultural Studies." In *Biblical Studies / Cultural Studies: The Third Sheffield Colloquium*, edited by Stephen D. Moore and J. Cheryl Exum. Sheffield Academic Press, 1998.

Moore, Stephen D., and Yvonne Sherwood. *The Invention of the Biblical Scholar: A Critical Manifesto*. Fortress Press, 2011.

Moses, A. Dirk. "Colonialism." In *The Oxford Handbook of Holocaust Studies*, edited by Peter Hayes and John K. Roth. Oxford University Press, 2010.

Moss, Candida. *God's Ghostwriters: Enslaved Christians and the Making of the Bible*. Little, Brown, 2024.

Munson, Henry. "Christianity, Antisemitism, and the Holocaust." *Religions* 9, no. 1 (2018): 26.

Mussolini, Benito. "Speech in Trieste, September 18, 1938." Translated by *Biblioteca Fascista*, March 4, 2012. https://bibliotecafascista.blogspot.com/2012/03/speech-in-trieste-september-18-1938.html.

Myles, Robert J. "The Fetish for a Subversive Jesus." *Journal for the Study of the Historical Jesus* 14, no. 1 (2016): 52–70.

Najman, Hindy. *Past Renewals: Interpretative Authority, Renewed Revelation and the Quest for Perfection in Jewish Antiquity*. Supplements to the *Journal for the Study of Judaism* 53. Brill, 2010.

Nanos, Mark D. "All Israel Will Be *Saved* or *Kept Safe*? (Rom 11:26): Israel's *Conversion* or *Irrevocable Calling to Gospel the Nations*?" In *Israel and the Nations: Paul's Gospel in the Context of Jewish Expectation*, edited by František Ábel. Lexington Books / Fortress Academic, 2021.

Nanos, Mark D. *The Irony of Galatians: Paul's Letter in First-Century Context*. Fortress Press, 2002.

Nanos, Mark D. "A Jewish View." In *Four Views on the Apostle Paul*, edited by Michael F. Bird. Counterpoints: Bible and Theology. Zondervan, 2012.

Nanos, Mark D. *The Mystery of Romans: The Jewish Context of Paul's Letters*. 1st ed. Fortress Press, 1996.

Nanos, Mark D. "Paul and Judaism: Why Not Paul's Judaism?" In *Paul Unbound: Other Perspectives on the Apostle*, edited by Mark D. Given. Hendrickson, 2010.

Nanos, Mark D. *Reading Paul Within Judaism: Collected Essays of Mark D. Nanos*, vol. 1. Wipf and Stock, 2017.

Nanos, Mark D., and Magnus Zetterholm, eds. *Paul Within Judaism: Restoring the First-Century Context to the Apostle*. Fortress Press, 2015.

Nasrallah, Laura Salah. *Ancient Christians and the Power of Curses: Magic, Aesthetics, and Justice*. Cambridge University Press, 2024.

Nienhuis, David R. *Not by Paul Alone: The Formation of the Catholic Epistle Collection and the Christian Canon*. reprint ed. Baylor University Press, 2007.

Nirenberg, David. *Communities of Violence: Persecution of Minorities in the Middle Ages*. Princeton University Press, 2015.

Noll, Mark A. "Review Essay: The Bible in America." *Journal of Biblical Literature* 106, no. 3 (1987): 496–498.

Novenson, Matthew V. "Anti-Judaism and Philo-Judaism in Pauline Studies, Then and Now." In *Protestant Bible Scholarship: Antisemitism, Philosemitism and Anti-Judaism*, edited by Arjen F. Bakker, René Bloch, Yael Fisch, Paula Fredriksen, and Hindy Najman. *Supplements to the Journal for the Study of Judaism* 200. Brill, 2022.

Novenson, Matthew V. *Christ Among the Messiahs: Christ Language in Paul and Messiah Language in Ancient Judaism*. Oxford University Press, 2012.

Novenson, Matthew V. *The Grammar of Messianism: An Ancient Jewish Political Idiom and Its Users*. Oxford University Press, 2017.

Novenson, Matthew V. *Paul and Judaism at the End of History*. Cambridge University Press, 2024.

Økland, Jorunn. *Women in Their Place: Paul and the Corinthian Discourse of Gender and Sanctuary Space*. T&T Clark, 2004.

Parker, Angela N. *If God Still Breathes, Why Can't I?: Black Lives Matter and Biblical Authority*. Eerdmans, 2021.

Parkes, James W. *Conflict of the Church and the Synagogue: A Study in the Origins of Anti-Semitism*. Soncino, 1934.

Parks, Sara. "'The Brooten Phenomenon': Moving Women from the Margins in Second-Temple and New Testament Scholarship." *The Bible & Critical Theory* 15 (2019): 46–64.

Parks, Sara, Shayna Sheinfeld, and Meredith J. C. Warren. *Jewish and Christian Women in the Ancient Mediterranean*. Routledge, 2021.

Patel, Shaily. "Magical Practices and Discourses of Magic in Early Christian Traditions: Jesus, Peter, and Paul." PhD diss., University of North Carolina, 2017.

Pearce, Andy. *Holocaust Consciousness in Contemporary Britain*. Routledge, 2014.

Peppard, Michael. "Bearing a 'Jewish Weight': A New Interpretation of a Greek Comedic Papyrus About Athletics (CPJ 3.519)." *Journal for Interdisciplinary Biblical Studies* 5, no. 2 (2024): 21–41.

Pharr, Clyde, trans. *The Theodosian Code and Novels, and the Sirmondian Constitutions*. The Lawbook Exchange, 2001.

Pinheiro, Marília P. Futre, Judith Perkins, and Richard Pervo, eds. *The Ancient Novel and Early Christian and Jewish Narrative: Fictional Intersections*. Barkhuis, 2012.

Pippin, Tina. *Death and Desire: The Rhetoric of Gender in the Apocalypse of John*. Westminster John Knox, 1992.

Probst, Christopher J. *Demonizing the Jews: Luther and the Protestant Church in Nazi Germany*. Indiana University Press, 2012.

Probst, Christopher J. "Luther Scholars, Jews, and Judaism During the Third Reich: From the Hallowed Halls of Academia to the Sacred Spaces of German

Protestantism." In *The Betrayal of the Humanities: The University During the Third Reich*, edited by Bernard M. Levinson and Robert P. Ericksen. Indiana University Press, 2022.

Rainey, Brian. *Religion, Ethnicity and Xenophobia in the Bible: A Theoretical, Exegetical and Theological Survey*. Routledge, 2020.

Reinarz, Jonathan. *Past Scents: Historical Perspectives on Smell*. University of Illinois Press, 2014.

Reinhartz, Adele. *Cast Out of the Covenant: Jews and Anti-Judaism in the Gospel of John*, illustrated ed. Lexington Books / Fortress Academic, 2018.

Reinhartz, Adele. "The Hermeneutics of Chutzpah: A Disquisition on the Value/s of 'Critical Investigation of the Bible.'" *Journal of Biblical Literature* 140, no. 1 (2021): 8–30.

Reinhartz, Adele. "What Are the Implications of the Within Judaism Perspective for the Study of the New Testament? And What Are the Implications of the Study of the New Testament for the Within Judaism Perspective?" Presentation at The New Testament Within Judaism conference, January 7, 2025. The Enoch Seminar, https://enochseminar.org/ntwithinjud/.

Riley-Smith, Jonathan. "Crusading as an Act of Love." *History* 65, no. 214 (1980): 177–192.

Rollens, Sarah. "Why We Have Failed to Theorize Scribes in Antiquity." In *Scribal Practices and Social Structures Among Jesus Adherents: Essays in Honour of John S. Kloppenborg*, edited by William E. Arnal, Richard S. Ascough, Robert A. Derrenbacker Jr., and Philip A. Harland. Peeters, 2016.

Rose, E. M. *The Murder of William of Norwich: The Origins of the Blood Libel in Medieval Europe*. 1st ed. Oxford University Press, 2015.

Rose, Emily M. "Crusades, Blood Libels, and Popular Violence." In *The Cambridge Companion to Antisemitism*, edited by Steven Katz. Cambridge Companions to Religion. Cambridge University Press, 2022.

Rozett, Robert, and Dan Michman. "The Unprecedented Nature of the Holocaust and Its Unique Features: Some Reflections Part I." January 3, 2021. https://www.yadvashem.org/blog/the-unprecedented-nature-of-the-holocaust.html.

Rubenstein, Richard L. "Holocaust and Holy War." *Annals of the American Academy of Political and Social Science* 548 (1996): 23–44.

Sanders, E. P. "Covenantal Nomism Revisited." *Jewish Studies Quarterly* 16, no. 1 (2009): 23–55.

Sanders, E. P. *Jesus and Judaism*. Fortress Press, 1985.

Sanders, E. P. *Paul and Palestinian Judaism: A Comparison of Patterns of Religion*. Fortress Press, 1977.

Sanders, E. P. "Paul's Attitude Toward the Jewish People." *Union Seminary Quarterly Review* 33, no. 3–4 (1978): 175–187.

Sanders, E. P. *Paul, the Law, and the Jewish People*. Fortress Press, 1983.

Sanders, E. P. *Paul: The Apostle's Life, Letters, and Thought*. Fortress Press, 2015.

Sands, Philippe. *The Ratline: The Exalted Life and Mysterious Death of a Nazi Fugitive*. Knopf, 2021.

Schäfer, Peter. "Diversity and Interaction: Messiahs in Early Judaism." In *Toward the Millennium: Messianic Expectations from the Bible to Waco*, edited by Peter Schäfer and Mark R. Cohen. SHR 77. Brill, 1998.

Schmid, Konrad. "The Interpretation of Second Temple Judaism as 'Spätjudentum' in Christian Biblical Scholarship." In *Confronting Antisemitism from the Perspectives of Christianity, Islam, and Judaism*, vol. 2, *An End to Antisemitism!*, edited by Armin Lange, Kerstin Mayerhofer, Dina Porat, and Lawrence H. Schiffman. De Gruyter, 2020.

Schramm, Brooks, and Kirsi I. Stjerna, eds. *Martin Luther, the Bible, and the Jewish People: A Reader*. illustrated ed. Fortress Press, 2012.

Schüssler Fiorenza, Elisabeth. *Rhetoric and Ethic: The Politics of Biblical Studies*. Fortress Press, 1999.

Schüssler Fiorenza, Elisabeth. *Wisdom Ways: Introducing Feminist Biblical Interpretation*. Orbis Books, 2001.

Schwartz, Ethan. "Mirrors of Moses in Isaiah 1–12." In *The History of Isaiah: The Formation of the Book and Its Presentation of the Past*, edited by Jacob Stromberg and James Todd Hibbard. Mohr Siebeck, 2021.

Schwartz, Seth. *Imperialism and Jewish Society: 200 B.C.E. to 640 C.E.* Princeton University Press, 2001.

Seesengood, Robert Paul. *Paul: A Brief History*. Wiley-Blackwell, 2010.

Segovia, Fernando F. "'And They Began to Speak in Other Tongues': Competing Modes of Discourse in Contemporary Biblical Criticism." In *Reading from This Place: Social Location and Biblical Interpretation in the United States*, edited by Fernando F. Segovia and Mary Ann Tolbert. Fortress Press, 1995.

Semler, Johann. *Abhandlung von freier Untersuchung des Canon*. Halle, 1771.

Setzer, Claudia, and David A. Shefferman. "Introduction." In *The Bible in the American Experience*, edited by Claudia Setzer and David A. Shefferman. SBL Press, 2020.

Shandler, Jeffrey. *Holocaust Memory in the Digital Age: Survivors' Stories and New Media Practices*. Stanford Studies in Jewish History and Culture. Stanford University Press, 2017.

Sharples, Caroline. "'Where, Exactly, Is Auschwitz?' British Confrontation with the Holocaust Through the Medium of the 1945 'Belsen' Trial." In *The Palgrave Handbook of Britain and the Holocaust*, edited by Tom Lawson and Andy Pearce. Palgrave Macmillan, 2020.

Sheehan, Jonathan. *The Enlightenment Bible: Translation, Scholarship, Culture*. Princeton University Press, 2013.

Sheinfeld, Shayna. "From Nomos to Logos: Torah in First-Century Jewish Texts." In *The Message of Paul the Apostle Within Second Temple Judaism*, edited by František Ábel. Lexington Books / Fortress Academic, 2020.

Sheinfeld, Shayna. "Messianism." In *End of Days: An Encyclopedia of the Apocalypse in World Religions*, edited by Wendell G. Johnson. Bloomsbury USA, 2017.

Sheinfeld, Shayna. "Who Is the Righteous Remnant in Romans 9–11?: The Concept of Remnant in Early Jewish Literature and Paul's Letter to the Romans." In *Paul the Jew: Rereading the Apostle as a Figure of Second Temple Judaism*, edited by Gabriele Boccaccini and Carlos A. Segovia. Fortress Press, 2016.

Sherwood, Yvonne. *Biblical Blaspheming: Trials of the Sacred for a Secular Age*. 1st ed. Cambridge University Press, 2012.

Sicher, Efraim, ed. *Race, Color, Identity: Rethinking Discourses About "Jews" in the Twenty-First Century*. Berghahn Books, 2013.

Sim, David. "Matthew's Use of Mark: Did Matthew Intend to Supplement or to Replace His Primary Source?" *New Testament Studies* 57 (2011): 176–179.

Smallwood, Christine. "A Reviewer's Life: The Material Constraints of Writing Criticism Today." *Yale Review*, June 10, 2024. https://yalereview.org/article/christine-smallwood-reviewers-life.

Smith, Eric C. *Paul the Progressive?: The Compassionate Christian's Guide to Reclaiming the Apostle as an Ally*. Chalice Press, 2019.

Smith, Mitzi J. *Chloe and Her People: A Womanist Critical Dialogue with First Corinthians*. Wipf and Stock, 2023.

Smith, Mitzi J., Yung Suk Kim, and Michael Willett Newheart. *Toward Decentering the New Testament*. Wipf and Stock, 2018.

Smith, Shanell T. *The Woman Babylon and the Marks of Empire: Reading Revelation with a Postcolonial Womanist Hermeneutics of Ambi*veilence. Fortress Press, 2014.

Smith, Stephen D. *Making Memory: Creating Britain's First Holocaust Centre*. Quill Press, 2002.

Solberg, Mary M., trans. *A Church Undone: Documents from the German Christian Faith Movement, 1932–1940*. Fortress Press, 2015.

Soon, Isaac T. *A Disabled Apostle: Impairment and Disability in the Letters of Paul*. Oxford University Press, 2023.

Stacey, Robert C. "Anti-Semitism and the Medieval English State." In *The Medieval State: Essays Presented to James Campbell*, edited by John Maddicott and David Palliser. The Hambledon Press, 2000.

Stacey, Robert C. "The Conversion of Jews to Christianity in Thirteenth-Century England." *Speculum* 67, no. 2 (1992): 263–283.

Staley, Jeffrey L. *Reading with a Passion: Rhetoric, Autobiography, and the American West in the Gospel of John*. Continuum, 1995.

Stanton, Elizabeth Cady. *The Woman's Bible: A Classic Feminist Perspective*. Dover Publications, 2003.

Staples, Jason A. *Paul and the Resurrection of Israel: Jews, Former Gentiles, Israelites*. Cambridge University Press, 2024.

Stein, Sarah Abrevaya. *Saharan Jews and the Fate of French Algeria*. University of Chicago Press, 2014.

Steigmann-Gall, Richard. *The Holy Reich: Nazi Conceptions of Christianity, 1919–1945*. Cambridge University Press, 2004.

Stendahl, Krister. *Final Account: Paul's Letter to the Romans*. Fortress Press, 1995.

Stendahl, Krister. *Paul Among Jews and Gentiles and Other Essays*. Fortress Press, 1976.

Storkey, Elaine. *Women in a Patriarchal World: Twenty-Five Empowering Stories from the Bible*. SPCK, 2020.

Stowers, Stanley. *A Rereading of Romans: Justice, Jews, and Gentiles*. Yale University Press, 1994.

Stowers, Stanley. "The Concept of 'Community' and the History of Early Christianity." *Method & Theory in the Study of Religion* 23 (2011): 238–256.

Stowers, Stanley. "Kinds of Myth, Meals, and Power: Paul and the Corinthians." In *Redescribing Paul and the Corinthians*, edited by Ron Cameron and Merrill P. Miller. Society of Biblical Literature, 2011.

Strauss, David Friedrich. *Das Leben Jesu Kritishch Bearbeitet*, vol. 1. C.F. Osiander, 1835.

Strauss, David Friedrich. *Das Leben Jesu Kritishch Bearbeitet*, vol. 2. C.F. Osiander, 1836.

Strozier, Charles B. *Apocalypse: On the Psychology of Fundamentalism in America*. Beacon Press, 1994.

Swancutt, Diana M. "Sexing the Pauline Body of Christ: Scriptural Sex in the Context of the American Christian Culture War." In *Toward a Theology of Eros: Transfiguring Passion at the Limits of Discipline*, edited by Virginia Burrus and Catherine Keller. Fordham University Press, 2006.

Szocik, Konrad, and Philip L. Walden. "The Attitude of the Catholic Church Toward the Jews: An Outline of a Turbulent History." *Numen* 64, no. 2–3 (2017): 209–228.

Tartakoff, Paola. "Testing Boundaries: Jewish Conversion and Cultural Fluidity in Medieval Europe, c. 1200–1391." *Speculum* 90, no. 3 (2015): 728–762.

Thielman, Frank. *From Plight to Solution: A Jewish Framework for Understanding Paul's View of the Law in Galatians and Romans*. E. J. Brill, 1989.

Thiessen, Matthew. *A Jewish Paul: The Messiah's Herald to the Gentiles*. Baker Academic, 2023.

Thiessen, Matthew. *Paul and the Gentile Problem*. Oxford University Press, 2016.

Thiessen, Matthew, and Paula Fredriksen. "Paul and Israel." In *The Oxford Handbook of Pauline Studies*, edited by Matthew V. Novenson and R. Barry Matlock. Oxford University Press, 2022.

Trachtenberg, Joshua. *The Devil and the Jews: The Medieval Conception of the Jew and Its Relation to Modern Anti-Semitism*. The Jewish Publication Society, 1983.

Trible, Phyllis. "Biblical Views: Wrestling with Faith." *Biblical Archeology Review*, September/October 2014. https://library.biblicalarchaeology.org/department/biblical-views-wrestling-with-faith/.

Trible, Phyllis. "Not a Jot, Not a Tittle: Genesis 2–3 After Twenty Years." In *Eve and Adam: Jewish, Christian, and Muslim Readings on Genesis and Gender.* 1st ed., edited by Kristen E. Kvam, Linda S. Schearing, and Valarie H. Ziegler. Indiana University Press, 1999.

Trible, Phyllis. *Texts of Terror: Literary-Feminist Readings of Biblical Narratives.* 40th ann. ed. Fortress Press, 2022.

Tertullian. *Apology. De Spectaculis. Minucius Felix: Octavius.* Translated by T. R. Glover and Gerald H. Rendall. Harvard University Press, 1931.

Tertullian. *Disciplinary, Moral, and Ascetical Works.* Translated by Rudolph Arbesmann, Emily Joseph Daly, and Edwin A. Quain. Fathers of the Church, 1959.

Tong, M Adryael. "Banishing Baur: The Antisemitic Origins of White Supremacy in Biblical Studies," *Political Theology Network*, December 3, 2020. https://politicaltheology.com/banishing-baur-the-antisemitic-origins-of-white-supremacy-in-biblical-studies/

van der Horst, Pieter Willem. *Early Jewish Prayers in Greek.* Commentaries on Early Jewish Literature. Walter de Gruyter, 2008.

Vatican Council II. "*Nostra Aetate:* Declaration on the Relationship of the Church to Non-Christian Religions." October 28, 1965. https://www.vatican.va/archive/hist_councils/ii_vatican_council/documents/vat-ii_decl_19651028_nostra-aetate_en.html.

Vermes, Geza, trans. *The Complete Dead Sea Scrolls in English.* Penguin Books, 2011.

Vinzent, Markus. *Christ's Torah.* English ed. Routledge, 2024.

Vinzent, Markus. *Paul's Literary Metamorphosis: Translations of Marcion's Apostolos and Canonical Counterparts*, version 1.01, edited by Jack Bull. Translated by Mark G. Bilby. LODLIB, 2023. https://doi.org/10.5281/zenodo.8271824.

Vinzent, Markus. *Resetting the Origins of Christianity: A New Theory of Sources and Beginnings.* Cambridge University Press, 2023.

Walsh, Robyn Faith. *The Origins of Early Christian Literature: Contextualizing the New Testament Within Greco-Roman Literary Culture.* Cambridge University Press, 2021.

Wan, Sze-kar. "Does Diaspora Identity Imply Some Sort of Universality? An Asian-American Reading of Galatians." In *Interpreting Beyond Borders*, edited by Fernando F. Segovia. The Bible and Postcolonialism. Sheffield Academic Press, 2000.

Weber, Ferdinand Wilhelm. *Jüdische Theologie auf Grund des Talmud und verwandter Schriften.* Dörffling & Franke, 1897.

Weems, Renita. *Battered Love: Marriage, Sex, and Violence in the Hebrew Prophets.* Fortress Press, 1995.

Wendt, Heidi. "Secrecy as Pauline Influence on the Gospel of Mark." *Journal of Biblical Literature* 140 (2021): 579–600.

West, Mark D. "Necro-Waste and Hauntology: Ghosts, Specters, and the Infinitive Responsibility of the Past." *Social Epistemology Review and Reply Collective* 12, no. 10 (2023): 65–75.

West, Nathaniel. "The Old Hebrew Theology." *Old Testament Student* 3, no. 1 (1883): 14–19.

Westerholm, Stephen. *Perspectives Old and New on Paul: The "Lutheran" Paul and His Critics*. Eerdmans, 2003.

Williams, Jeremy L. *Criminalization in Acts of the Apostles: Race, Rhetoric, and the Prosecution of an Early Christian Movement*. Cambridge University Press, 2023.

Winant, Howard. "Behind Blue Eues: Whiteness and Contemporary US Racial Politics." In *Off White: Readings on Power, Privilege, and Resistance*. 2nd ed., edited by Michelle Fine, Lois Weis, Linda Powell Pruitt, and April Burns. Routledge, 2004.

Wright, Benjamin Givens. *Praise Israel for Wisdom and Instruction: Essays on Ben Sira and Wisdom, the Letter of Aristeas and the Septuagint*. Brill, 2008.

Wright, N. T. *The Climax of the Covenant: Christ and the Law in Pauline Theology*. T&T Clark, 1993.

Wright, N. T. *Paul and the Faithfulness of God*. Fortress Press, 2013.

Wright, N. T. *Paul: In Fresh Perspective*. Fortress Press, 2009.

Wright, N. T. "The Paul of History and the Apostle of Faith." *Tyndale Bulletin* 29, no. 1 (1978): 61–88.

Wright, N. T. "Romans 9–11 and the 'New Perspective.'" In *Between Gospel and Election: Explorations in the Interpretation of Romans 9–11*, edited by Florian Wilk and J. Ross Wagner. Mohr Siebeck, 2010.

Wu, Ashley Shannon. "Whoopi Goldberg Returns to *The View* After Her Suspension." *Vulture*, February 14, 2022. https://www.vulture.com/2022/02/whoopi-goldberg-holocaust-comments-late-night-show.html.

Yinger, Kent L. *Paul, Judaism, and Judgment According to Deeds*. Cambridge University Press, 1999.

Young, Stephen L. "Ethnic Ethics: Paul's Eschatological Myth of Jewish Sin." *New Testament Studies* 70 (2024): 235–248.

Young, Stephen L. "Let's Take the Text Seriously: The Protectionist Doxa of Mainstream New Testament Studies." *Method & Theory in the Study of Religion* 32, no. 4/5 (2020): 328–363.

Young, Stephen L. "'Make Rome Great Again' Preceded 'Make America Great Again': The Ancient Romo-Nationalism of Biblical Writers." *Interpretation* 78, no. 4 (2024): 321–334.

Young, Stephen L. *Paul Among the Mythmakers: Sins, Gods, and Scriptures*. Studies in Religion in Antiquity. Edinburgh University Press, forthcoming.

Young, Stephen L. "Paul's Ethnic Discourse on 'Faith': Christ's Faithfulness and Gentile Access to the Judean God in Romans." *Harvard Theological Review* 108 (2015): 30–51.

Young, Stephen L. "So Radically Jewish That He's an Evangelical Christian: N. T. Wright's Judeophobic and Privileged Paul." *Interpretation* 76 (2022): 339–351.

Zetterholm, Magnus. *Approaches to Paul: A Student's Guide to Recent Scholarship.* Fortress Press, 2009.

Zetterholm, Magnus. "The Paul Within Judaism Perspective." In *Perspectives on Paul: Five Views*, edited by Scot McKnight and B. J. Oropeza. Baker Academic, 2020.

Zetterholm, Magnus. "Paul Within Judaism: The State of the Questions." In *Paul Within Judaism: Restoring the First-Century Context to the Apostle*, edited by Mark D. Nanos and Magnus Zetterholm. Fortress Press, 2015.

Žižek, Slavoj. *The Puppet and the Dwarf: The Perverse Core of Christianity.* Short Circuits. MIT Press, 2003.

Zonszein, Mairav. "The 'Israel Fetish': Singling Out Jews and Israelis for Hate and Love." *+972 Magazine*, March 15, 2011. https://www.972mag.com/the-israel-fetish/.

Zwiep, Arie W. "Judas and the Jews: Anti-Semitic Interpretation of Judas Iscariot Past and Present." In *Jesus and Paul: Global Perspectives in Honor of James D. G. Dunn. A Festschrift for His 70th Birthday*, edited by B. J. Oropeza, C. K. Robertson, and D. C. Mohrmann. Library of New Testament Studies. T&T Clark International, 2009.

Zwiep, Arie W. *Judas en de joden: Een onderzoek naar antisemitische interpretaties van Judas Iskariot* (Onderzoeksverslag in opdracht van het Openbaar Ministerie n.a.v. de preek van ds. N.C. Mos, gehouden op zondag 13 maart 2005 in de Messiaskerk te Wassenaar; februari 2007).

ANCIENT SOURCES INDEX

MODERN AUTHORS INDEX

SUBJECT INDEX